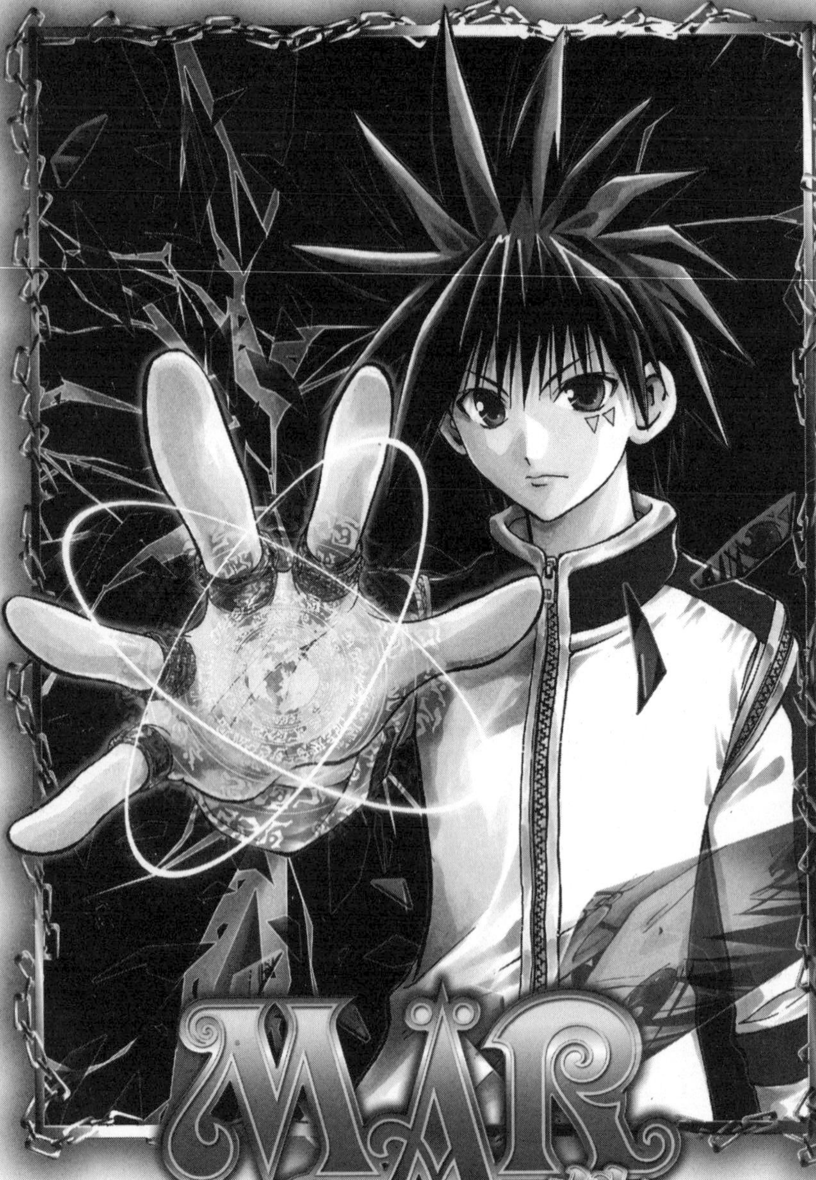

MÄR

MÄRCHEN AWAKENS ROMANCE

Vol.5

Nobuyuki Anzai

Characters

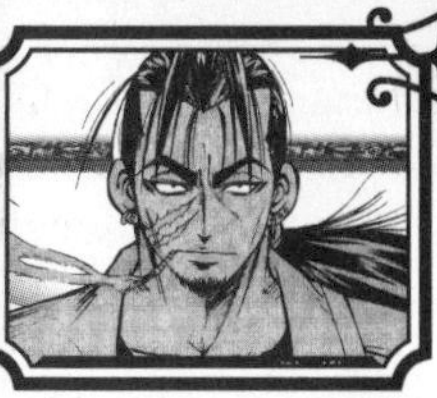

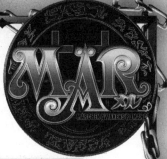

Edward (Human)

A warrior who played a major role in the war six years ago. Back then his name was Alan, but then a curse trapped him in the form of a dog.

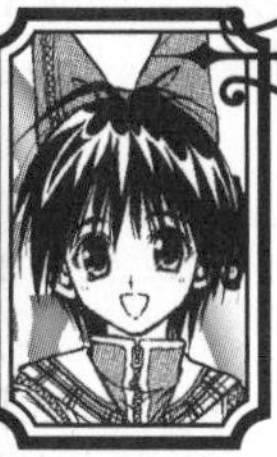

Snow

The Princess of the Great Kingdom of Lestava. Rescued from a frozen state by Ginta.

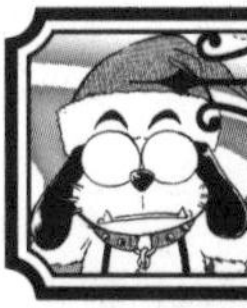

Edward (Canine)

Devotedly serves Princess Snow. He returns to human form by sleeping three times.

Alviss

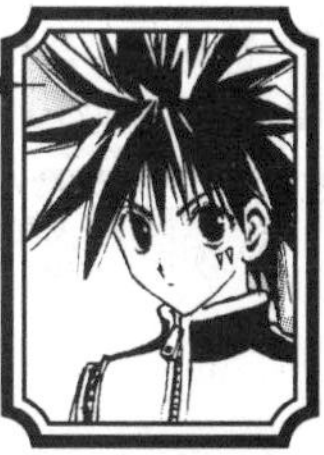

He called Ginta to Mär Heaven using the Dimension ÄRM "Gate Keeper Clown."

Nanashi

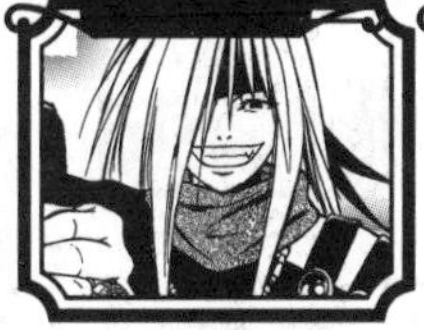

Leader of the Thieves Guild, Luberia. Detests the Chess Pieces.

Dorothy

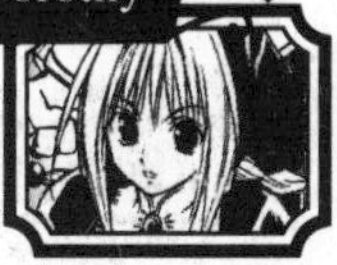

A witch. Although she used Ginta to help her find Babbo, could she have some real feelings for him…?

Babbo

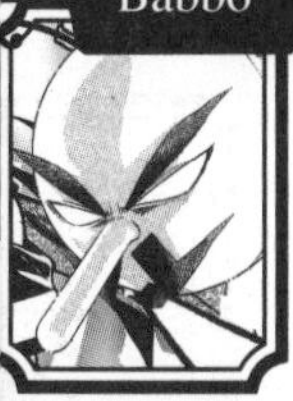

A talking ÄRM, rare throughout the world. He has a dark past…

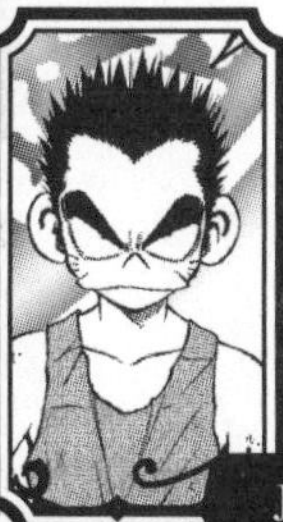

A farmboy who left his mother and his farm to go on an adventure with Ginta.

Jack

Ginta Toramizu

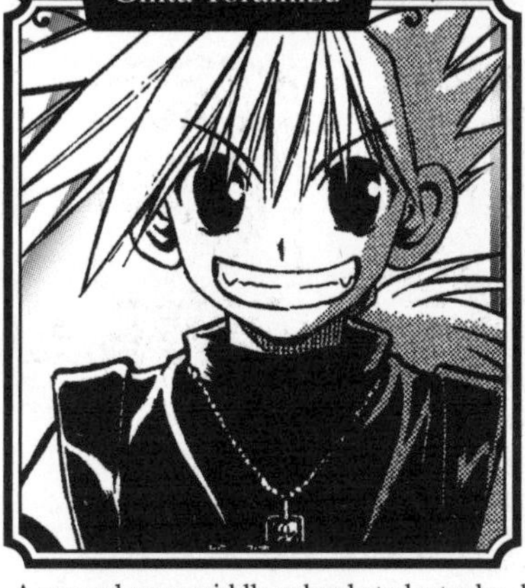

A second-year middle school student who dreams about the world of fairy tales—and suddenly finds himself there.

Previous Volume

Ginta jumps through a "door" that suddenly appears in his classroom finds himself in Märchen, the magical world of his dreams. In keeping with a prophecy known by Princess Snow, Ginta becomes one of eigh warriors who must battle the Chess Pieces to save the world of MÄR Heaven. Just as they did once before, the Chess Pieces declare that the conflict will be settled by the "War Games." Now Ginta and his fello Mär warriors must pass a test to confirm whether or not they are wortl to participate…!

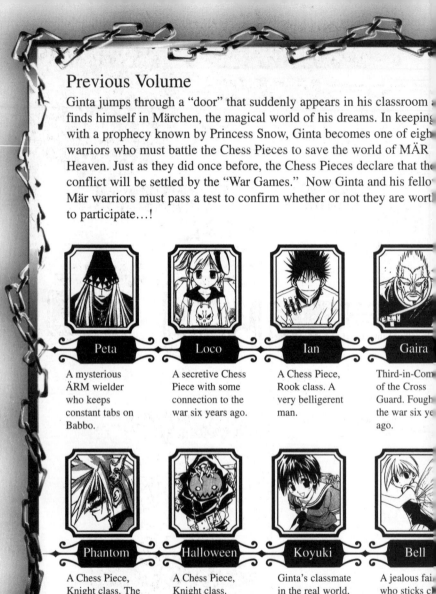

Peta
A mysterious ÄRM wielder who keeps constant tabs on Babbo.

Loco
A secretive Chess Piece with some connection to the war six years ago.

Ian
A Chess Piece, Rook class. A very belligerent man.

Gaira
Third-in-Com of the Cross Guard. Fough the war six ye ago.

Phantom
A Chess Piece, Knight class. The most powerful of the group, and the leader of its combat force.

Halloween
A Chess Piece, Knight class.

Koyuki
Ginta's classmate in the real world, and the only one who really listens to Ginta's stories about his dreams.

Bell
A jealous fai who sticks cl to Alviss.

CONTENTS

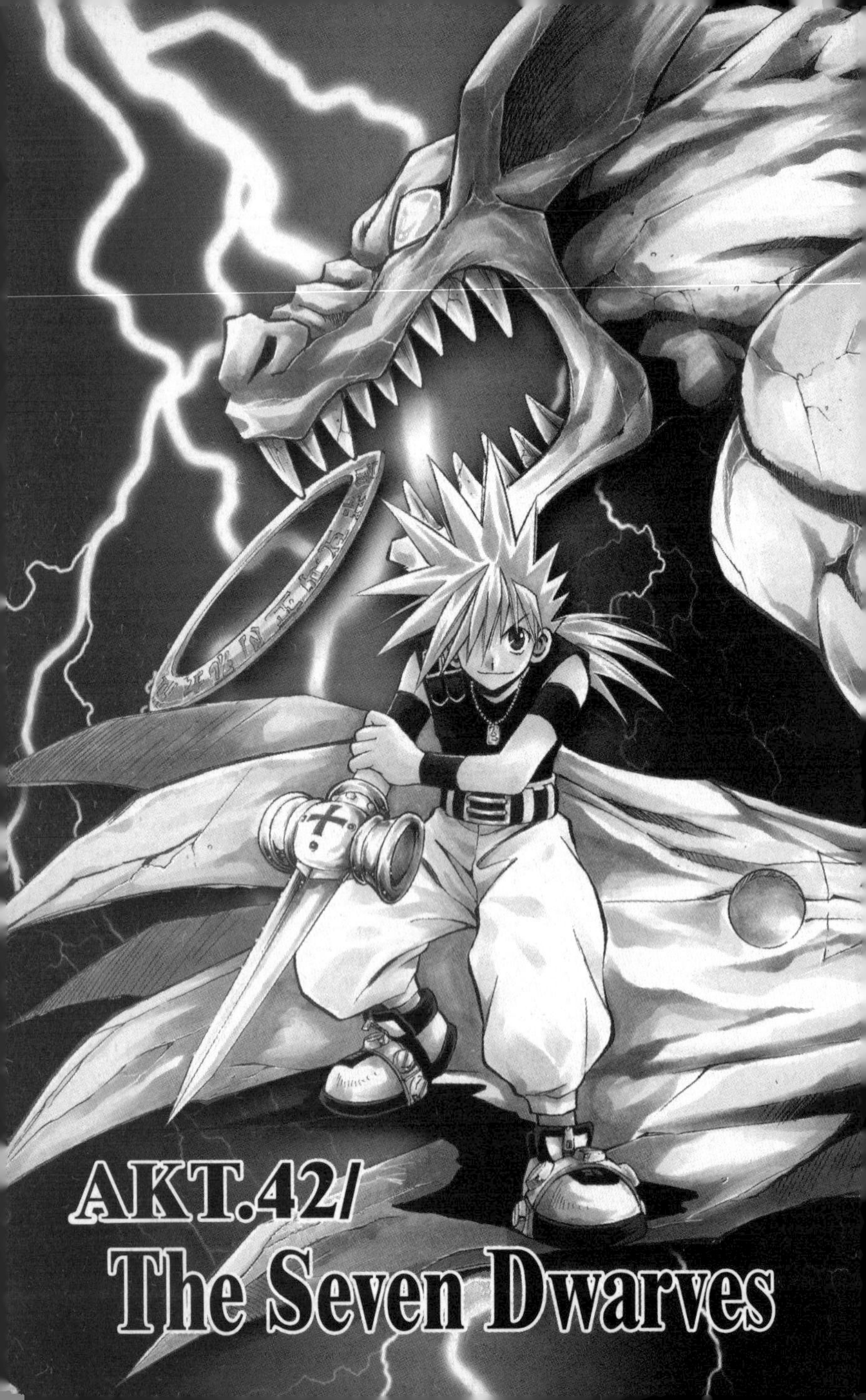
AKT.42/
The Seven Dwarves

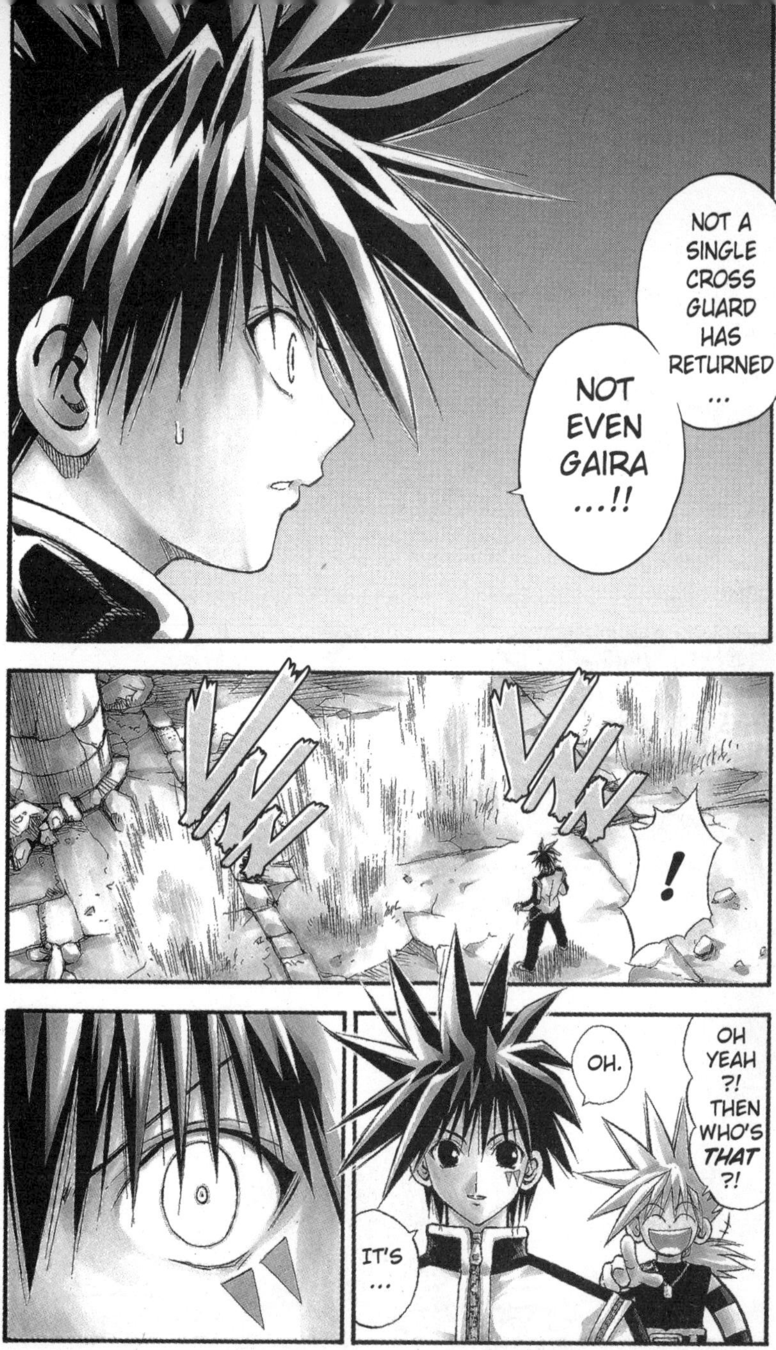
NOT A SINGLE CROSS GUARD HAS RETURNED ...
NOT EVEN GAIRA ...!!
!
OH YEAH ?! THEN WHO'S *THAT* ?!
OH.
IT'S ...

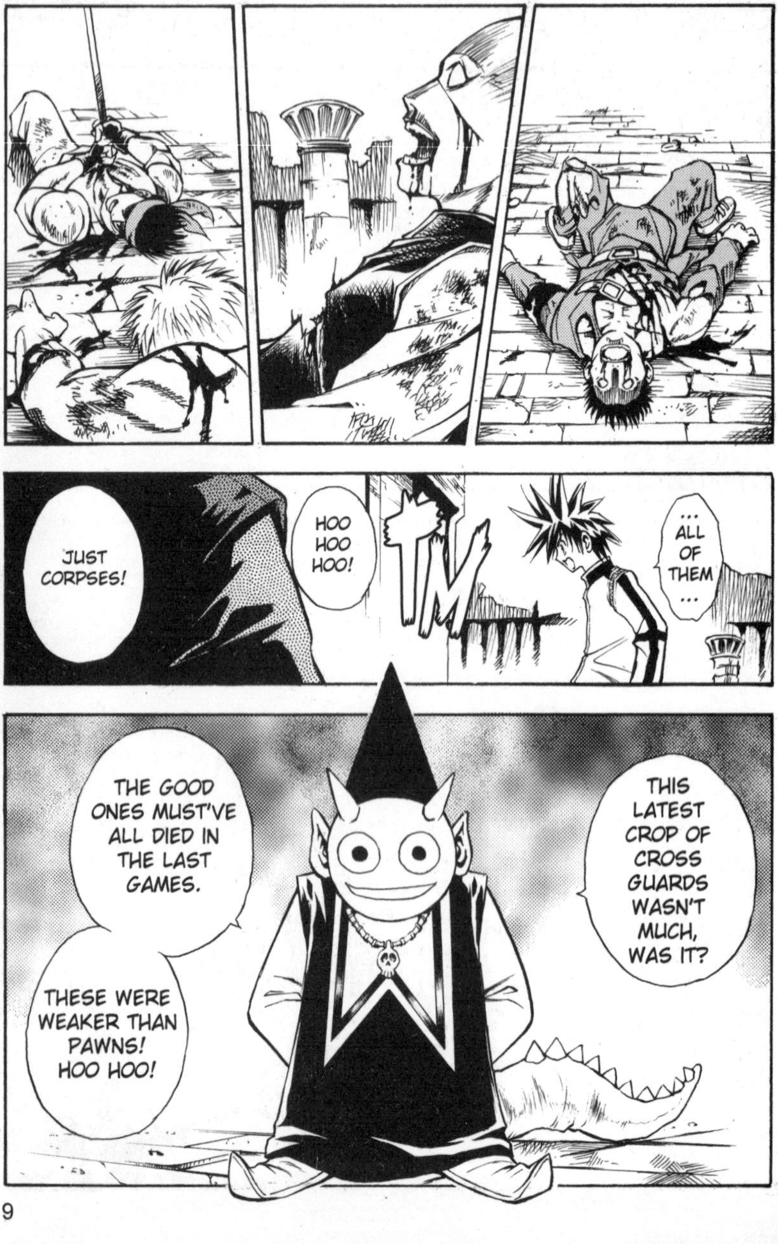
... ALL OF THEM ...
TM
HOO HOO HOO!
JUST CORPSES!
THIS LATEST CROP OF CROSS GUARDS WASN'T MUCH, WAS IT?
THE GOOD ONES MUST'VE ALL DIED IN THE LAST GAMES.
THESE WERE WEAKER THAN PAWNS! HOO HOO!

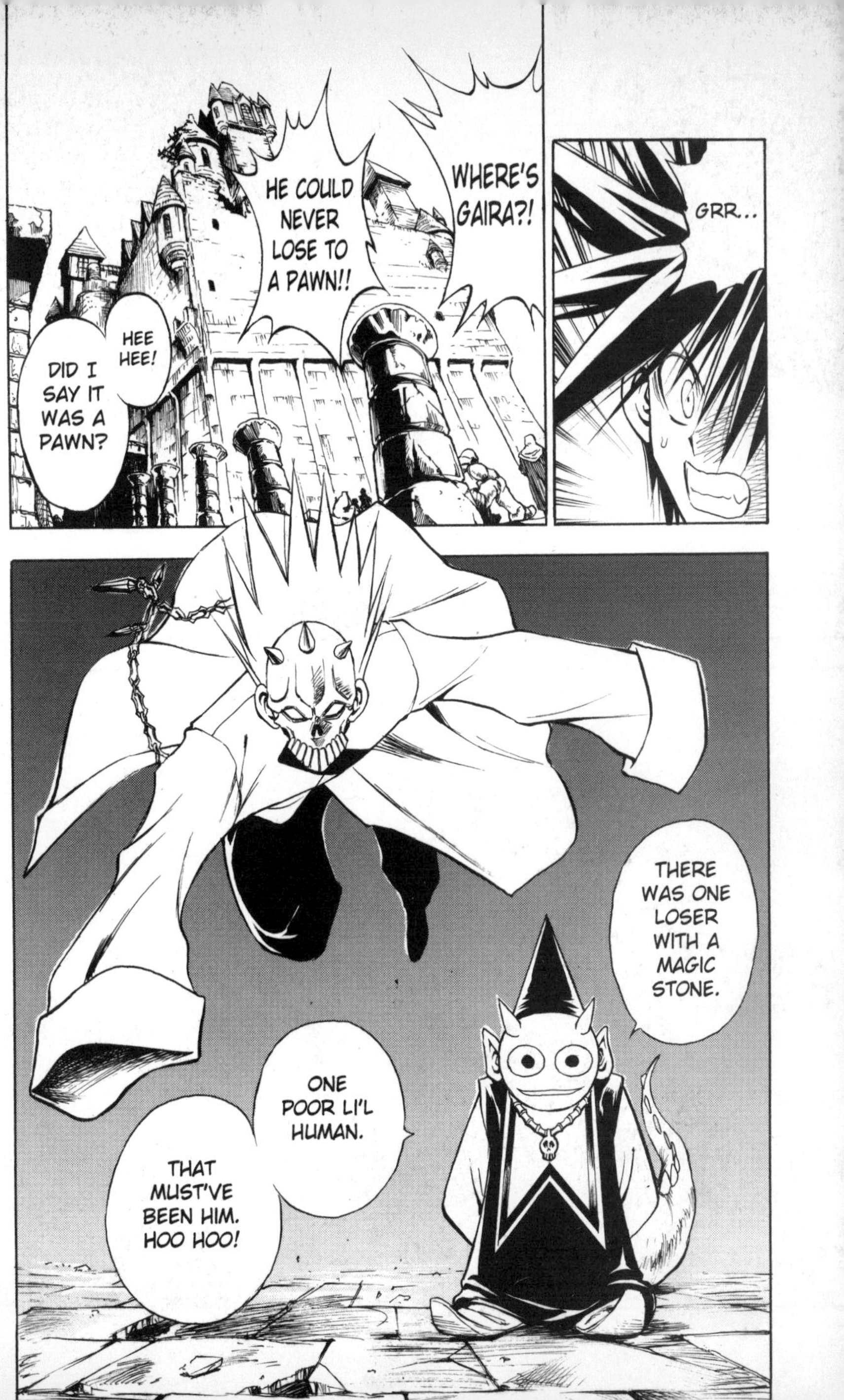
GRR...
WHERE'S GAIRA?!
HE COULD NEVER LOSE TO A PAWN!!
HEE HEE!
DID I SAY IT WAS A PAWN?
THERE WAS ONE LOSER WITH A MAGIC STONE.
ONE POOR LI'L HUMAN.
THAT MUST'VE BEEN HIM. HOO HOO!

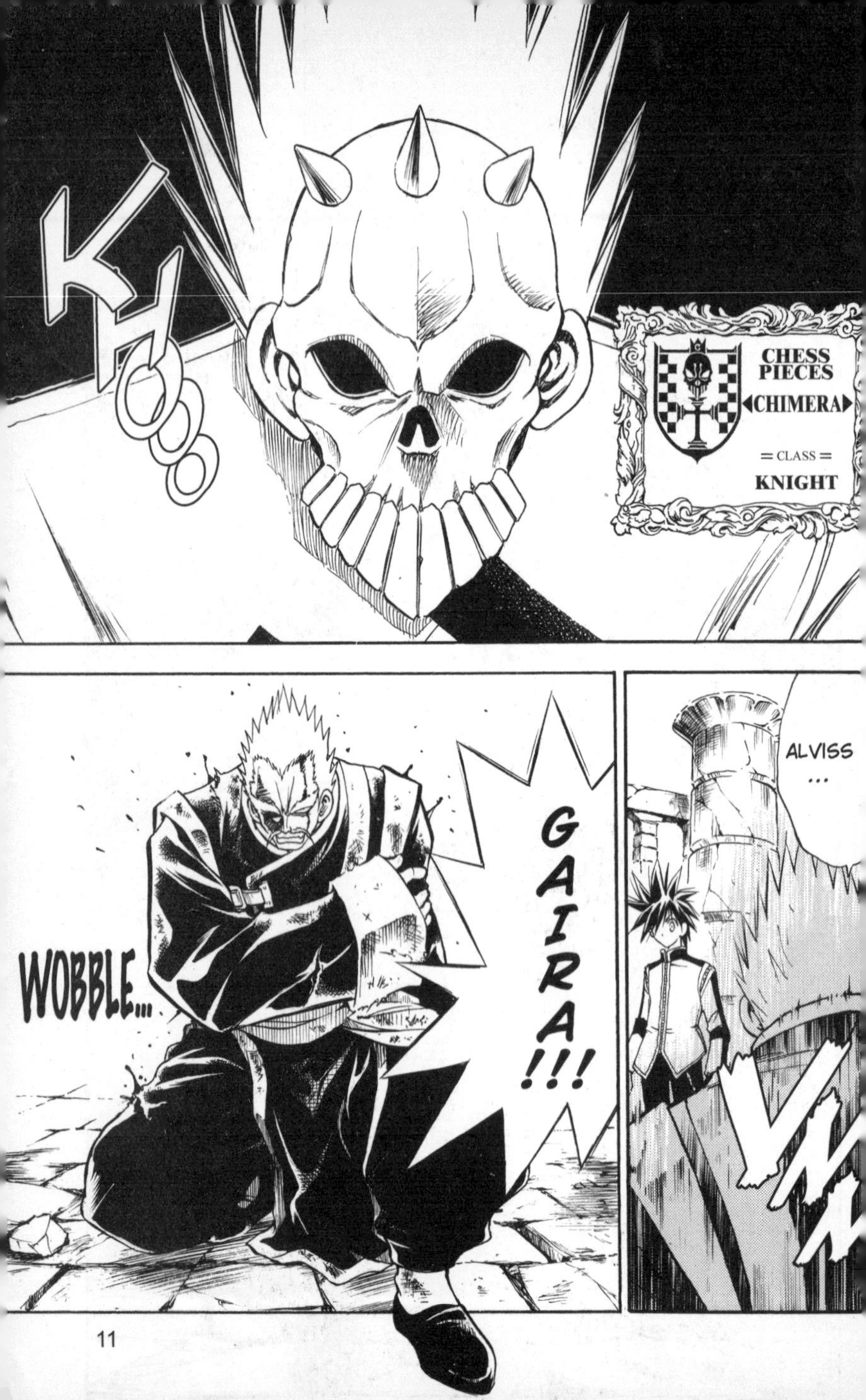
KHOOOO
CHESS PIECES
◀CHIMERA▶
= CLASS =
KNIGHT
ALVISS ...
GAIRA!!!
WOBBLE...

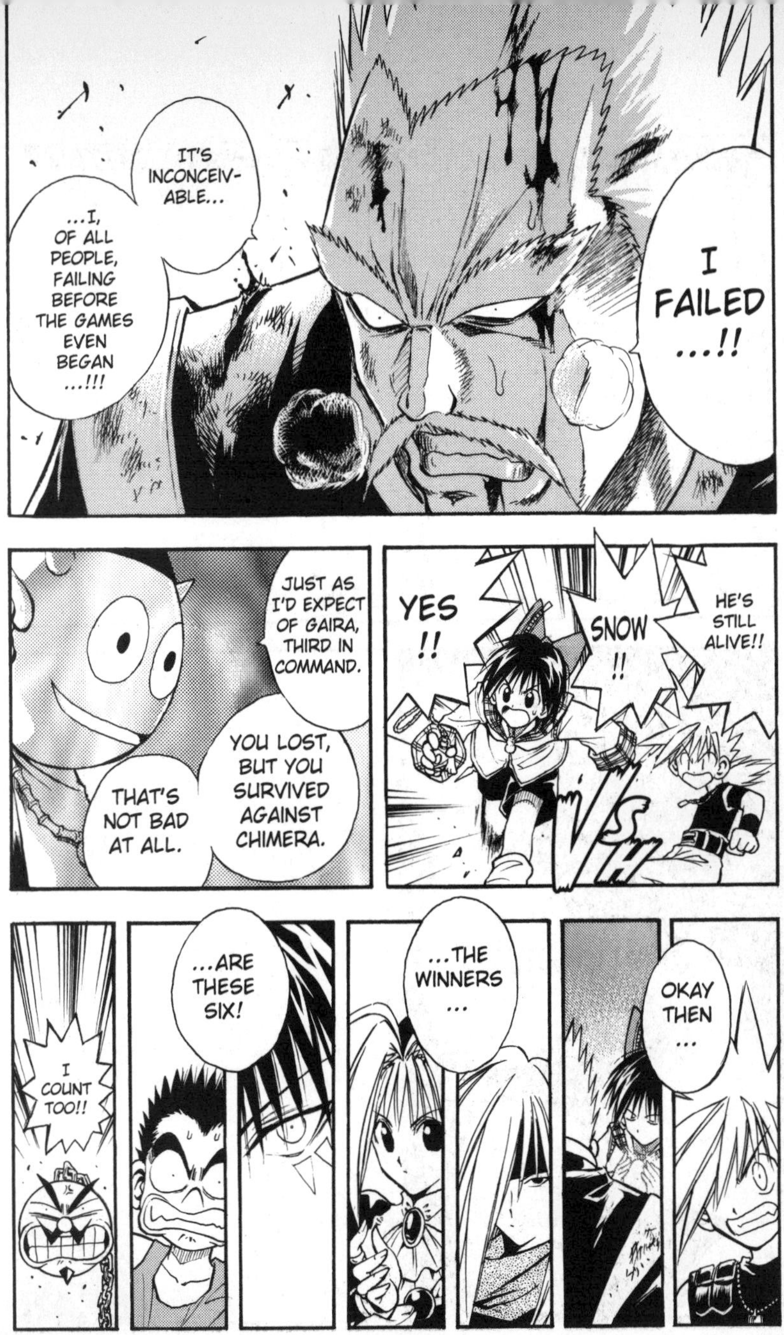
I FAILED ...!!
IT'S INCONCEIVABLE...
...I, OF ALL PEOPLE, FAILING BEFORE THE GAMES EVEN BEGAN ...!!!
HE'S STILL ALIVE!!
SNOW !!
YES !!
JUST AS I'D EXPECT OF GAIRA, THIRD IN COMMAND.
YOU LOST, BUT YOU SURVIVED AGAINST CHIMERA.
THAT'S NOT BAD AT ALL.
OKAY THEN ...
...THE WINNERS ...
...ARE THESE SIX!
I COUNT TOO!!

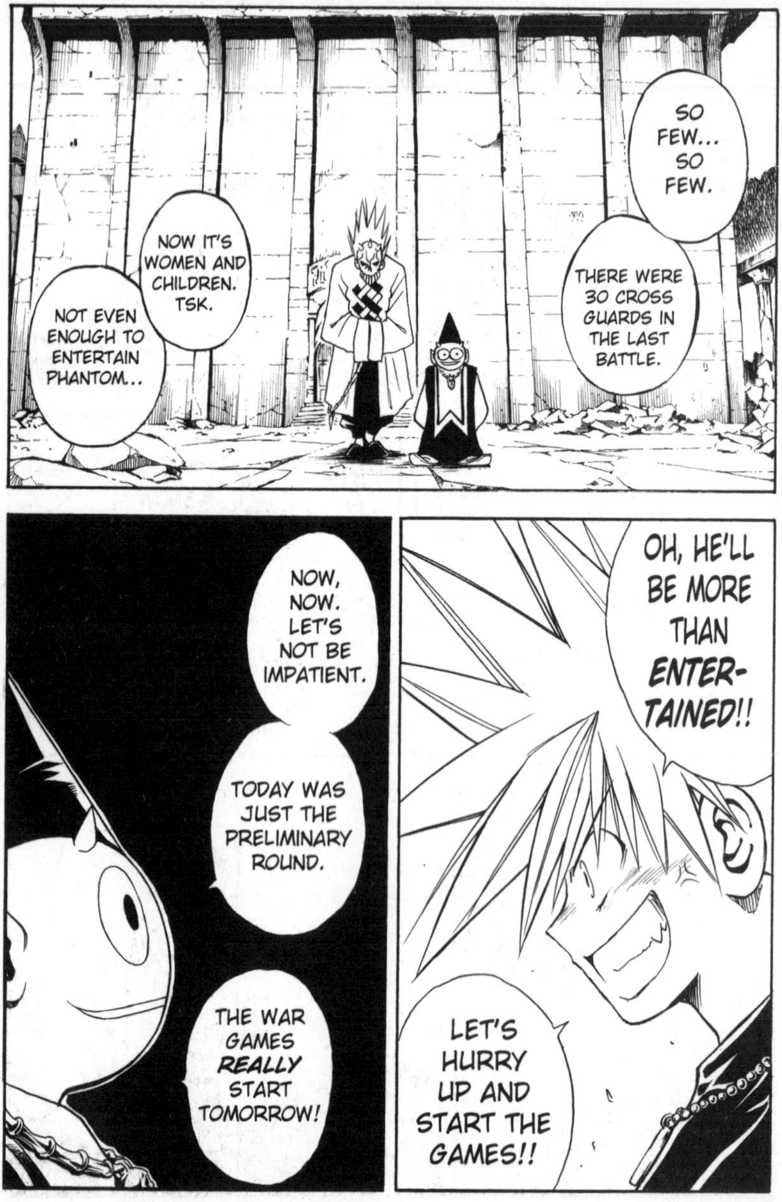
SO FEW... SO FEW.
THERE WERE 30 CROSS GUARDS IN THE LAST BATTLE.
NOW IT'S WOMEN AND CHILDREN. TSK.
NOT EVEN ENOUGH TO ENTERTAIN PHANTOM...
OH, HE'LL BE MORE THAN ENTER-TAINED!!
LET'S HURRY UP AND START THE GAMES!!
NOW, NOW. LET'S NOT BE IMPATIENT.
TODAY WAS JUST THE PRELIMINARY ROUND.
THE WAR GAMES REALLY START TOMORROW!

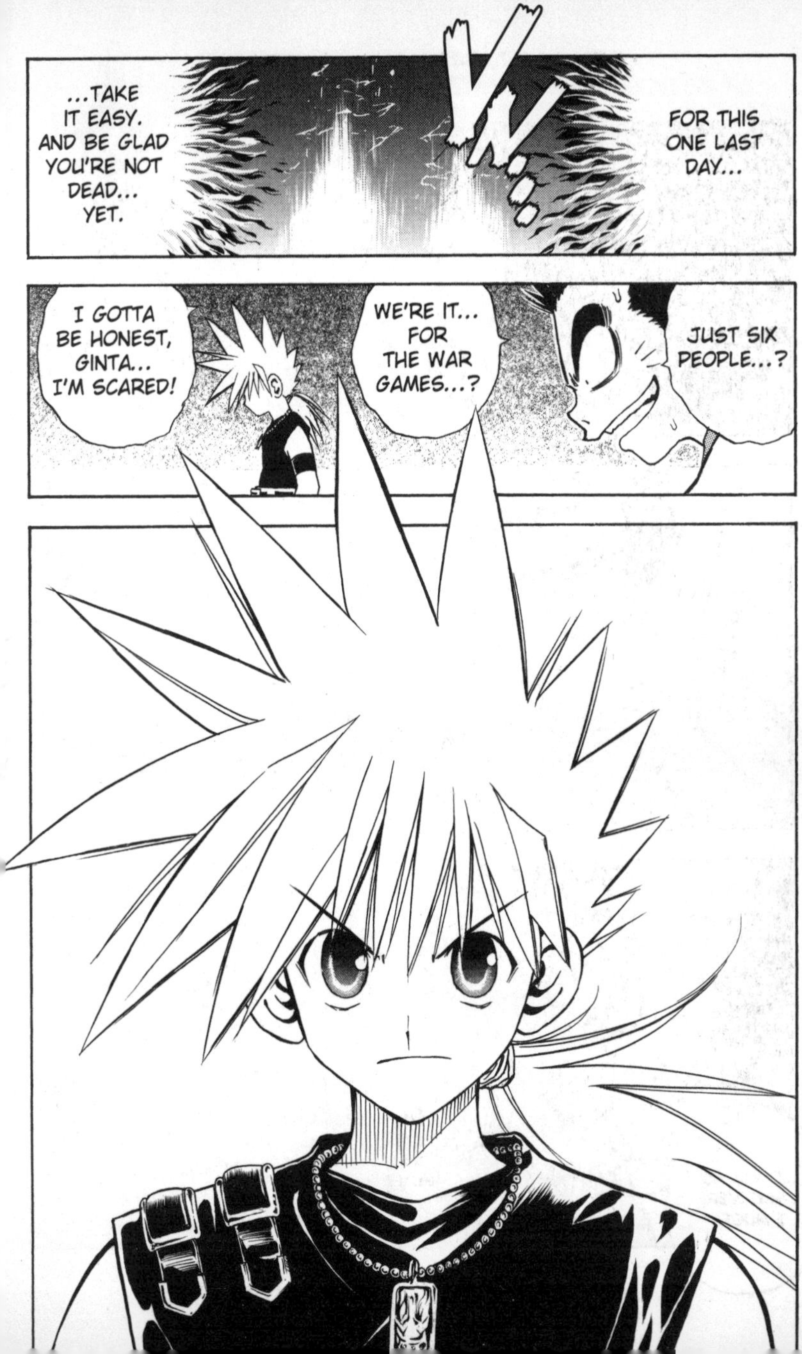
FOR THIS ONE LAST DAY...
...TAKE IT EASY. AND BE GLAD YOU'RE NOT DEAD... YET.
JUST SIX PEOPLE...?
WE'RE IT... FOR THE WAR GAMES...?
I GOTTA BE HONEST, GINTA... I'M SCARED!

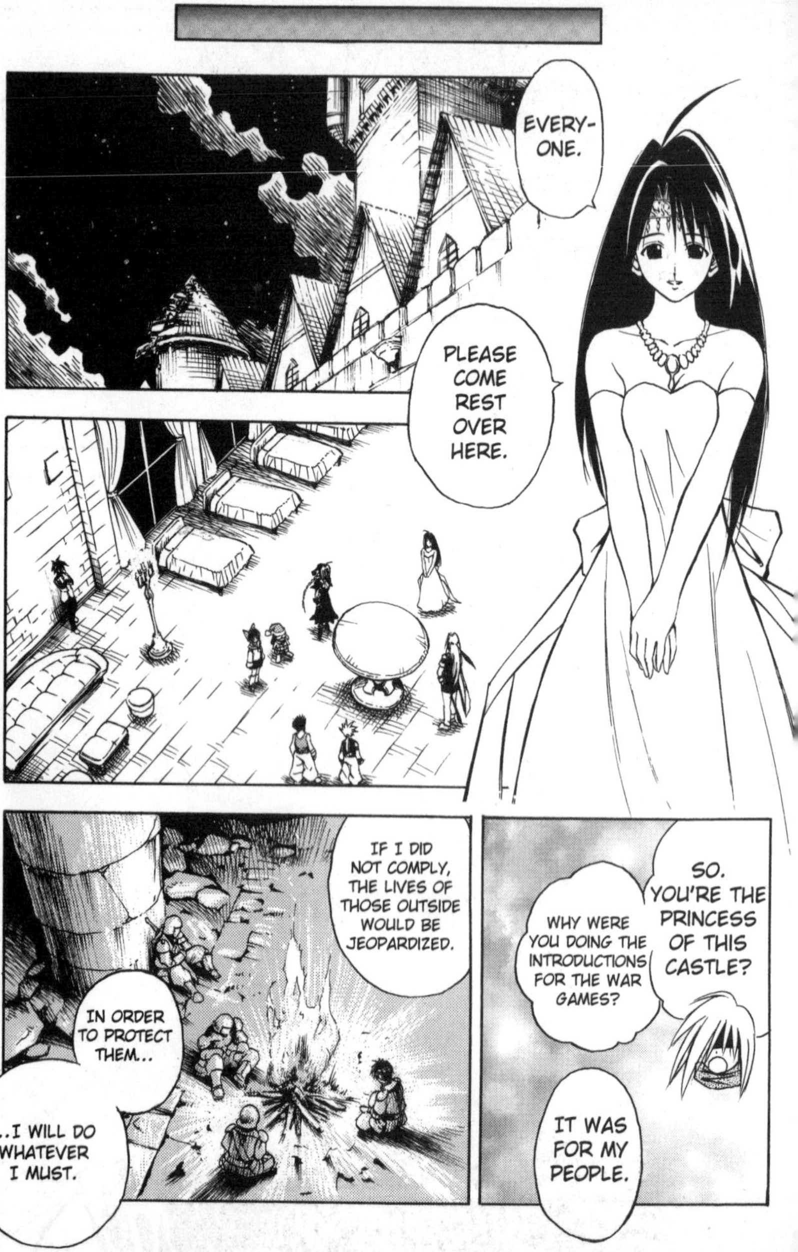
EVERY-ONE.
PLEASE COME REST OVER HERE.
SO. YOU'RE THE PRINCESS OF THIS CASTLE?
WHY WERE YOU DOING THE INTRODUCTIONS FOR THE WAR GAMES?
IT WAS FOR MY PEOPLE.
IF I DID NOT COMPLY, THE LIVES OF THOSE OUTSIDE WOULD BE JEOPARDIZED.
IN ORDER TO PROTECT THEM..
...I WILL DO WHATEVER I MUST.

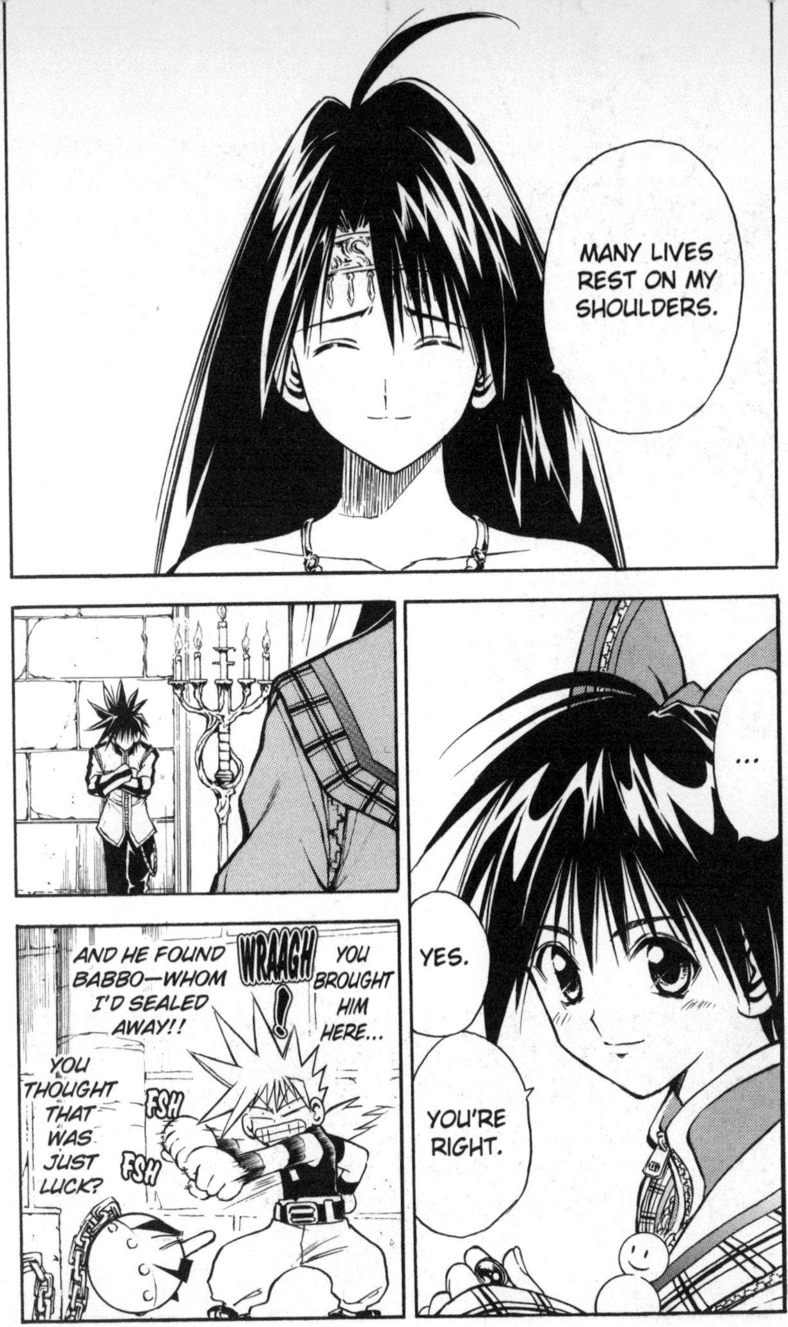
MANY LIVES REST ON MY SHOULDERS.
...
YES.
YOU'RE RIGHT.
YOU BROUGHT HIM HERE...
WRAAGH
!
AND HE FOUND BABBO—WHOM I'D SEALED AWAY!!
YOU THOUGHT THAT WAS JUST LUCK?
FSH
FSH

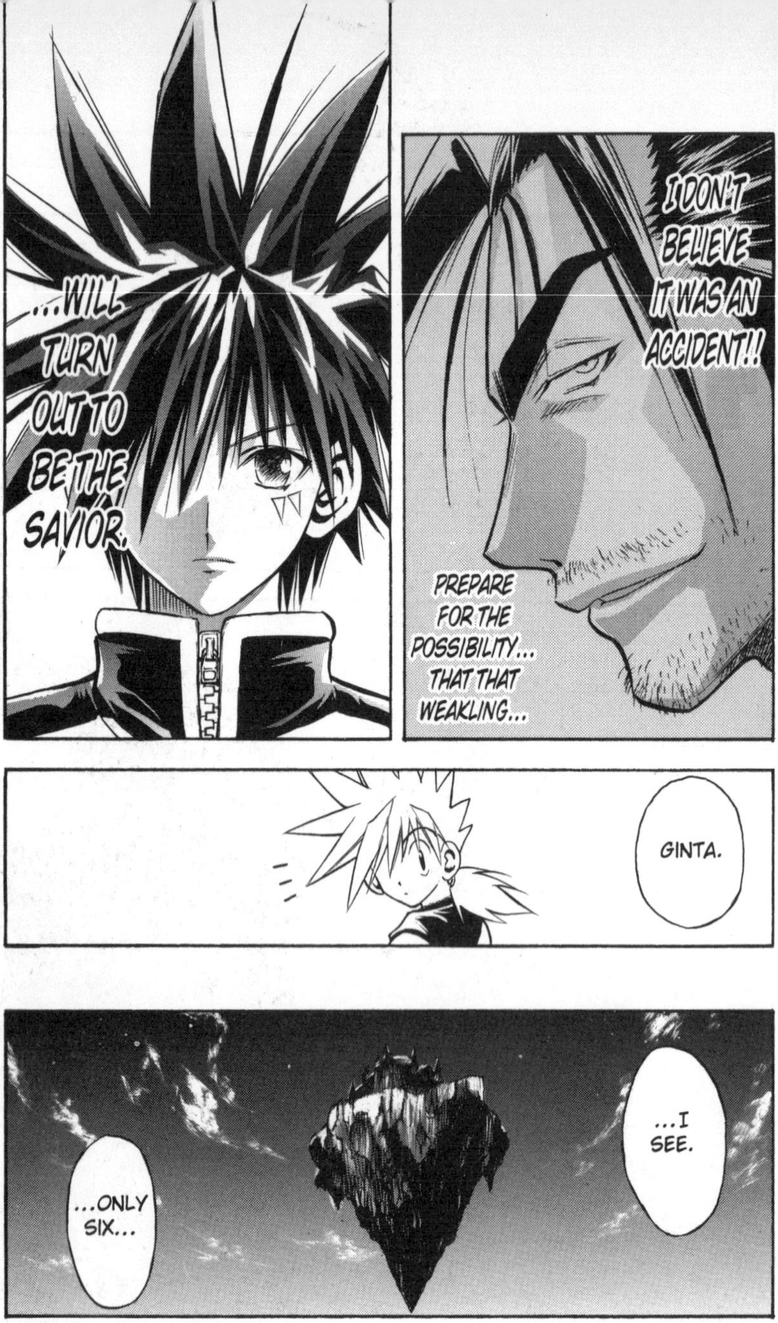
I DON'T BELIEVE IT WAS AN ACCIDENT!!
PREPARE FOR THE POSSIBILITY... THAT THAT WEAKLING...
...WILL TURN OUT TO BE THE SAVIOR.
GINTA.
...I SEE.
...ONLY SIX...

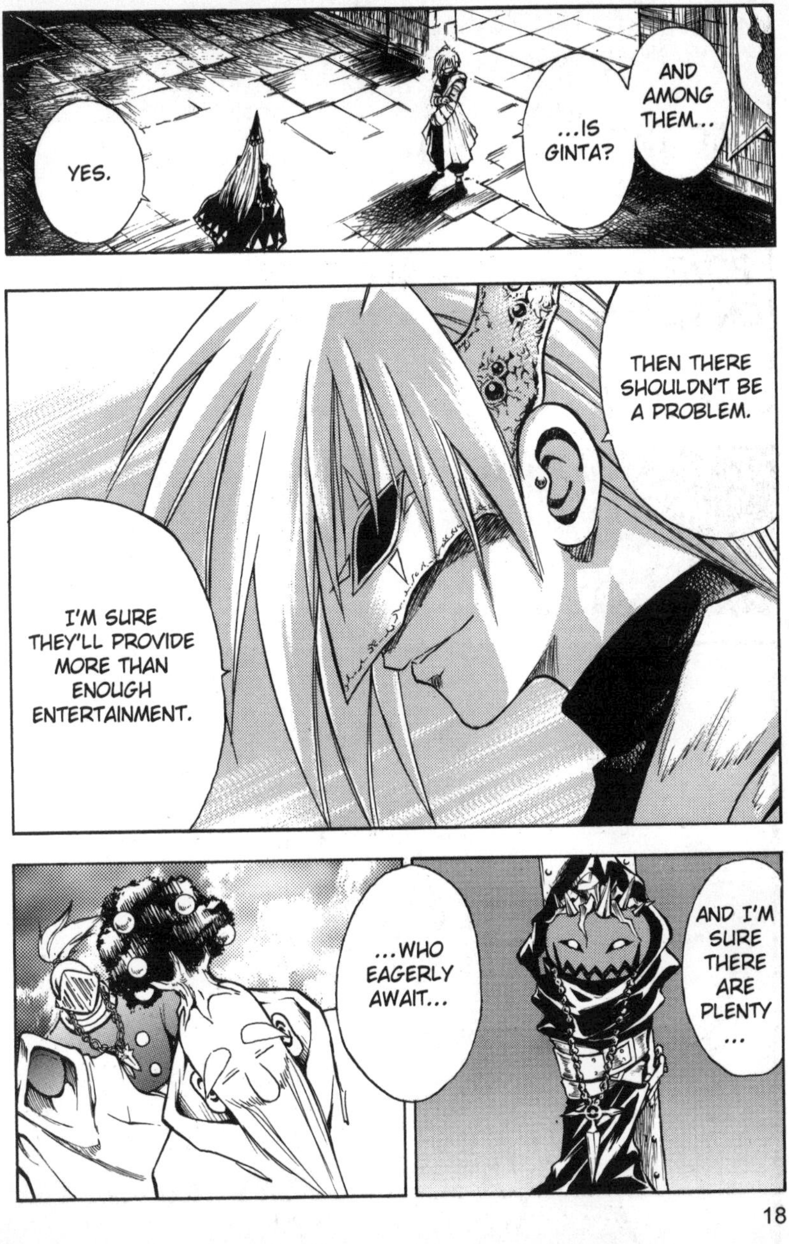
AND AMONG THEM...
...IS GINTA?
YES.
THEN THERE SHOULDN'T BE A PROBLEM.
I'M SURE THEY'LL PROVIDE MORE THAN ENOUGH ENTERTAINMENT.
AND I'M SURE THERE ARE PLENTY ...
...WHO EAGERLY AWAIT...

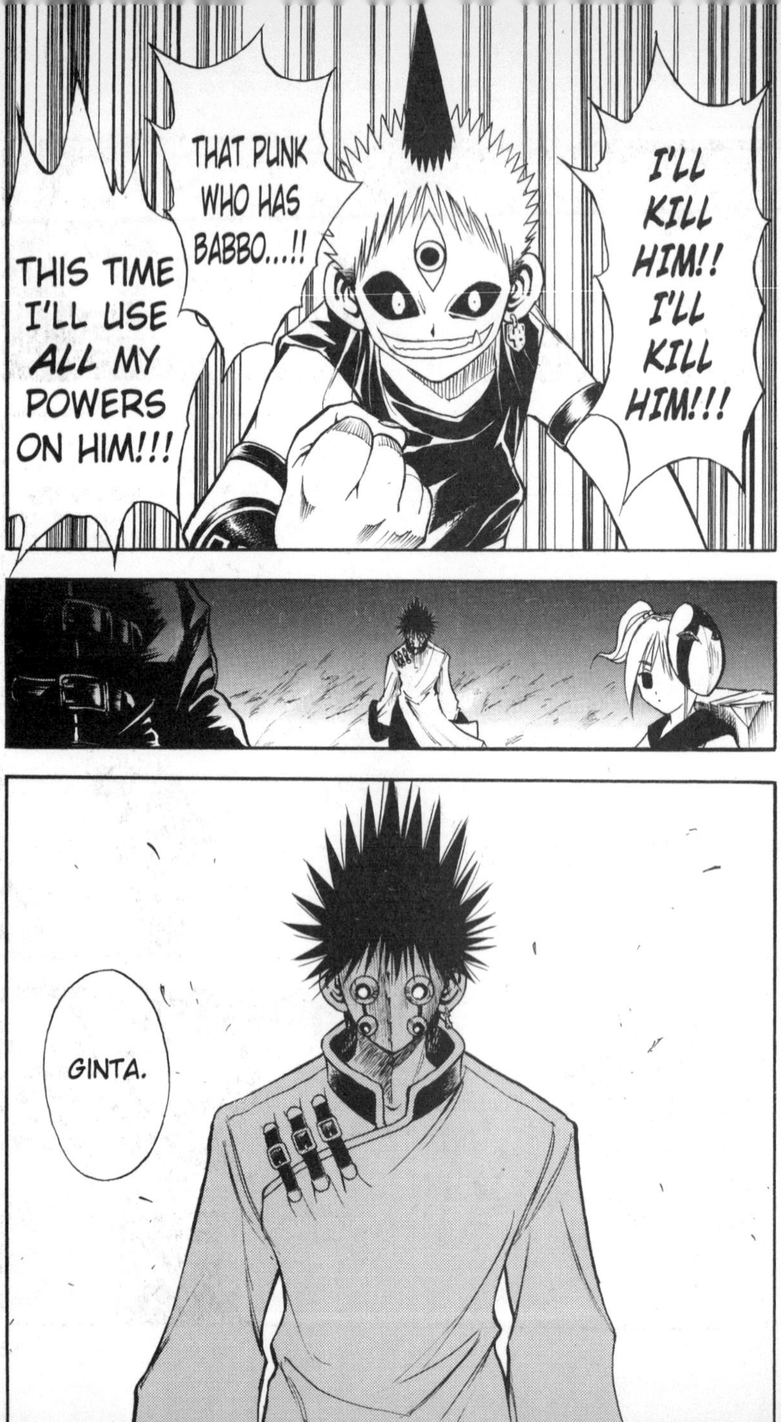
I'LL KILL HIM!! I'LL KILL HIM!!!
THAT PUNK WHO HAS BABBO...!!
THIS TIME I'LL USE ALL MY POWERS ON HIM!!!
GINTA.

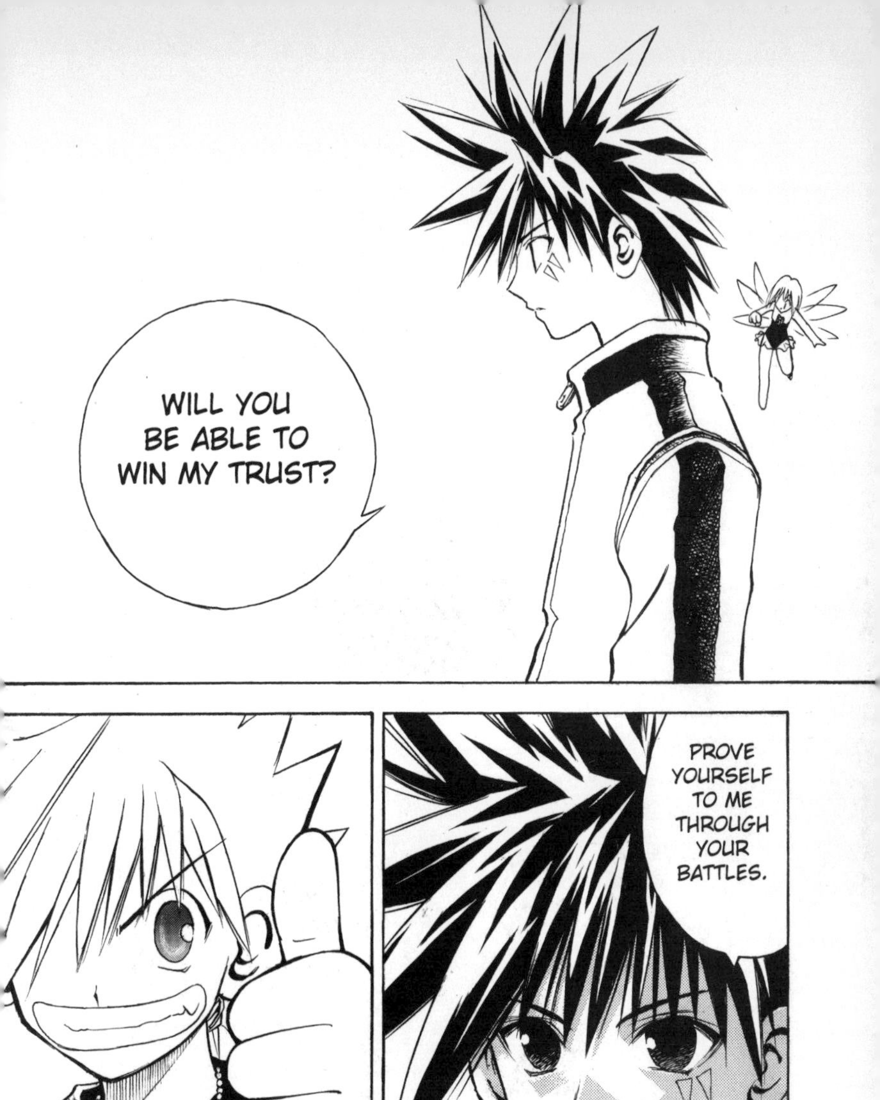
WILL YOU BE ABLE TO WIN MY TRUST?
PROVE YOURSELF TO ME THROUGH YOUR BATTLES.
I'LL BE WATCHING YOU...
THAT'S WHAT HE SAYS—BUT THE TRUTH IS THAT AL HAS HIGH HOPES FOR YOU, SHRIMP!

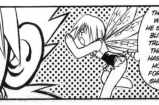

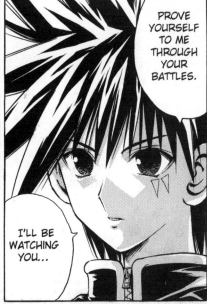

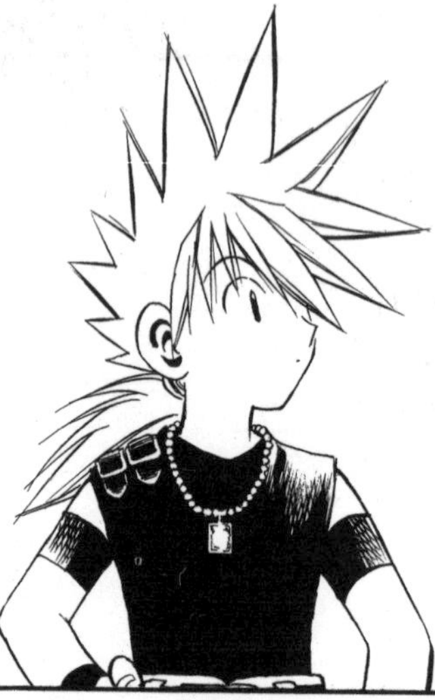

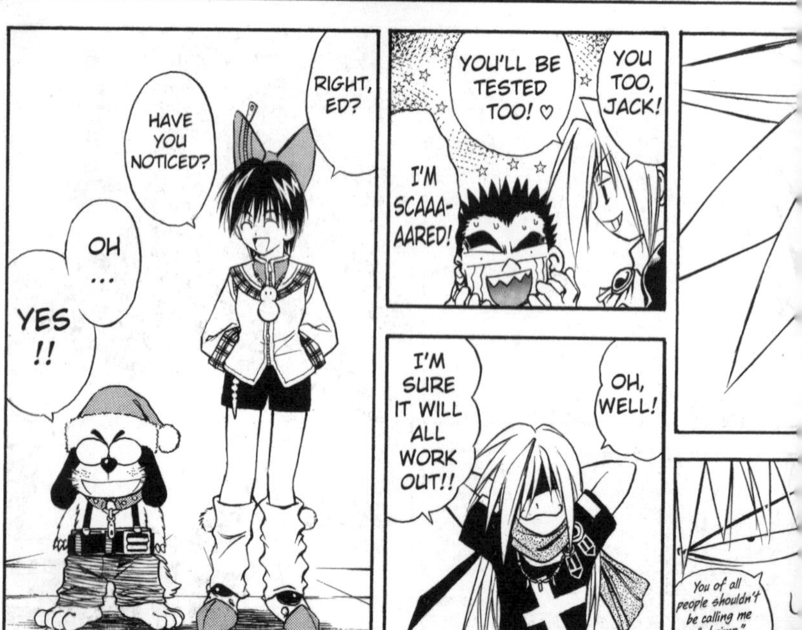
You of all people shouldn't be calling me "shrimp."
YOU TOO, JACK!
YOU'LL BE TESTED TOO! ♡
I'M SCAAA-AARED!
OH, WELL!
I'M SURE IT WILL ALL WORK OUT!!
RIGHT, ED?
HAVE YOU NOTICED?
OH ...
YES !!

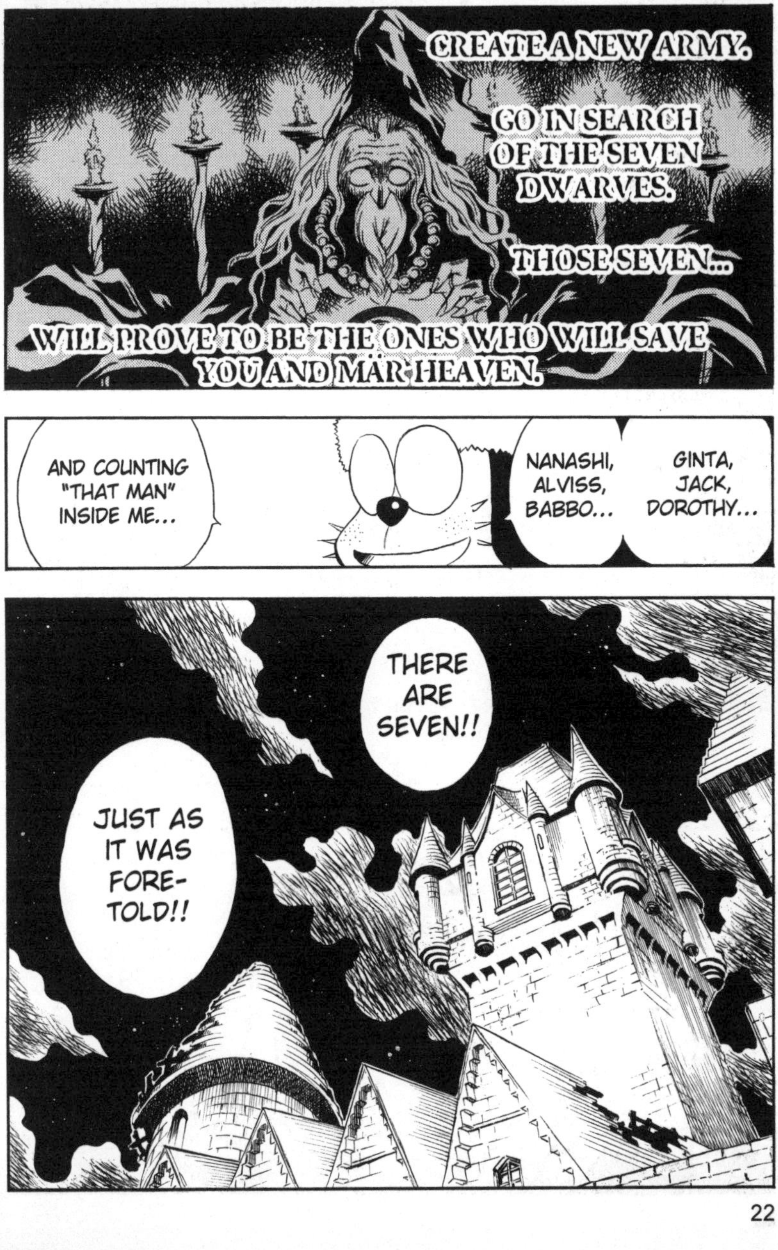
CREATE A NEW ARMY.
GO IN SEARCH OF THE SEVEN DWARVES.
THOSE SEVEN...
WILL PROVE TO BE THE ONES WHO WILL SAVE YOU AND MÄR HEAVEN.
GINTA, JACK, DOROTHY...
NANASHI, ALVISS, BABBO...
AND COUNTING "THAT MAN" INSIDE ME...
THERE ARE SEVEN!!
JUST AS IT WAS FORE-TOLD!!

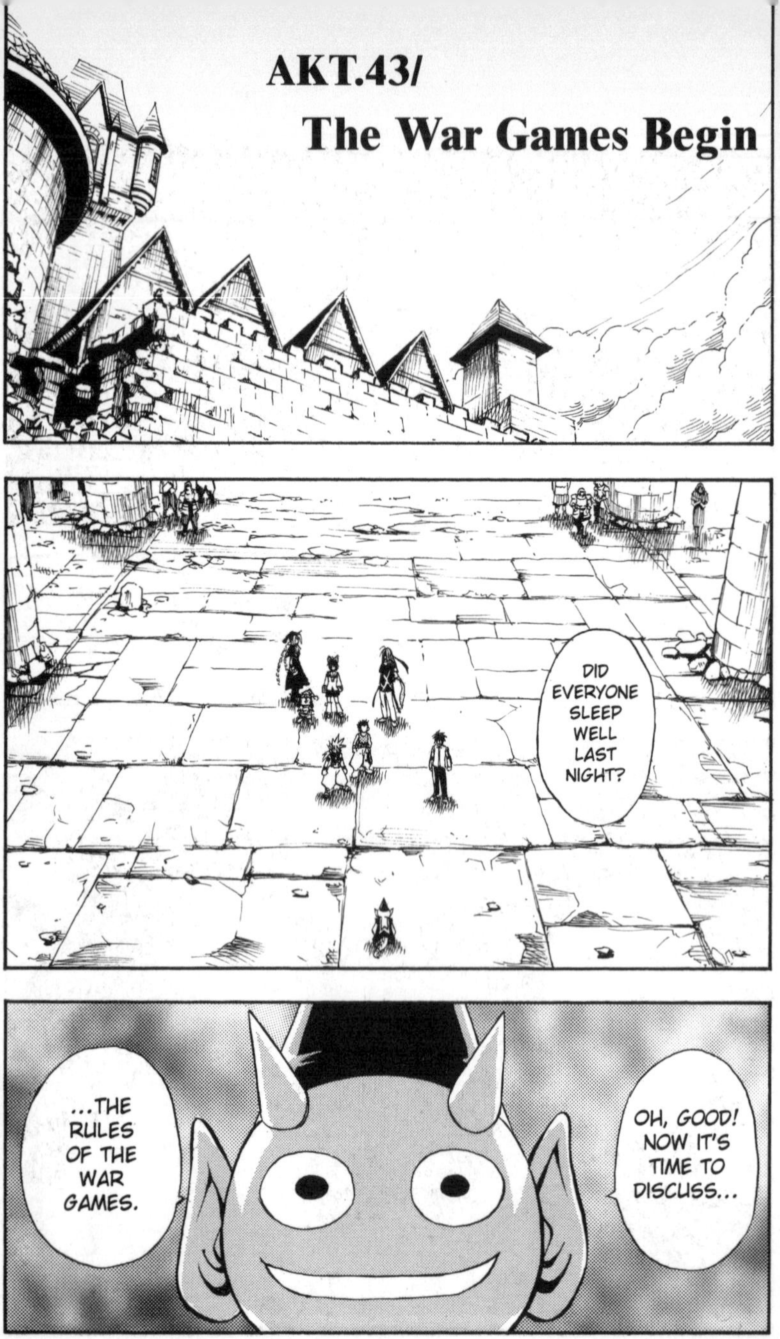
AKT.43/
The War Games Begin
DID EVERYONE SLEEP WELL LAST NIGHT?
OH, GOOD! NOW IT'S TIME TO DISCUSS...
...THE RULES OF THE WAR GAMES.

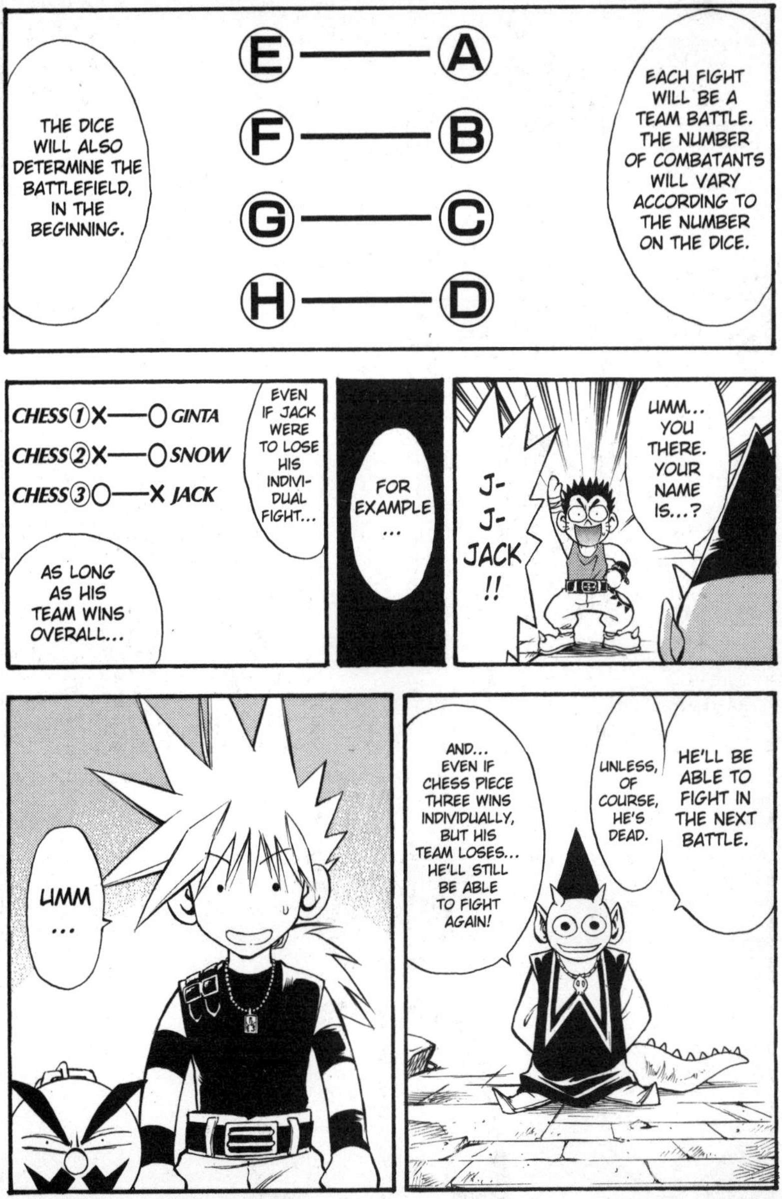
EACH FIGHT WILL BE A TEAM BATTLE. THE NUMBER OF COMBATANTS WILL VARY ACCORDING TO THE NUMBER ON THE DICE.
E—A
F—B
G—C
H—D
THE DICE WILL ALSO DETERMINE THE BATTLEFIELD, IN THE BEGINNING.
UMM... YOU THERE. YOUR NAME IS...?
J-J-JACK!!
FOR EXAMPLE...
EVEN IF JACK WERE TO LOSE HIS INDIVI-DUAL FIGHT...
CHESS① X—O GINTA
CHESS② X—O SNOW
CHESS③ O—X JACK
AS LONG AS HIS TEAM WINS OVERALL...
HE'LL BE ABLE TO FIGHT IN THE NEXT BATTLE.
UNLESS, OF COURSE, HE'S DEAD.
AND... EVEN IF CHESS PIECE THREE WINS INDIVIDUALLY, BUT HIS TEAM LOSES... HE'LL STILL BE ABLE TO FIGHT AGAIN!
UMM...

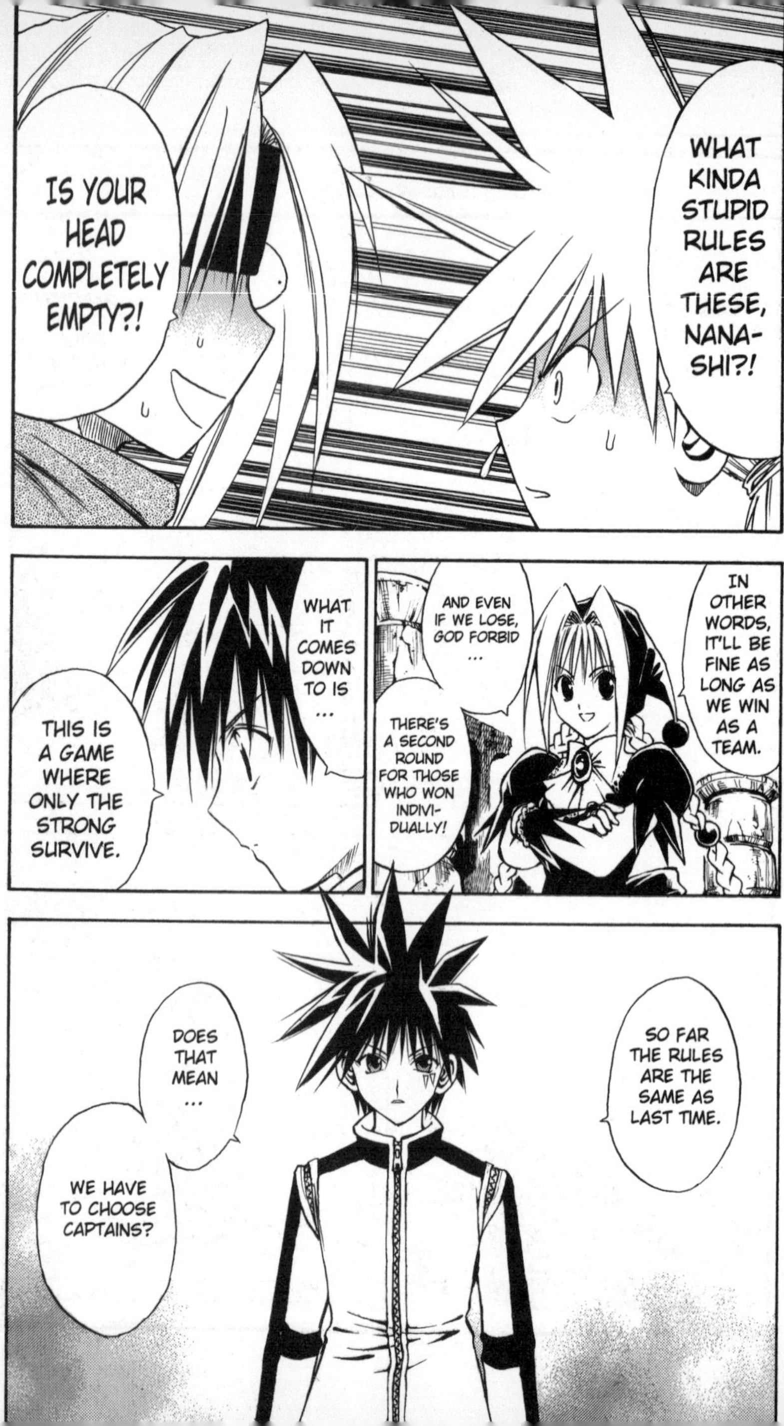
WHAT KINDA STUPID RULES ARE THESE, NANA-SHI?!
IS YOUR HEAD COMPLETELY EMPTY?!
IN OTHER WORDS, IT'LL BE FINE AS LONG AS WE WIN AS A TEAM.
AND EVEN IF WE LOSE, GOD FORBID ...
THERE'S A SECOND ROUND FOR THOSE WHO WON INDIVIDUALLY!
WHAT IT COMES DOWN TO IS ...
THIS IS A GAME WHERE ONLY THE STRONG SURVIVE.
SO FAR THE RULES ARE THE SAME AS LAST TIME.
DOES THAT MEAN ...
WE HAVE TO CHOOSE CAPTAINS?

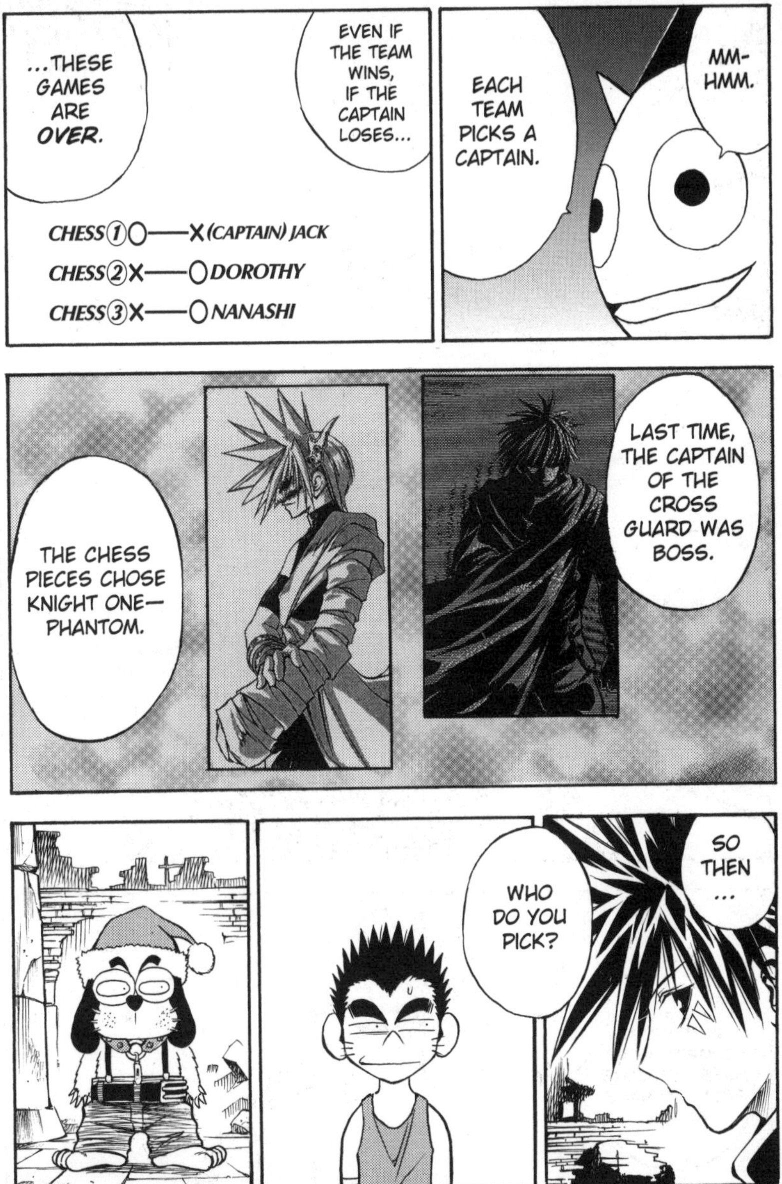
MM-HMM.
EACH TEAM PICKS A CAPTAIN.
EVEN IF THE TEAM WINS, IF THE CAPTAIN LOSES...
...THESE GAMES ARE OVER.
CHESS① ○——X (CAPTAIN) JACK
CHESS② X——○ DOROTHY
CHESS③ X——○ NANASHI
LAST TIME, THE CAPTAIN OF THE CROSS GUARD WAS BOSS.
THE CHESS PIECES CHOSE KNIGHT ONE—PHANTOM.
SO THEN ...
WHO DO YOU PICK?

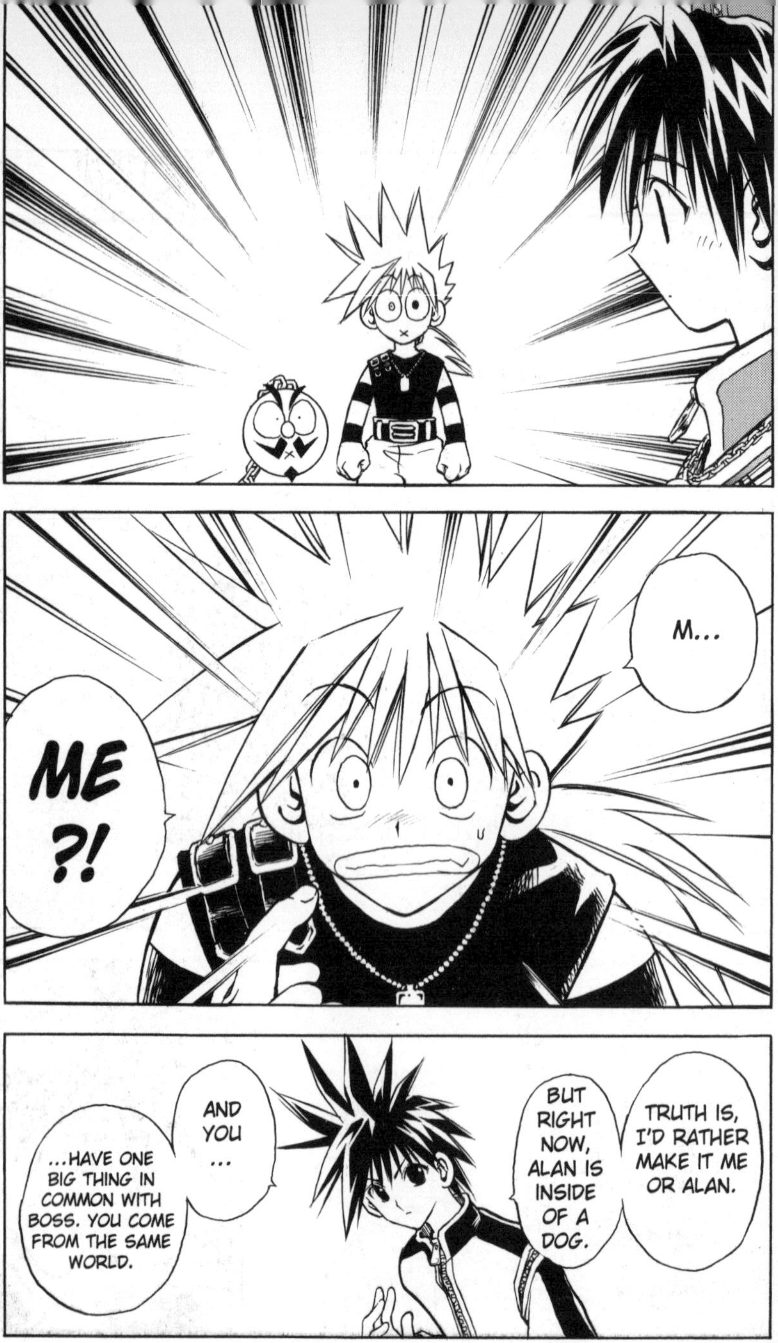
M...
ME ?!
TRUTH IS, I'D RATHER MAKE IT ME OR ALAN.
BUT RIGHT NOW, ALAN IS INSIDE OF A DOG.
AND YOU ...
...HAVE ONE BIG THING IN COMMON WITH BOSS. YOU COME FROM THE SAME WORLD.

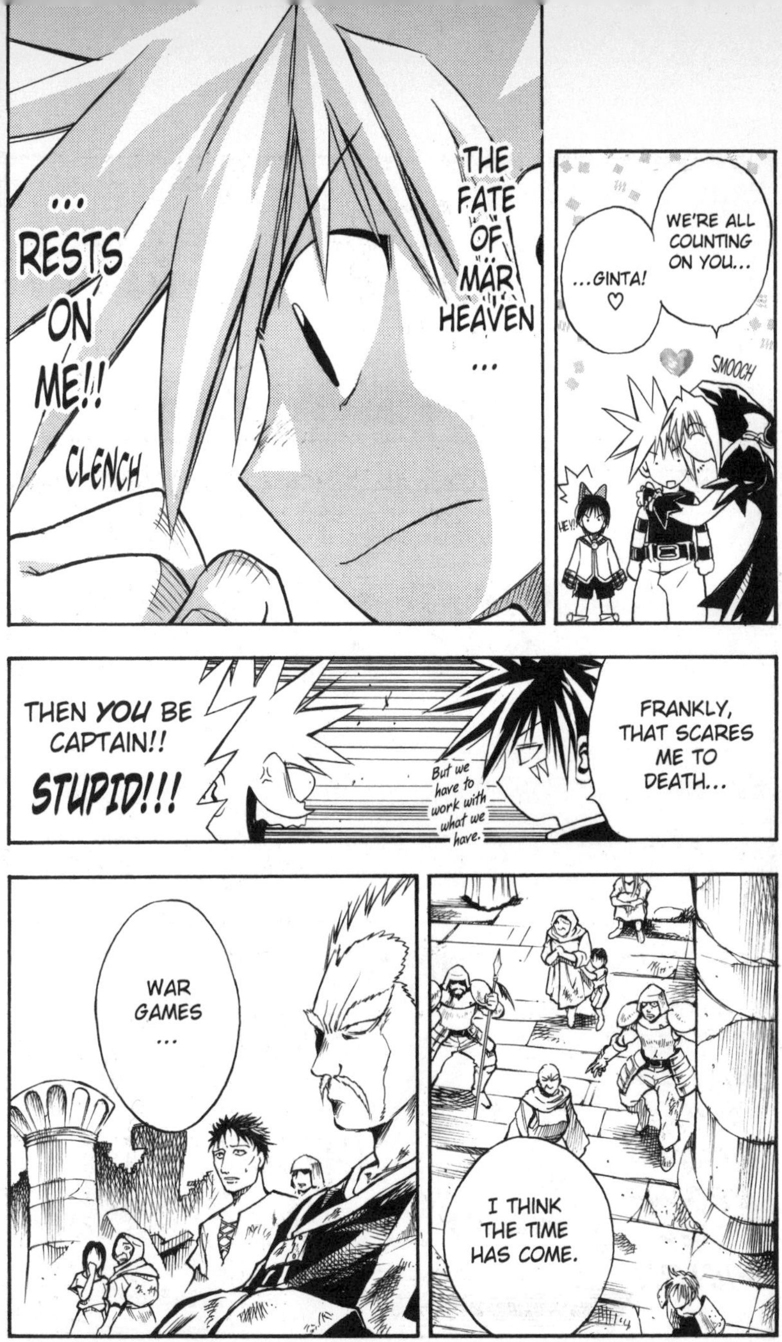
WE'RE ALL COUNTING ON YOU...
...GINTA! ♡
SMOOCH
HEY!
THE FATE OF MÄR HEAVEN...
...RESTS ON ME!!
CLENCH
FRANKLY, THAT SCARES ME TO DEATH...
But we have to work with what we have.
THEN *YOU* BE CAPTAIN!! **STUPID!!!**
I THINK THE TIME HAS COME.
WAR GAMES...

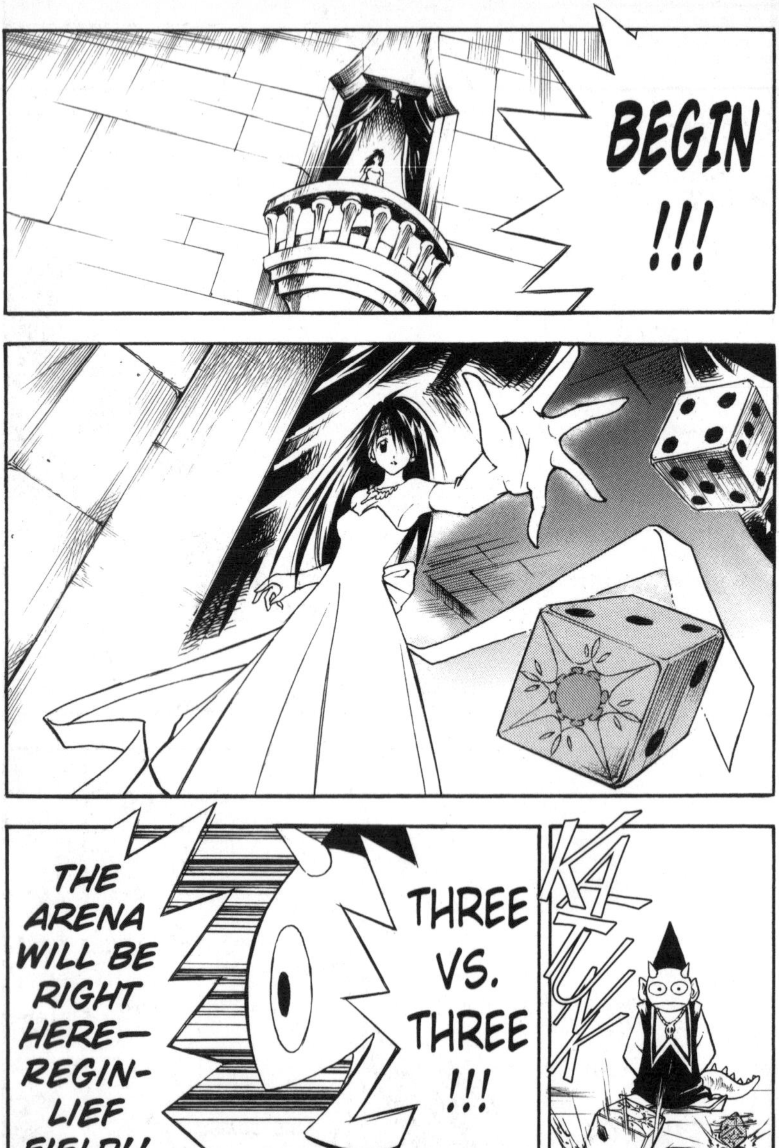
BEGIN!!!
KA-TUNK
THREE VS. THREE!!!
THE ARENA WILL BE RIGHT HERE—REGIN-LIEF FIELD!!

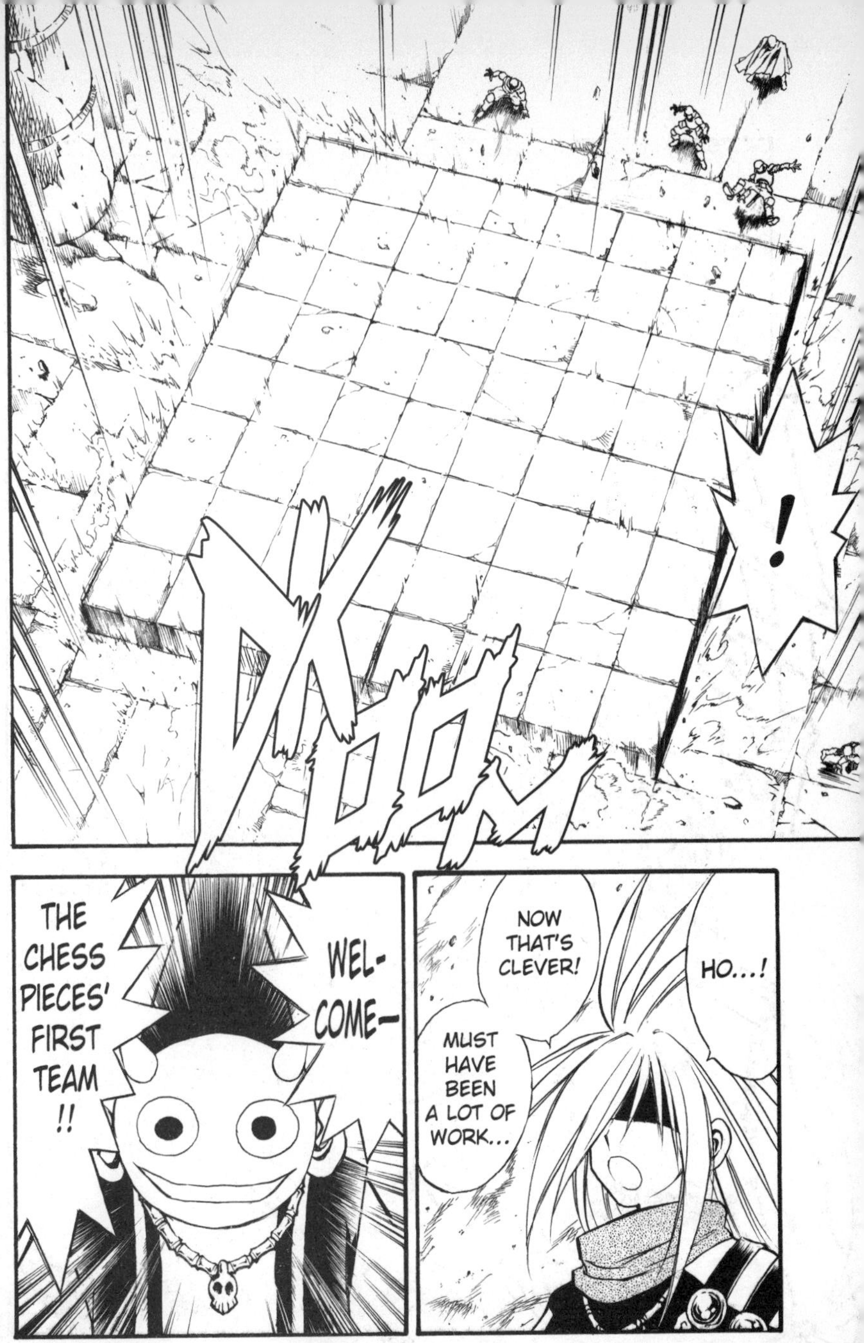
!
HO...!
NOW THAT'S CLEVER!
MUST HAVE BEEN A LOT OF WORK...
WEL-COME—
THE CHESS PIECES' FIRST TEAM !!

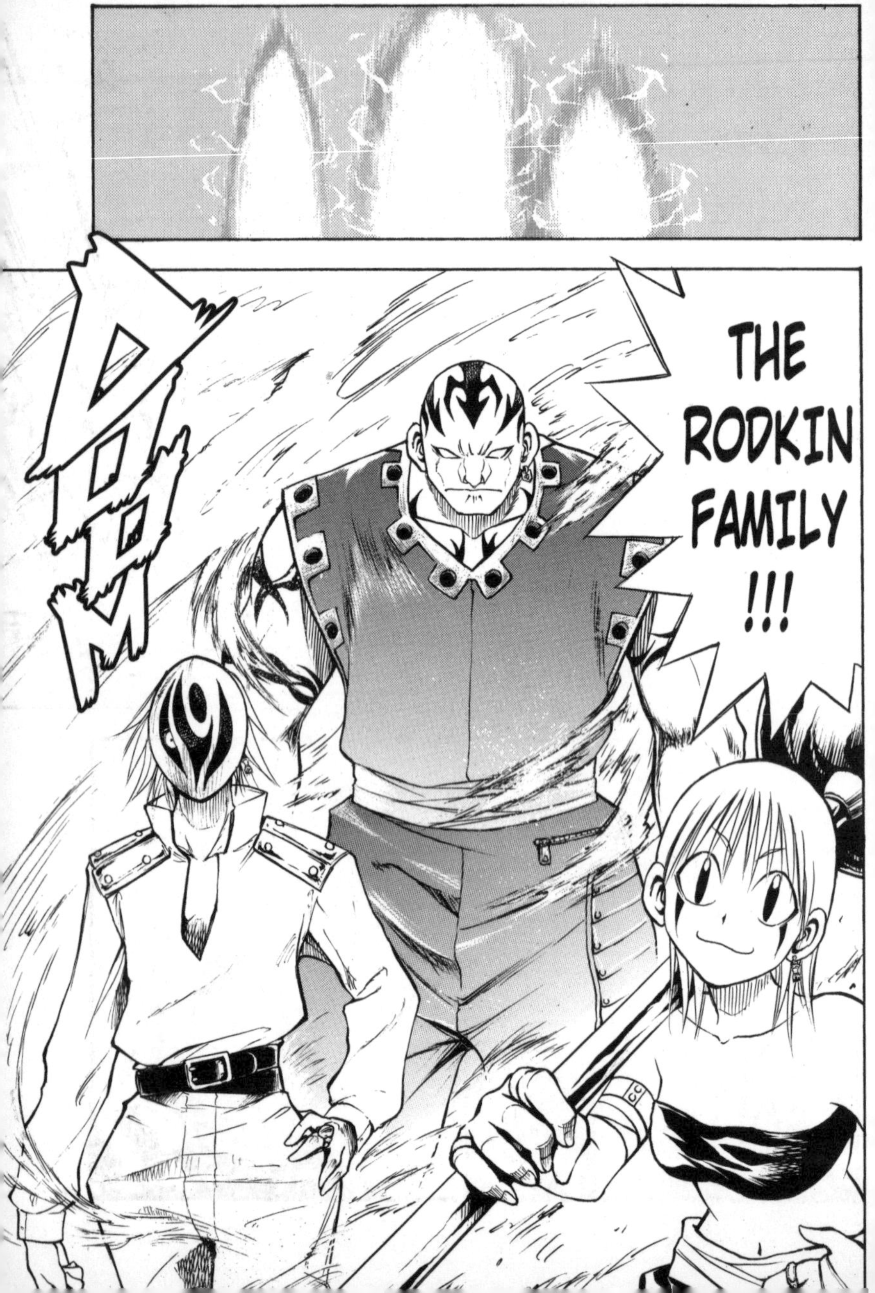
THE RODKIN FAMILY !!!
DOOM

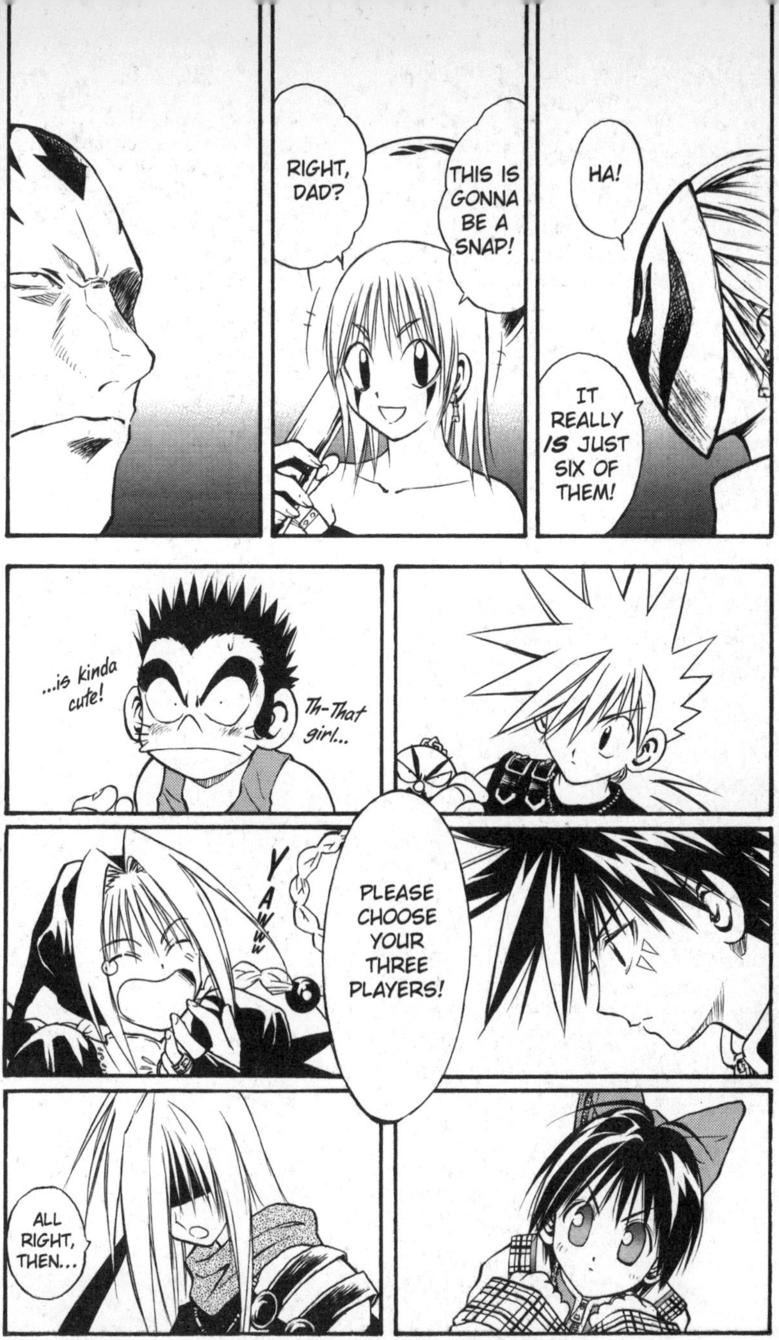
HA!
IT REALLY IS JUST SIX OF THEM!
THIS IS GONNA BE A SNAP!
RIGHT, DAD?
Th-That girl...
...is kinda cute!
PLEASE CHOOSE YOUR THREE PLAYERS!
YAWWW
ALL RIGHT, THEN...

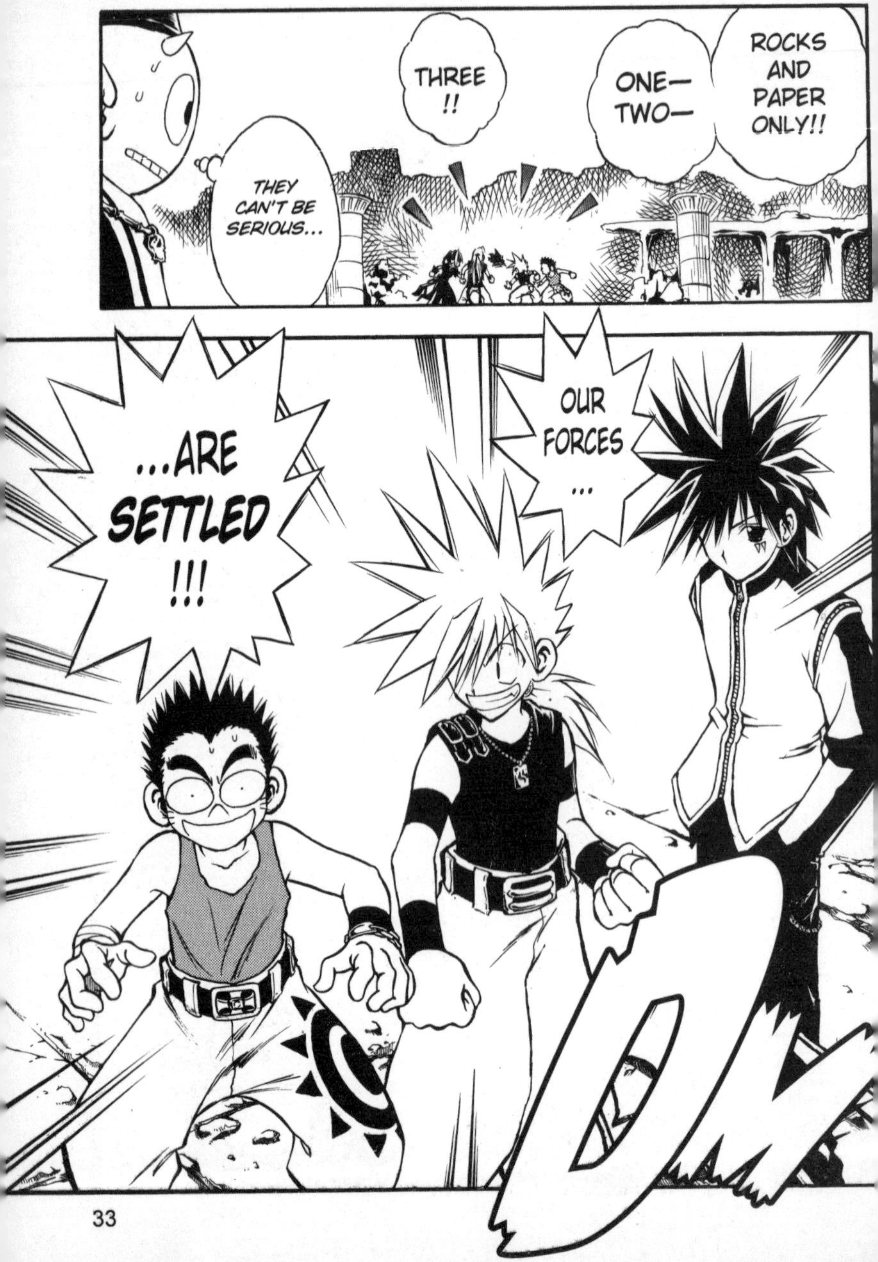
ROCKS AND PAPER ONLY!!
ONE— TWO—
THREE !!
THEY CAN'T BE SERIOUS...
OUR FORCES ...
...ARE SETTLED !!!

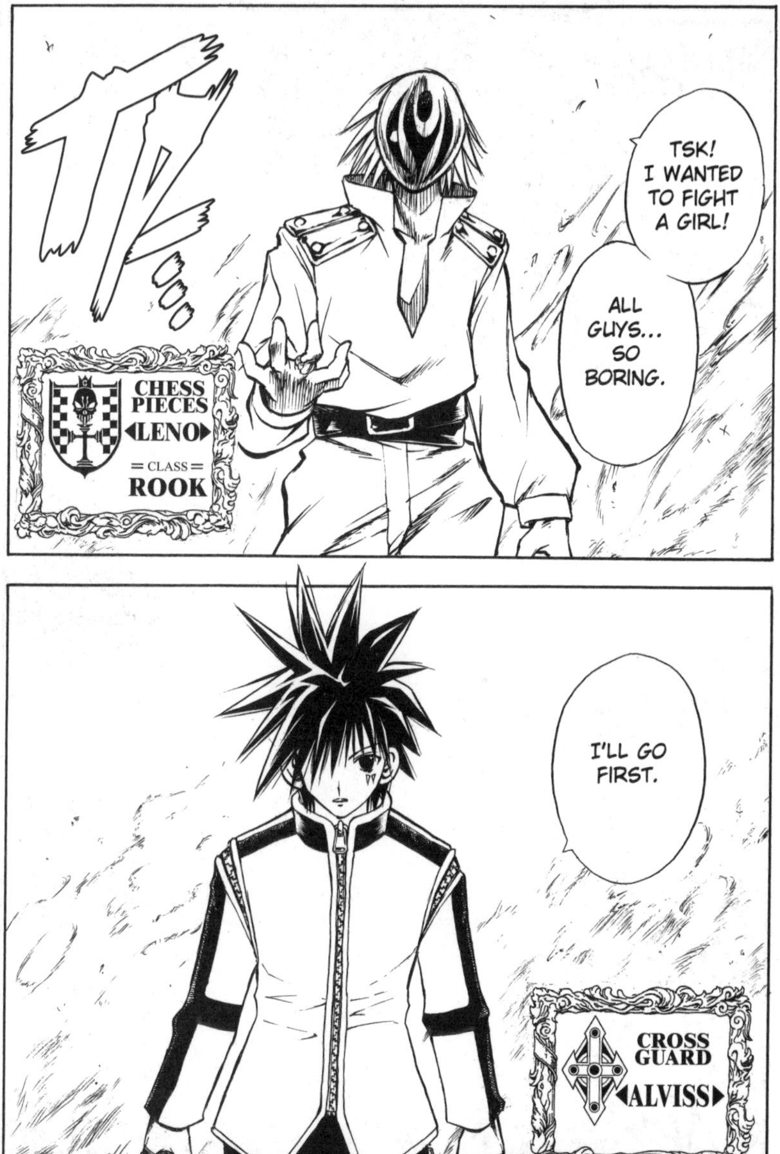
TSK! I WANTED TO FIGHT A GIRL!
ALL GUYS... SO BORING.
CHESS PIECES
◀LENO▶
=CLASS=
ROOK
I'LL GO FIRST.
CROSS GUARD
◀ALVISS▶

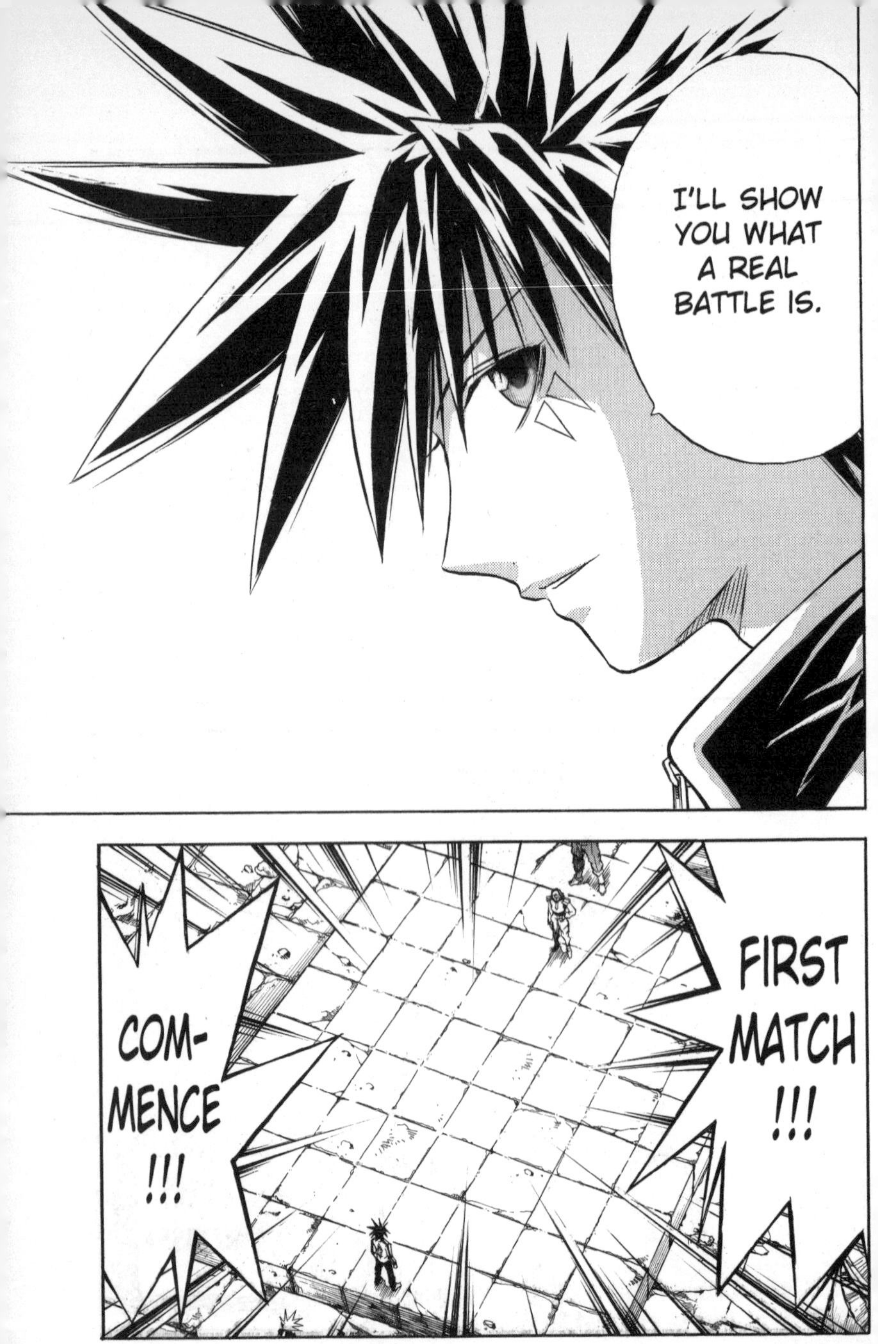
I'LL SHOW YOU WHAT A REAL BATTLE IS.
FIRST MATCH !!!
COM-MENCE !!!

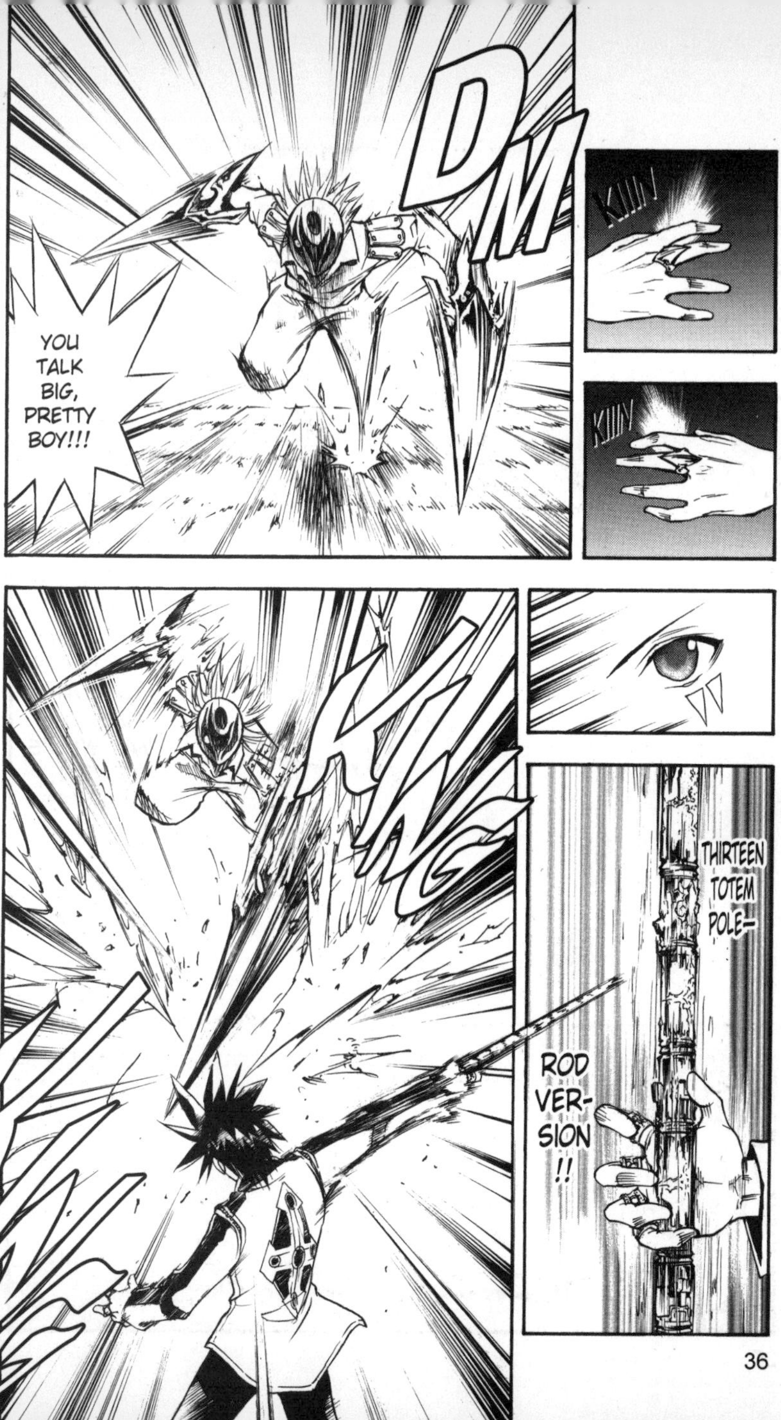
KIIIN
KIIIN
DM
YOU TALK BIG, PRETTY BOY!!!
THIRTEEN TOTEM POLE—
ROD VERSION!!

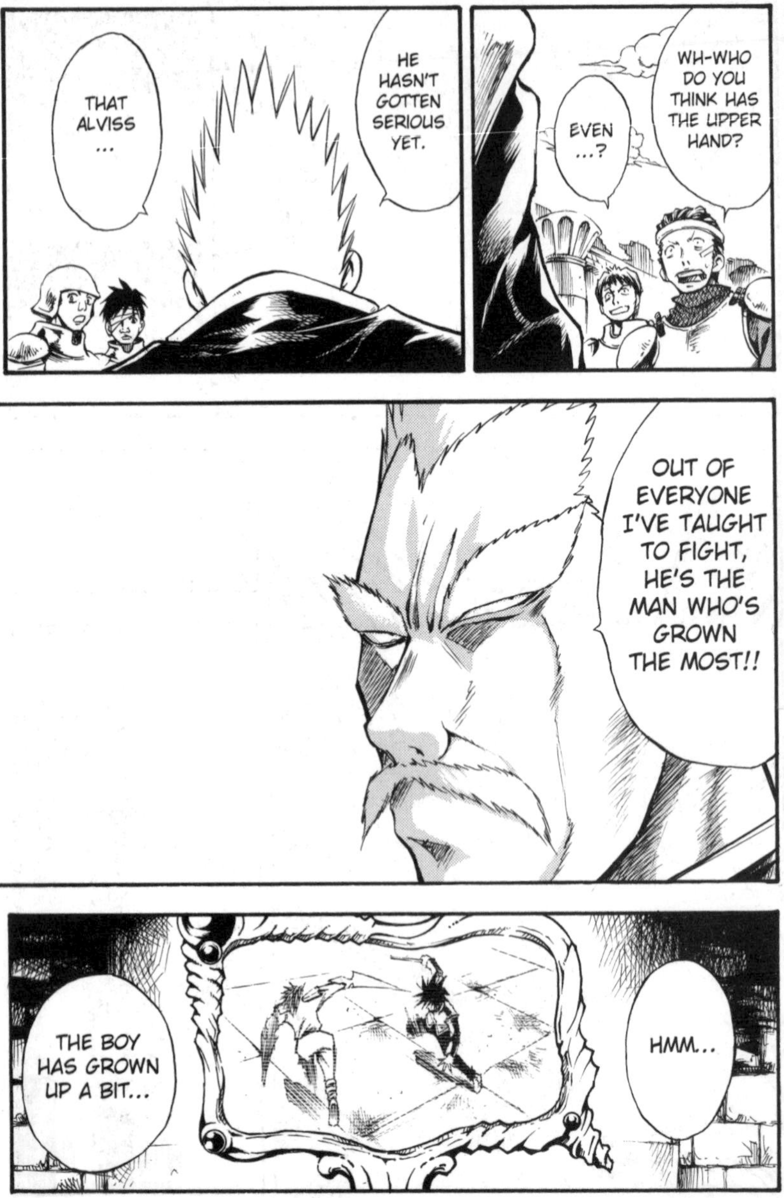
WH-WHO DO YOU THINK HAS THE UPPER HAND?
EVEN ...?
HE HASN'T GOTTEN SERIOUS YET.
THAT ALVISS ...
OUT OF EVERYONE I'VE TAUGHT TO FIGHT, HE'S THE MAN WHO'S GROWN THE MOST!!
HMM...
THE BOY HAS GROWN UP A BIT...

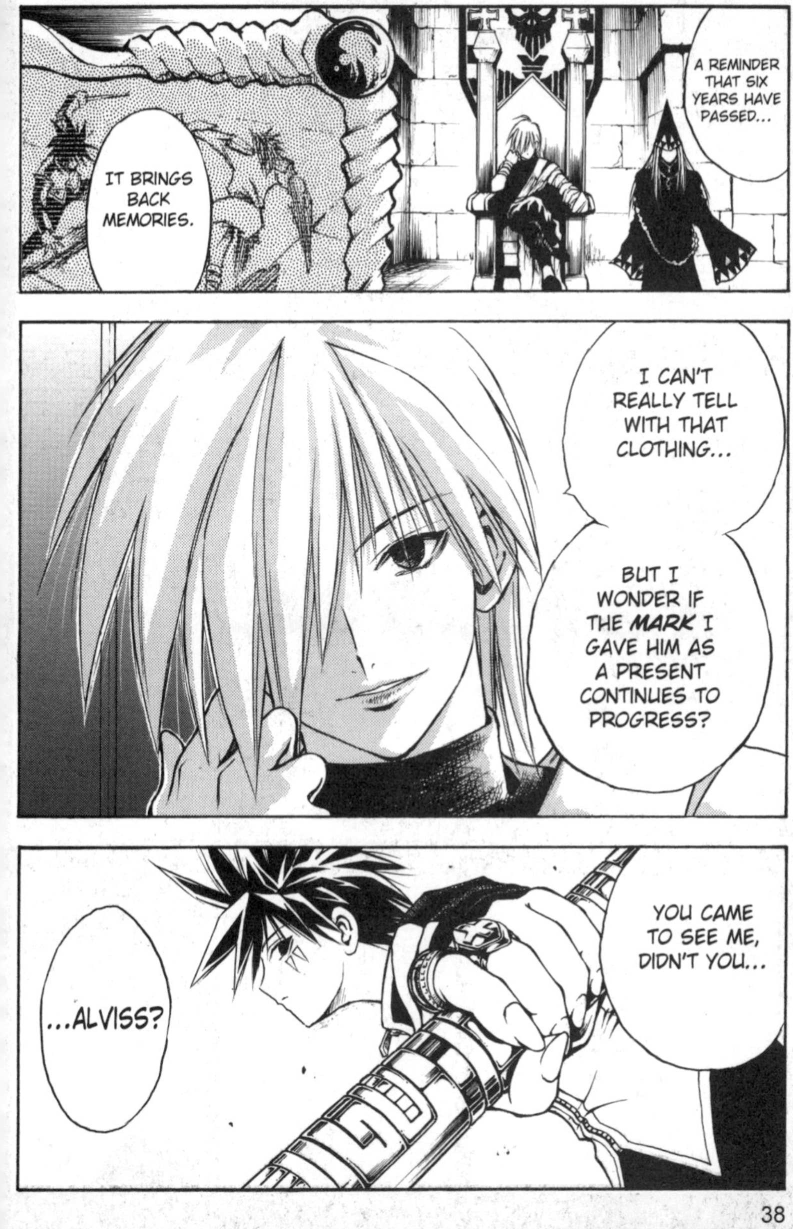
A REMINDER THAT SIX YEARS HAVE PASSED...
IT BRINGS BACK MEMORIES.
I CAN'T REALLY TELL WITH THAT CLOTHING...
BUT I WONDER IF THE **MARK** I GAVE HIM AS A PRESENT CONTINUES TO PROGRESS?
YOU CAME TO SEE ME, DIDN'T YOU...
...ALVISS?

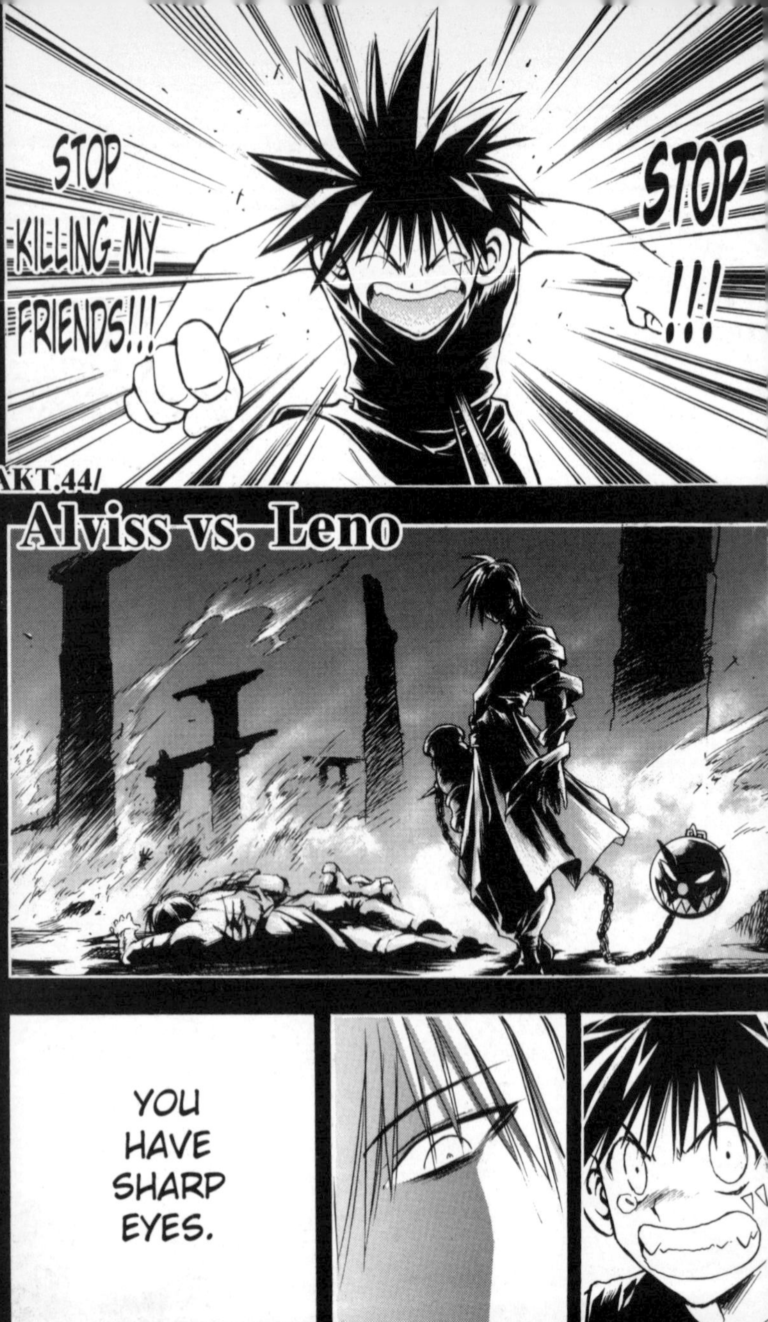
STOP!!!
STOP KILLING MY FRIENDS!!!
AKT.44/
Alviss vs. Leno
YOU HAVE SHARP EYES.

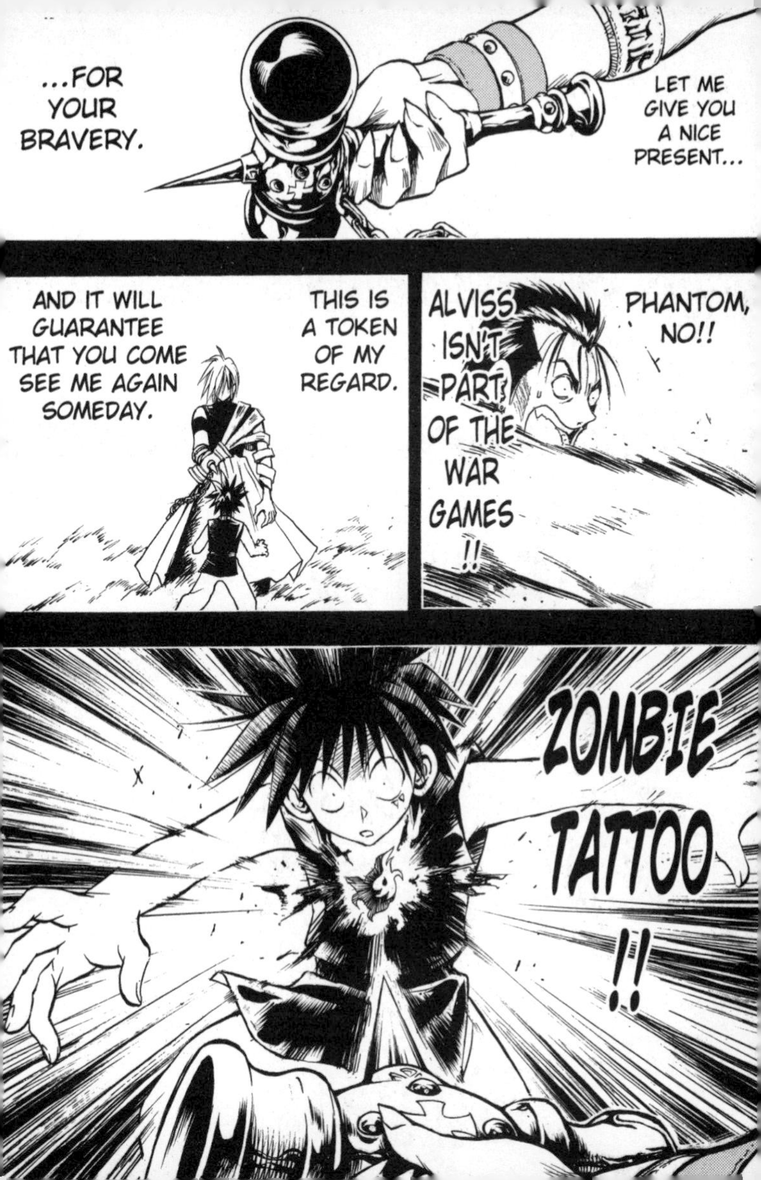
LET ME GIVE YOU A NICE PRESENT...
...FOR YOUR BRAVERY.
PHANTOM, NO!!
ALVISS ISN'T PART OF THE WAR GAMES!!
THIS IS A TOKEN OF MY REGARD.
AND IT WILL GUARANTEE THAT YOU COME SEE ME AGAIN SOMEDAY.
ZOMBIE TATTOO!!

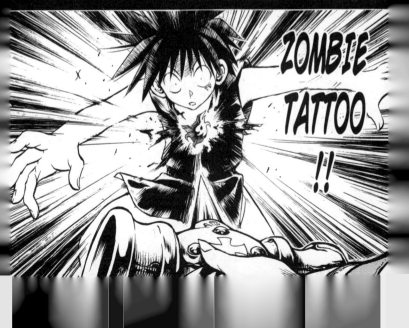

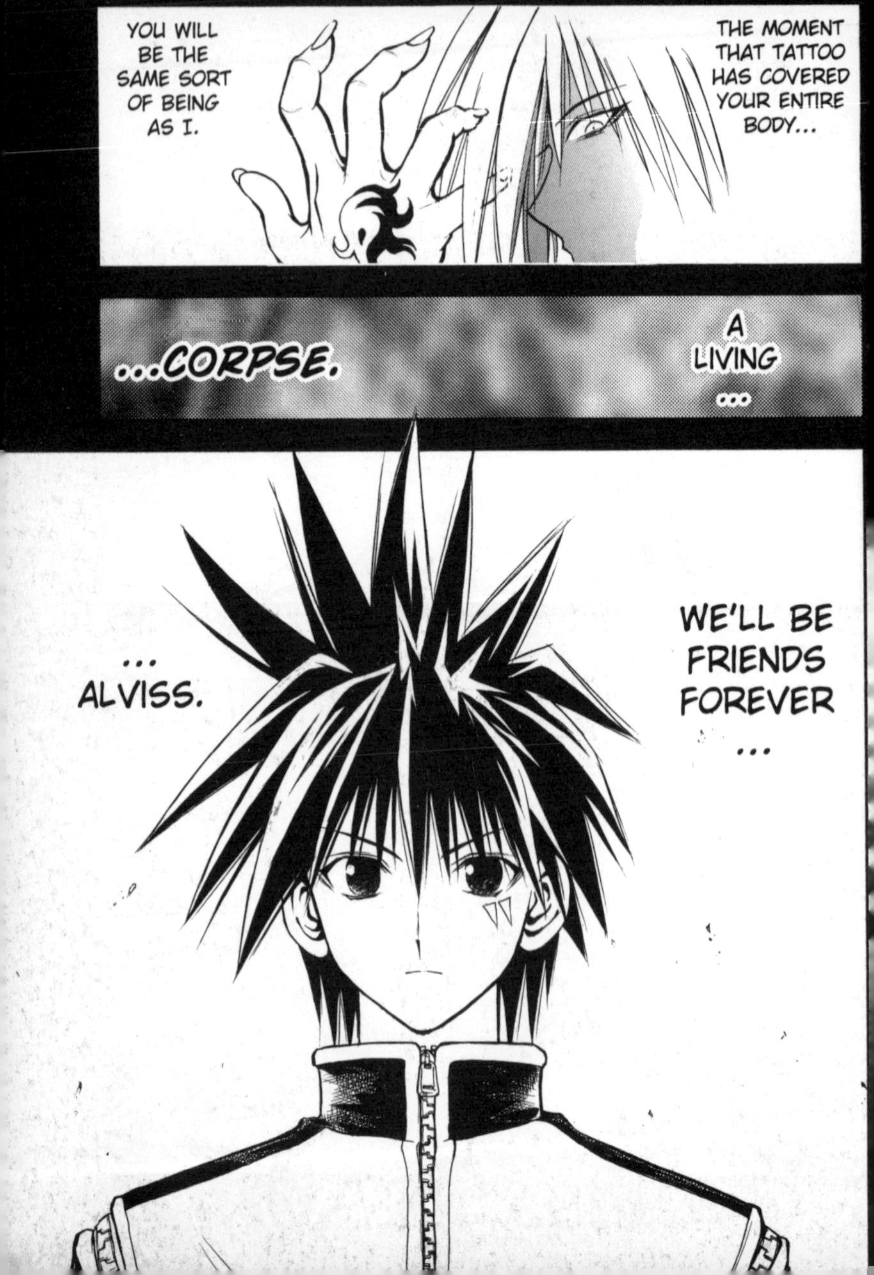
THE MOMENT THAT TATTOO HAS COVERED YOUR ENTIRE BODY...
YOU WILL BE THE SAME SORT OF BEING AS I.
A LIVING ...
...CORPSE.
WE'LL BE FRIENDS FOREVER ...
... ALVISS.

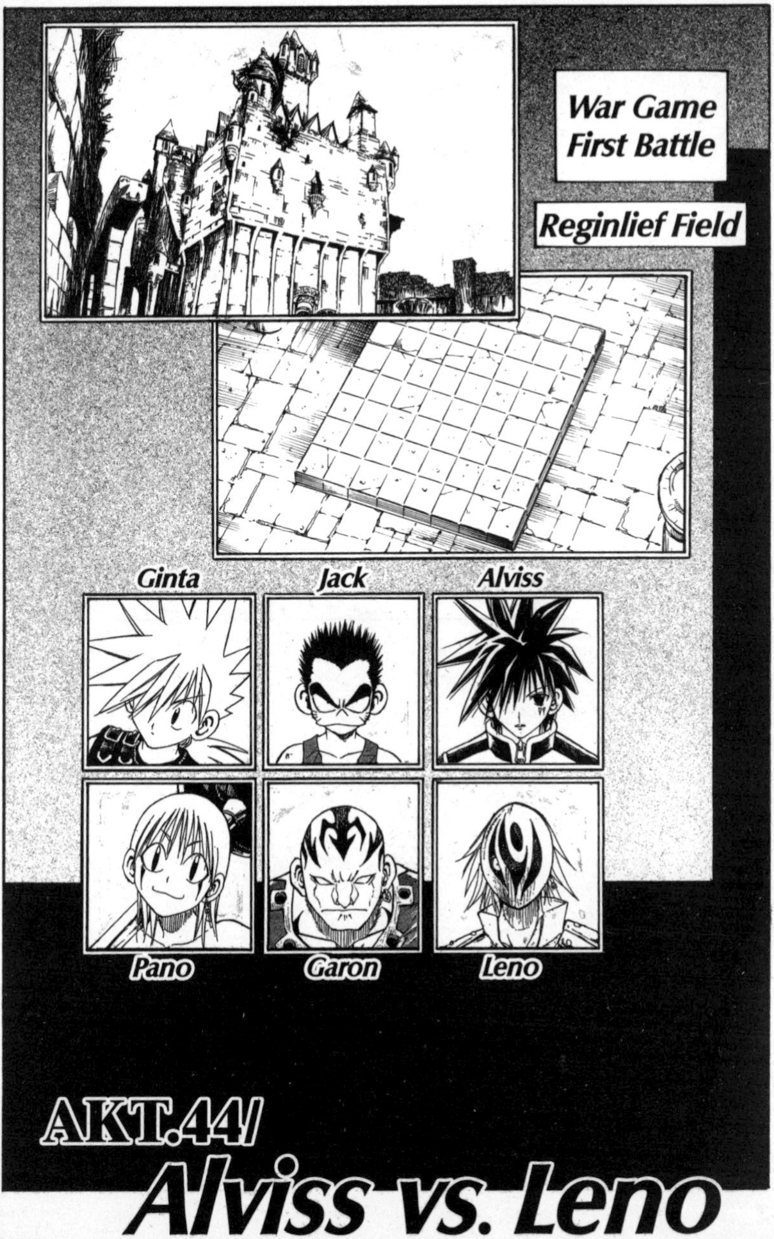
War Game
First Battle
Reginlief Field
Alviss
Jack
Ginta
Leno
Garon
Pano

AKT.44/ Alviss vs. Leno

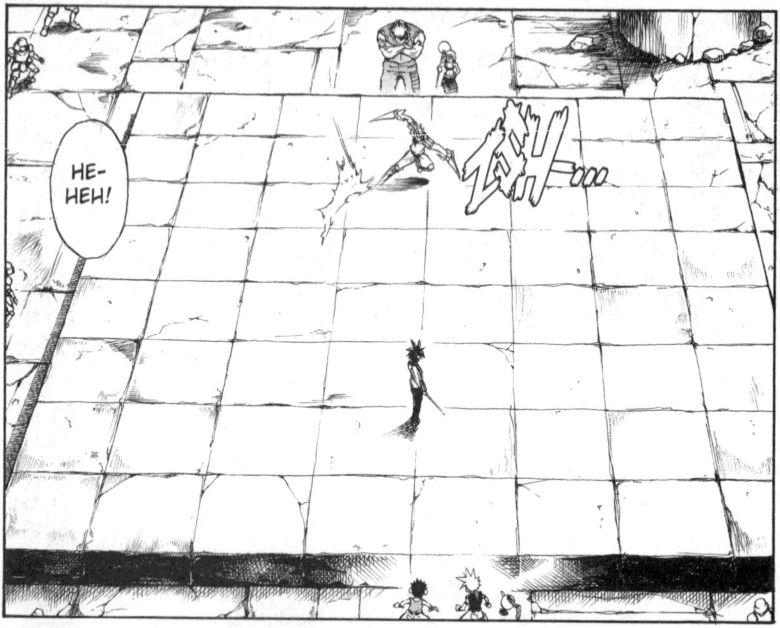
HE-HEH!

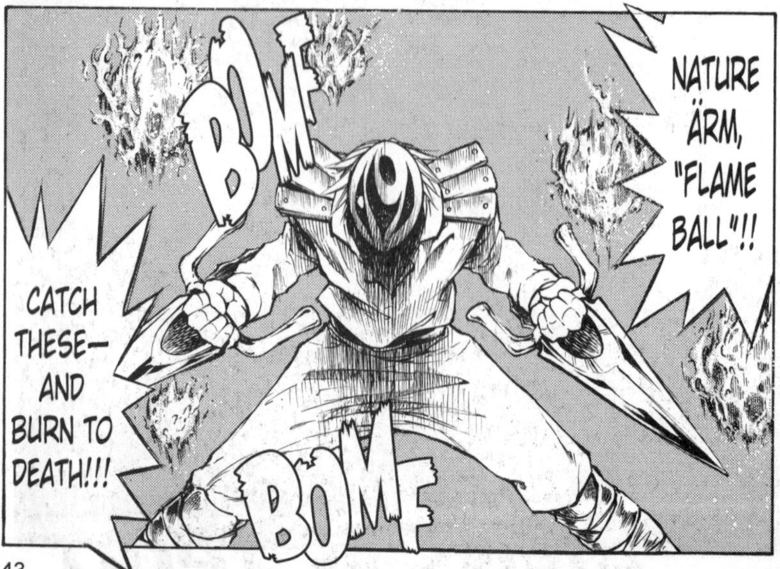
NATURE ÄRM, "FLAME BALL"!!
BOMF
CATCH THESE— AND BURN TO DEATH!!!
BOMF

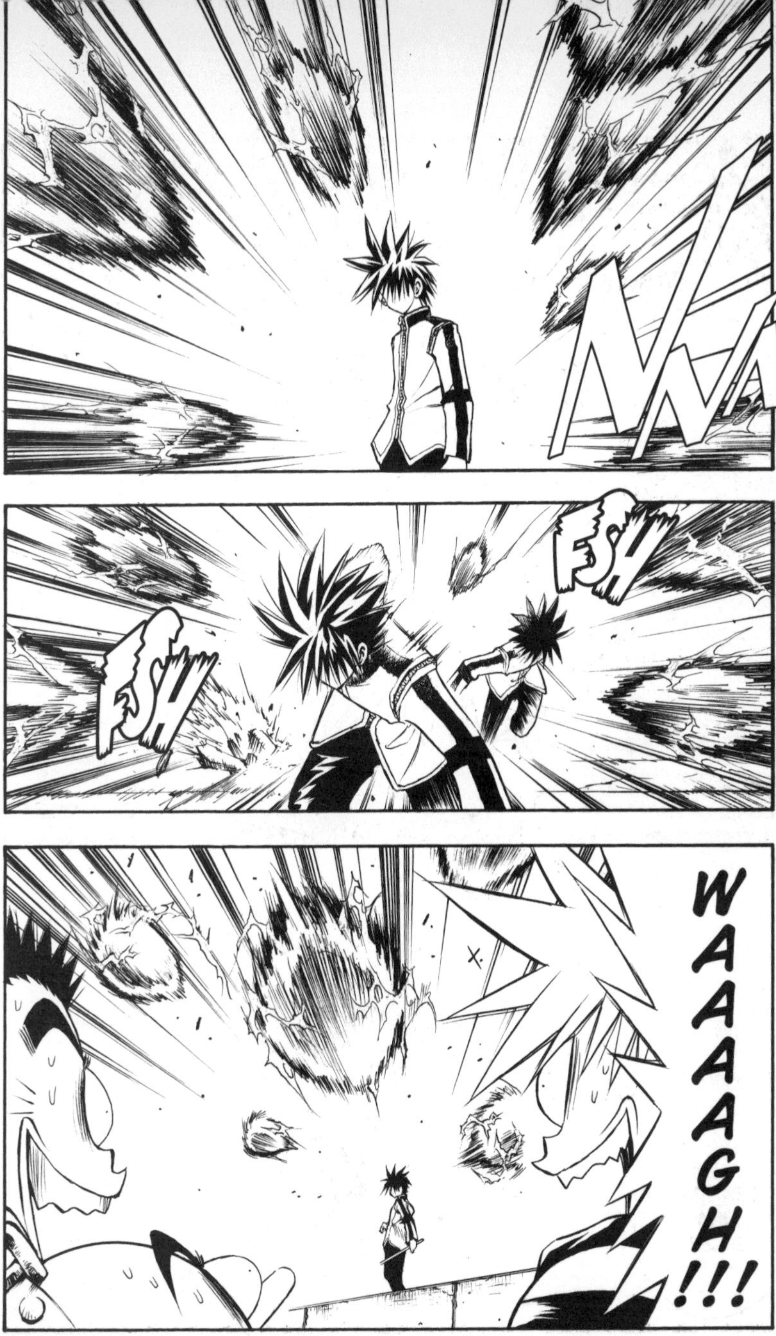
NNN
FSH
FSH
WAAAAAGH!!!

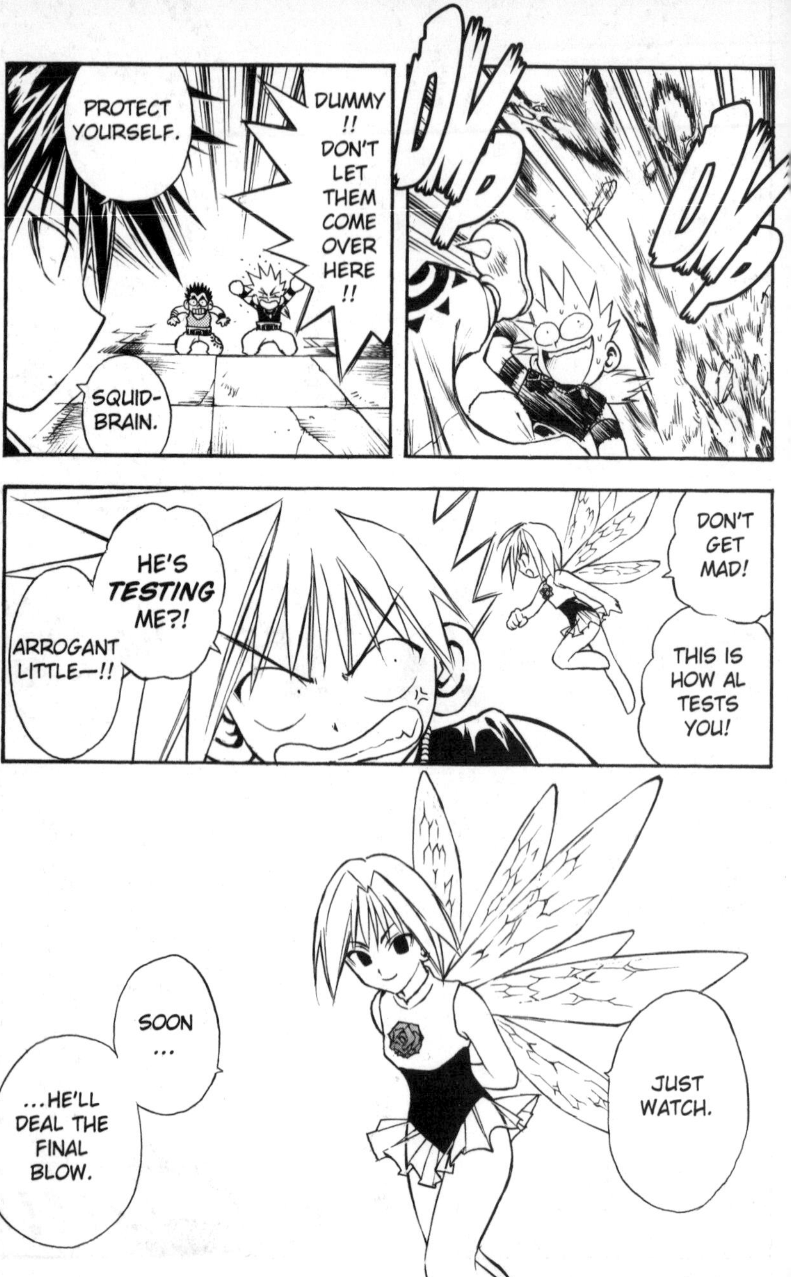
DUMMY!! DON'T LET THEM COME OVER HERE!!
PROTECT YOURSELF.
SQUID-BRAIN.
DON'T GET MAD!
THIS IS HOW AL TESTS YOU!
HE'S TESTING ME?!
ARROGANT LITTLE—!!
JUST WATCH.
SOON ...
...HE'LL DEAL THE FINAL BLOW.

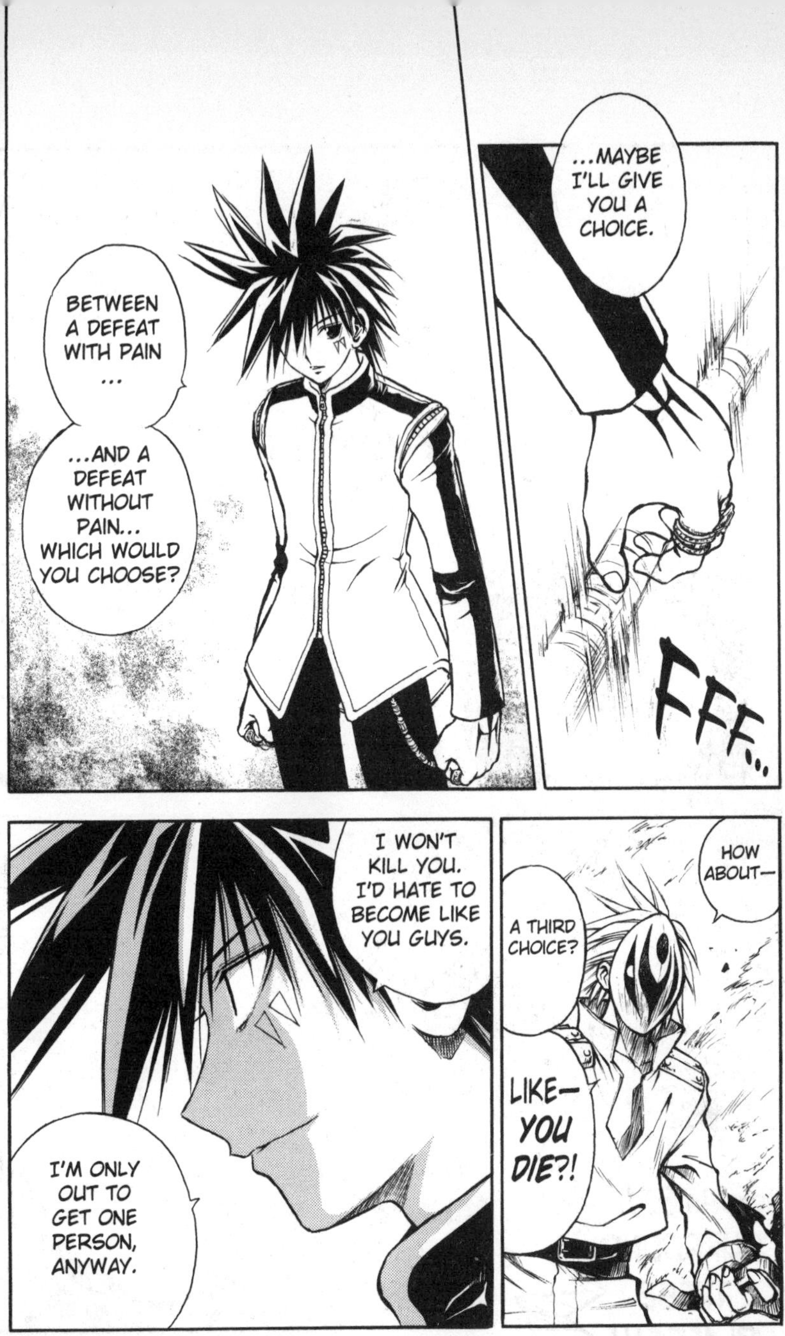
...MAYBE I'LL GIVE YOU A CHOICE.
FFF...
BETWEEN A DEFEAT WITH PAIN ...
...AND A DEFEAT WITHOUT PAIN... WHICH WOULD YOU CHOOSE?
HOW ABOUT—
A THIRD CHOICE?
LIKE— YOU DIE?!
I WON'T KILL YOU. I'D HATE TO BECOME LIKE YOU GUYS.
I'M ONLY OUT TO GET ONE PERSON, ANYWAY.

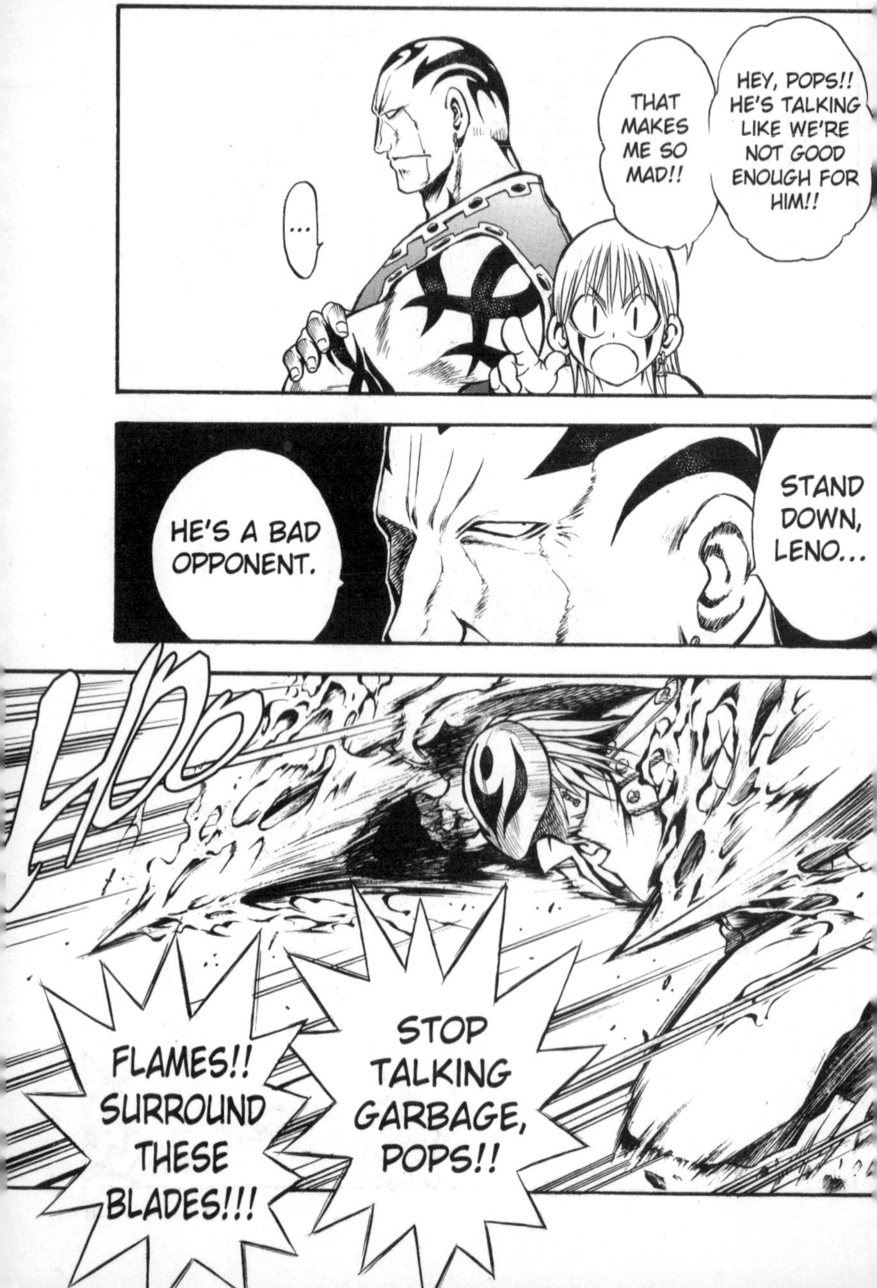
HEY, POPS!! HE'S TALKING LIKE WE'RE NOT GOOD ENOUGH FOR HIM!!
THAT MAKES ME SO MAD!!
...
STAND DOWN, LENO...
HE'S A BAD OPPONENT.
STOP TALKING GARBAGE, POPS!!
FLAMES!! SURROUND THESE BLADES!!!

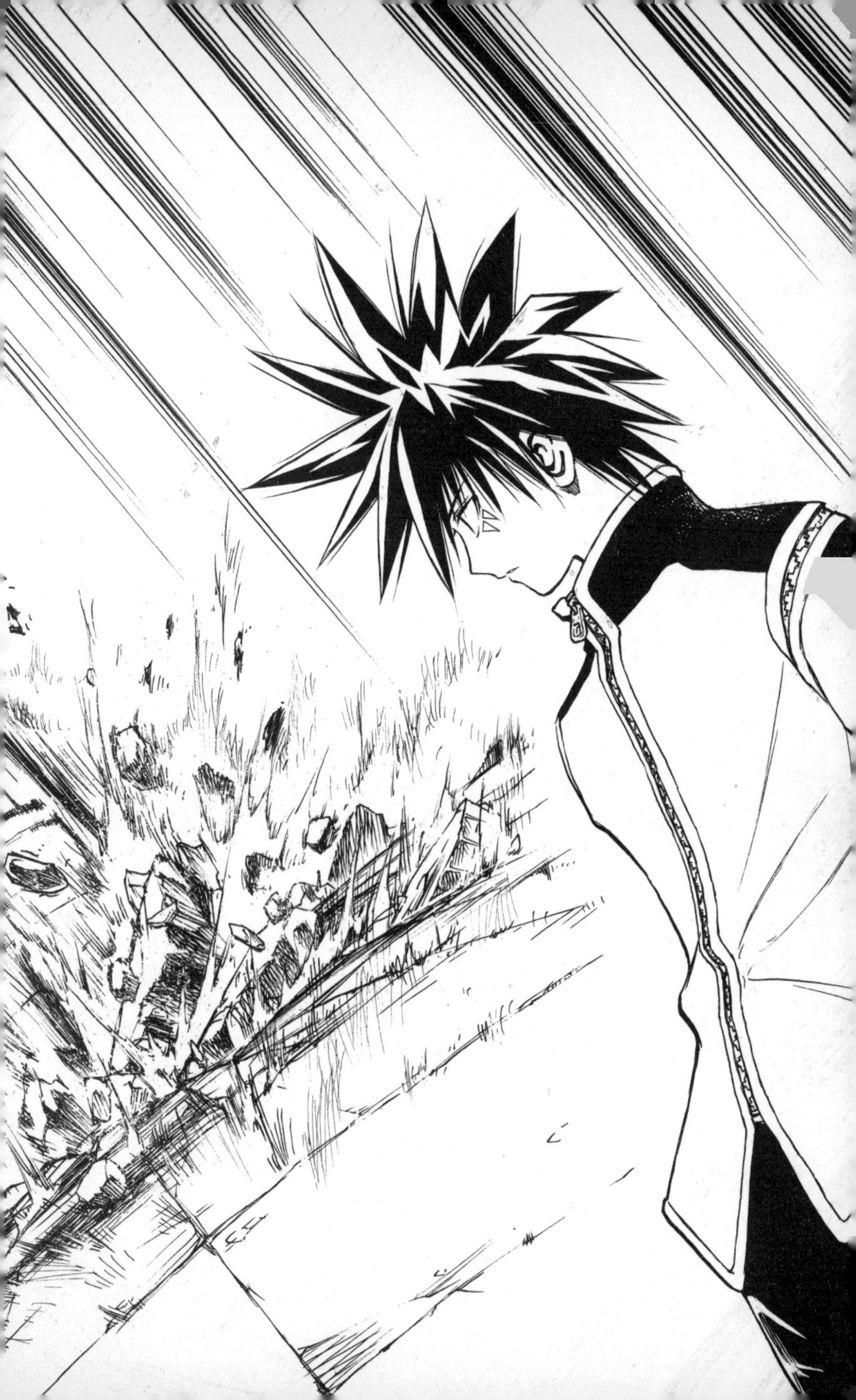

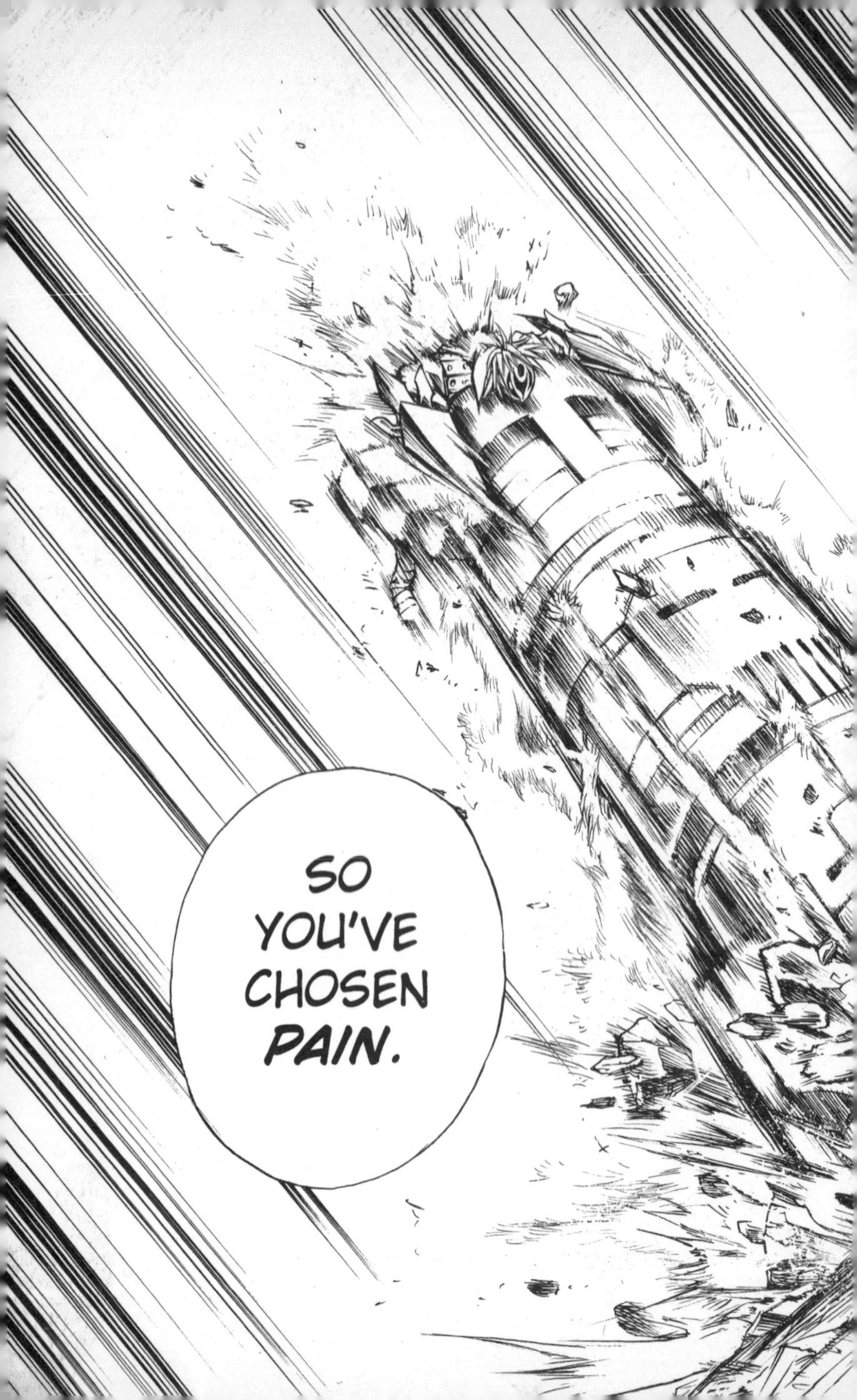
SO YOU'VE CHOSEN *PAIN.*

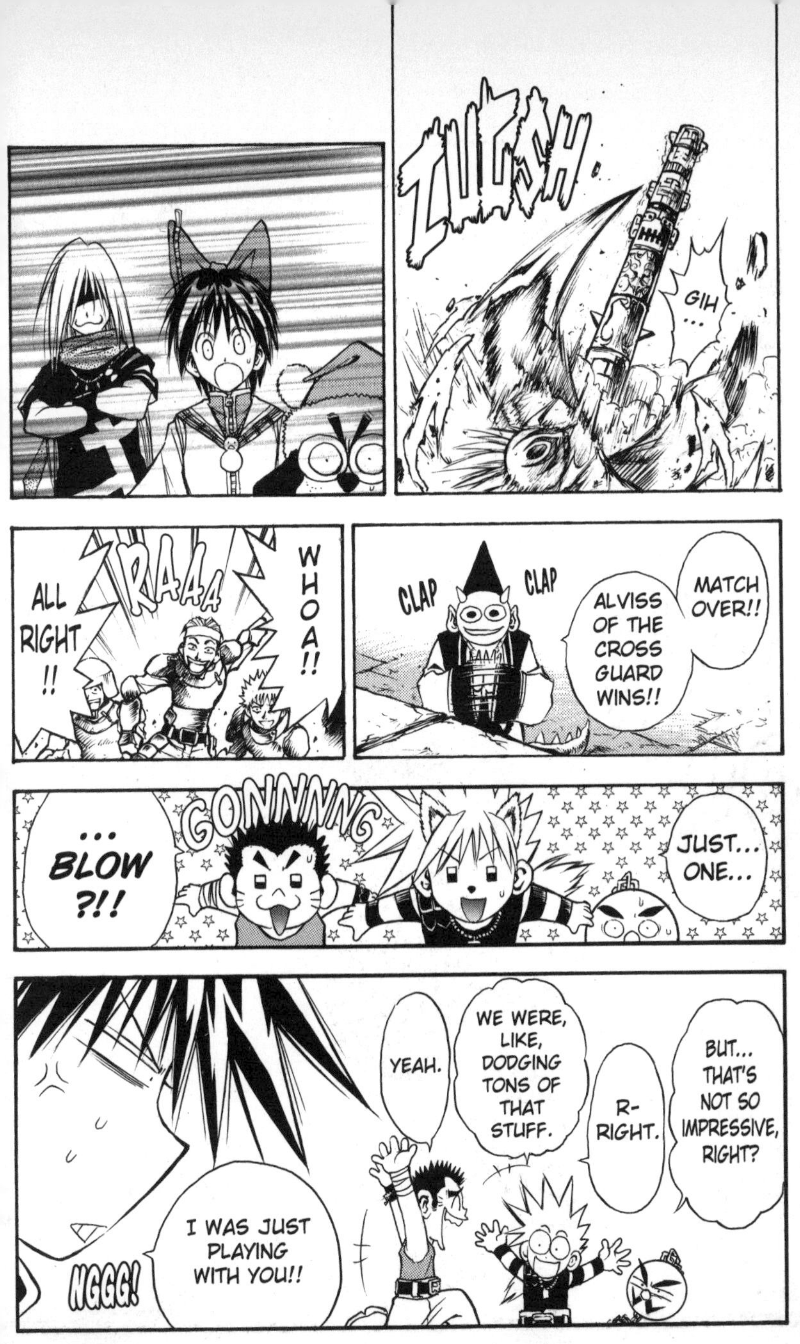
ZUGSH
GIH ...
CLAP
CLAP
MATCH OVER!!
ALVISS OF THE CROSS GUARD WINS!!
WHOA!!
RAAA
ALL RIGHT!!
JUST... ONE...
GONNNNG
... BLOW ?!!
BUT... THAT'S NOT SO IMPRESSIVE, RIGHT?
R-RIGHT.
WE WERE, LIKE, DODGING TONS OF THAT STUFF.
YEAH.
I WAS JUST PLAYING WITH YOU!!
NGGG!

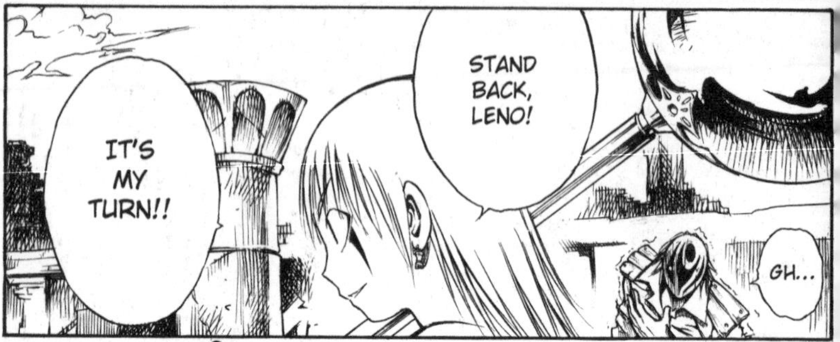
STAND BACK, LENO!
GH...
IT'S MY TURN!!

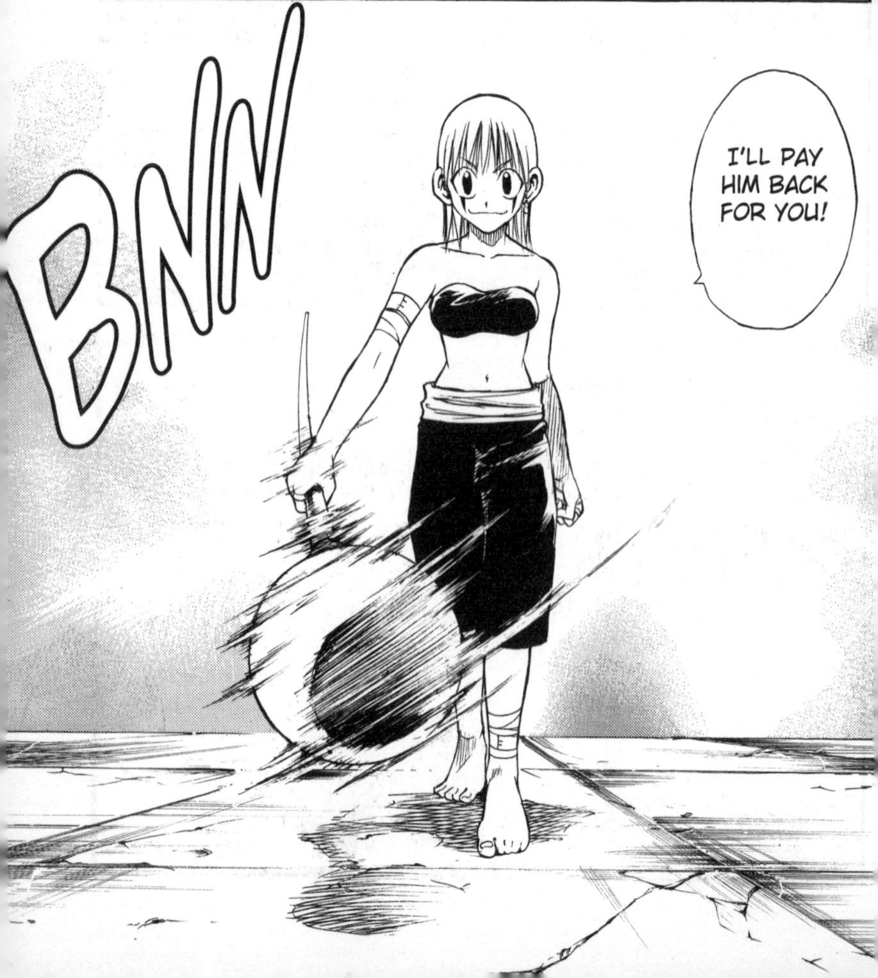
I'LL PAY HIM BACK FOR YOU!
BNN

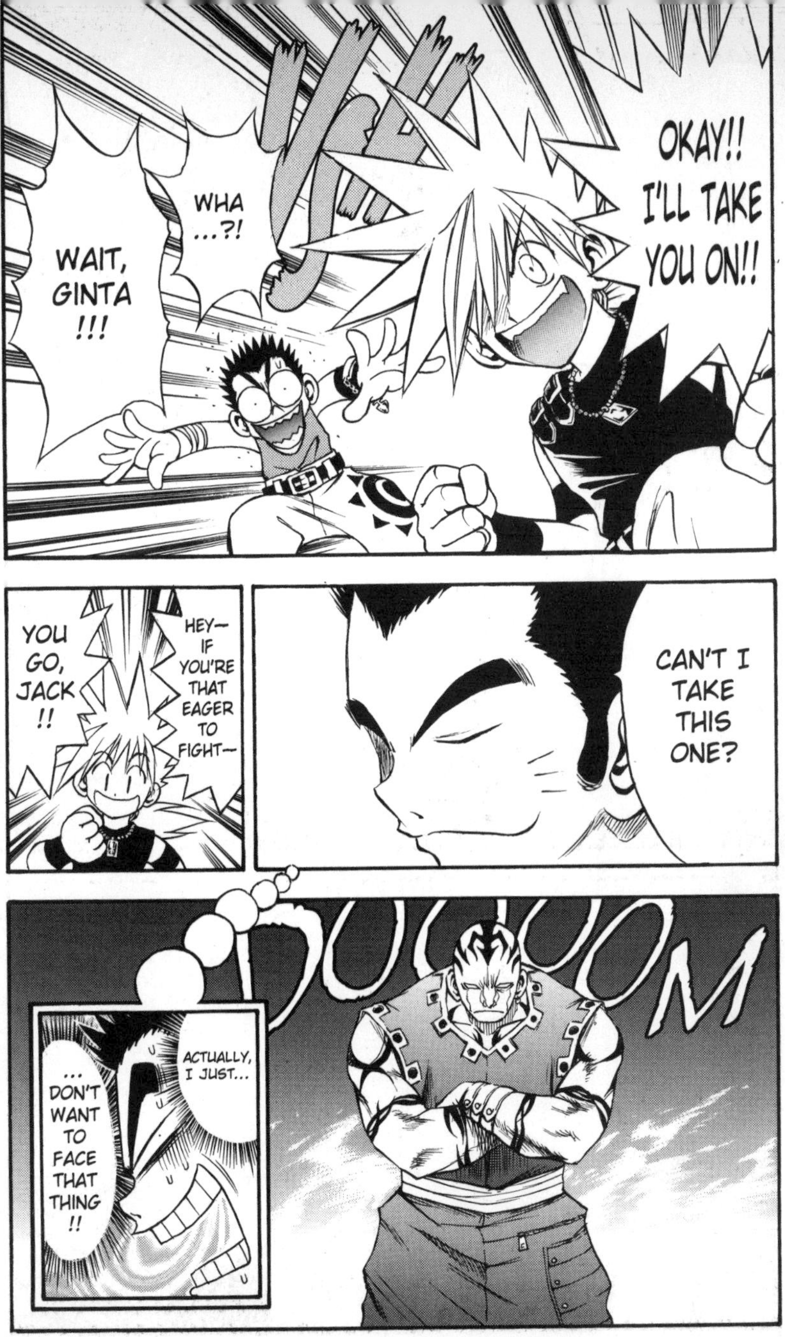
OKAY!! I'LL TAKE YOU ON!!
WHA ...?!
WAIT, GINTA !!!
CAN'T I TAKE THIS ONE?
HEY— IF YOU'RE THAT EAGER TO FIGHT—
YOU GO, JACK !!
DOOOOM
ACTUALLY, I JUST...
... DON'T WANT TO FACE THAT THING !!

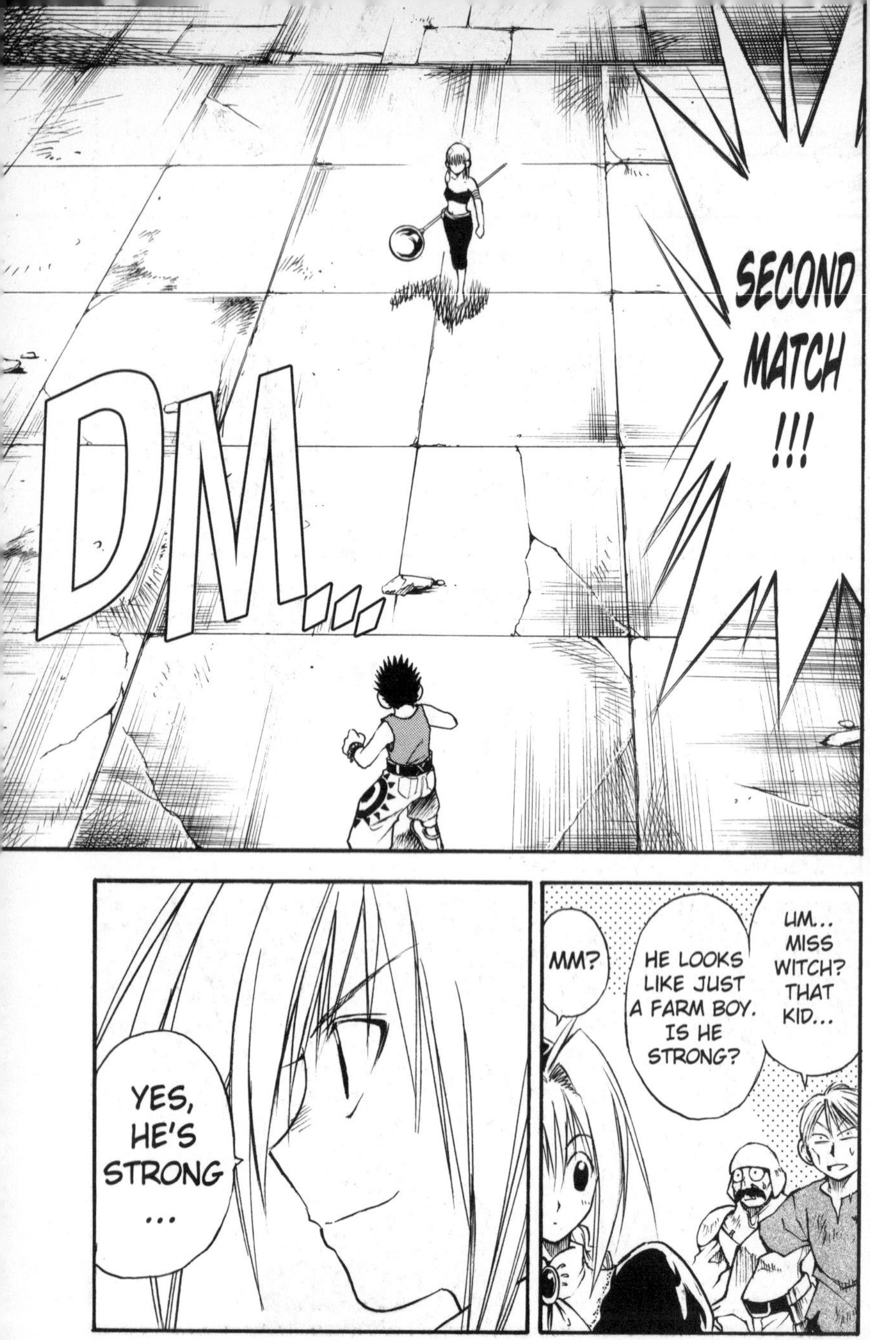
SECOND MATCH !!!
DM...
UM... MISS WITCH? THAT KID...
HE LOOKS LIKE JUST A FARM BOY. IS HE STRONG?
MM?
YES, HE'S STRONG ...

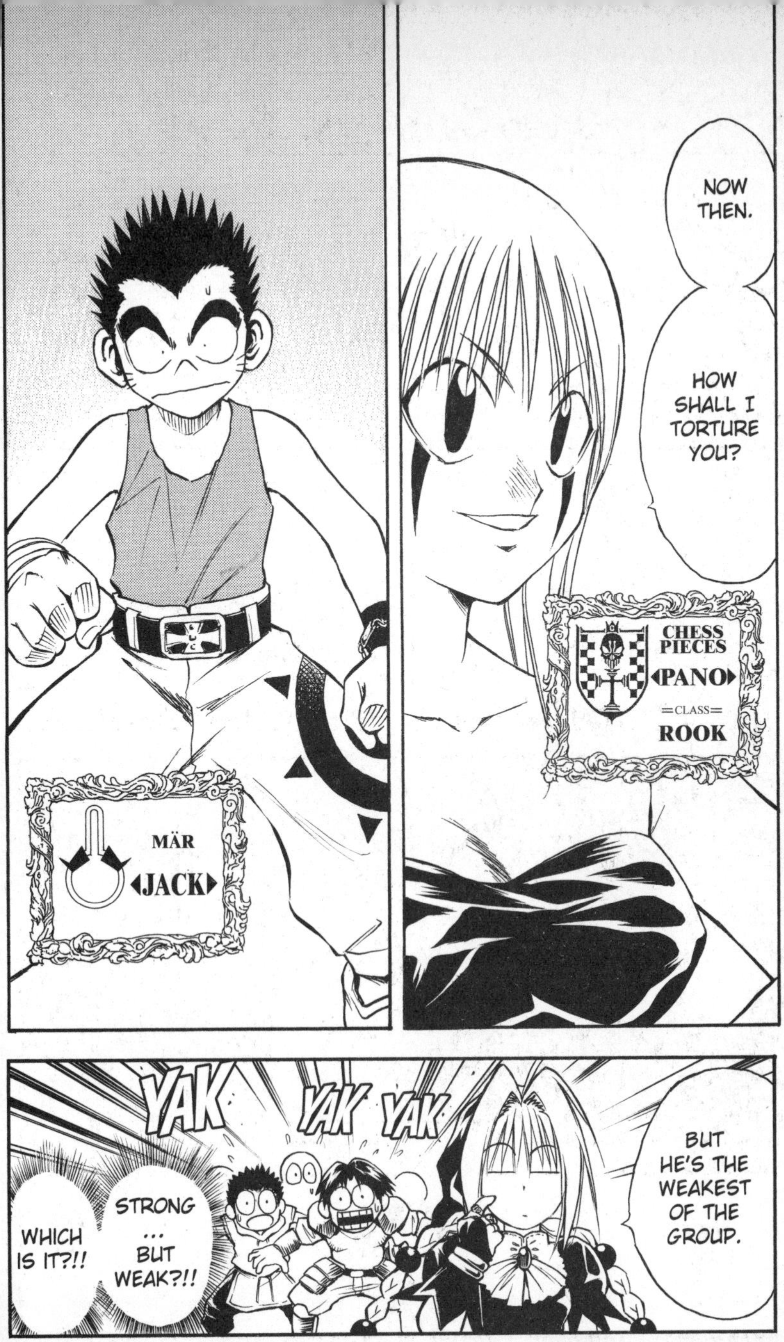
NOW THEN.
HOW SHALL I TORTURE YOU?
CHESS PIECES
◂PANO▸
=CLASS=
ROOK
MÄR
◂JACK▸
BUT HE'S THE WEAKEST OF THE GROUP.
YAK YAK YAK
STRONG ... BUT WEAK?!!
WHICH IS IT?!!

AKT.45/ Jack vs. Pano

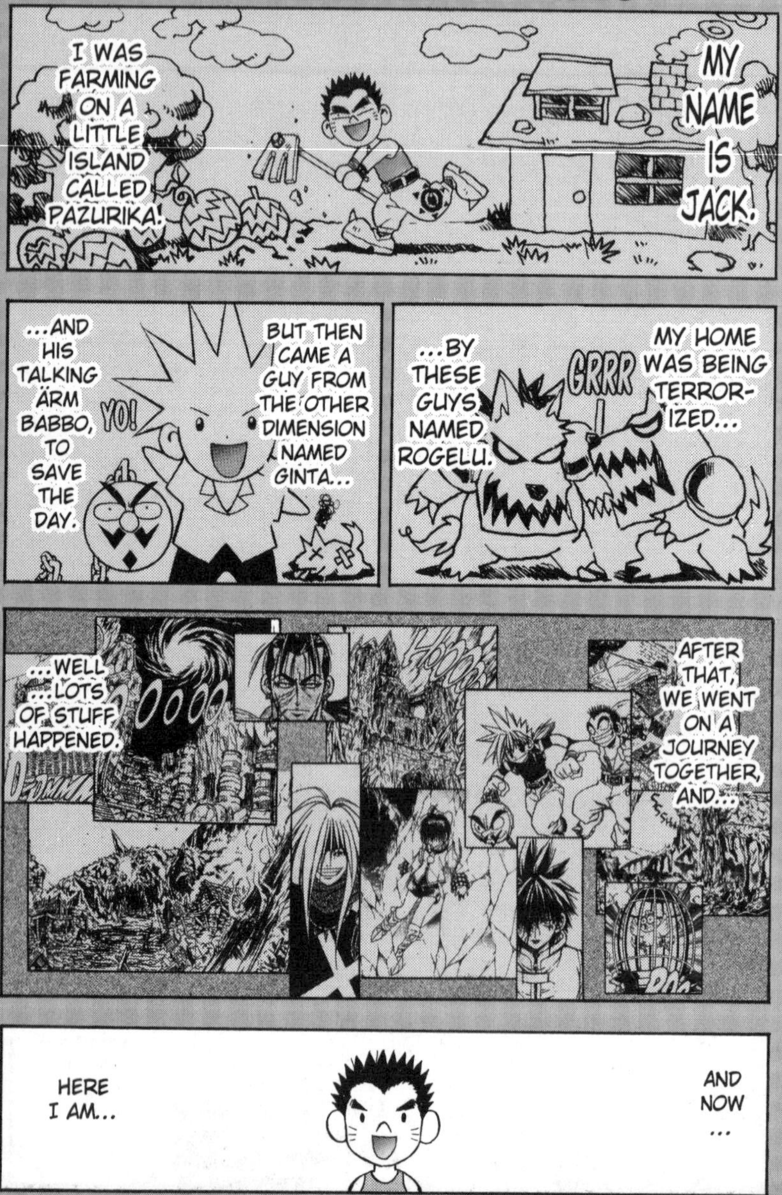
MY NAME IS JACK.
I WAS FARMING ON A LITTLE ISLAND CALLED PAZURIKA!
MY HOME WAS BEING TERROR-IZED...
GRRR
...BY THESE GUYS NAMED ROGELU.
BUT THEN CAME A GUY FROM THE OTHER DIMENSION NAMED GINTA...
YO!
...AND HIS TALKING ÄRM BABBO, TO SAVE THE DAY.
AFTER THAT, WE WENT ON A JOURNEY TOGETHER, AND...
...WELL ...LOTS OF STUFF HAPPENED.
AND NOW ...
HERE I AM...

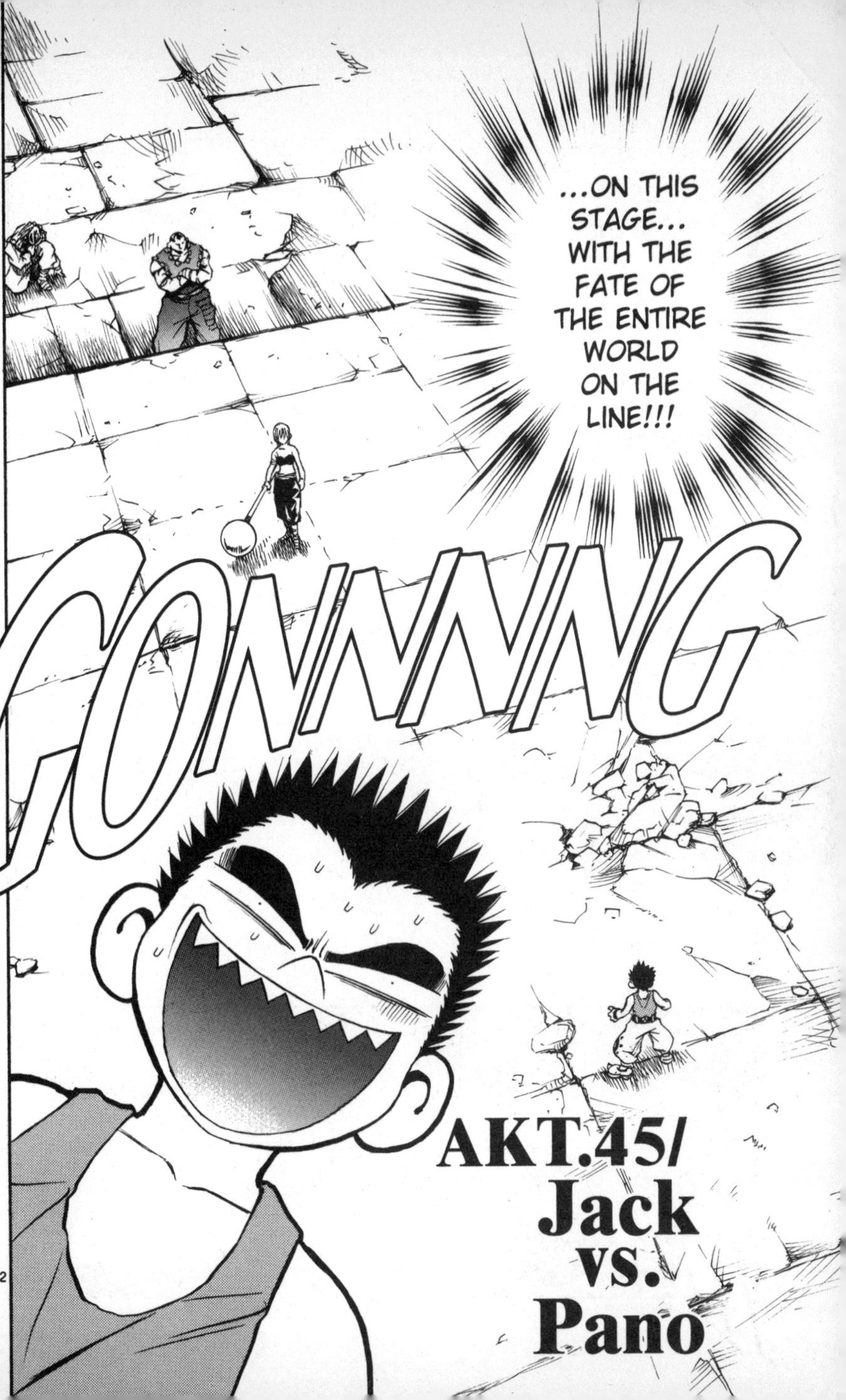

...ON THIS STAGE... WITH THE FATE OF THE ENTIRE WORLD ON THE LINE!!!
GONNNNG
AKT.45/ Jack vs. Pano

2

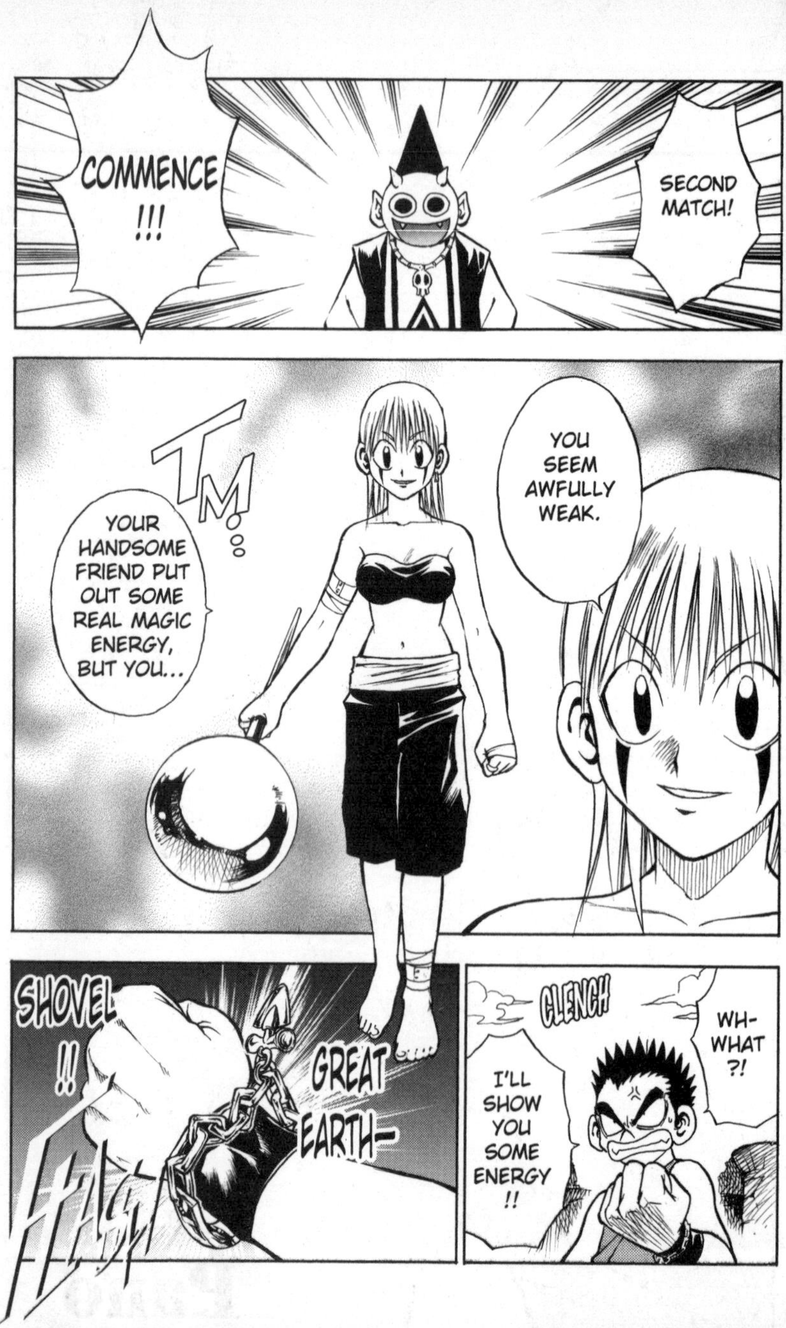
SECOND MATCH!
COMMENCE !!!
YOU SEEM AWFULLY WEAK.
TM
YOUR HANDSOME FRIEND PUT OUT SOME REAL MAGIC ENERGY, BUT YOU...
CLENCH
WH-WHAT ?!
I'LL SHOW YOU SOME ENERGY !!
GREAT EARTH-
SHOVEL !!
FLASH

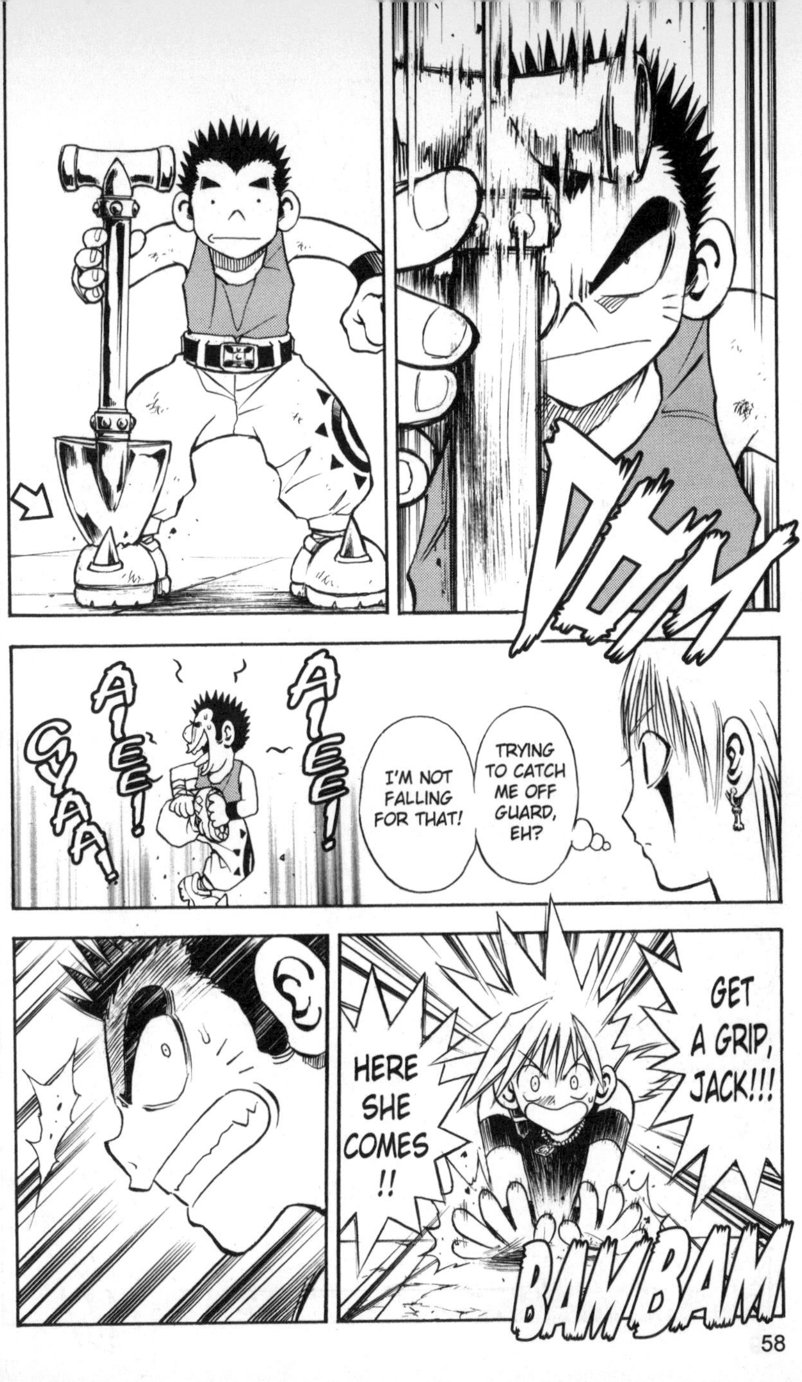
DOM
TRYING TO CATCH ME OFF GUARD, EH?
I'M NOT FALLING FOR THAT!
AIEE!
AIEE!
GYAAA!
GET A GRIP, JACK!!!
HERE SHE COMES !!
BAMBAM

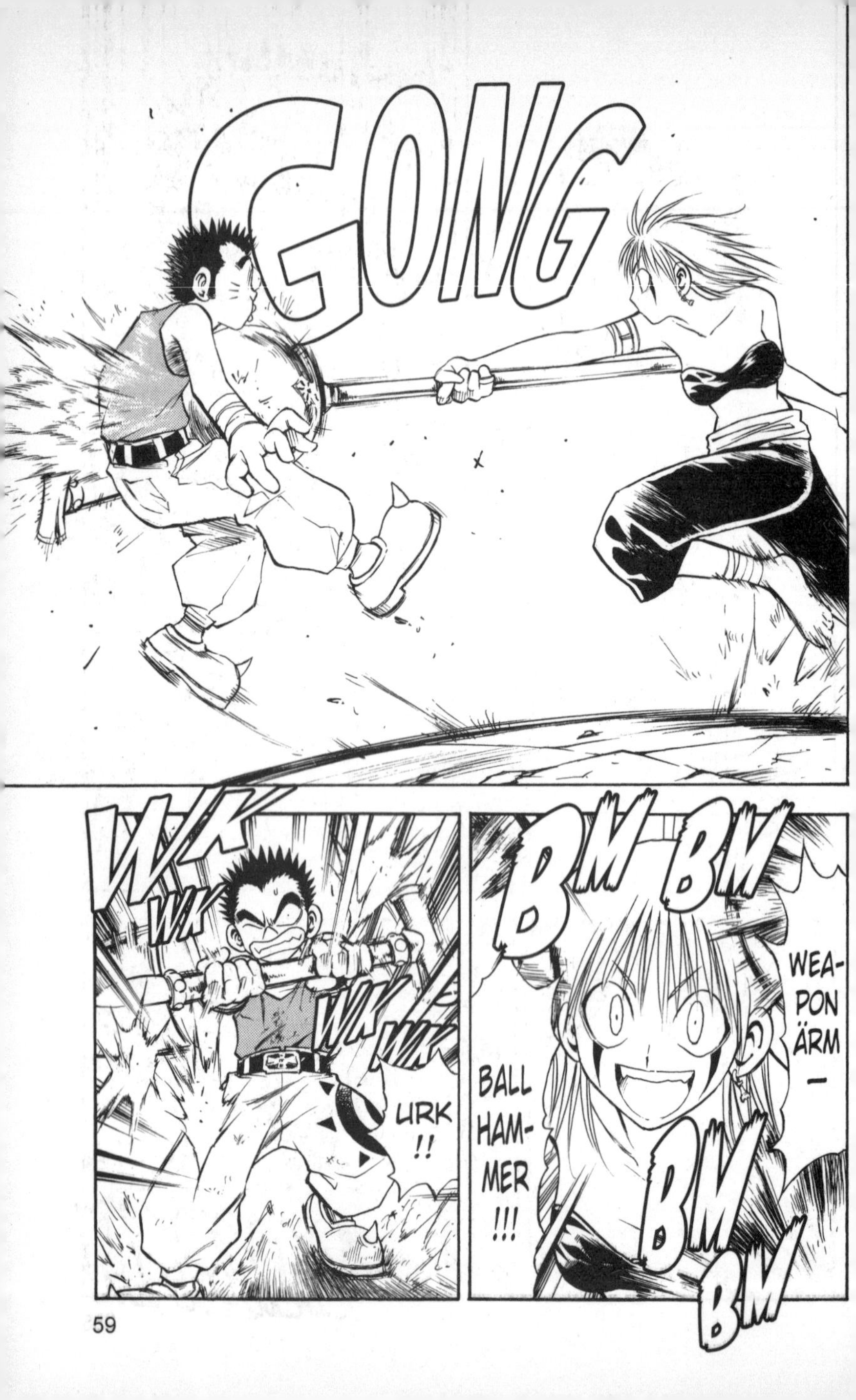
GONG
BM BM BM
WEA-PON ÄRM —
BALL HAM-MER !!!
BM BM
WK WK
WK WK
URK !!

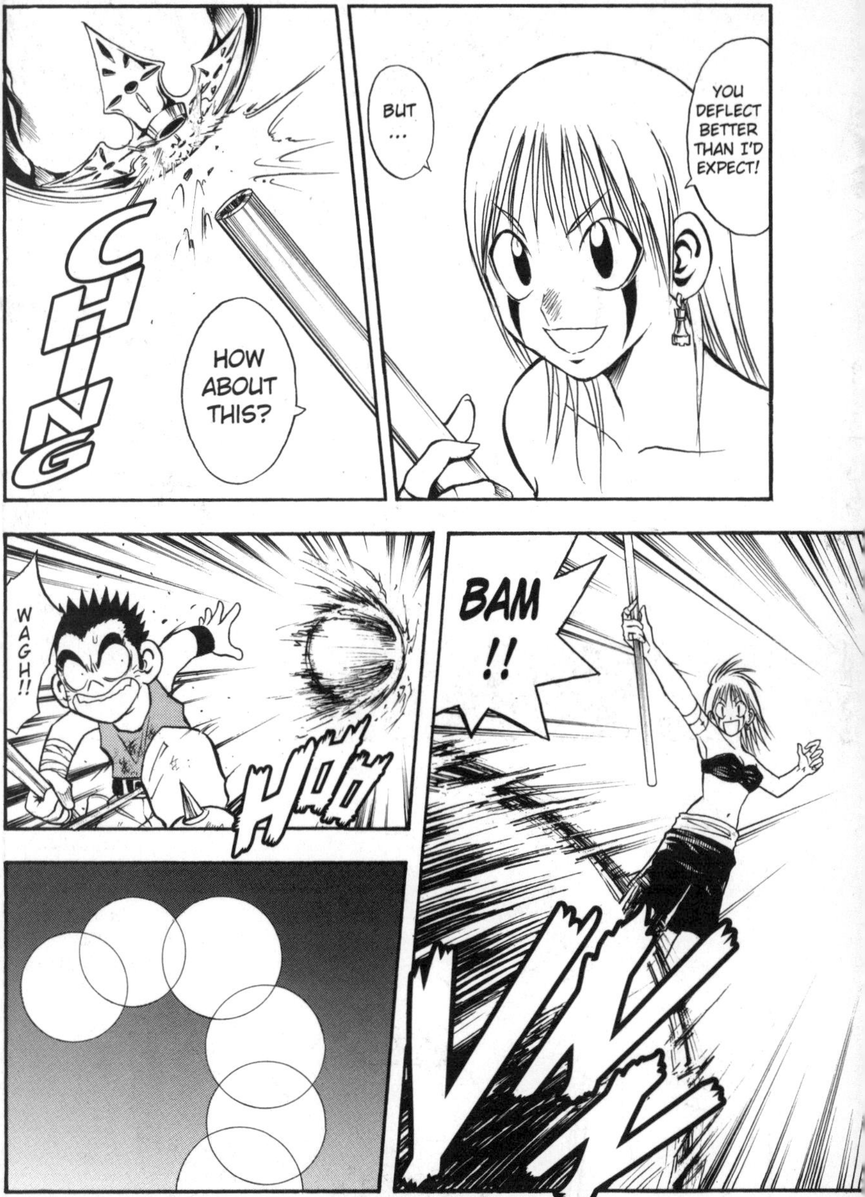
YOU DEFLECT BETTER THAN I'D EXPECT!
BUT ...
CHING
HOW ABOUT THIS?
BAM !!
WAGH!!
HOO

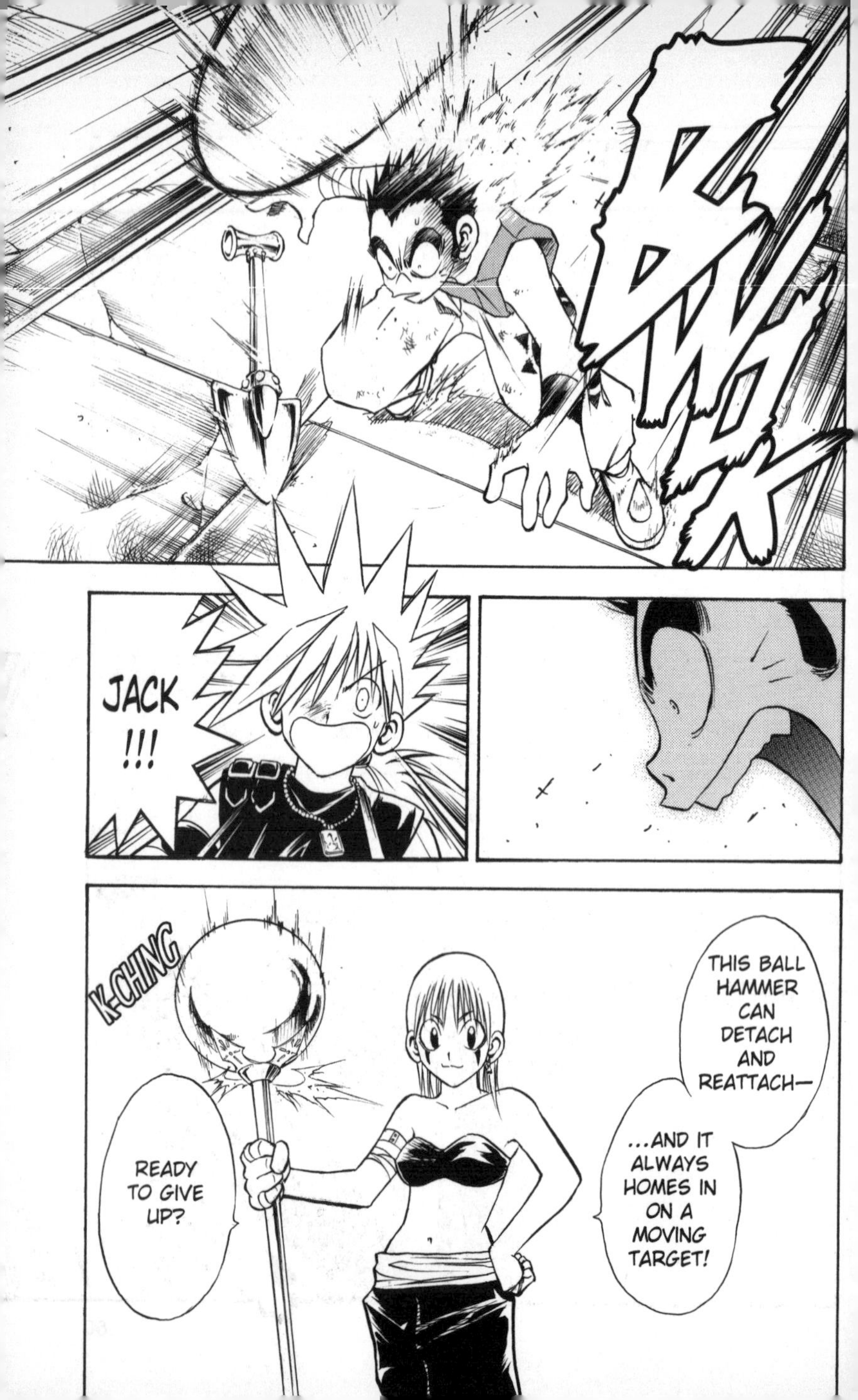
JACK !!!
THIS BALL HAMMER CAN DETACH AND REATTACH—
...AND IT ALWAYS HOMES IN ON A MOVING TARGET!
K-CHING
READY TO GIVE UP?

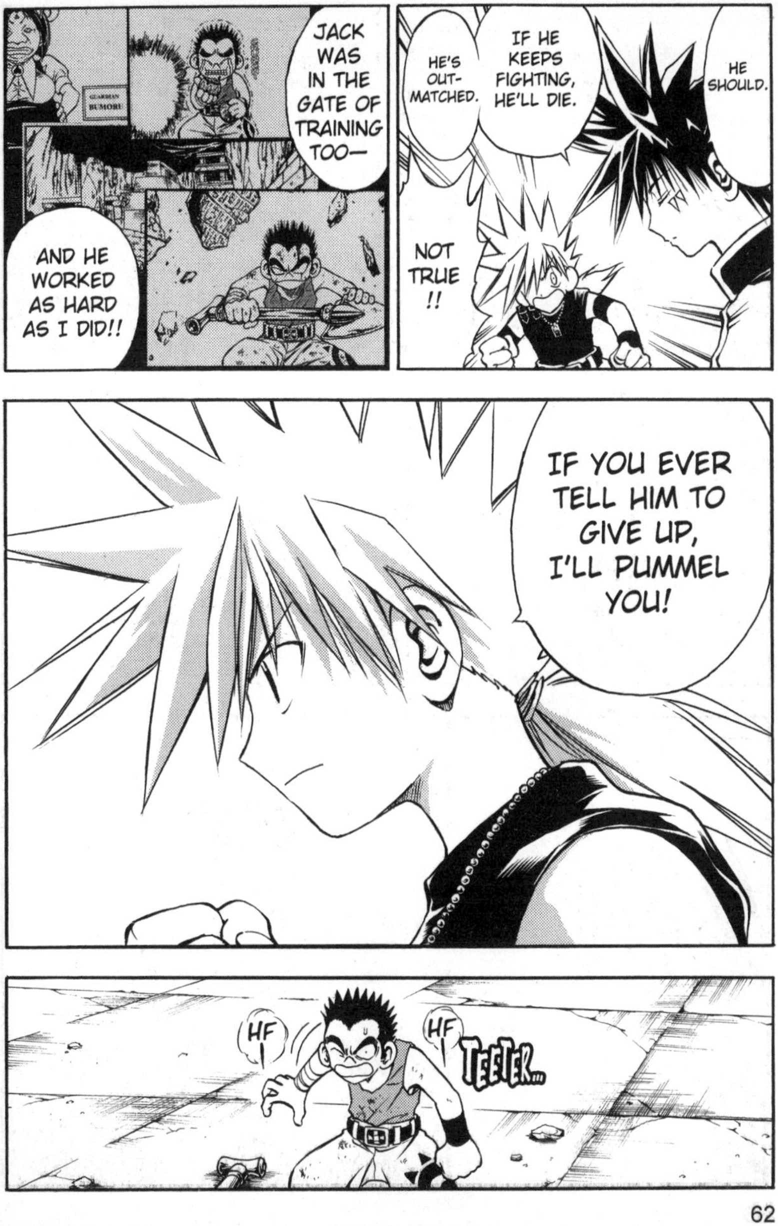
HE SHOULD.
IF HE KEEPS FIGHTING, HE'LL DIE.
HE'S OUT-MATCHED.
NOT TRUE!!
JACK WAS IN THE GATE OF TRAINING TOO—
GUARDIAN BUMORU
AND HE WORKED AS HARD AS I DID!!
IF YOU EVER TELL HIM TO GIVE UP, I'LL PUMMEL YOU!
TEETER...
HF
HF

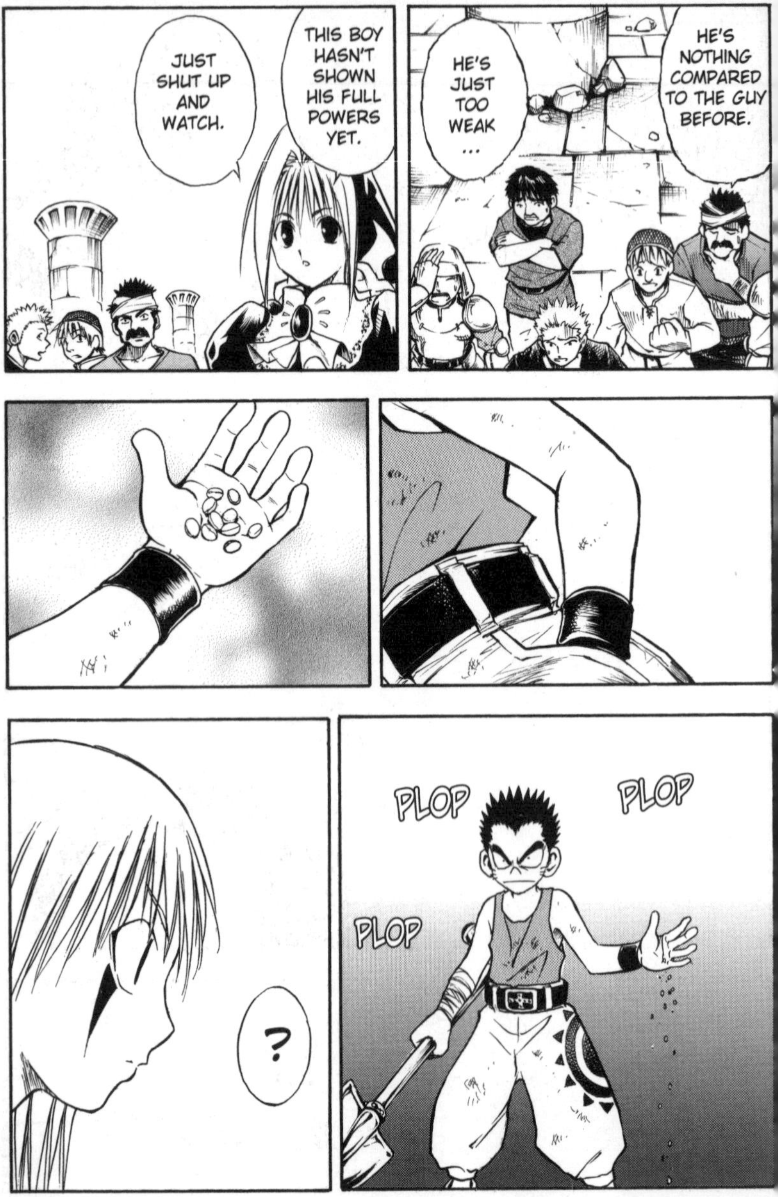
HE'S NOTHING COMPARED TO THE GUY BEFORE.
HE'S JUST TOO WEAK ...
THIS BOY HASN'T SHOWN HIS FULL POWERS YET.
JUST SHUT UP AND WATCH.
PLOP
PLOP
PLOP
?

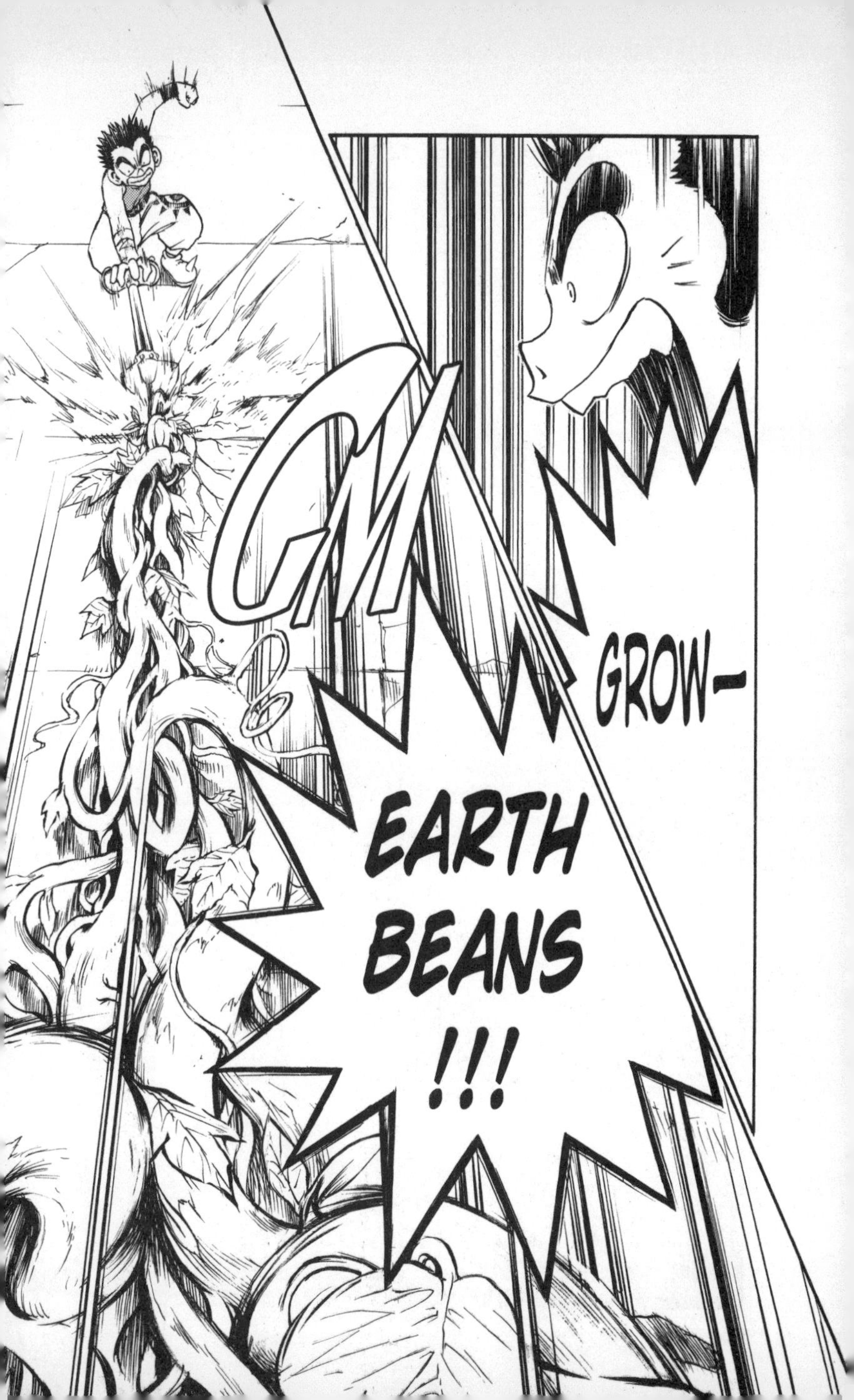
GROW-
EARTH BEANS !!!
GM

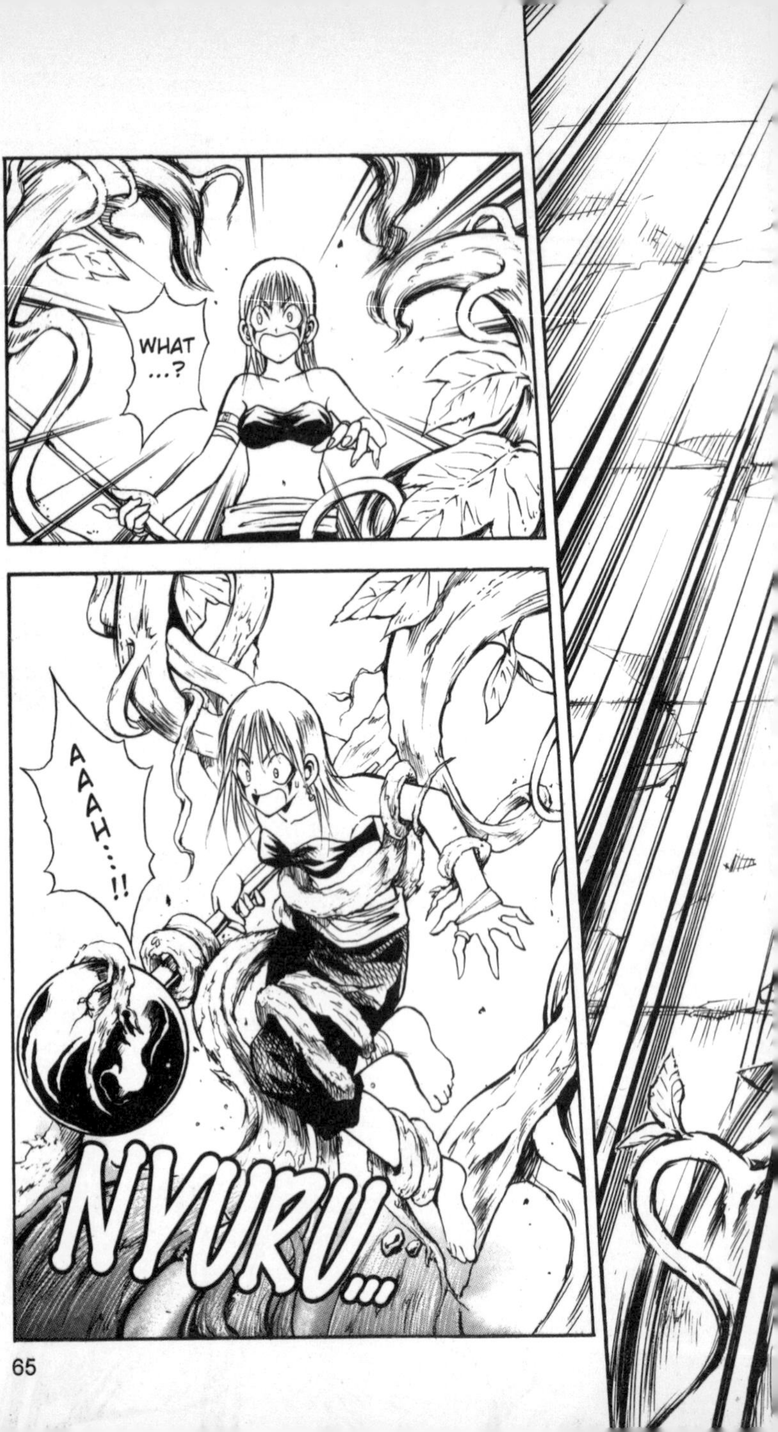
WHAT ...?
AAAAH...!!
NYURU...

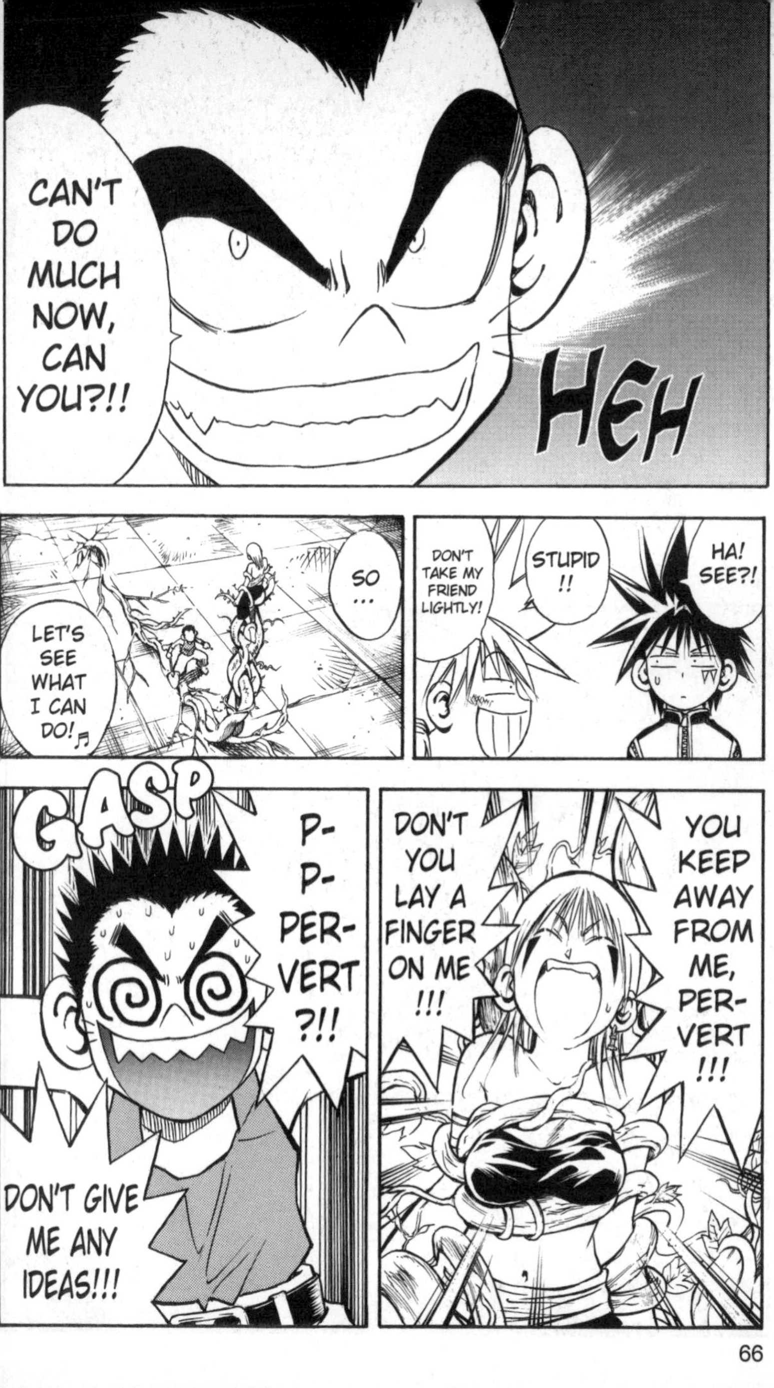
CAN'T DO MUCH NOW, CAN YOU?!!
HEH
HA! SEE?!
STUPID !!
DON'T TAKE MY FRIEND LIGHTLY!
SO ...
LET'S SEE WHAT I CAN DO! ♬
YOU KEEP AWAY FROM ME, PER-VERT !!!
DON'T YOU LAY A FINGER ON ME !!!
GASP
P-P-PER-VERT ?!!
DON'T GIVE ME ANY IDEAS!!!

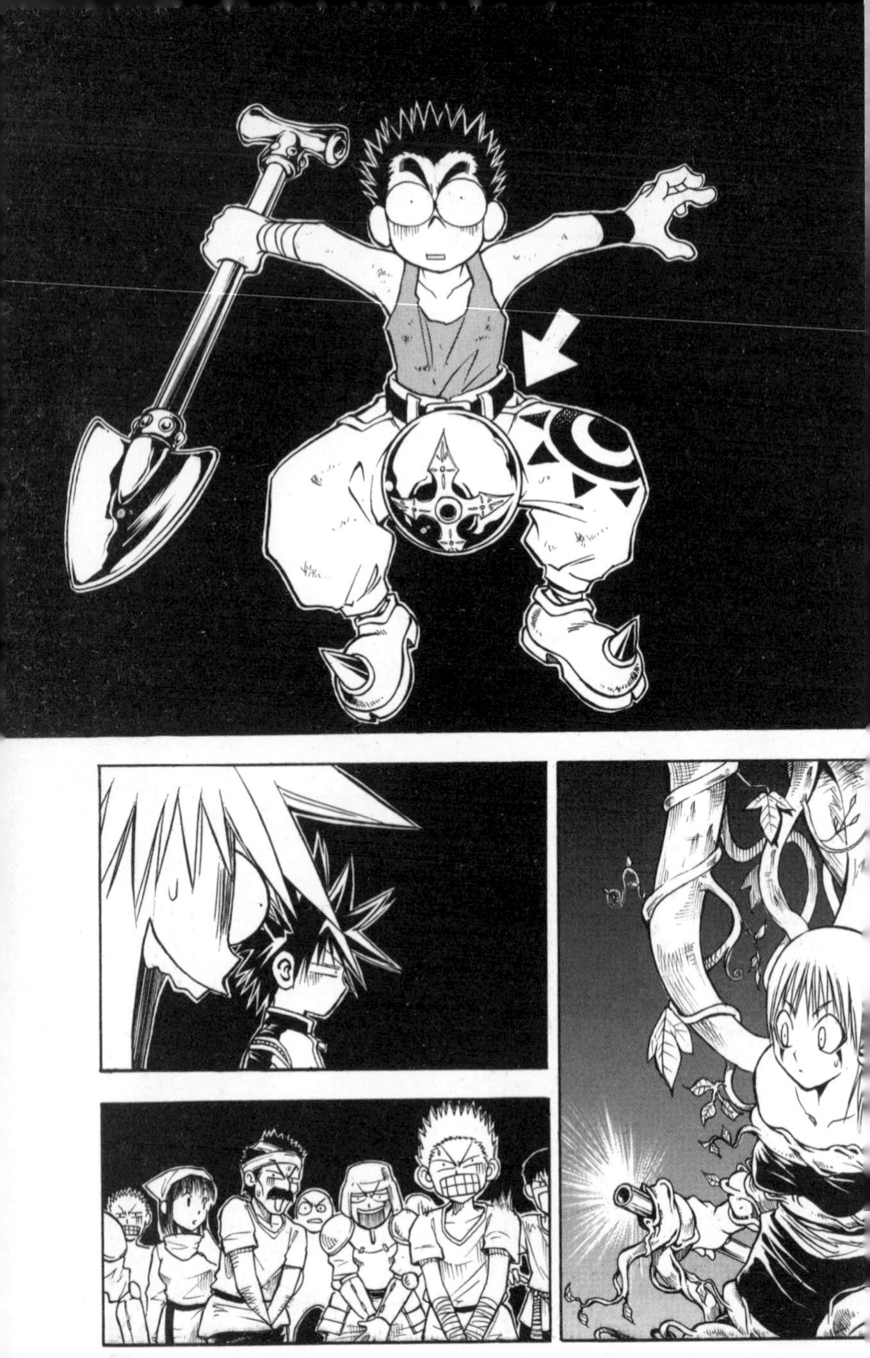

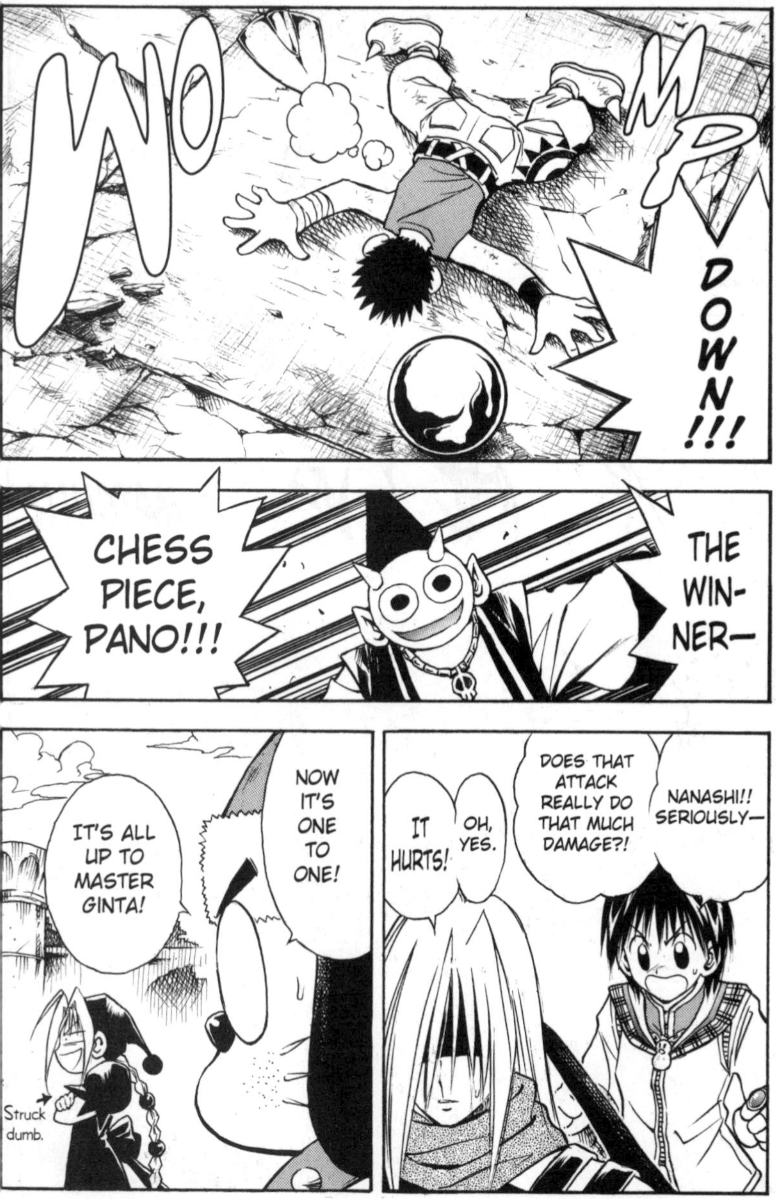
WOMP
DOWN!!!
THE WINNER—
CHESS PIECE, PANO!!!
NANASHI!! SERIOUSLY—
DOES THAT ATTACK REALLY DO THAT MUCH DAMAGE?!
OH, YES.
IT HURTS!
NOW IT'S ONE TO ONE!
IT'S ALL UP TO MASTER GINTA!
Struck dumb.

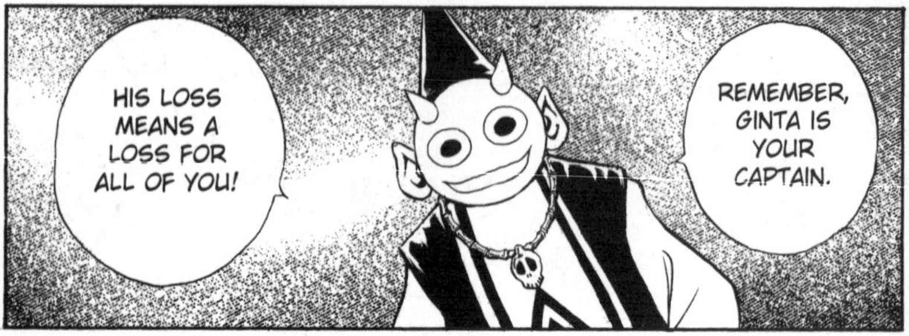
REMEMBER, GINTA IS YOUR CAPTAIN.
HIS LOSS MEANS A LOSS FOR ALL OF YOU!

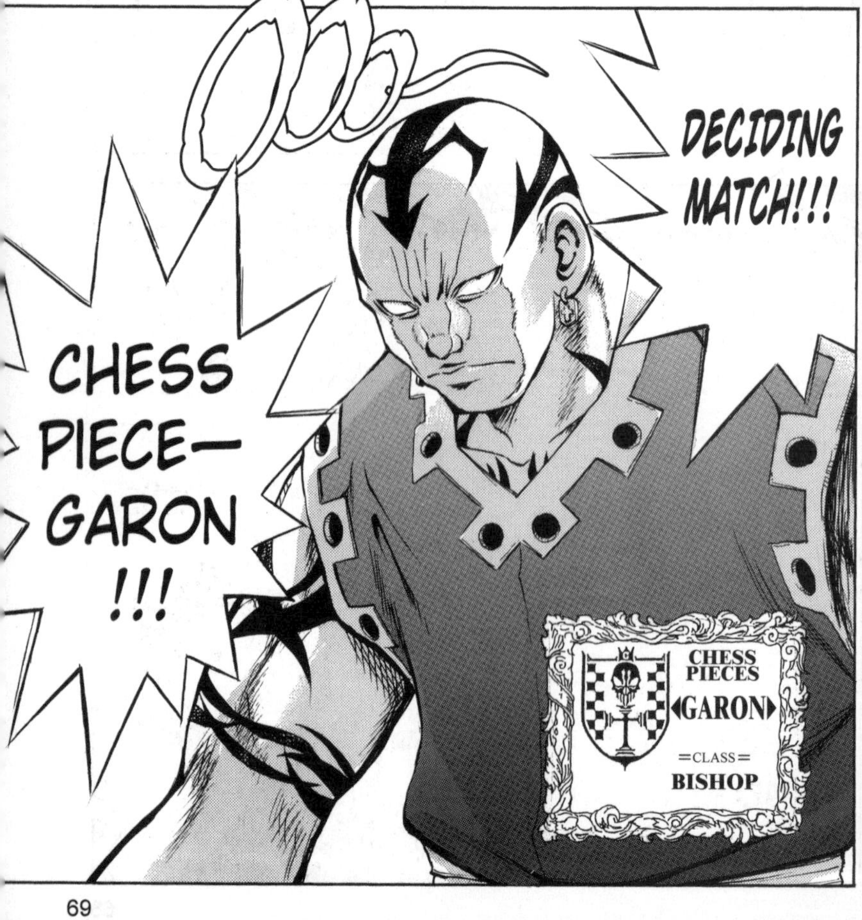
DECIDING MATCH!!!
CHESS PIECE—GARON !!!
CHESS PIECES
GARON
=CLASS=
BISHOP

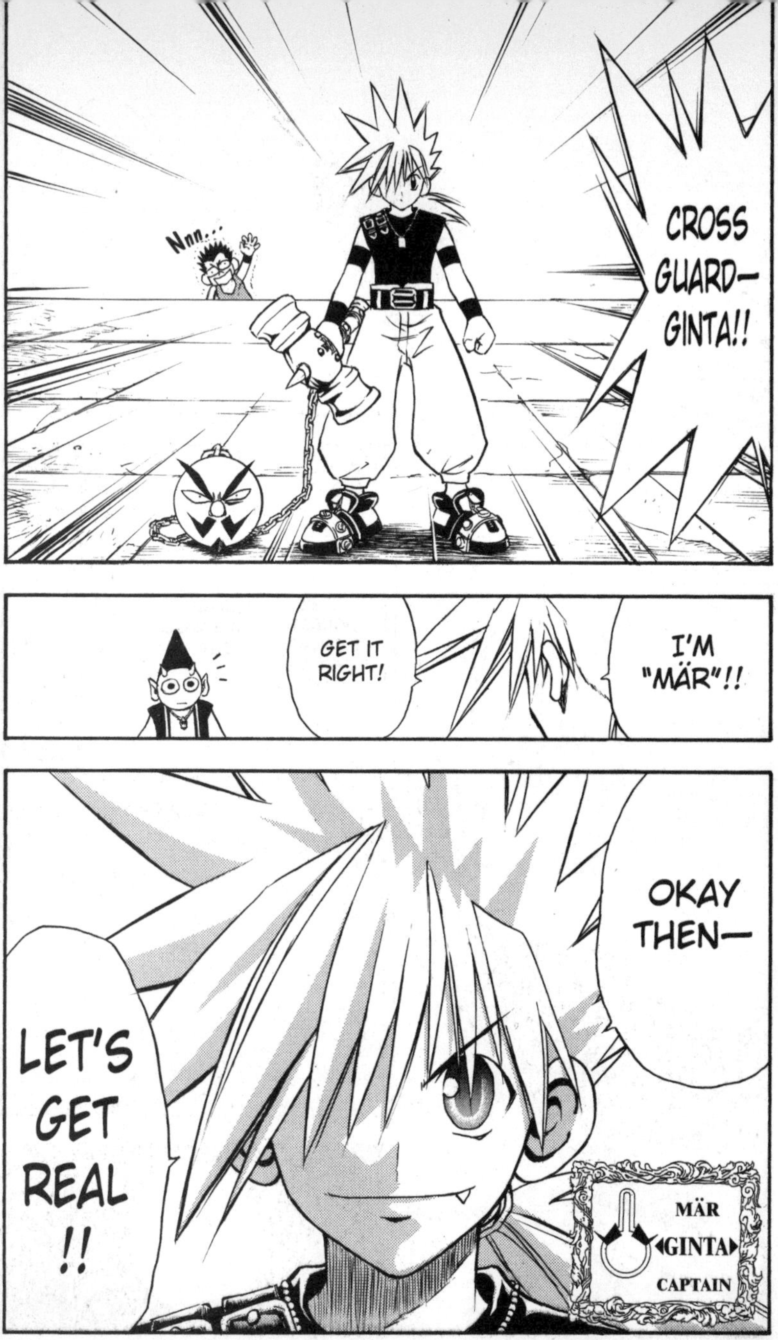
CROSS GUARD-GINTA!!
Nnn...
I'M "MÄR"!!
GET IT RIGHT!
OKAY THEN—
LET'S GET REAL!!
MÄR
GINTA
CAPTAIN

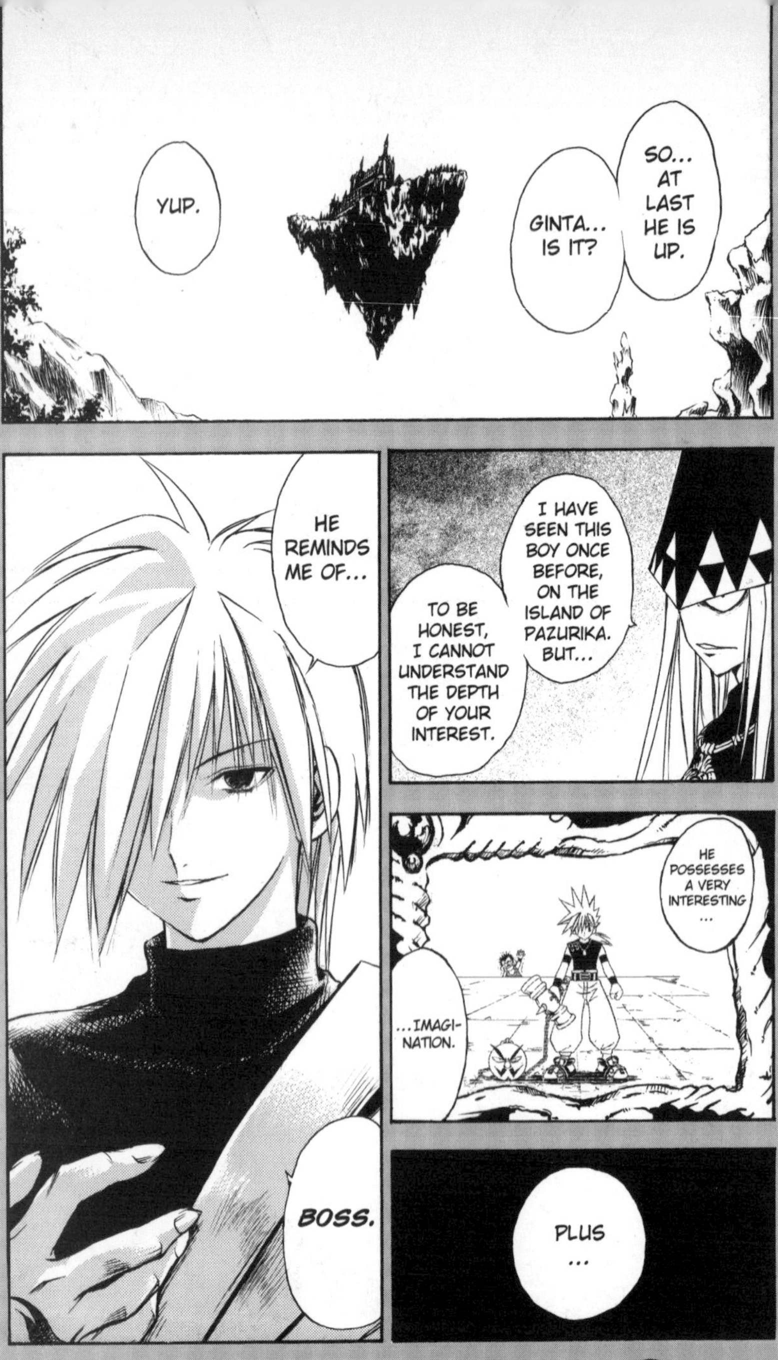
SO... AT LAST HE IS UP.
GINTA... IS IT?
YUP.
I HAVE SEEN THIS BOY ONCE BEFORE, ON THE ISLAND OF PAZURIKA. BUT...
TO BE HONEST, I CANNOT UNDERSTAND THE DEPTH OF YOUR INTEREST.
HE POSSESSES A VERY INTERESTING ...
...IMAGINATION.
PLUS ...
HE REMINDS ME OF...
BOSS.

AKT.46/ Ginta vs. Garon ①

AKT.46/ Ginta vs. Garon ①

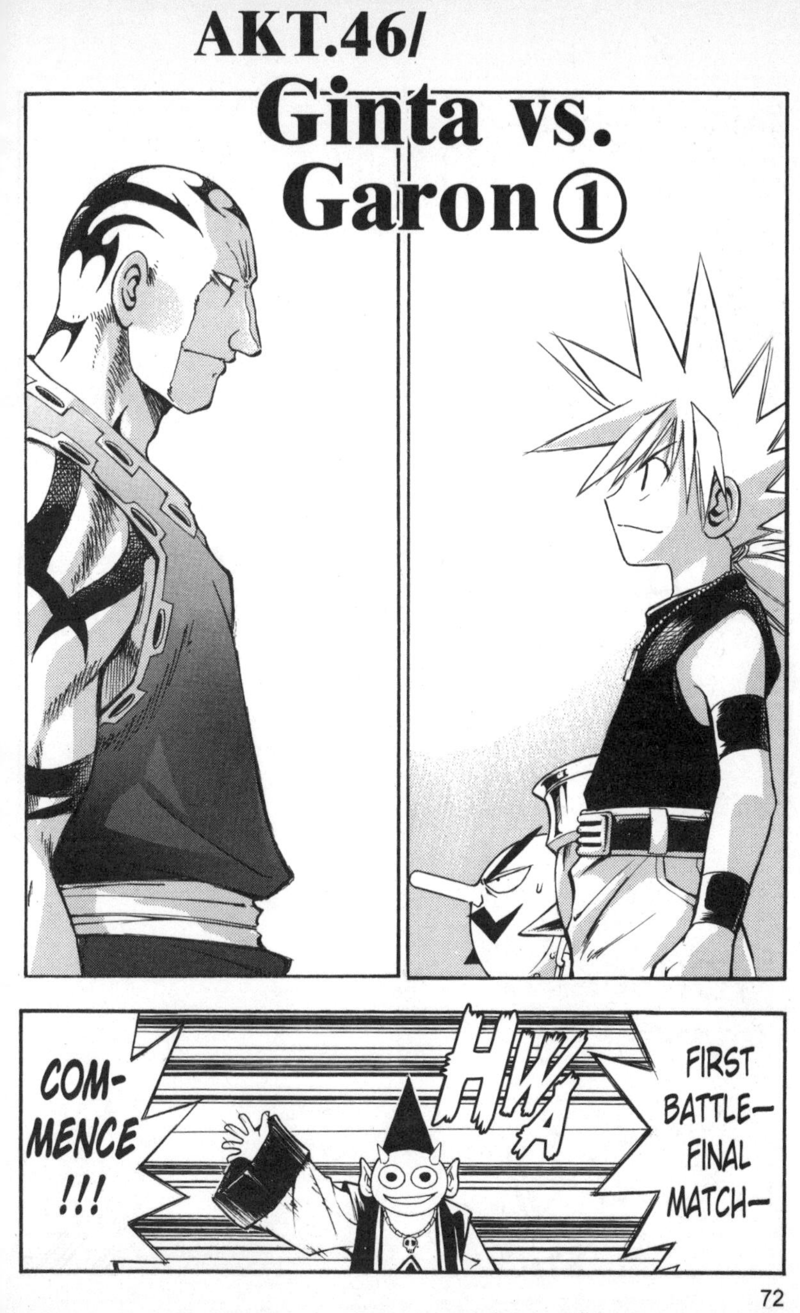
FIRST BATTLE— FINAL MATCH—
HWA
COM-MENCE !!!

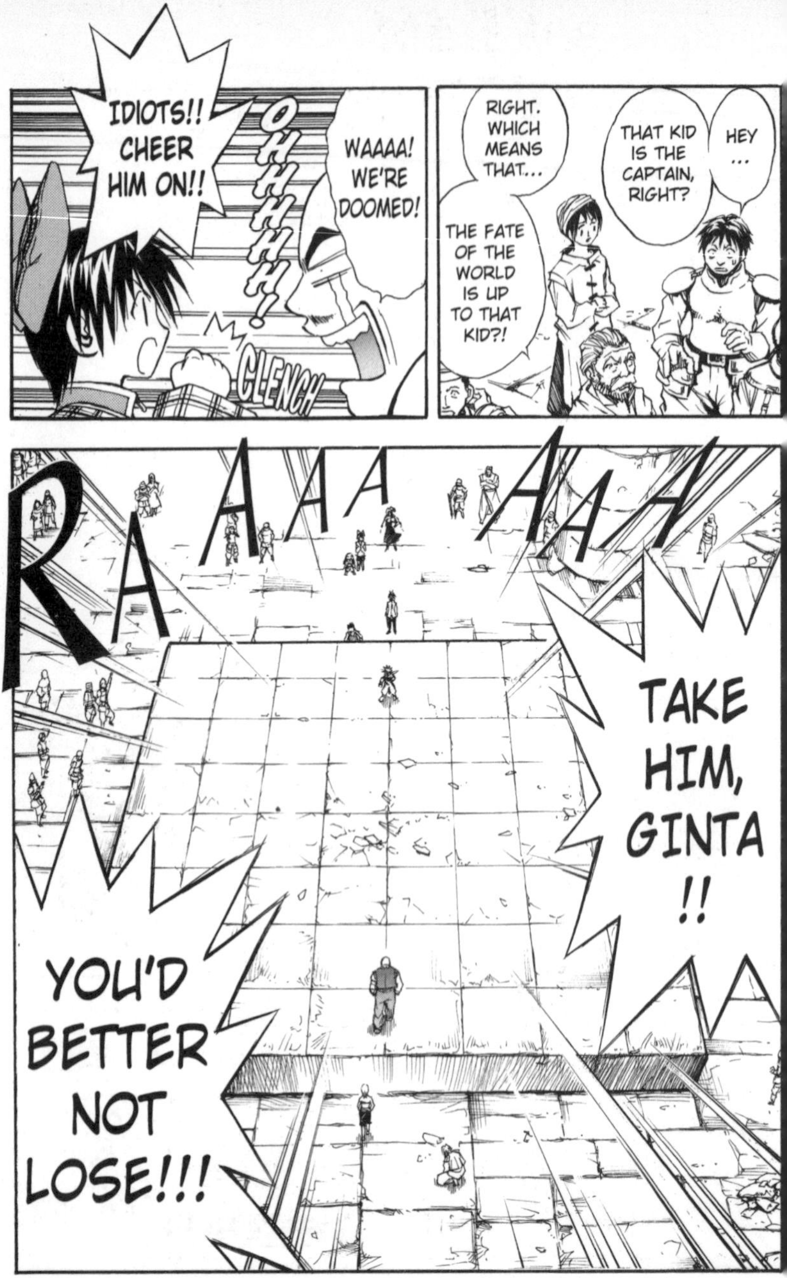
HEY ...
THAT KID IS THE CAPTAIN, RIGHT?
RIGHT. WHICH MEANS THAT...
THE FATE OF THE WORLD IS UP TO THAT KID?!
WAAAA! WE'RE DOOMED!
OHHHHHH!
IDIOTS!! CHEER HIM ON!!
CLENCH
RAAAAAAA
TAKE HIM, GINTA!!
YOU'D BETTER NOT LOSE!!!

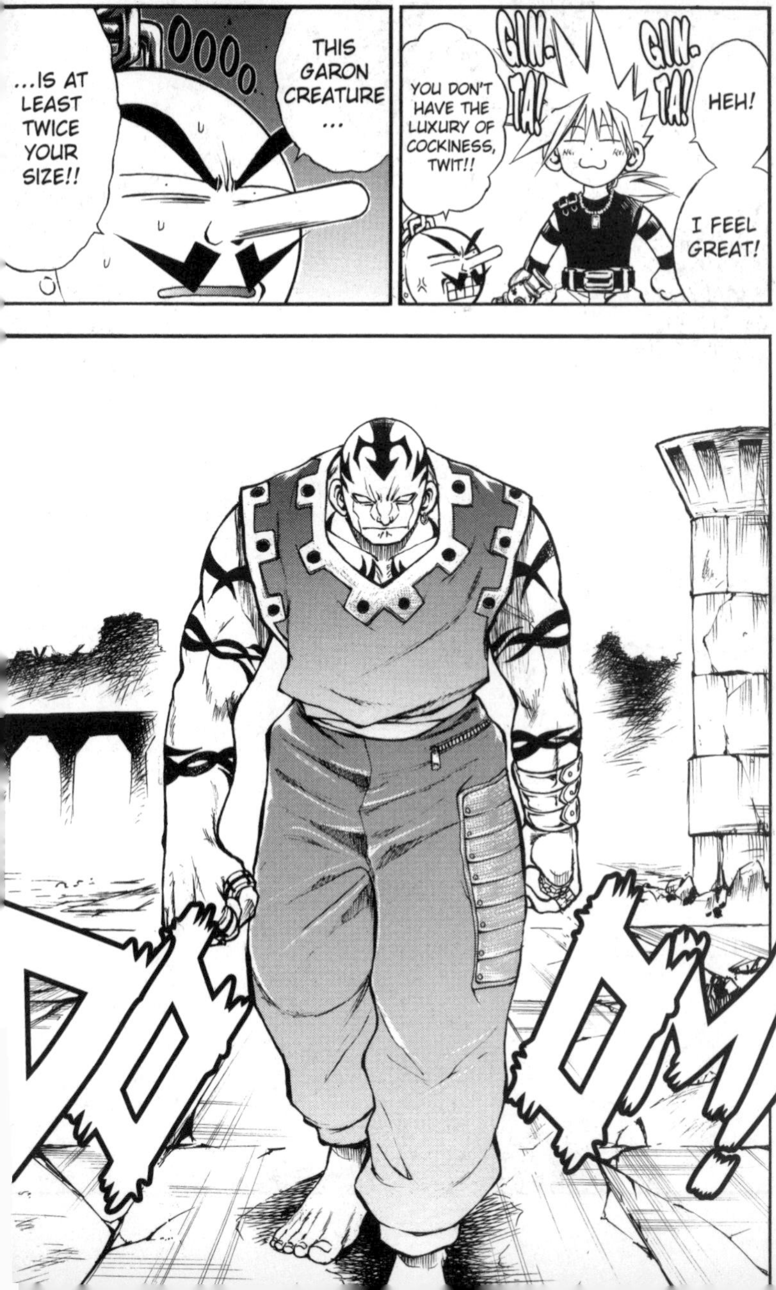
GIN. TA!
GIN. TA!
HEH!
I FEEL GREAT!
YOU DON'T HAVE THE LUXURY OF COCKINESS, TWIT!!
THIS GARON CREATURE...
...IS AT LEAST TWICE YOUR SIZE!!

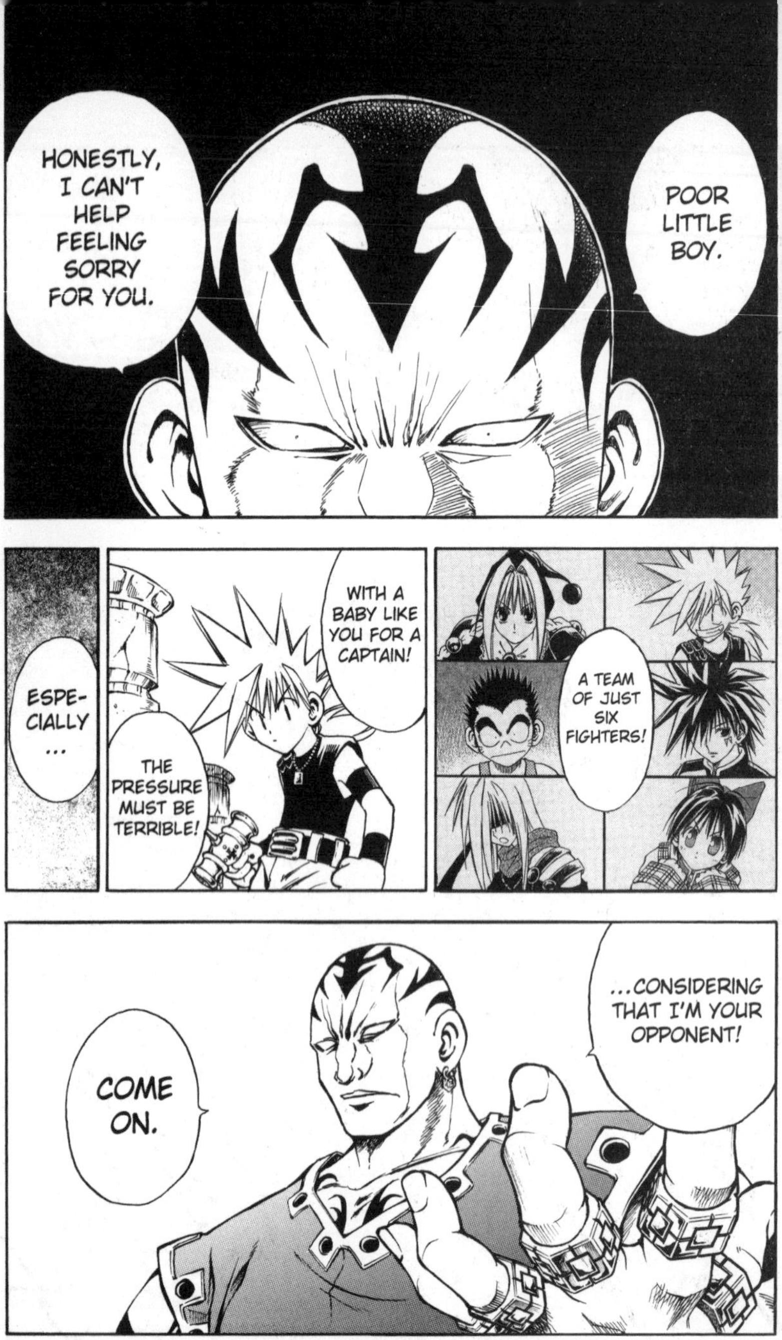
POOR LITTLE BOY.
HONESTLY, I CAN'T HELP FEELING SORRY FOR YOU.
A TEAM OF JUST SIX FIGHTERS!
WITH A BABY LIKE YOU FOR A CAPTAIN!
THE PRESSURE MUST BE TERRIBLE!
ESPE-CIALLY...
...CONSIDERING THAT I'M YOUR OPPONENT!
COME ON.

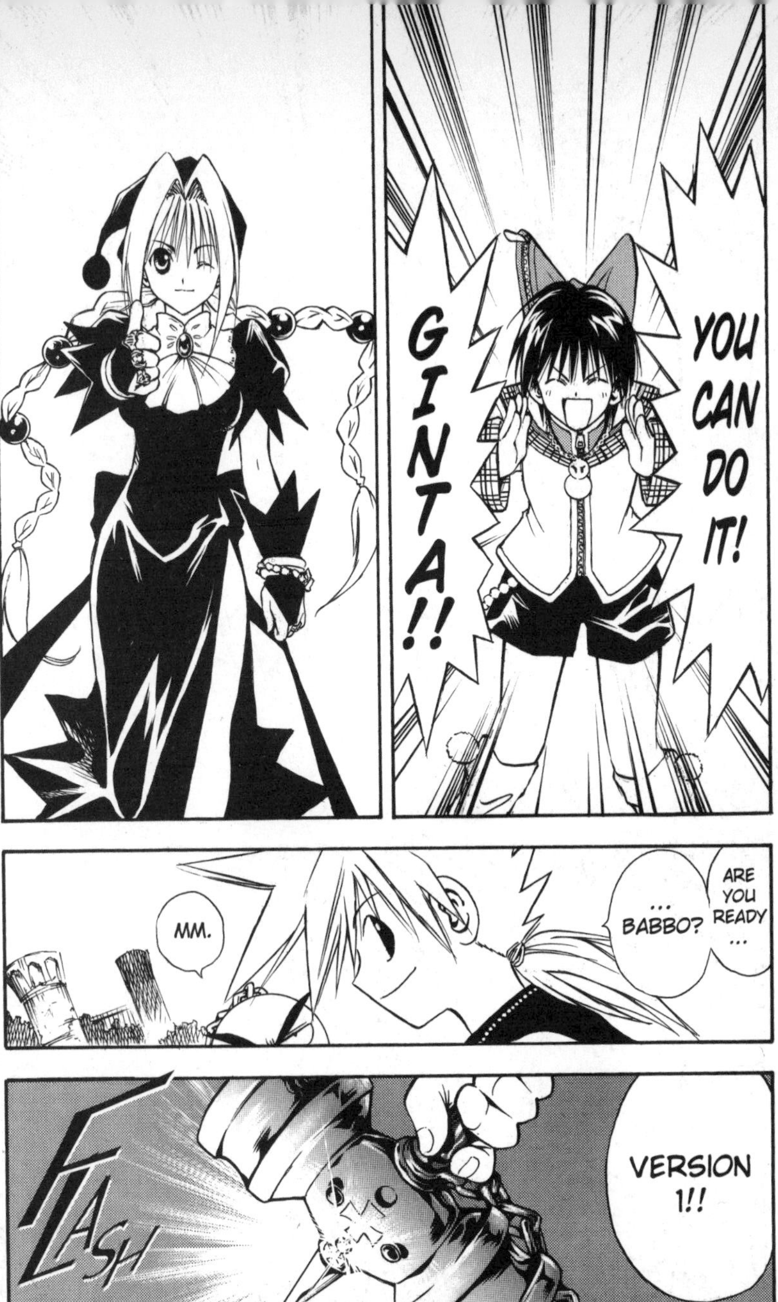
YOU CAN DO IT!
GINTA!!
ARE YOU READY ...
... BABBO?
MM.
VERSION 1!!
FLASH

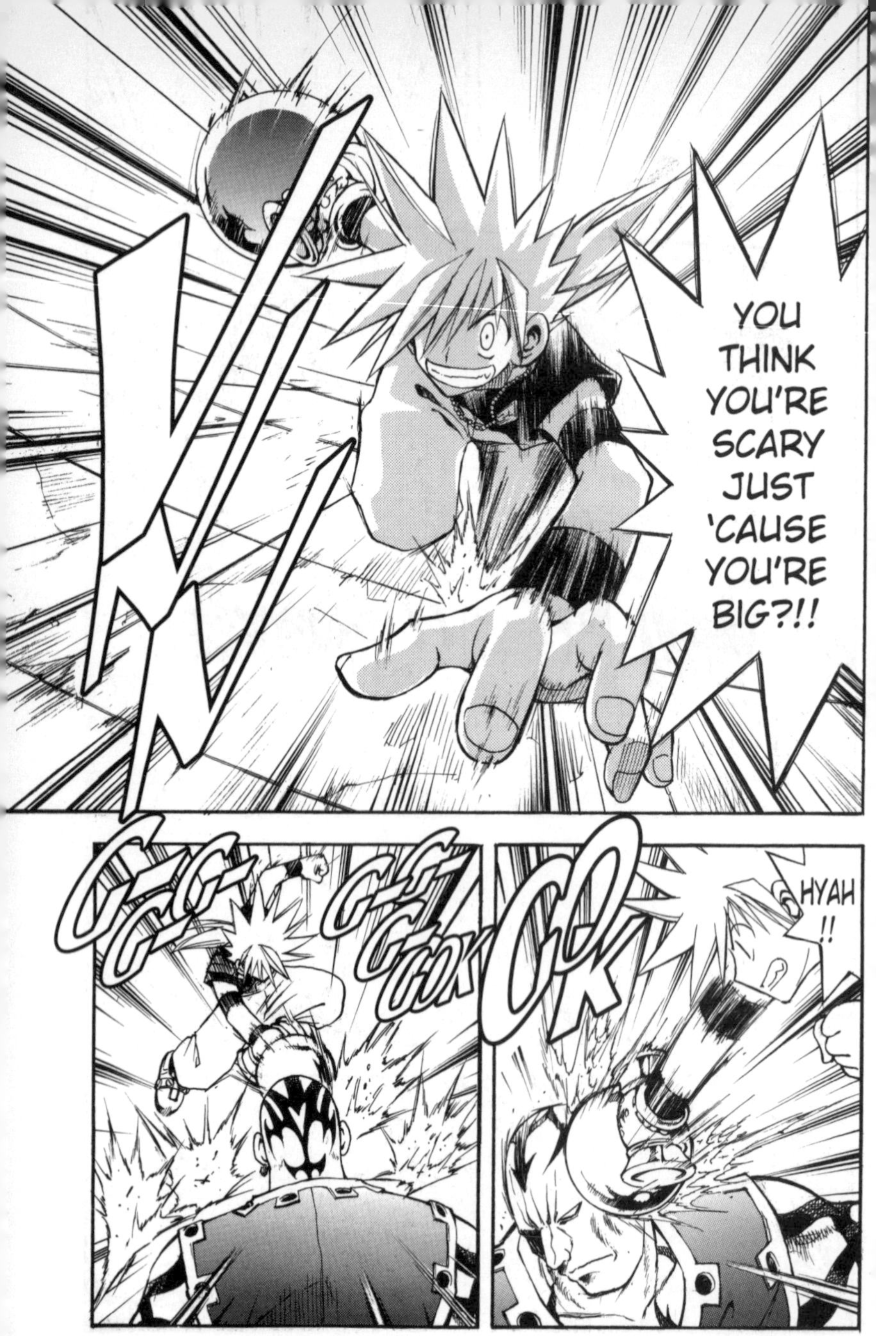
YOU THINK YOU'RE SCARY JUST 'CAUSE YOU'RE BIG?!!
HYAH !!

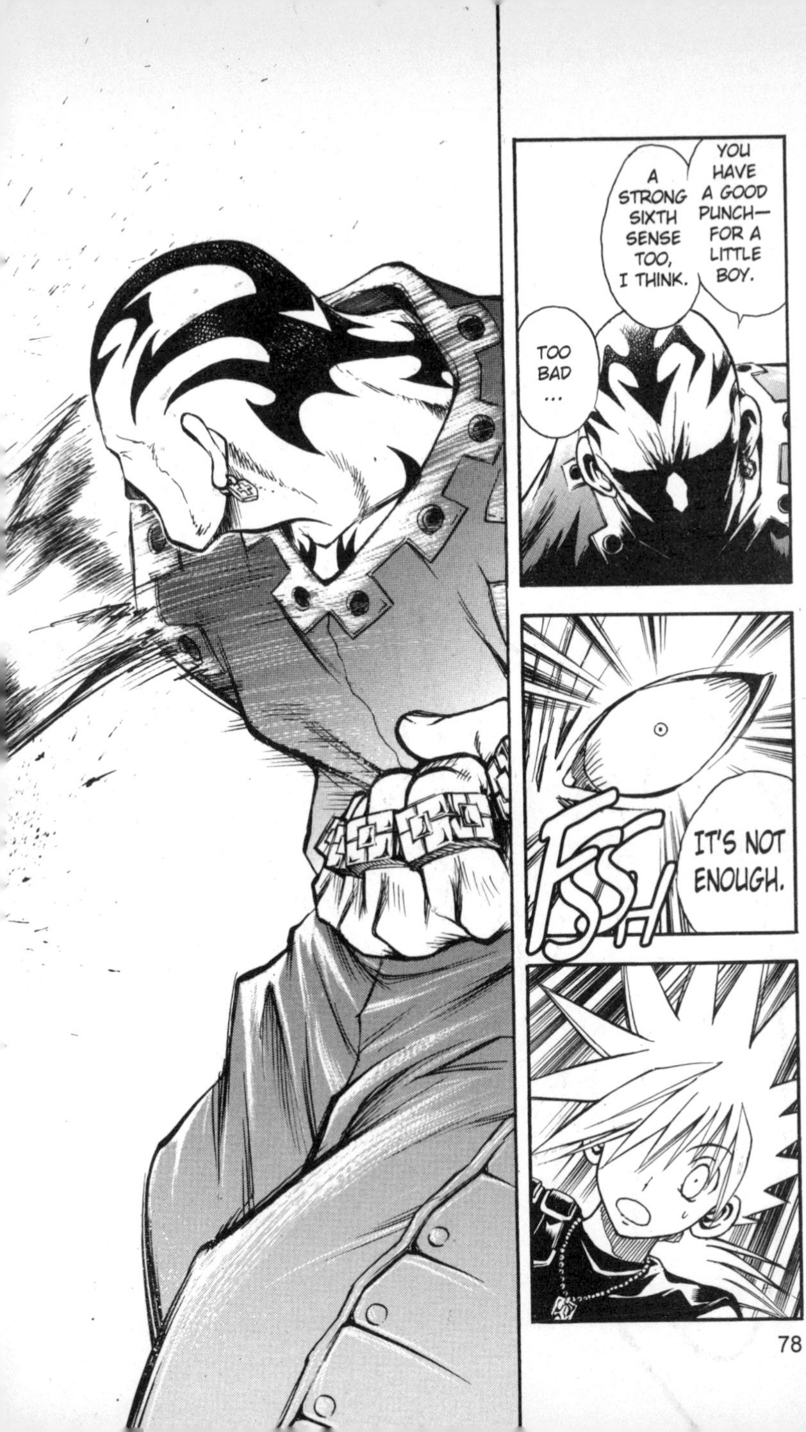
YOU HAVE A GOOD PUNCH— FOR A LITTLE BOY.
A STRONG SIXTH SENSE TOO, I THINK.
TOO BAD ...
IT'S NOT ENOUGH.
FSSH

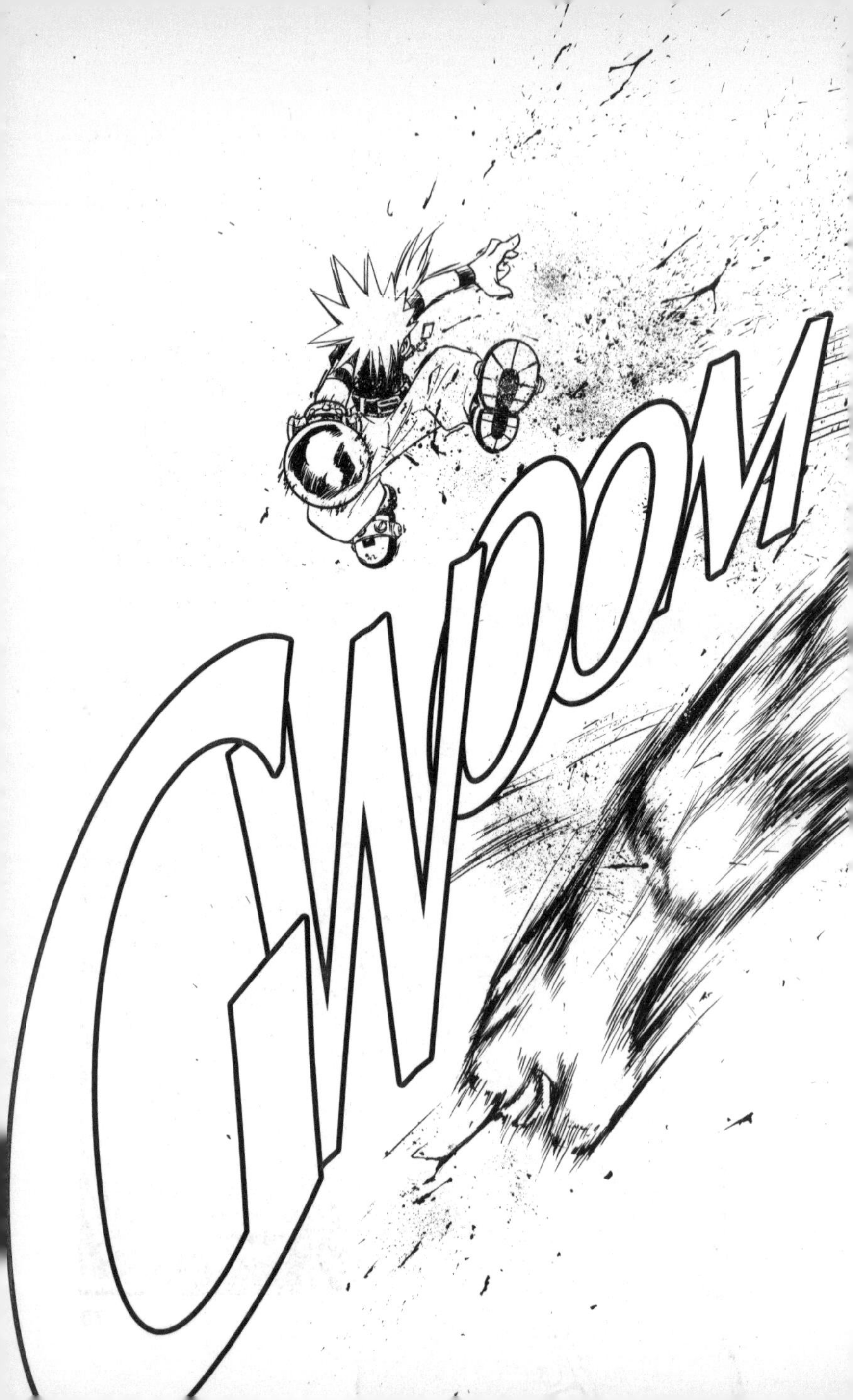
CWOOM

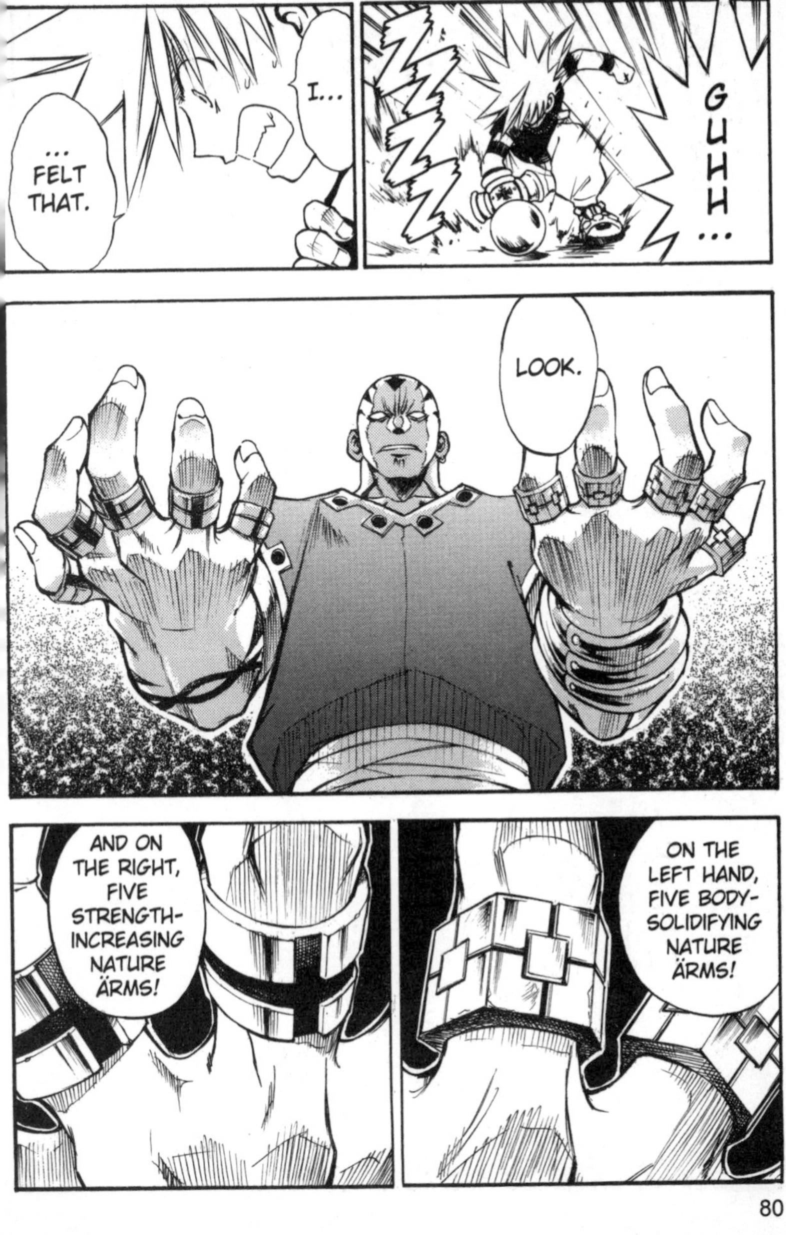
GUHH...
I...
...FELT THAT.
LOOK.
ON THE LEFT HAND, FIVE BODY-SOLIDIFYING NATURE ÄRMS!
AND ON THE RIGHT, FIVE STRENGTH-INCREASING NATURE ÄRMS!

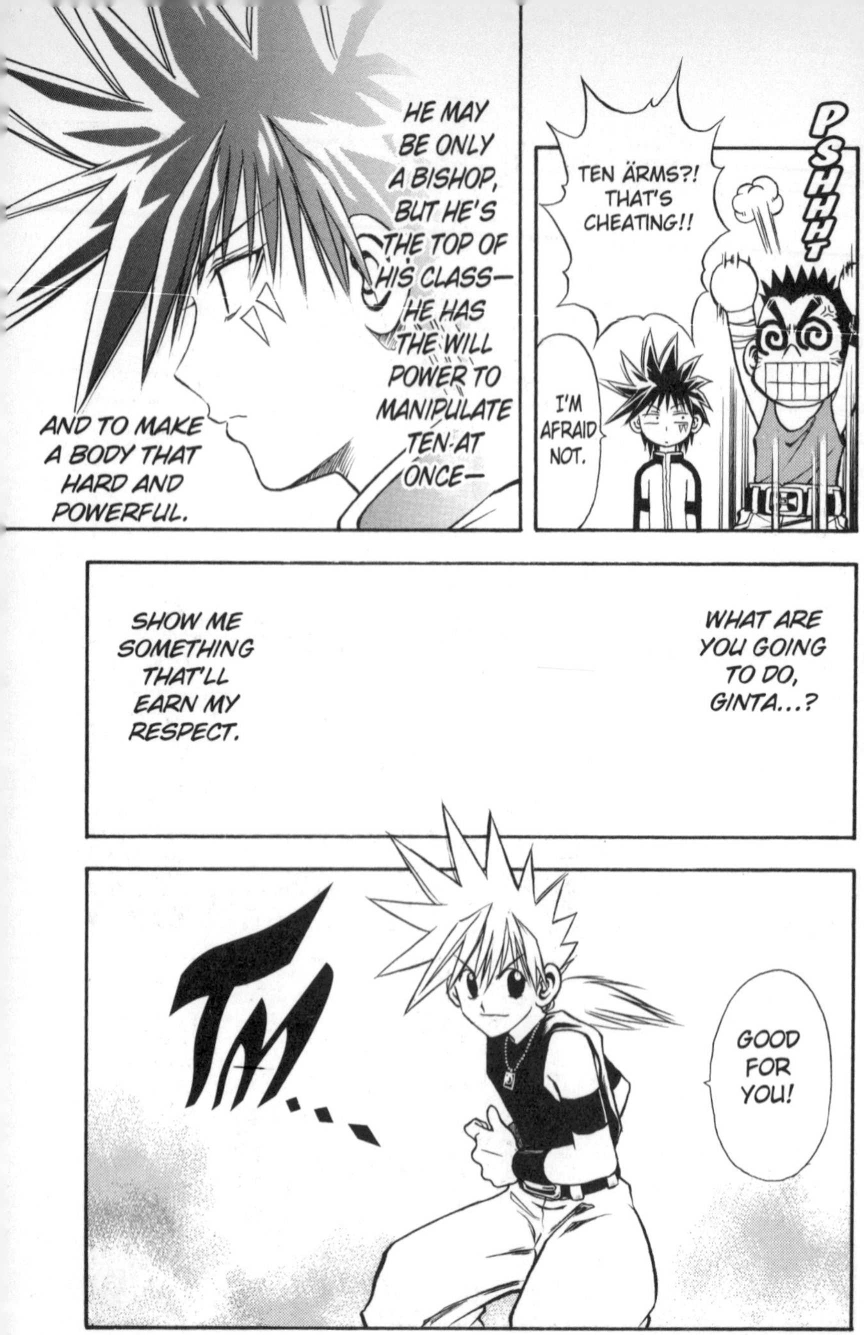
PSHHHT
TEN ÄRMS?! THAT'S CHEATING!!
I'M AFRAID NOT.
HE MAY BE ONLY A BISHOP, BUT HE'S THE TOP OF HIS CLASS—HE HAS THE WILL POWER TO MANIPULATE TEN AT ONCE—
AND TO MAKE A BODY THAT HARD AND POWERFUL.
WHAT ARE YOU GOING TO DO, GINTA...?
SHOW ME SOMETHING THAT'LL EARN MY RESPECT.
GOOD FOR YOU!
TM...

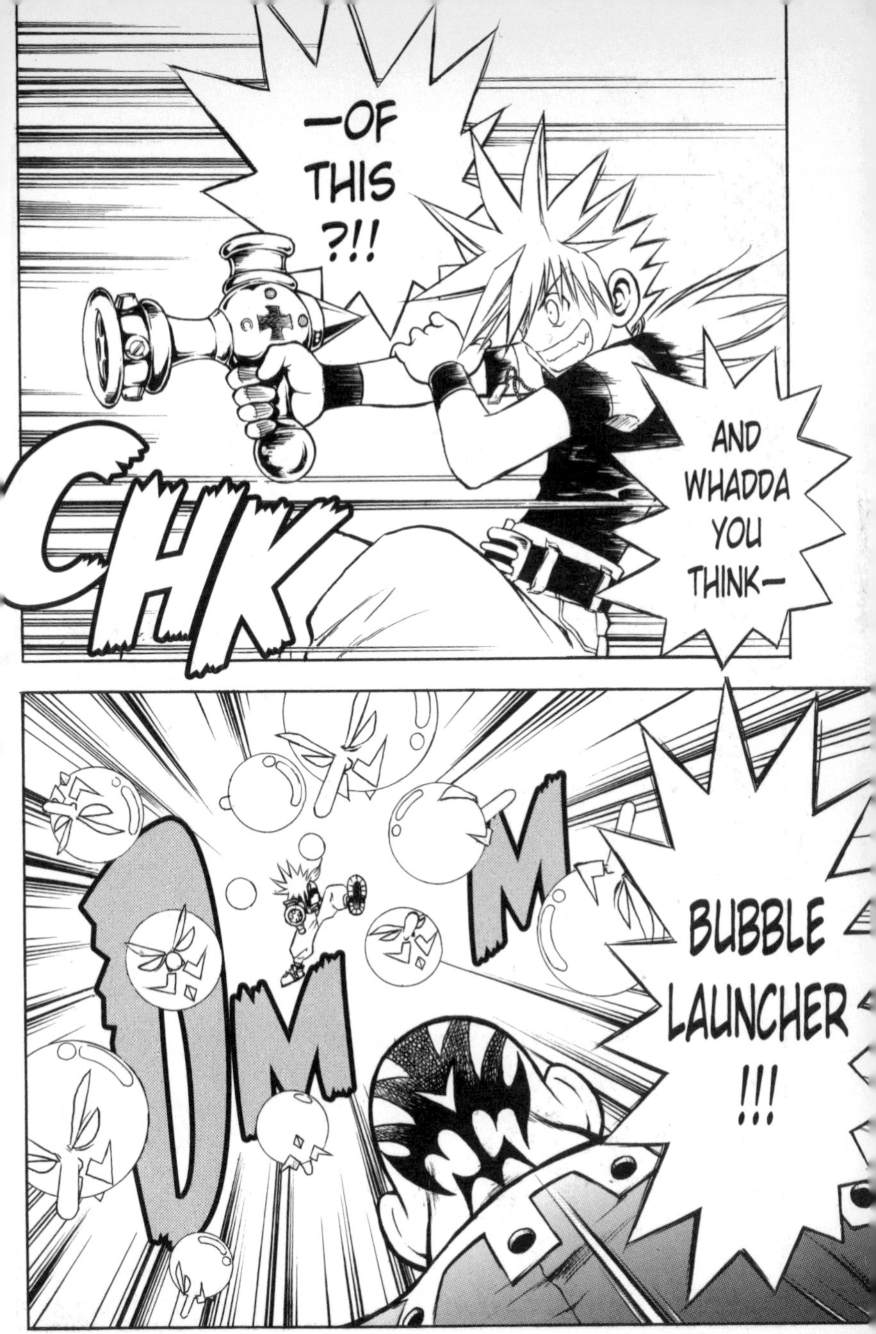
AND WHADDA YOU THINK—
—OF THIS ?!!
CHK
BUBBLE LAUNCHER !!!
UMM

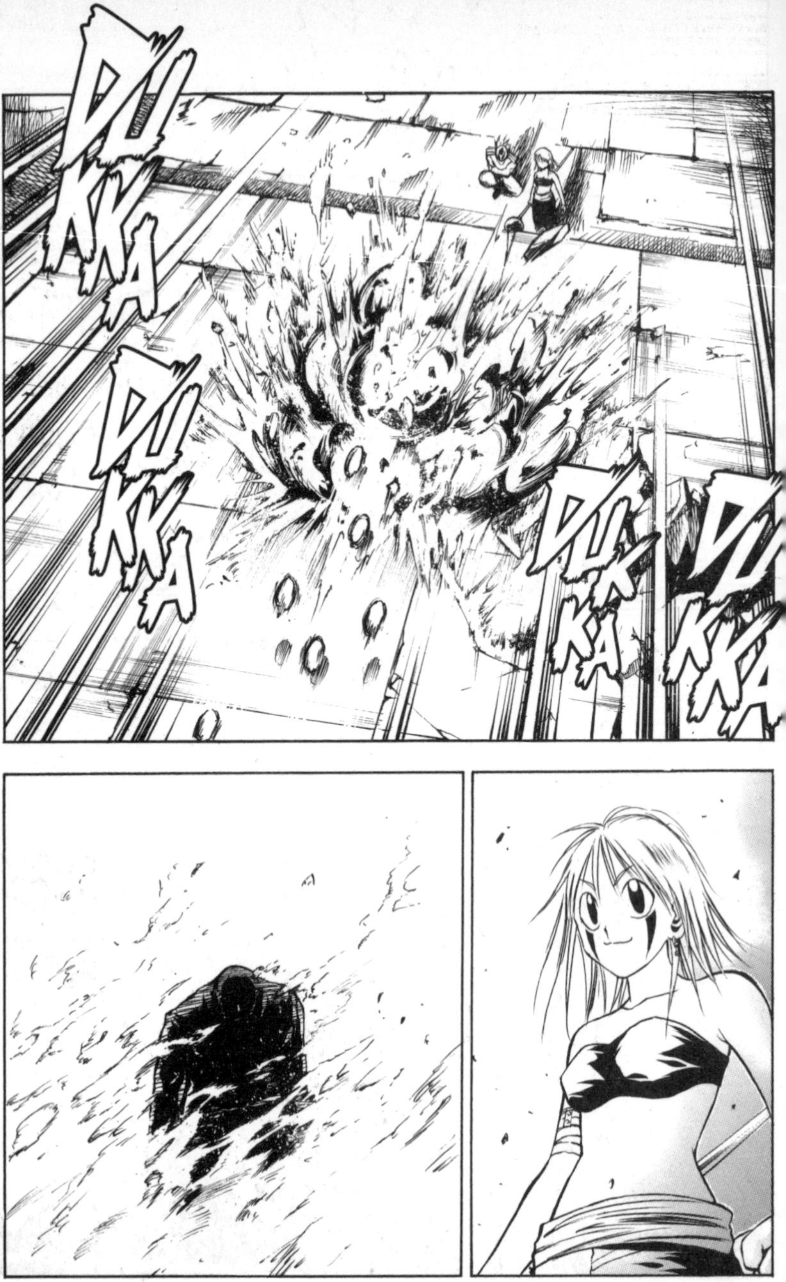
DUKKA
DUKKA
DUKKA
DUKKA

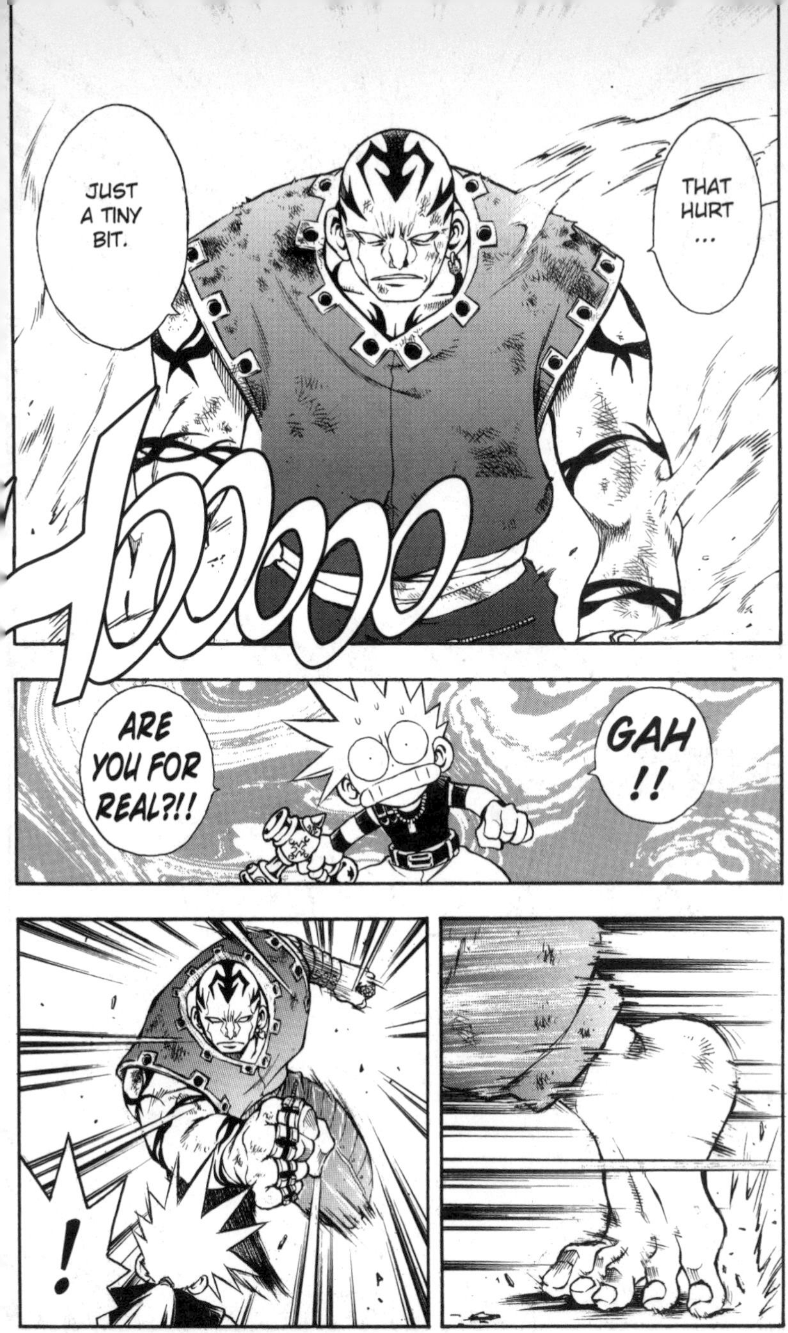
THAT HURT ...
JUST A TINY BIT.
GAH !!
ARE YOU FOR REAL?!!
!

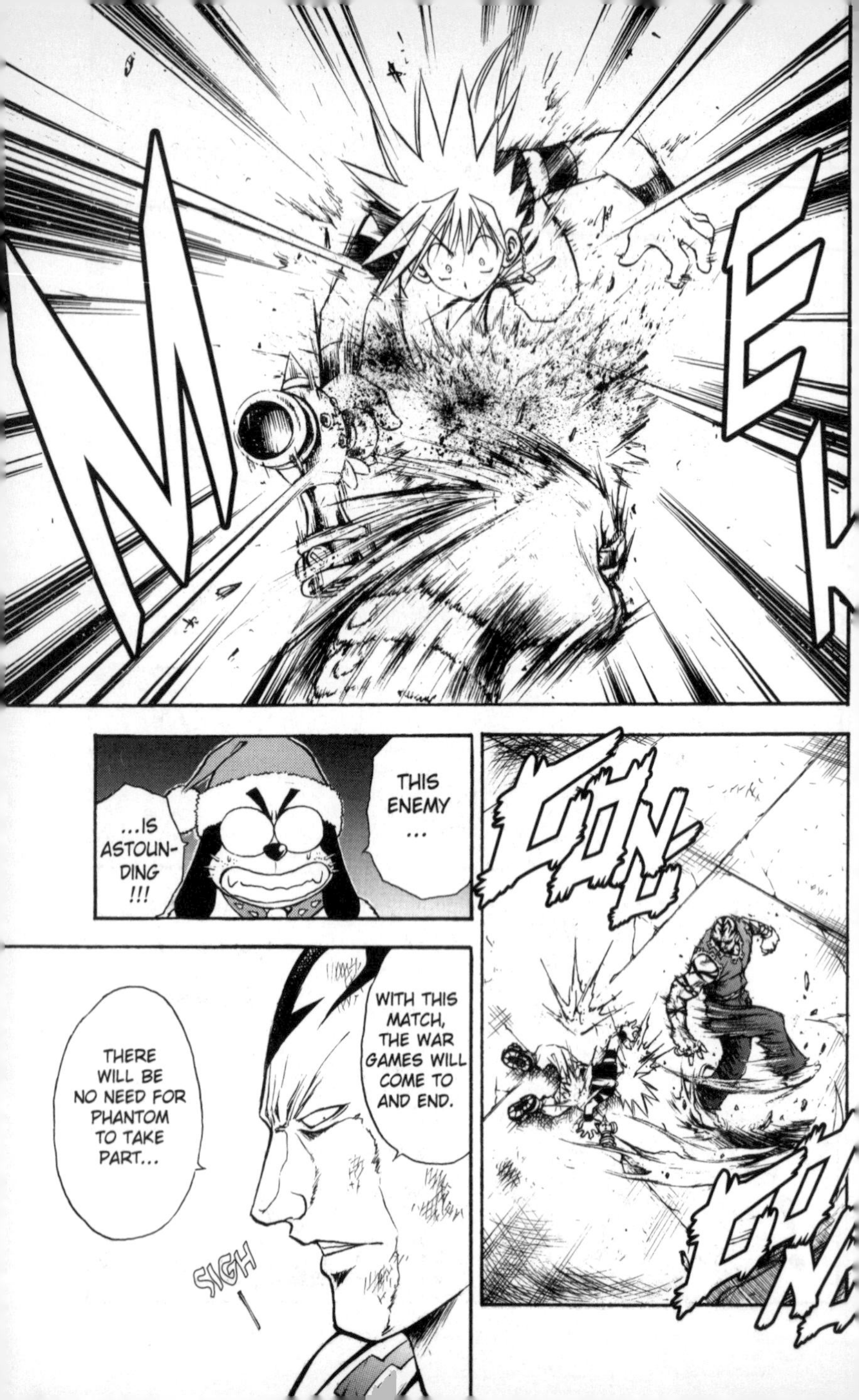

THIS ENEMY ...
...IS ASTOUN-DING !!!
WITH THIS MATCH, THE WAR GAMES WILL COME TO AND END.
THERE WILL BE NO NEED FOR PHANTOM TO TAKE PART...
SIGH

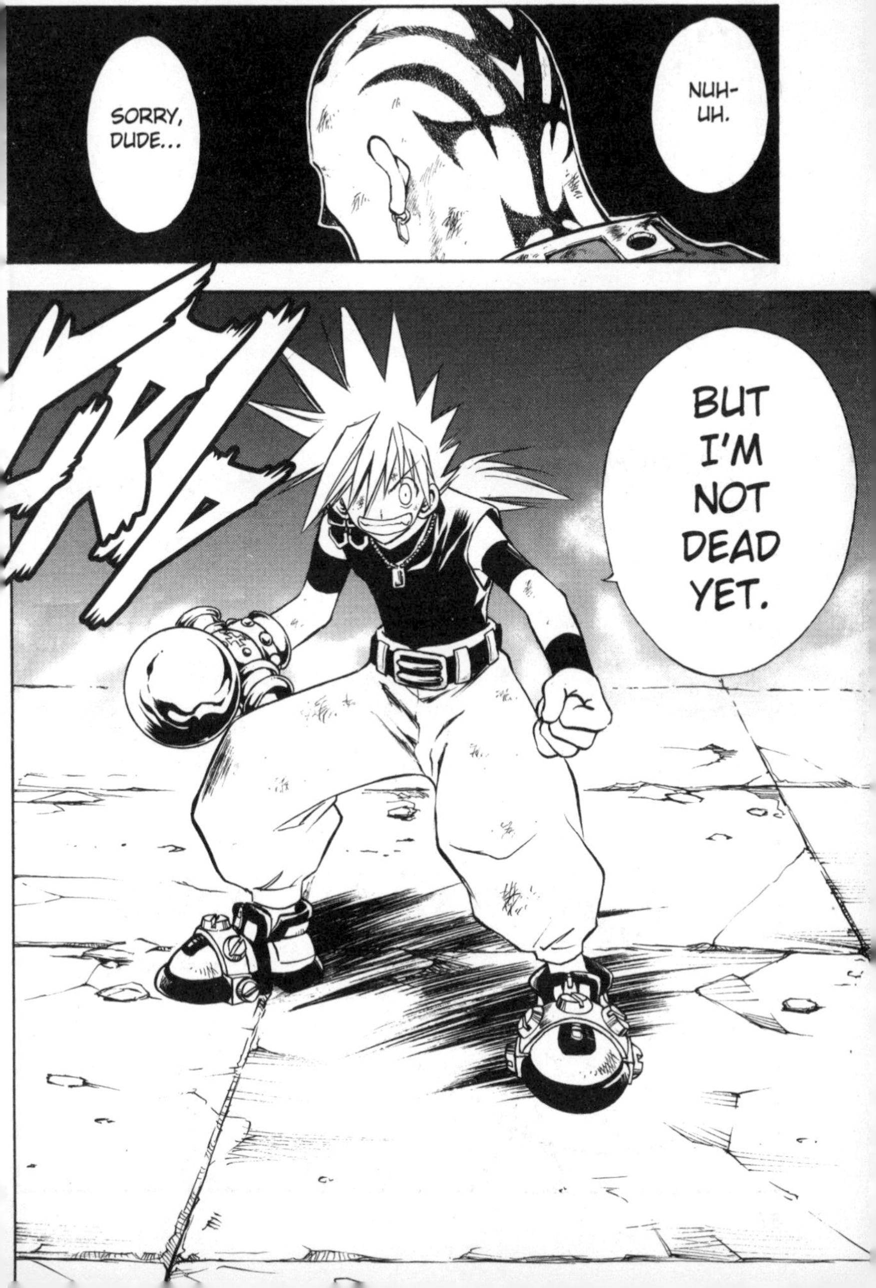
NUH-UH.
SORRY, DUDE...
BUT I'M NOT DEAD YET.

AKT.47/ Ginta vs. Garon②

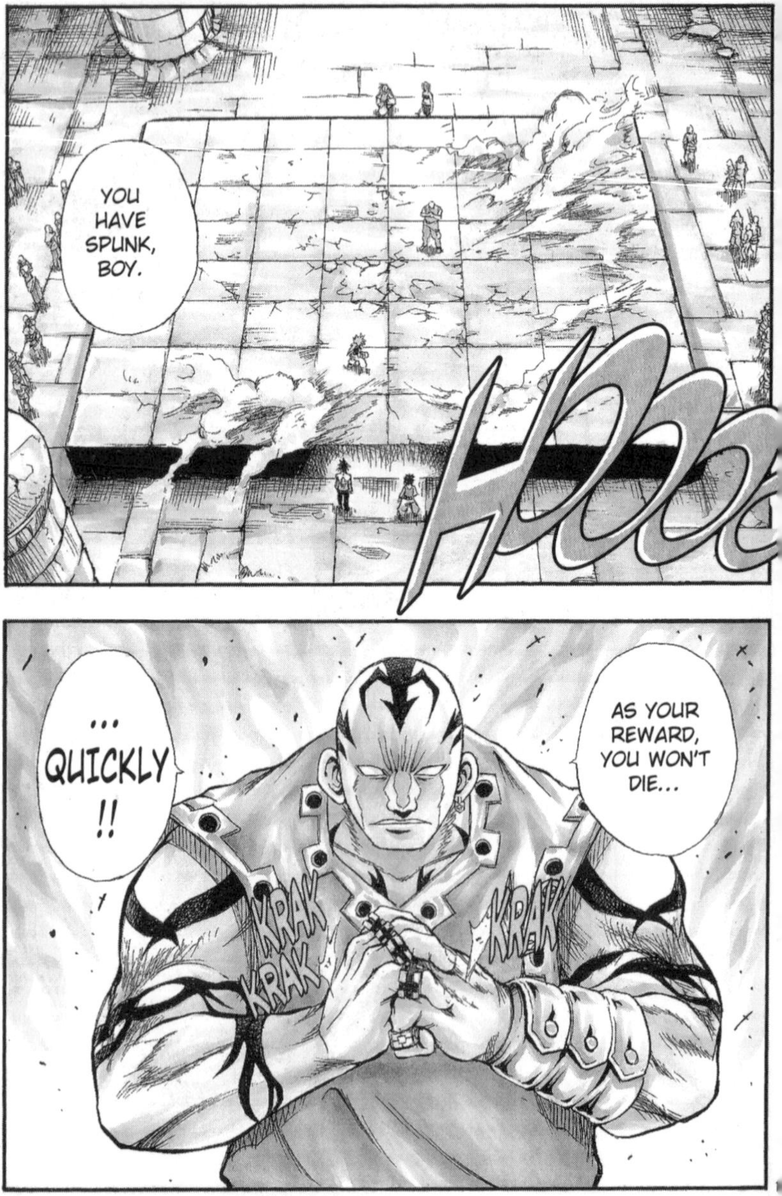
YOU HAVE SPUNK, BOY.
HOOO
AS YOUR REWARD, YOU WON'T DIE...
... QUICKLY !!
KRAK
KRAK KRAK

AKT.47/ Ginta vs. Garon②

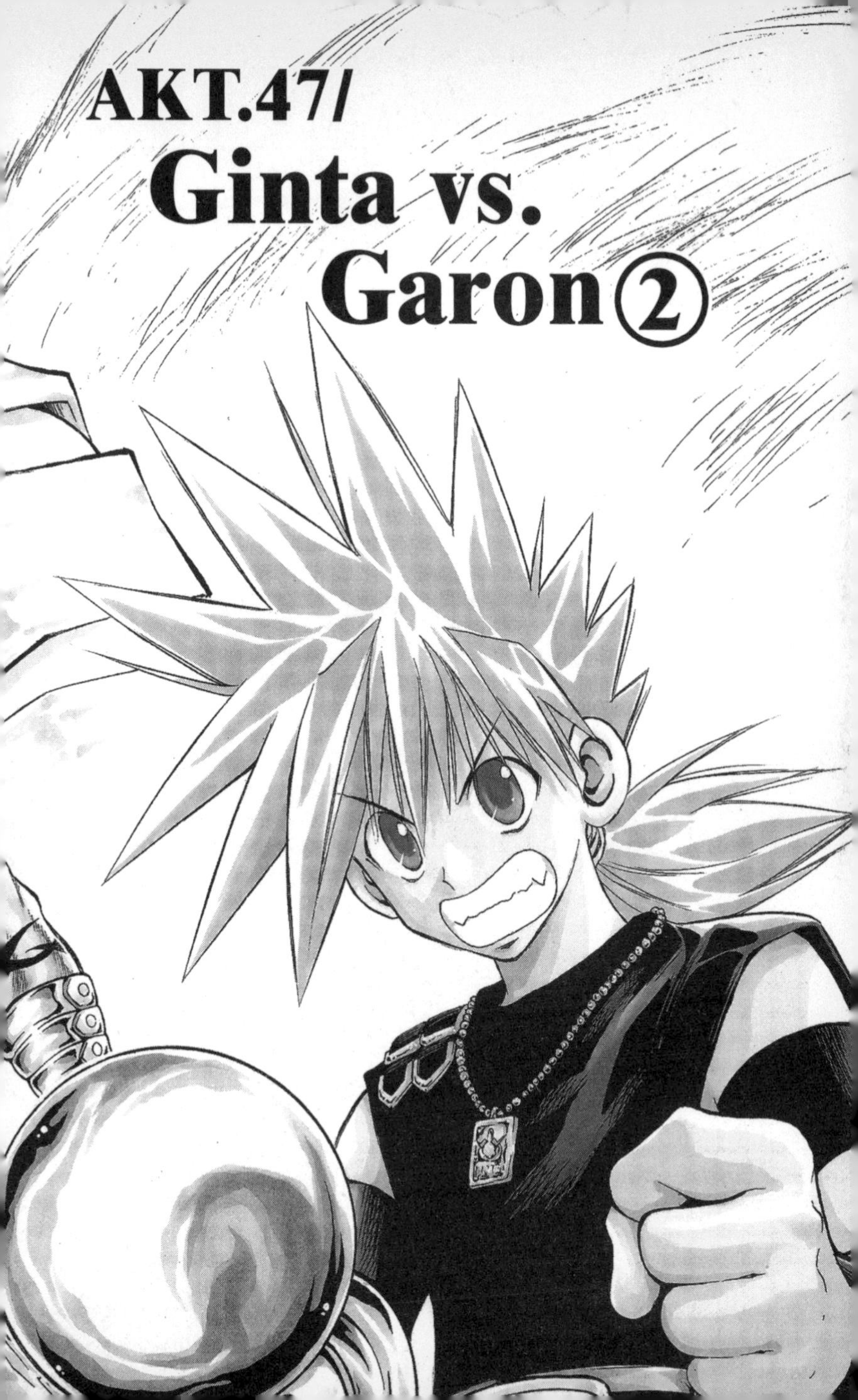

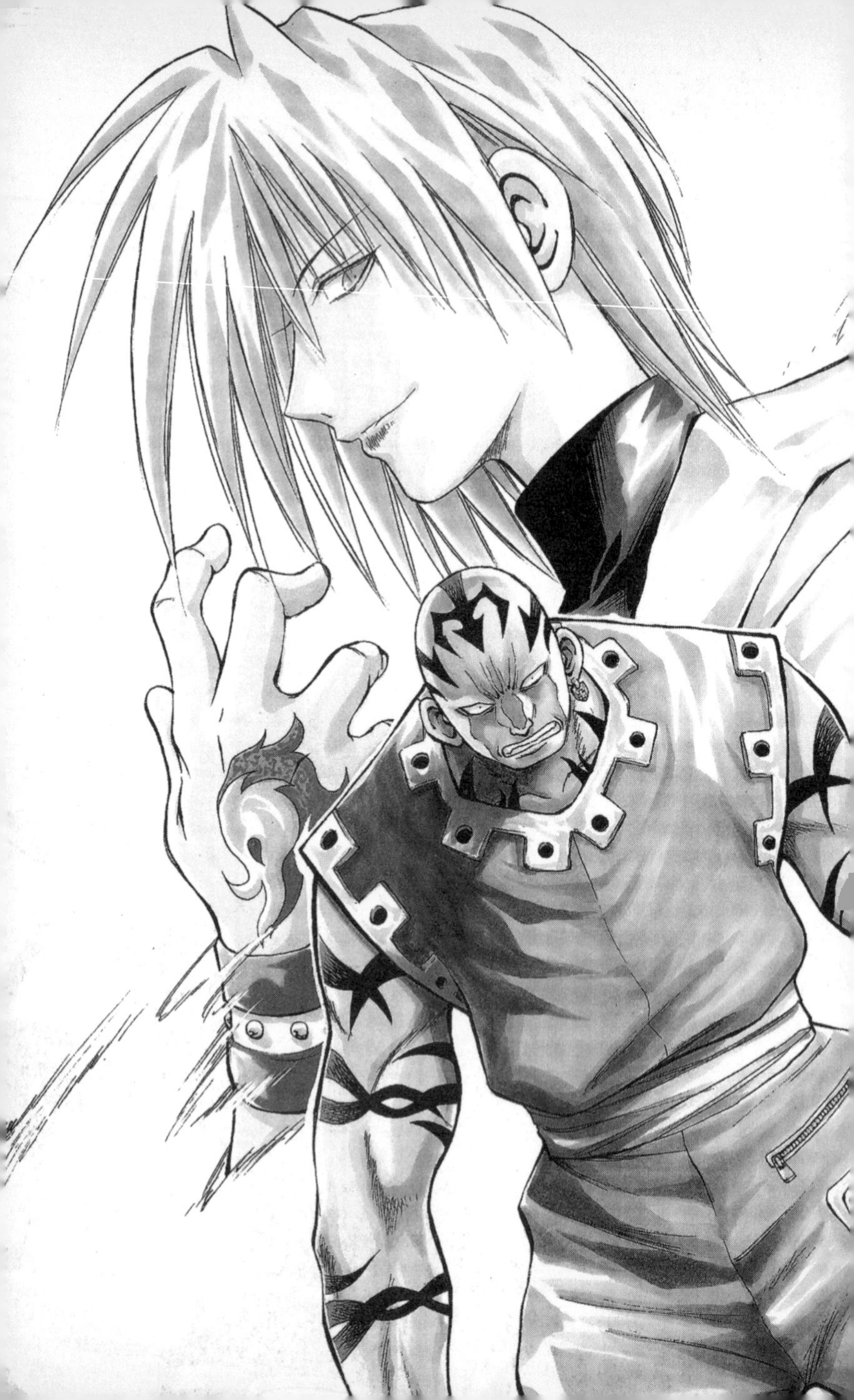

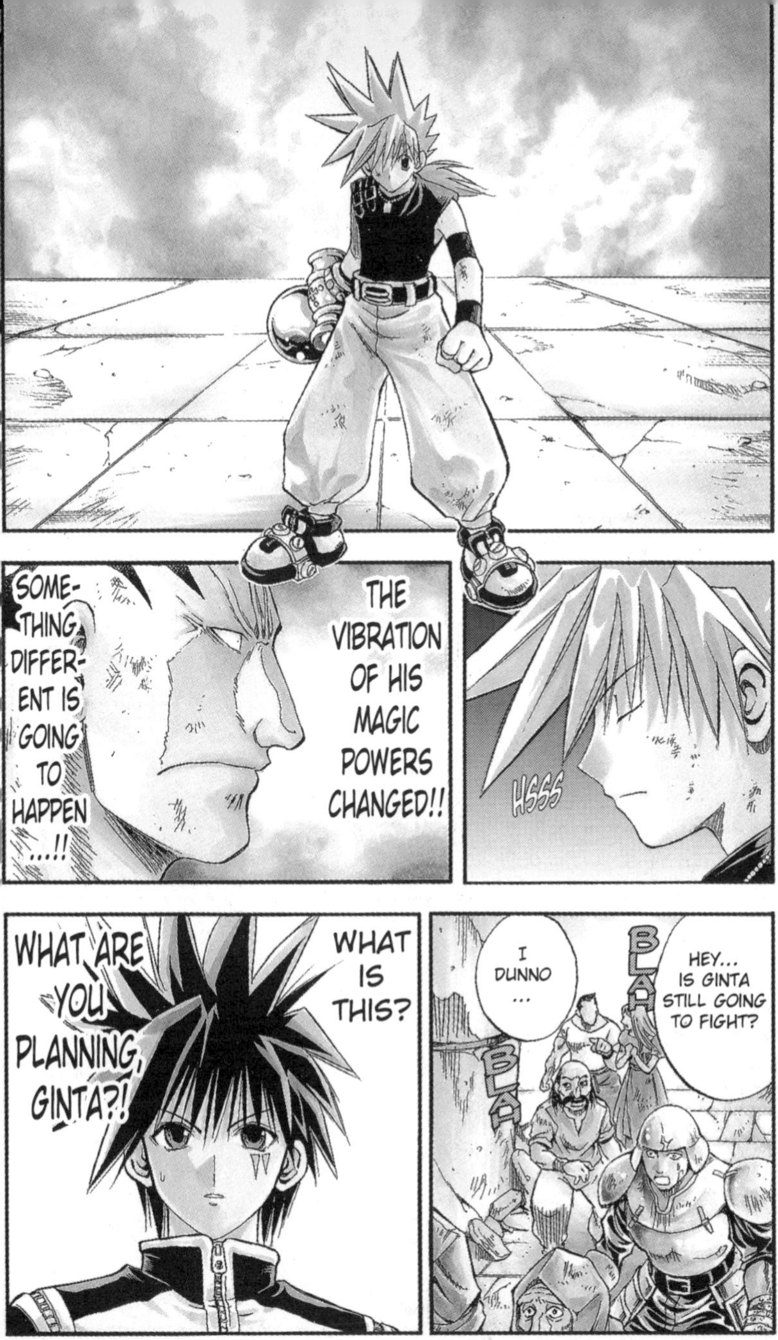
HSSS
THE VIBRATION OF HIS MAGIC POWERS CHANGED!!
SOME-THING DIFFER-ENT IS GOING TO HAPPEN ...!!
HEY... IS GINTA STILL GOING TO FIGHT?
BLA BLA
I DUNNO ...
WHAT IS THIS?
WHAT ARE YOU PLANNING, GINTA?!

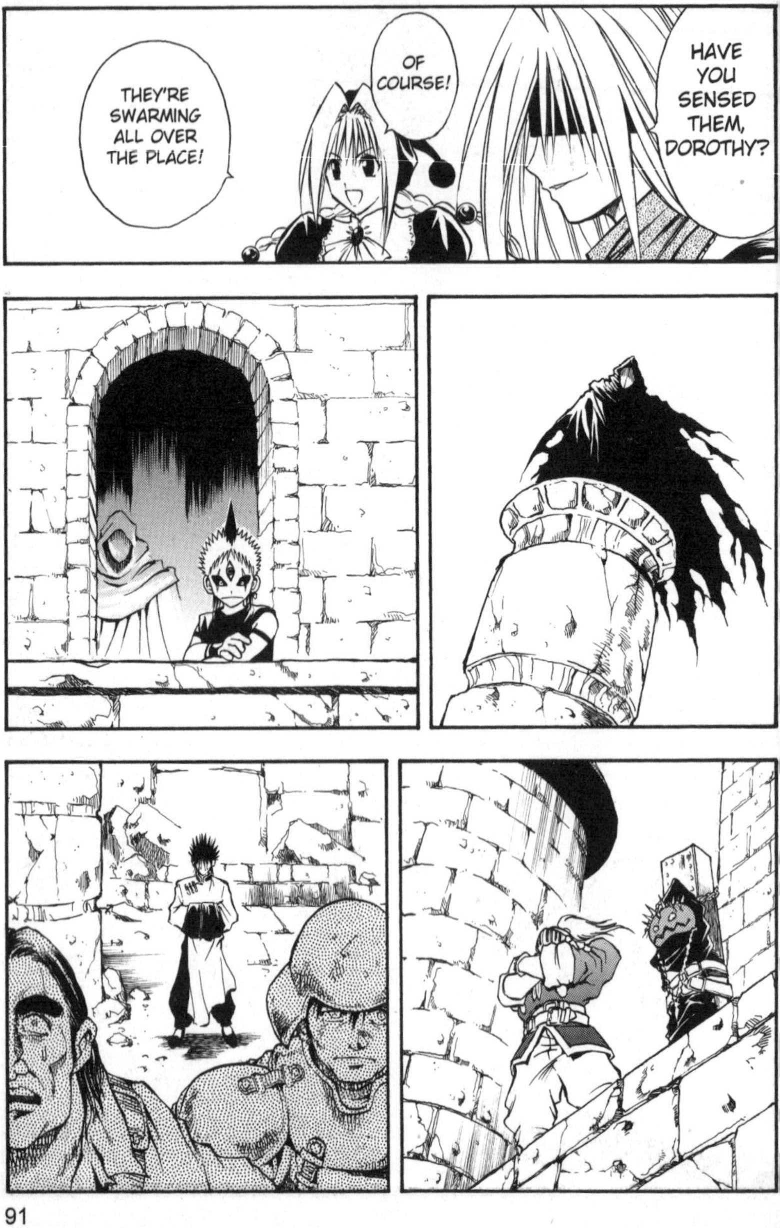
HAVE YOU SENSED THEM, DOROTHY?
OF COURSE!
THEY'RE SWARMING ALL OVER THE PLACE!

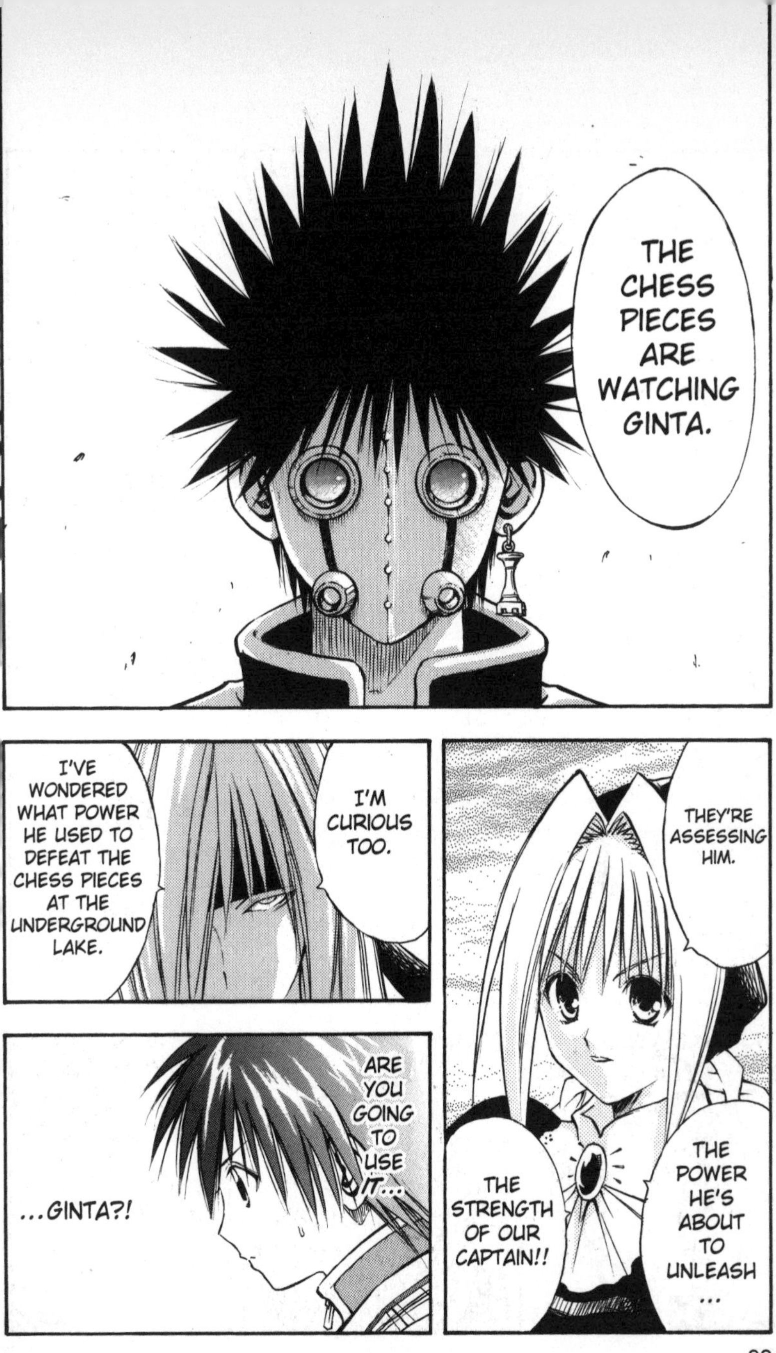
THE CHESS PIECES ARE WATCHING GINTA.
THEY'RE ASSESSING HIM.
THE POWER HE'S ABOUT TO UNLEASH ...
THE STRENGTH OF OUR CAPTAIN!!
I'M CURIOUS TOO.
I'VE WONDERED WHAT POWER HE USED TO DEFEAT THE CHESS PIECES AT THE UNDERGROUND LAKE.
ARE YOU GOING TO USE IT...
...GINTA?!

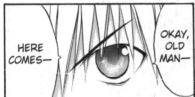

HERE COMES—

OKAY, OLD MAN—

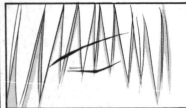

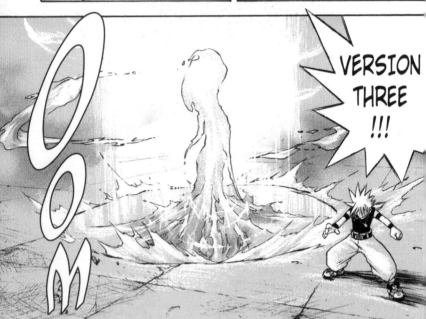

VERSION THREE !!!

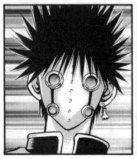

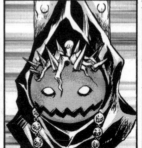

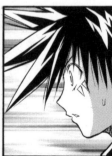

93

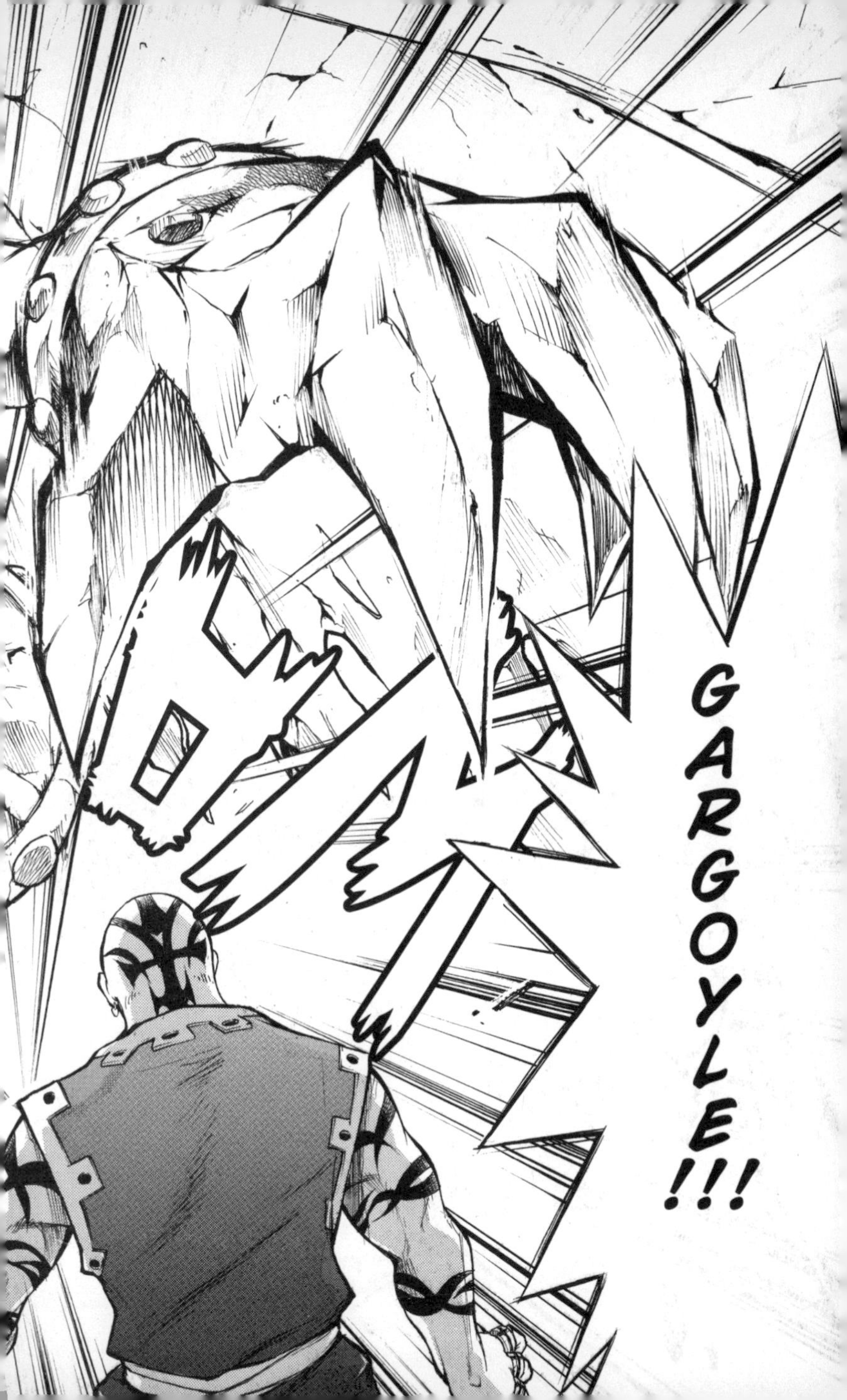
GARGOYLE!!!

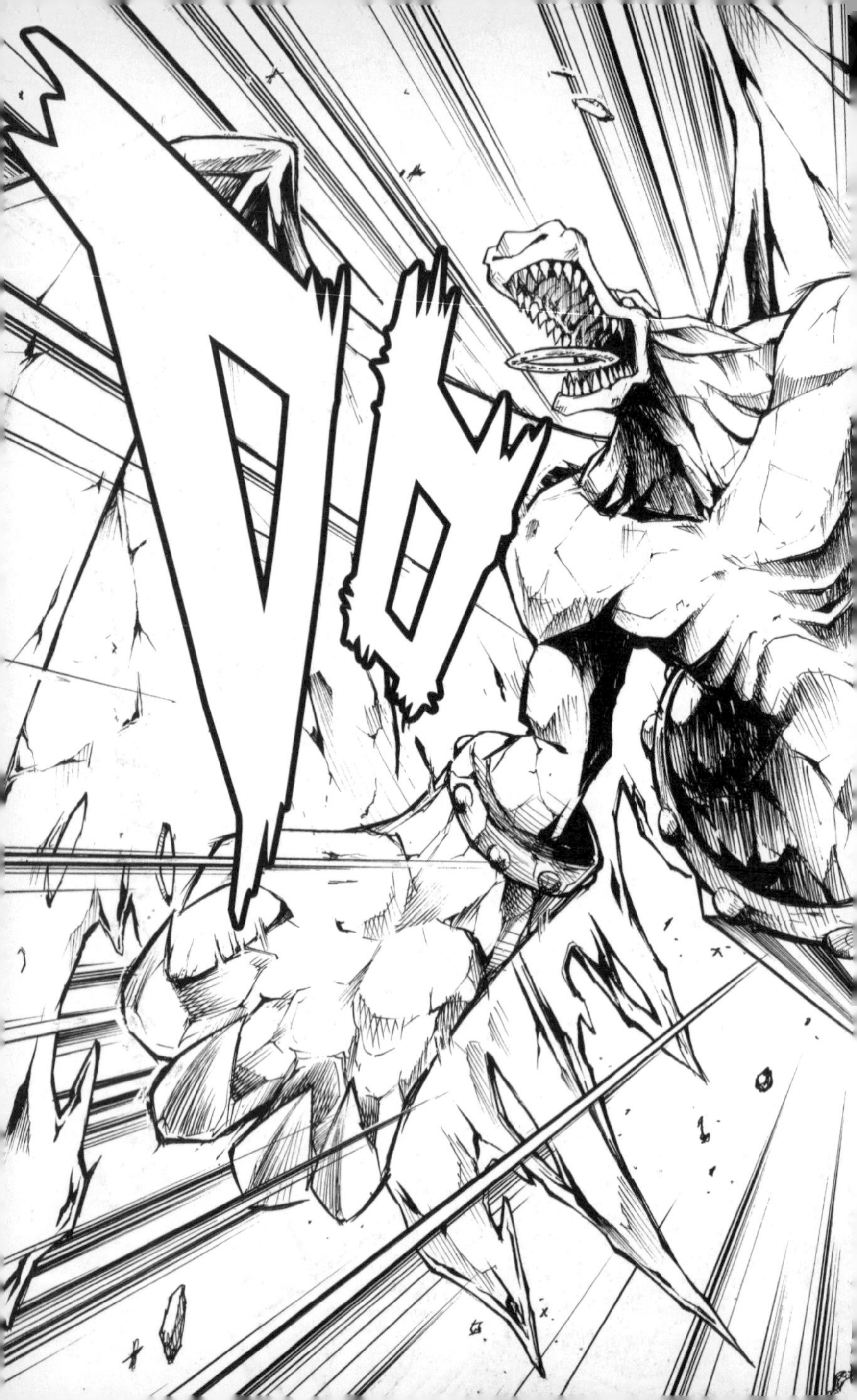

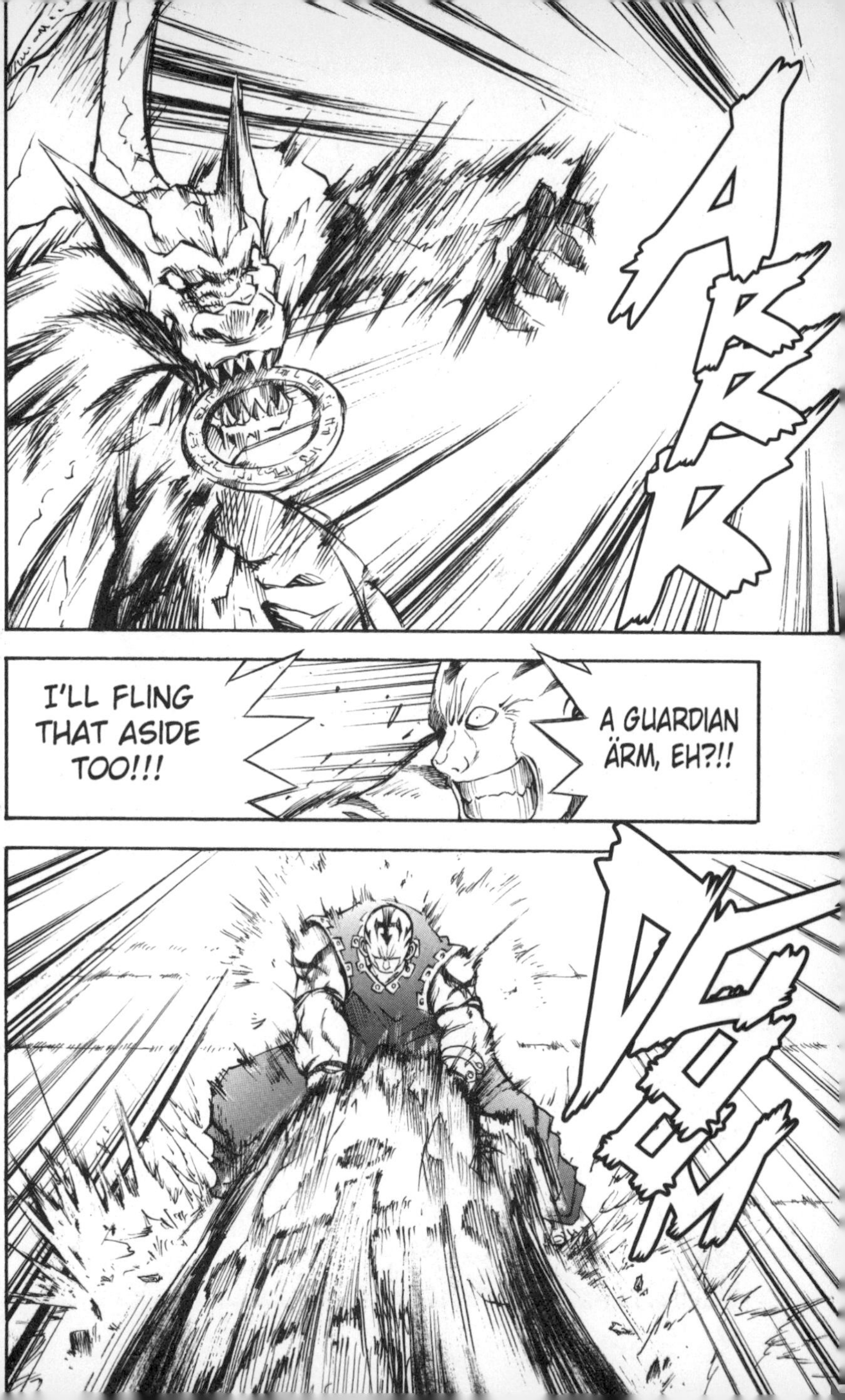
ARRR
A GUARDIAN ÄRM, EH?!!
I'LL FLING THAT ASIDE TOO!!!

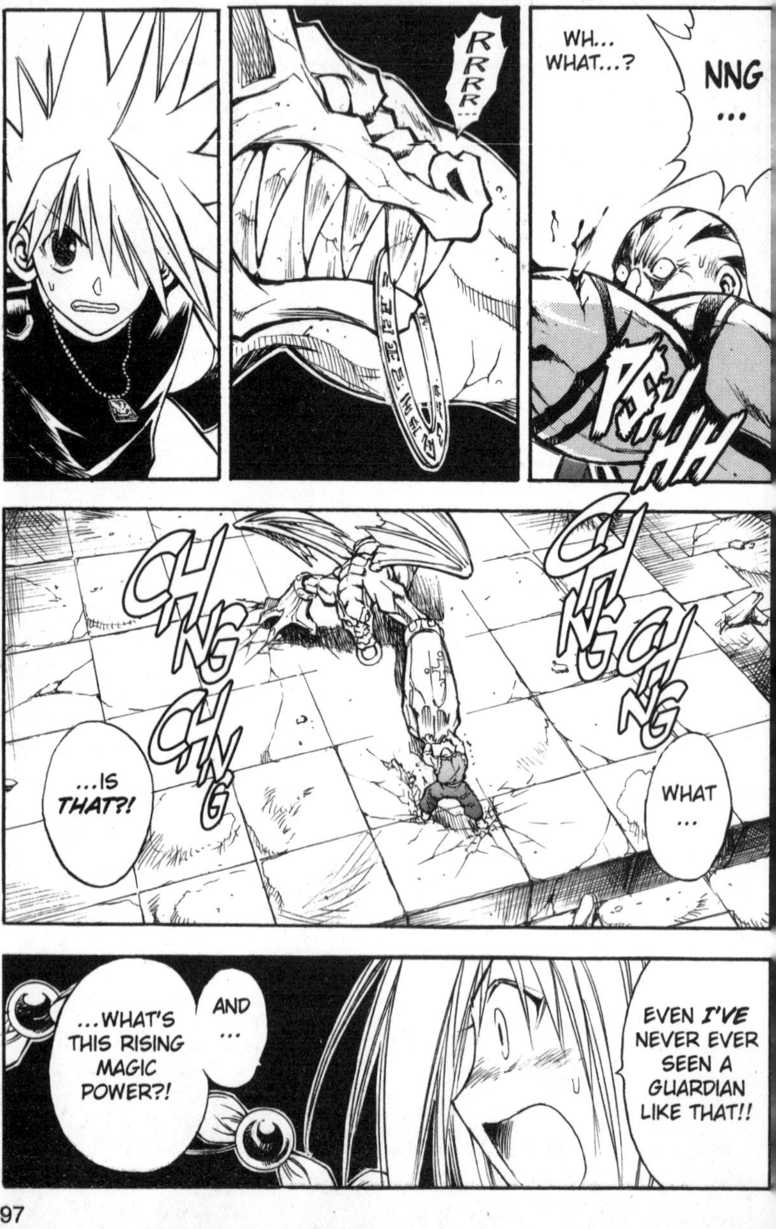
NNG ...
WH... WHAT...?
PSHHH
RRRR...
CHING
CHING
WHAT ...
CHING
CHING
...IS *THAT?!*
EVEN *I'VE* NEVER EVER SEEN A GUARDIAN LIKE THAT!!
AND ...
...WHAT'S THIS RISING MAGIC POWER?!

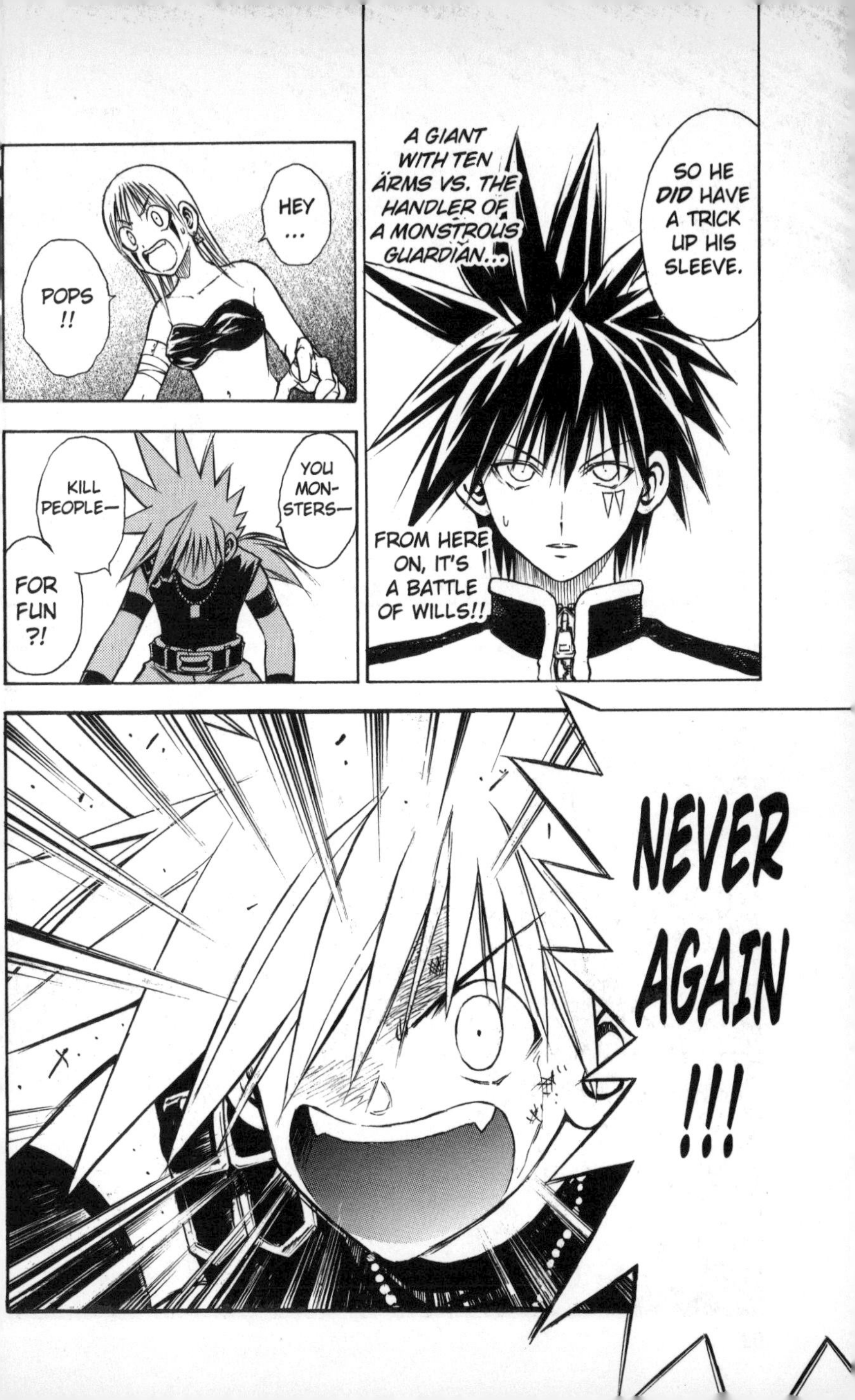
SO HE DID HAVE A TRICK UP HIS SLEEVE.
A GIANT WITH TEN ARMS VS. THE HANDLER OF A MONSTROUS GUARDIAN...
FROM HERE ON, IT'S A BATTLE OF WILLS!!
HEY...
POPS!!
YOU MON-STERS—
KILL PEOPLE—
FOR FUN?!
NEVER AGAIN!!!

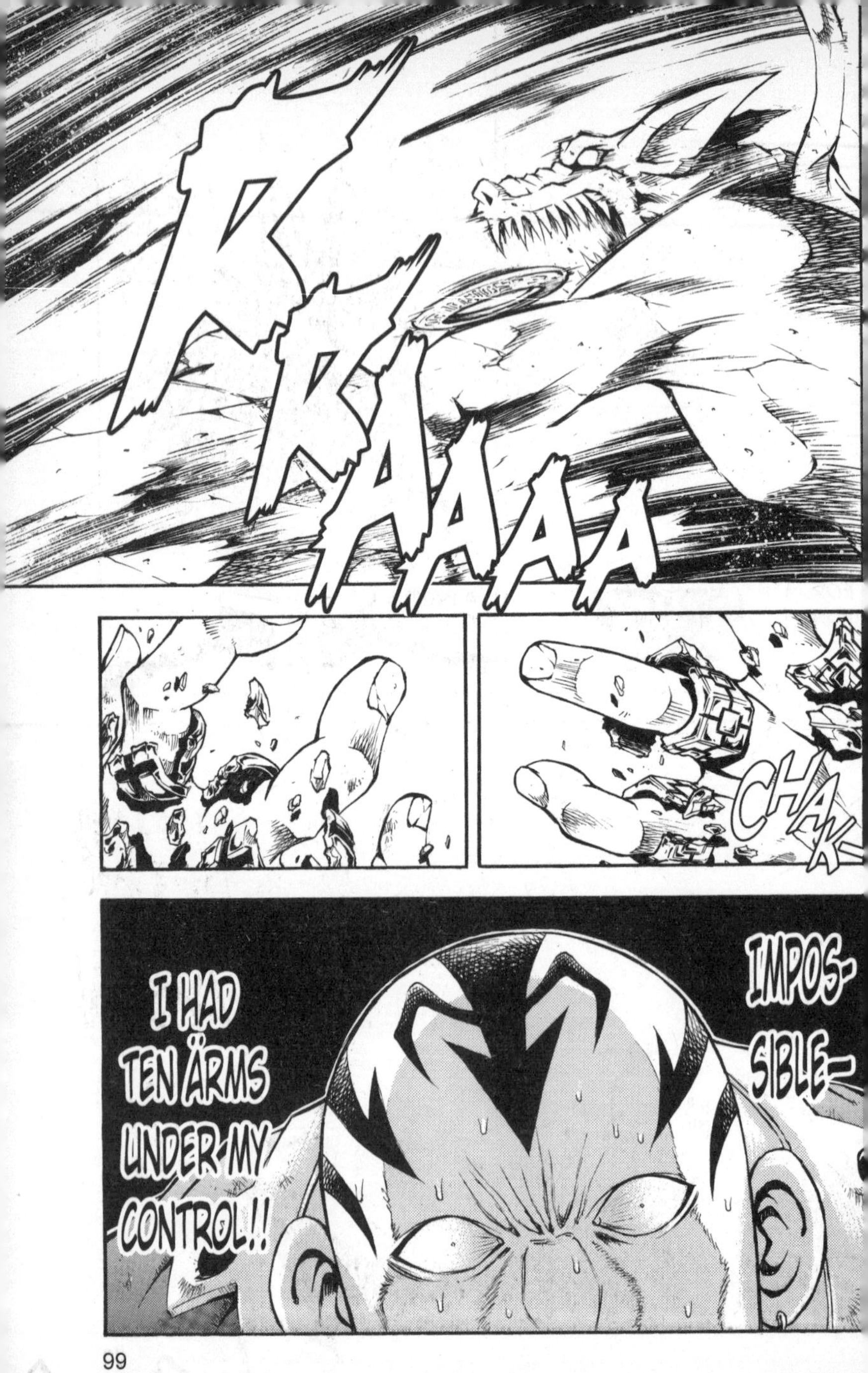

RRAAAA
CHAK
IMPOS-SIBLE—
I HAD TEN ÄRMS UNDER MY CONTROL!!

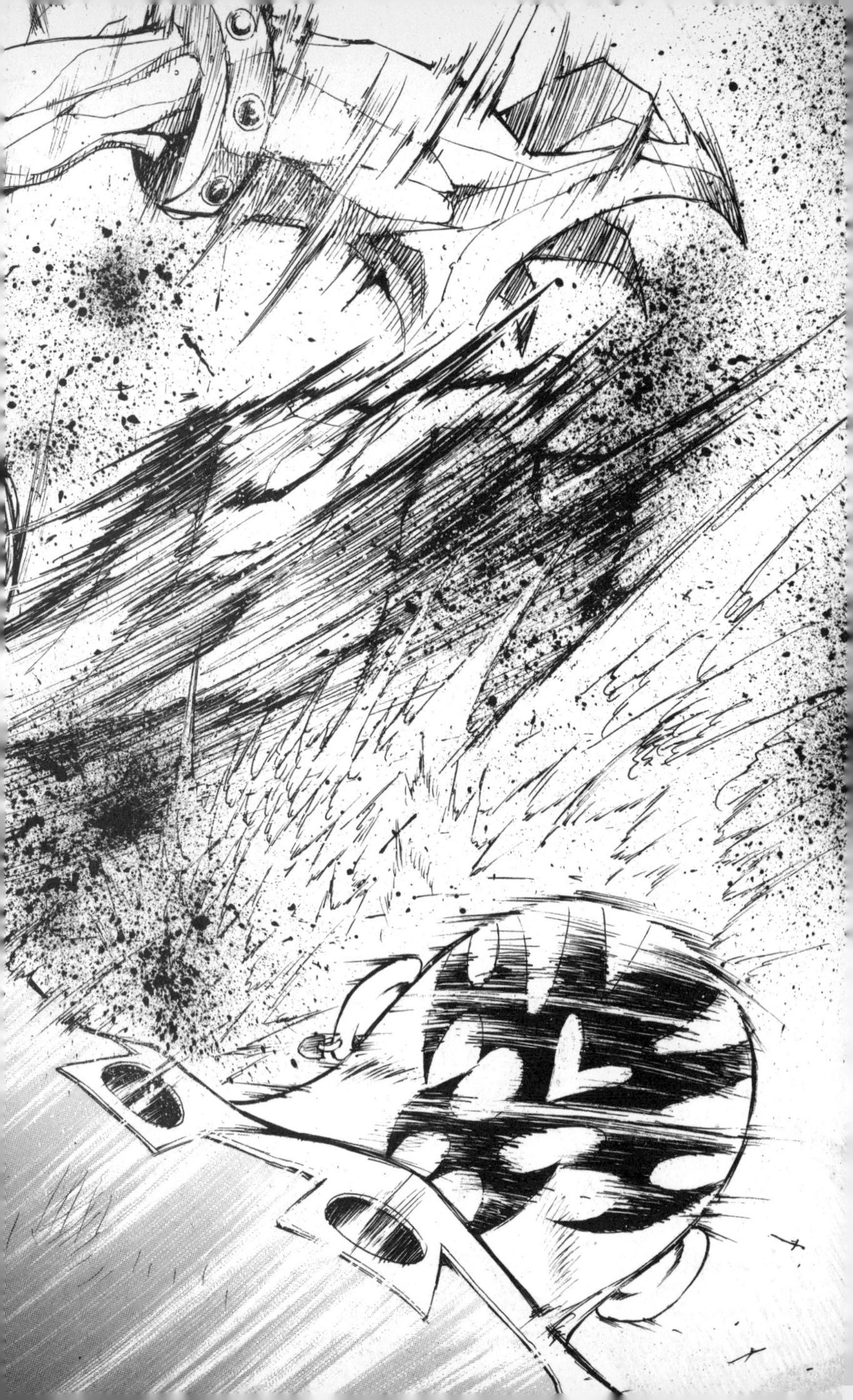

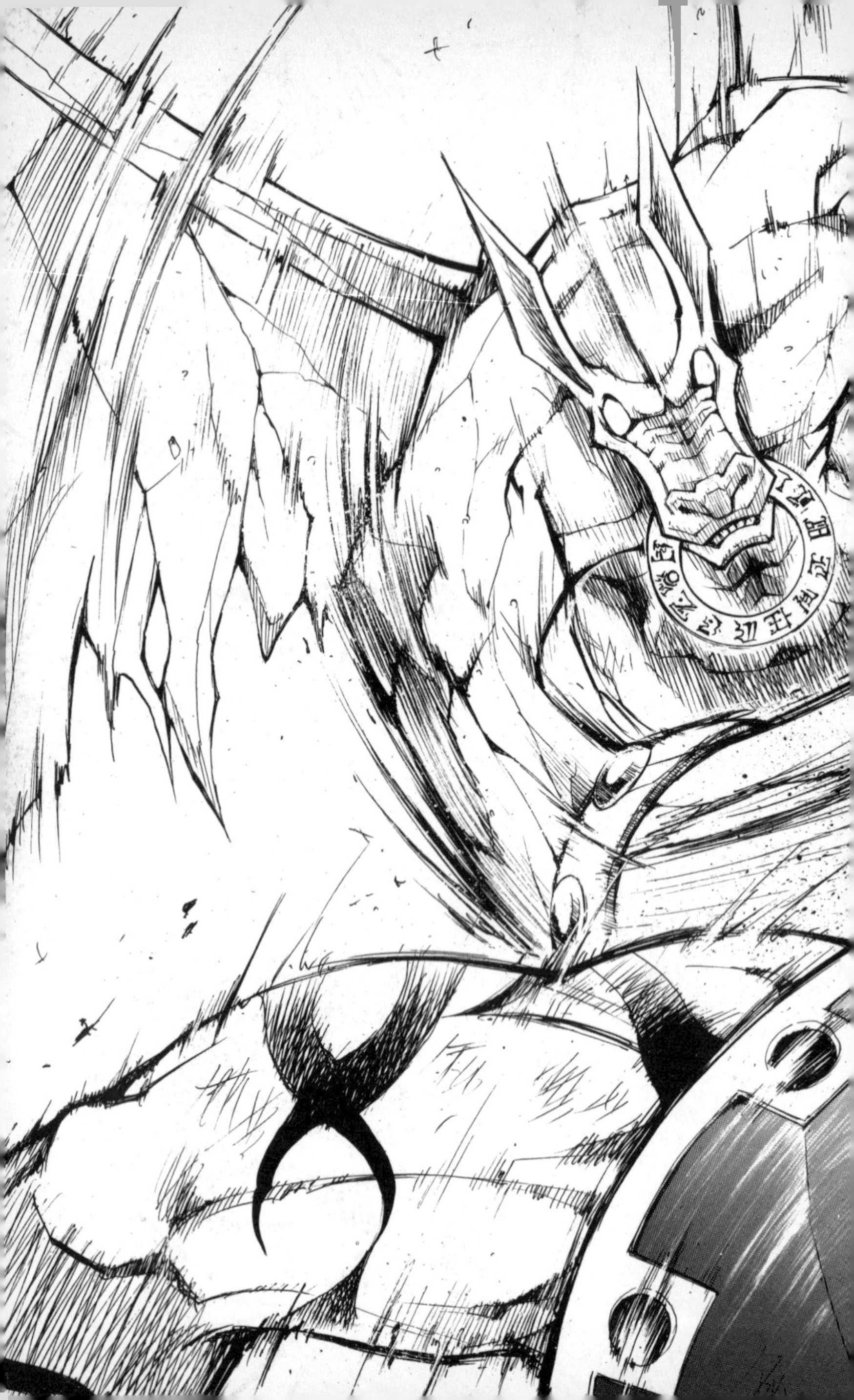

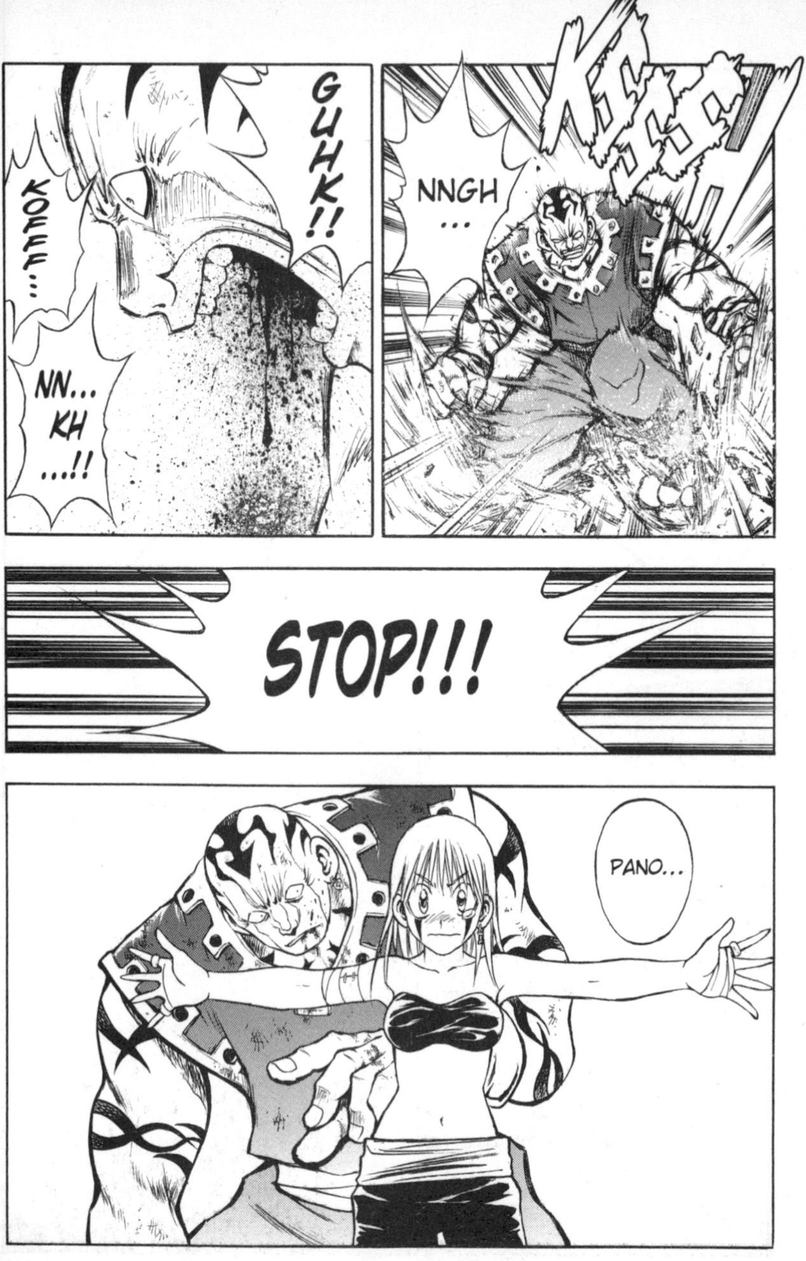
NNGH ...
GUHK!!
KOFFF...
NN... KH ...!!
STOP!!!
PANO...

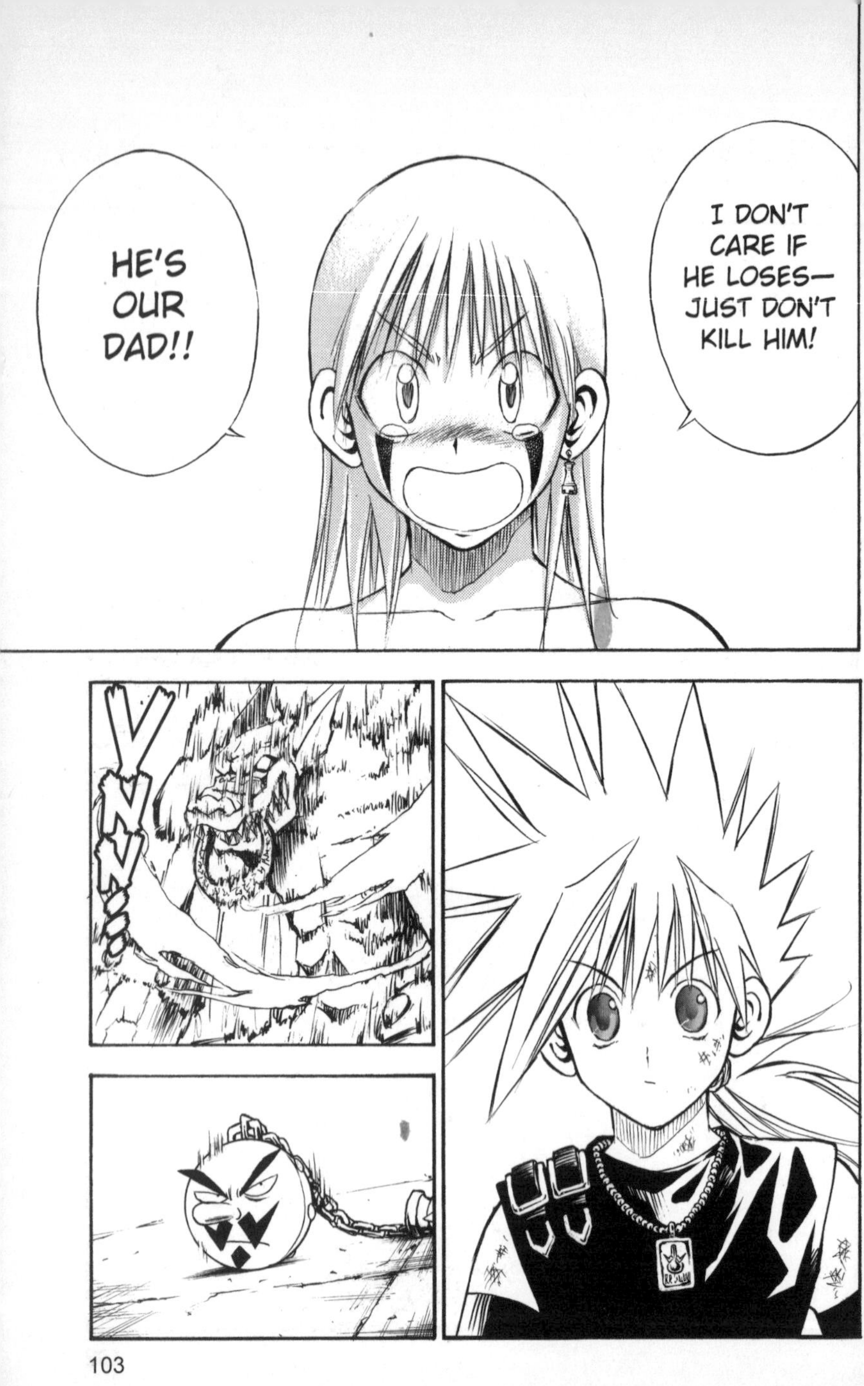
I DON'T CARE IF HE LOSES—JUST DON'T KILL HIM!
HE'S OUR DAD!!
VNNOOO

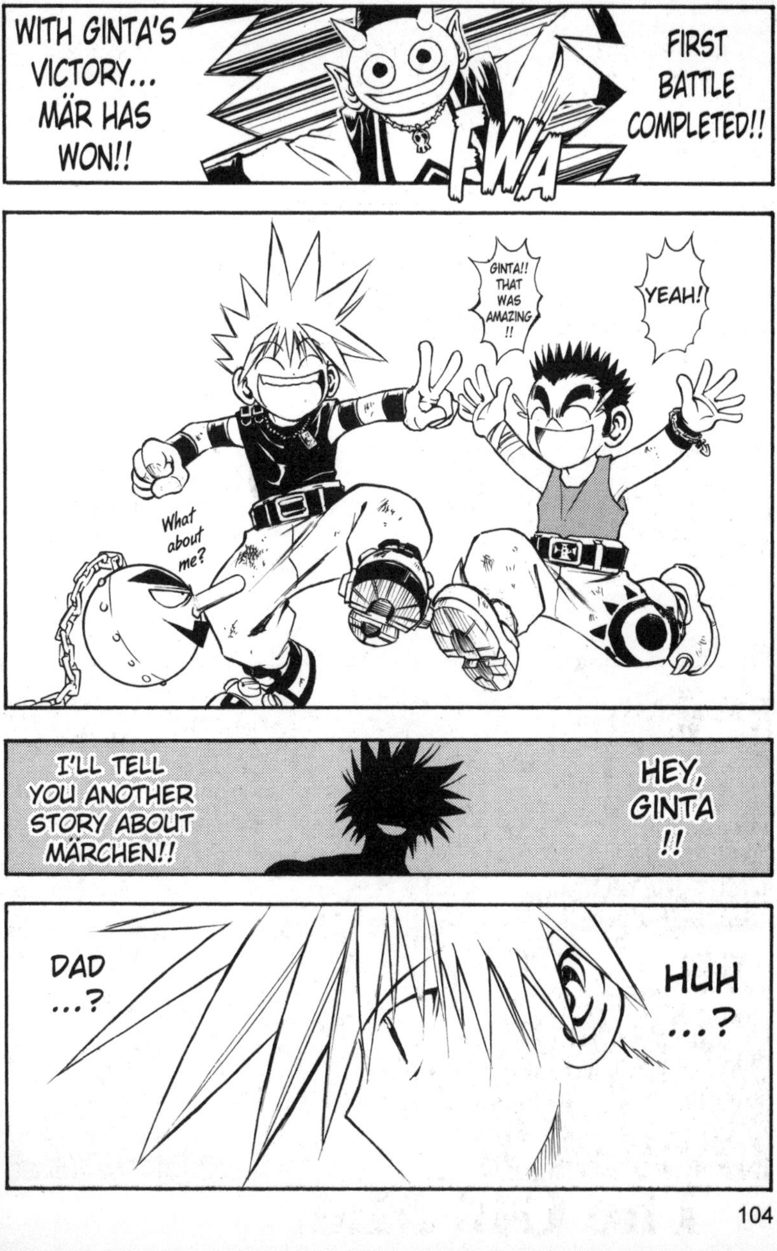
FIRST BATTLE COMPLETED!!
FWA
WITH GINTA'S VICTORY... MÄR HAS WON!!
YEAH!
GINTA!! THAT WAS AMAZING!!
What about me?
HEY, GINTA!!
I'LL TELL YOU ANOTHER STORY ABOUT MÄRCHEN!!
HUH ...?
DAD ...?

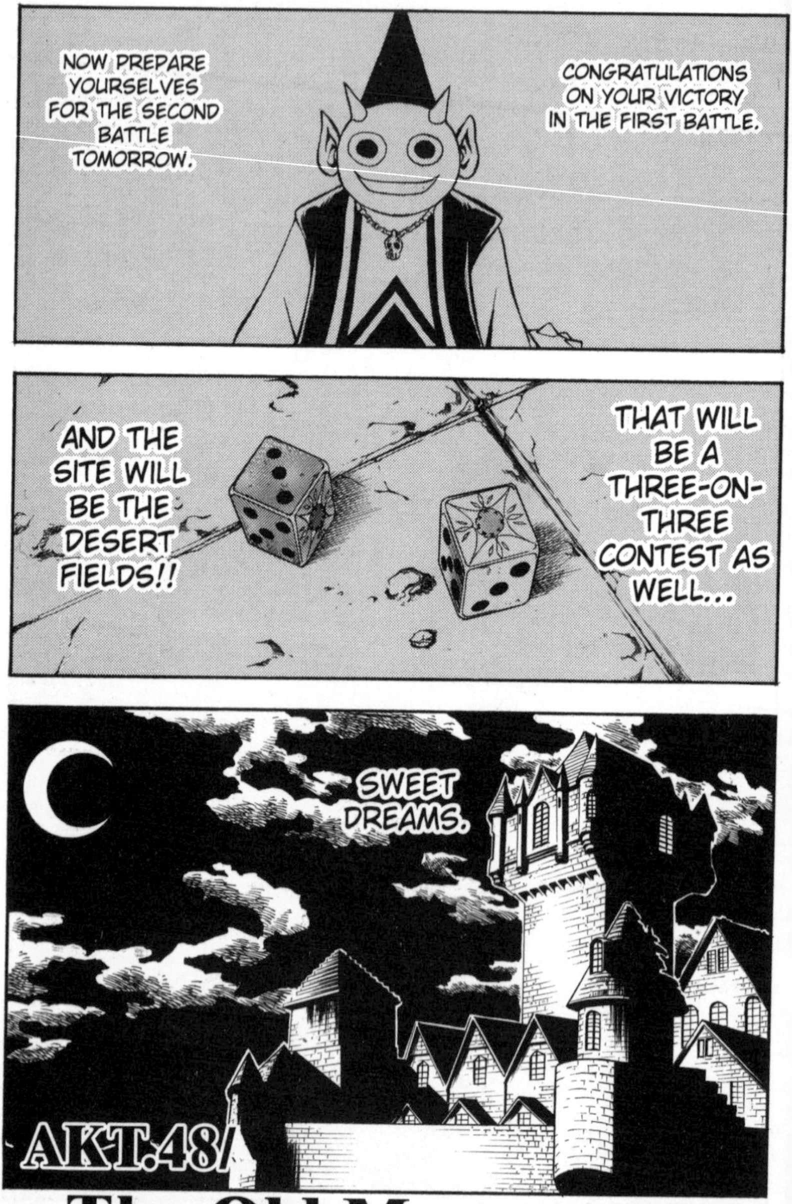
CONGRATULATIONS ON YOUR VICTORY IN THE FIRST BATTLE.
NOW PREPARE YOURSELVES FOR THE SECOND BATTLE TOMORROW.
THAT WILL BE A THREE-ON-THREE CONTEST AS WELL...
AND THE SITE WILL BE THE DESERT FIELDS!!
SWEET DREAMS.
AKT.48/

The Old Man

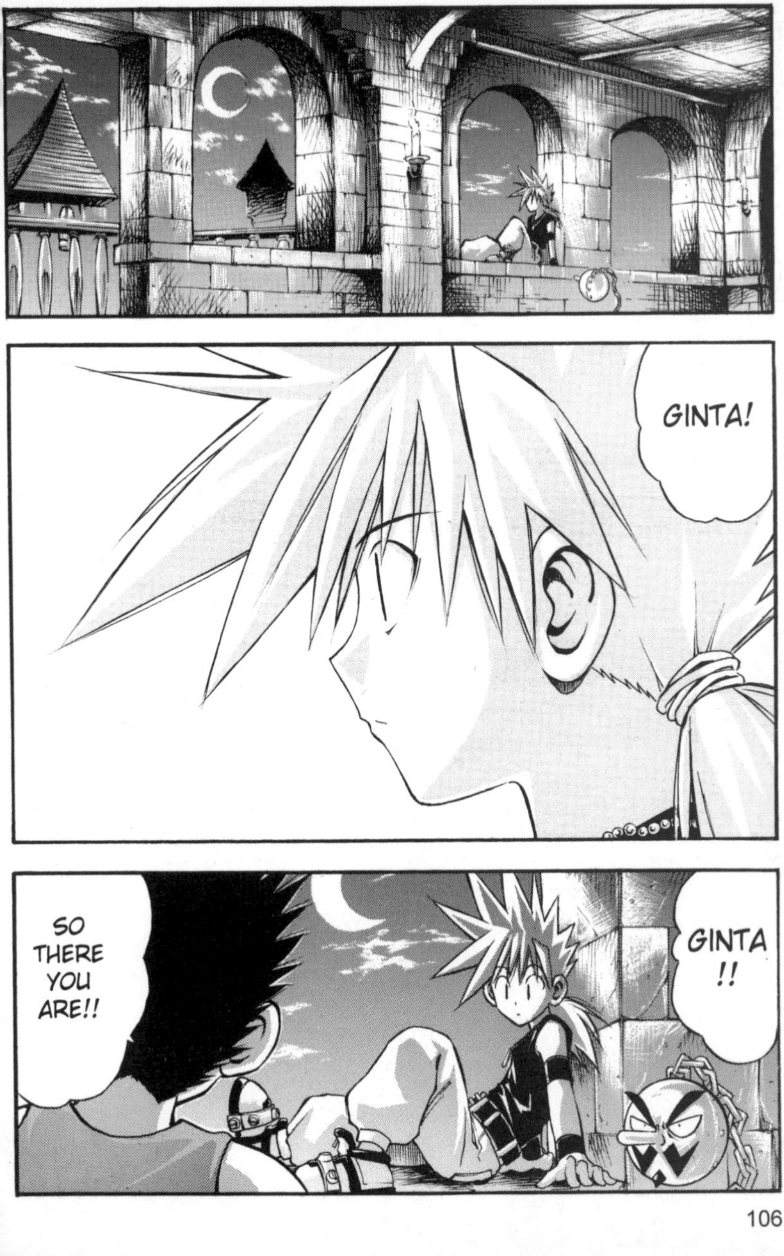
GINTA!
GINTA!!
SO THERE YOU ARE!!

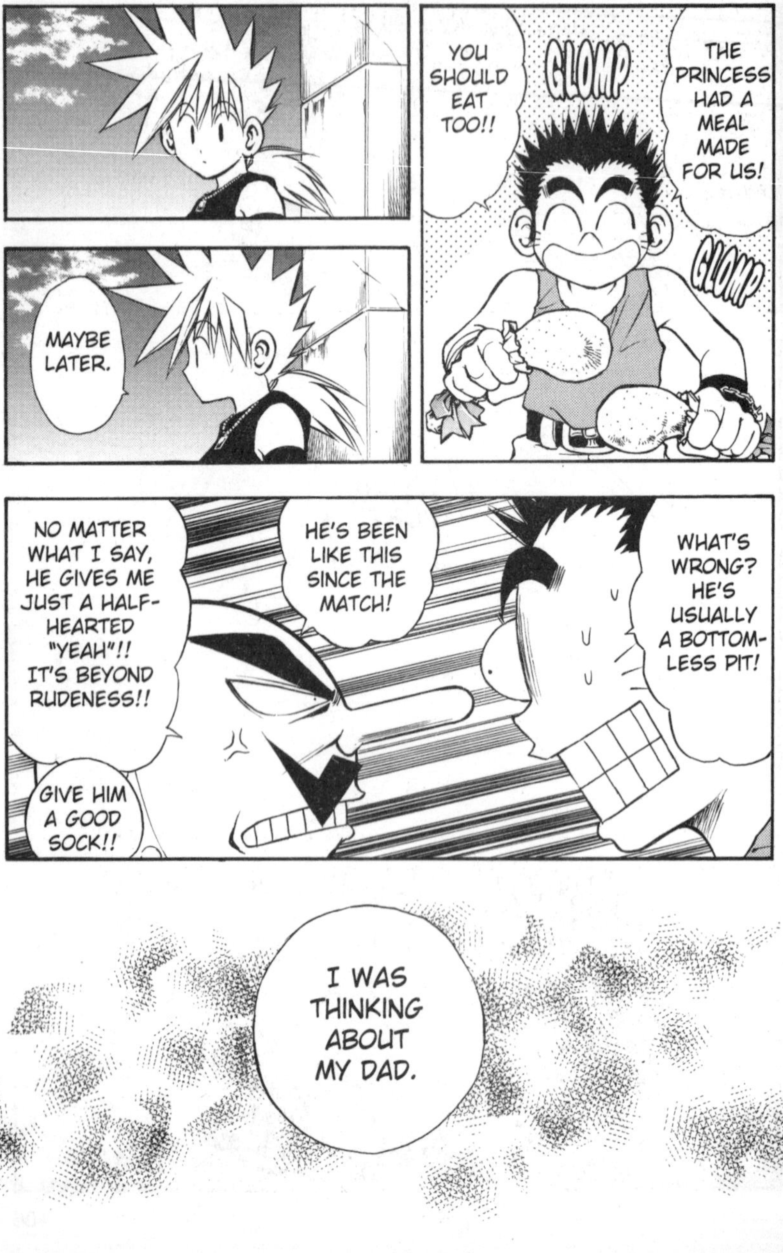
THE PRINCESS HAD A MEAL MADE FOR US!
GLOMP
YOU SHOULD EAT TOO!!
GLOMP
MAYBE LATER.
WHAT'S WRONG? HE'S USUALLY A BOTTOM-LESS PIT!
HE'S BEEN LIKE THIS SINCE THE MATCH!
NO MATTER WHAT I SAY, HE GIVES ME JUST A HALF-HEARTED "YEAH"!! IT'S BEYOND RUDENESS!!
GIVE HIM A GOOD SOCK!!
I WAS THINKING ABOUT MY DAD.

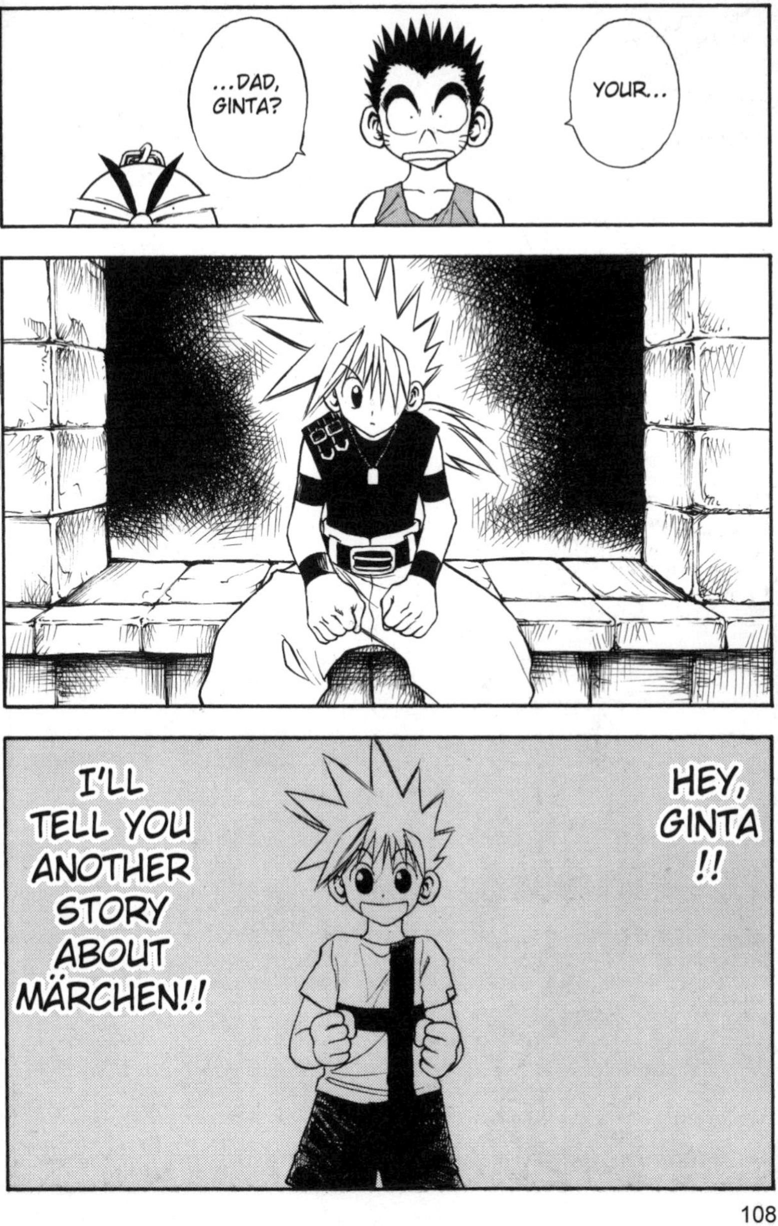
YOUR...
...DAD, GINTA?
HEY, GINTA!!
I'LL TELL YOU ANOTHER STORY ABOUT MÄRCHEN!!

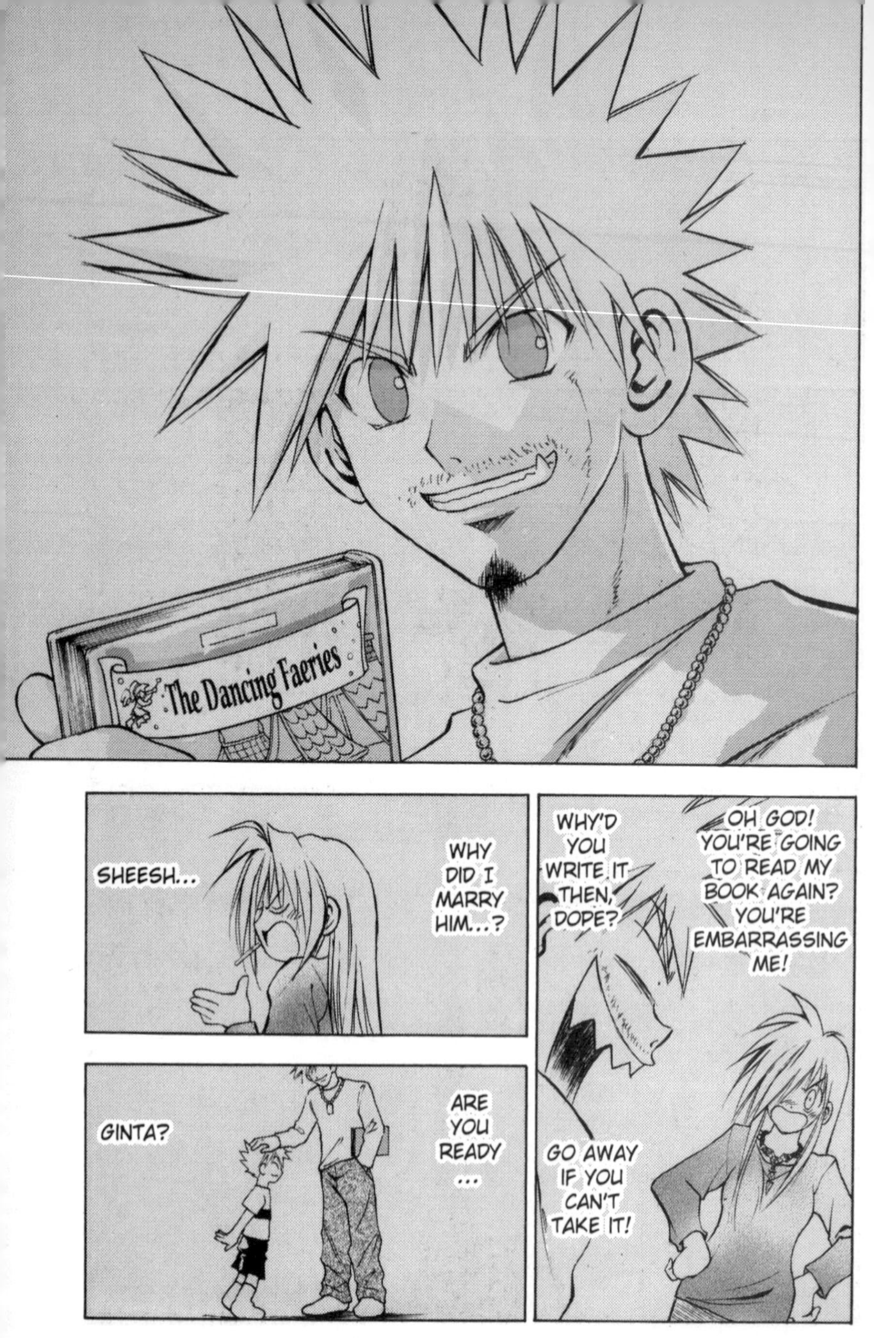
The Dancing Faeries
OH GOD! YOU'RE GOING TO READ MY BOOK AGAIN? YOU'RE EMBARRASSING ME!
WHY'D YOU WRITE IT THEN, DOPE?
GO AWAY IF YOU CAN'T TAKE IT!
WHY DID I MARRY HIM...?
SHEESH...
ARE YOU READY ...
GINTA?

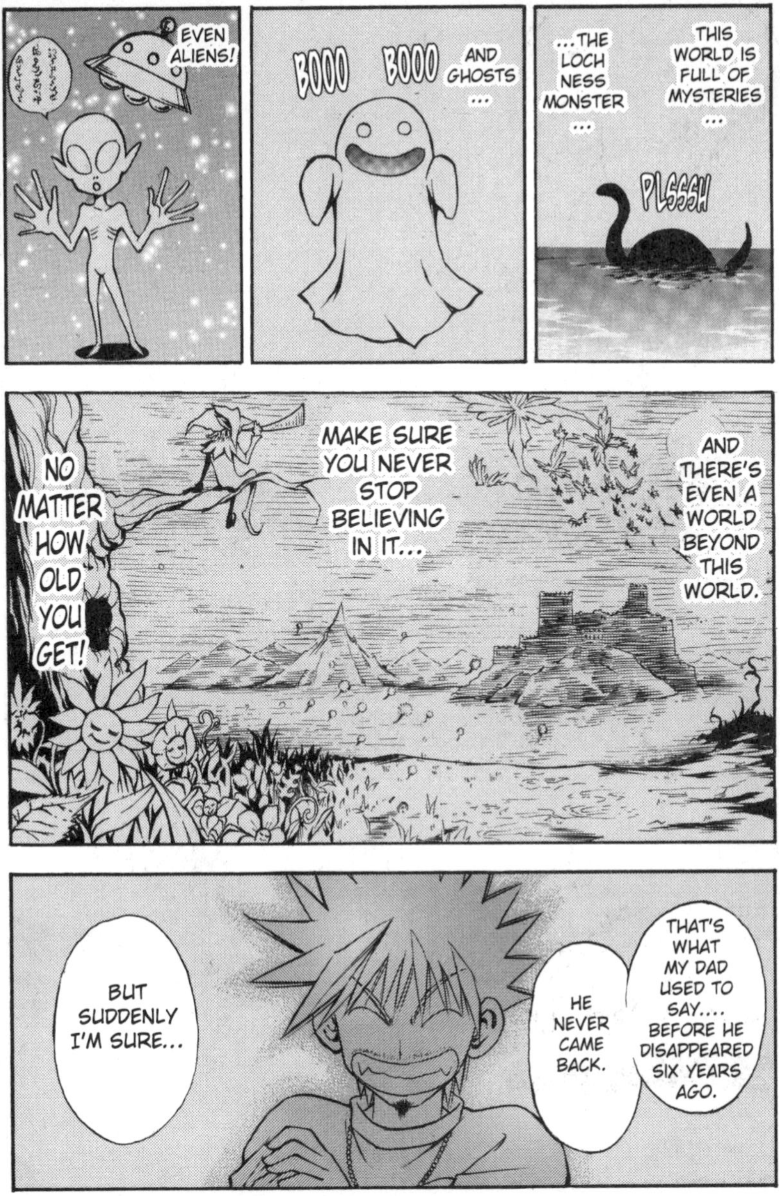
THIS WORLD IS FULL OF MYSTERIES...
...THE LOCH NESS MONSTER...
PLSSSH
BOOO
BOOO
AND GHOSTS...
EVEN ALIENS!
AND THERE'S EVEN A WORLD BEYOND THIS WORLD.
MAKE SURE YOU NEVER STOP BELIEVING IN IT...
NO MATTER HOW OLD YOU GET!
THAT'S WHAT MY DAD USED TO SAY.... BEFORE HE DISAPPEARED SIX YEARS AGO.
HE NEVER CAME BACK.
BUT SUDDENLY I'M SURE...

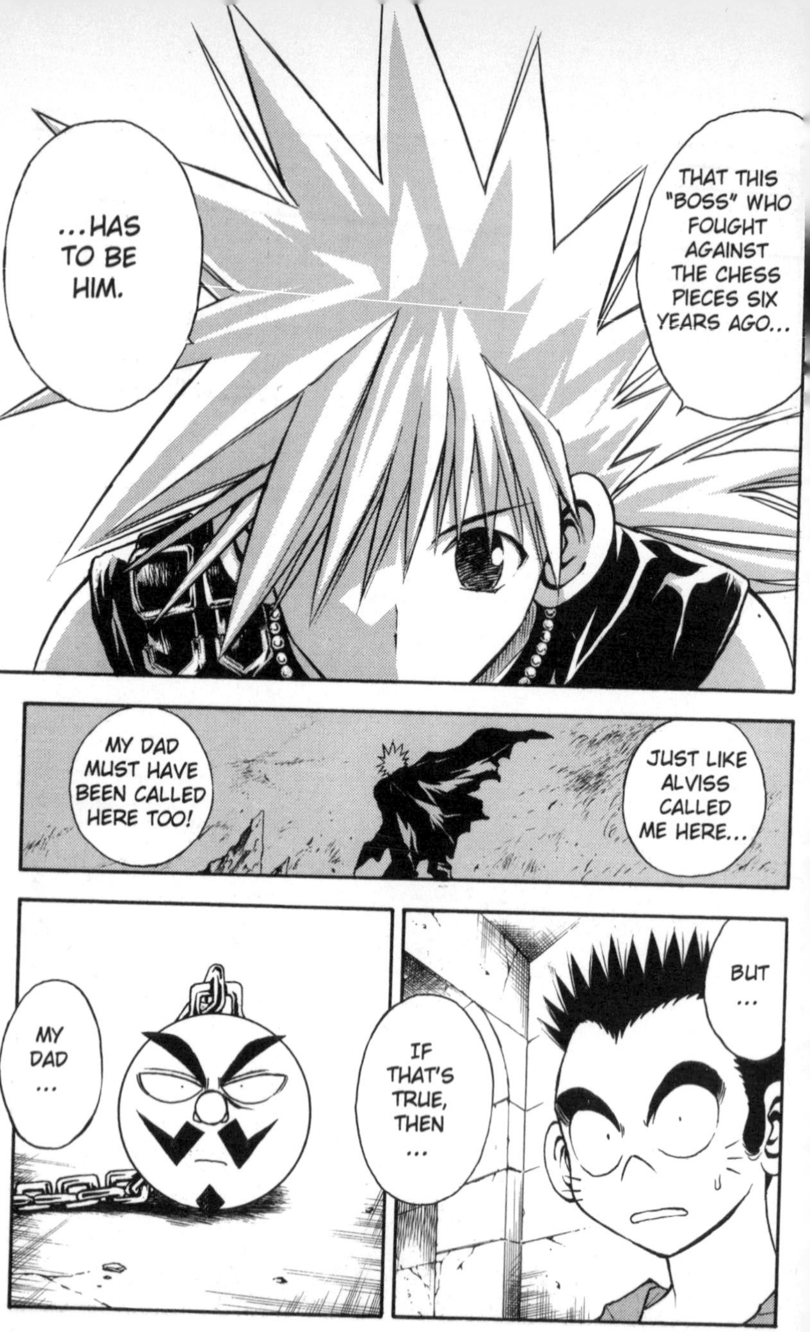
THAT THIS "BOSS" WHO FOUGHT AGAINST THE CHESS PIECES SIX YEARS AGO...
...HAS TO BE HIM.
JUST LIKE ALVISS CALLED ME HERE...
MY DAD MUST HAVE BEEN CALLED HERE TOO!
BUT ...
IF THAT'S TRUE, THEN ...
MY DAD ...

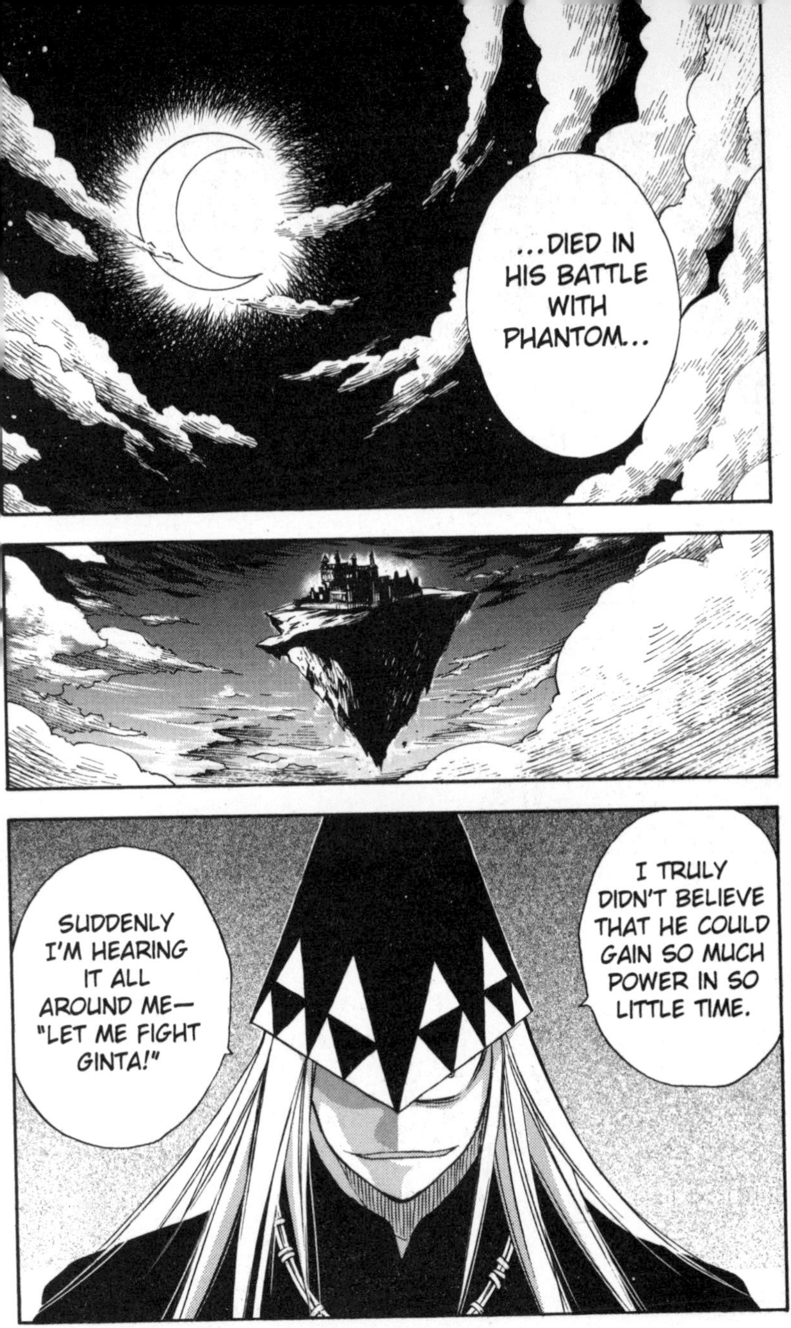
...DIED IN HIS BATTLE WITH PHANTOM...
I TRULY DIDN'T BELIEVE THAT HE COULD GAIN SO MUCH POWER IN SO LITTLE TIME.
SUDDENLY I'M HEARING IT ALL AROUND ME—"LET ME FIGHT GINTA!"

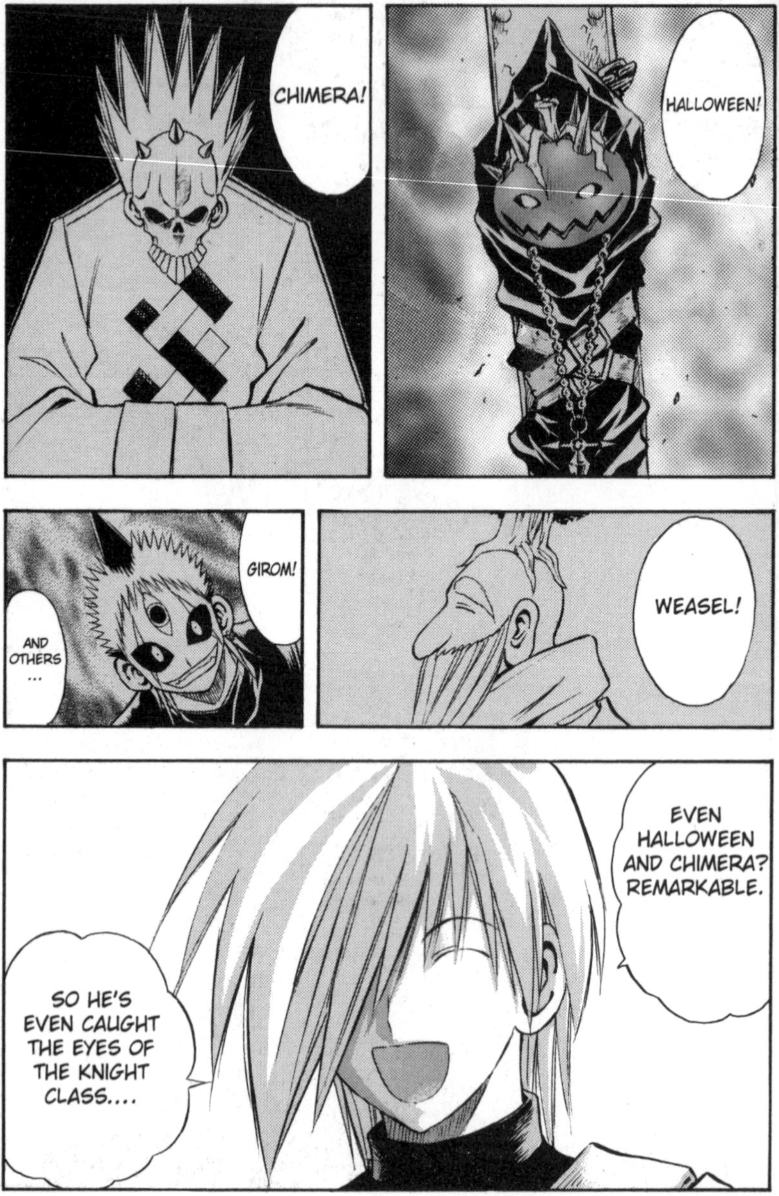
HALLOWEEN!
CHIMERA!
WEASEL!
GIROM!
AND OTHERS ...
EVEN HALLOWEEN AND CHIMERA? REMARKABLE.
SO HE'S EVEN CAUGHT THE EYES OF THE KNIGHT CLASS....

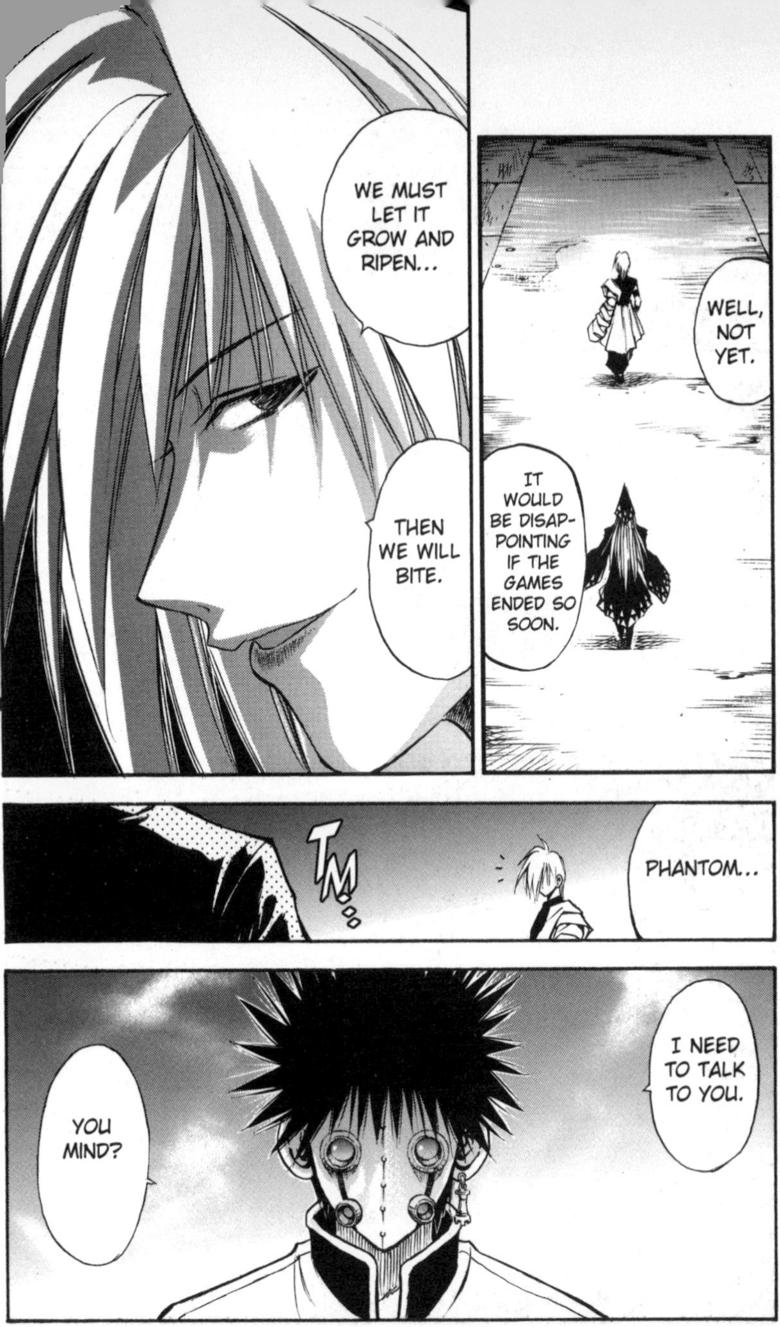
WELL, NOT YET.
IT WOULD BE DISAP-POINTING IF THE GAMES ENDED SO SOON.
WE MUST LET IT GROW AND RIPEN...
THEN WE WILL BITE.
PHANTOM...
TM...
I NEED TO TALK TO YOU.
YOU MIND?

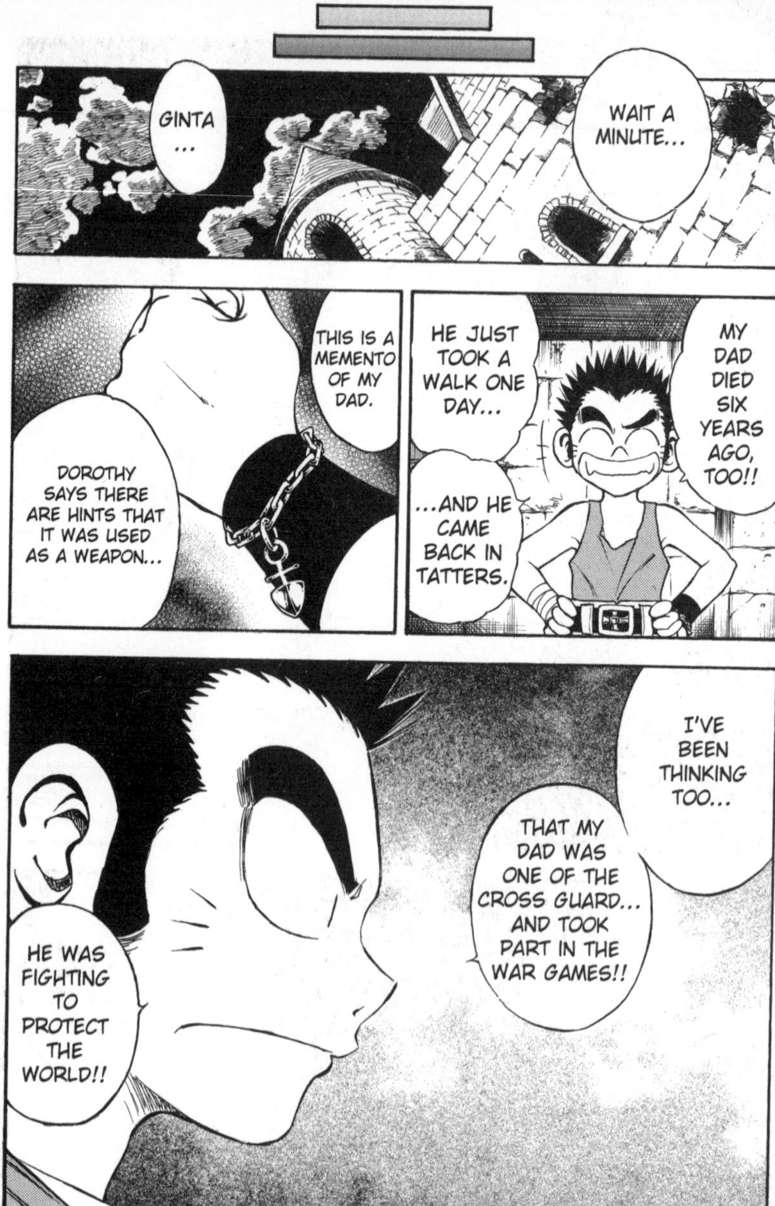
WAIT A MINUTE...
GINTA ...
MY DAD DIED SIX YEARS AGO, TOO!!
HE JUST TOOK A WALK ONE DAY...
...AND HE CAME BACK IN TATTERS.
THIS IS A MEMENTO OF MY DAD.
DOROTHY SAYS THERE ARE HINTS THAT IT WAS USED AS A WEAPON...
I'VE BEEN THINKING TOO...
THAT MY DAD WAS ONE OF THE CROSS GUARD... AND TOOK PART IN THE WAR GAMES!!
HE WAS FIGHTING TO PROTECT THE WORLD!!

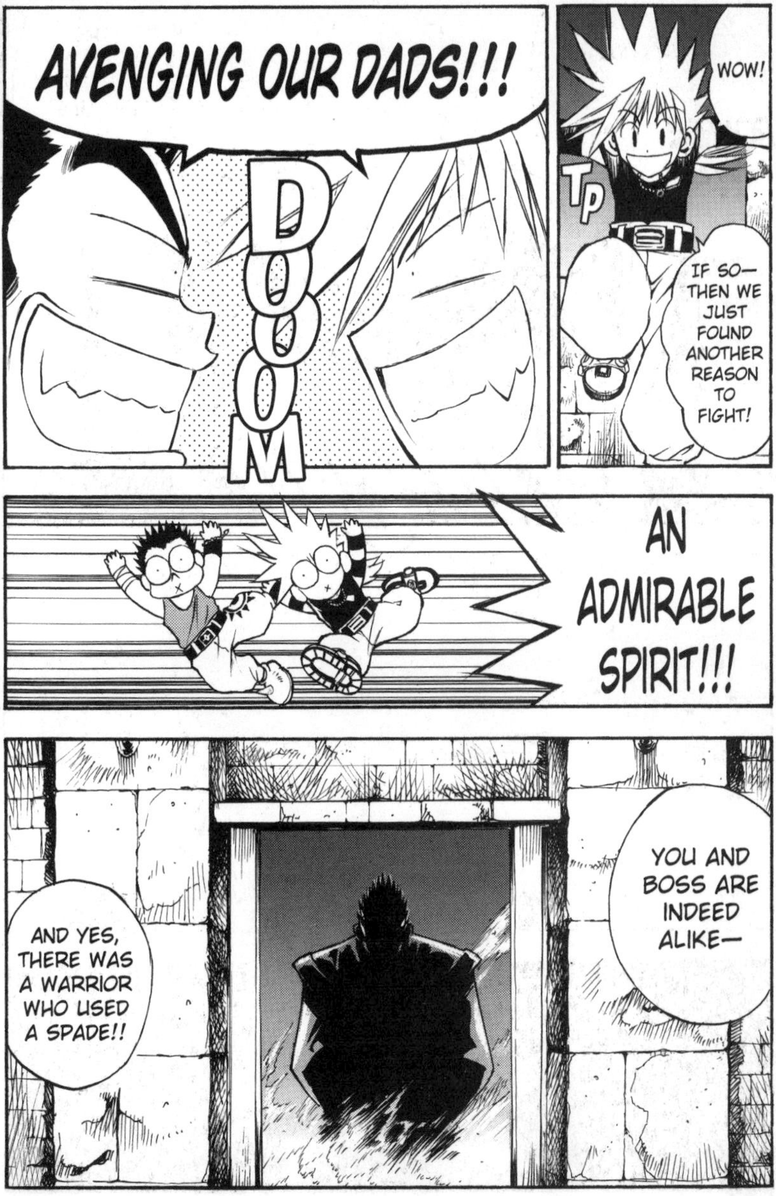
WOW!
TP
IF SO— THEN WE JUST FOUND ANOTHER REASON TO FIGHT!
AVENGING OUR DADS!!!
DOOOOM
AN ADMIRABLE SPIRIT!!!
YOU AND BOSS ARE INDEED ALIKE—
AND YES, THERE WAS A WARRIOR WHO USED A SPADE!!

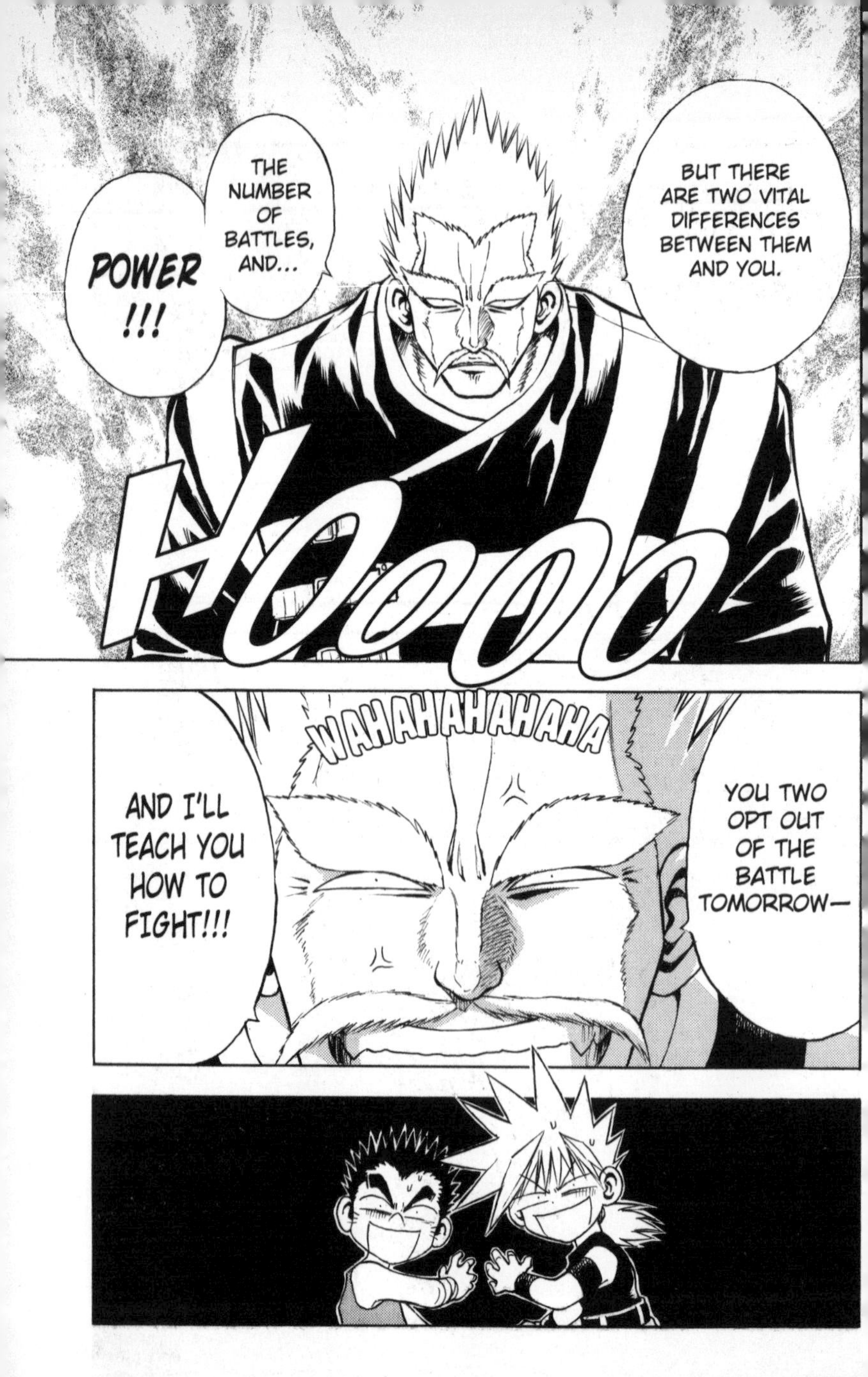
BUT THERE ARE TWO VITAL DIFFERENCES BETWEEN THEM AND YOU.
THE NUMBER OF BATTLES, AND...
POWER!!!
HOOOOO
YOU TWO OPT OUT OF THE BATTLE TOMORROW—
WAHAHAHAHAHA
AND I'LL TEACH YOU HOW TO FIGHT!!!

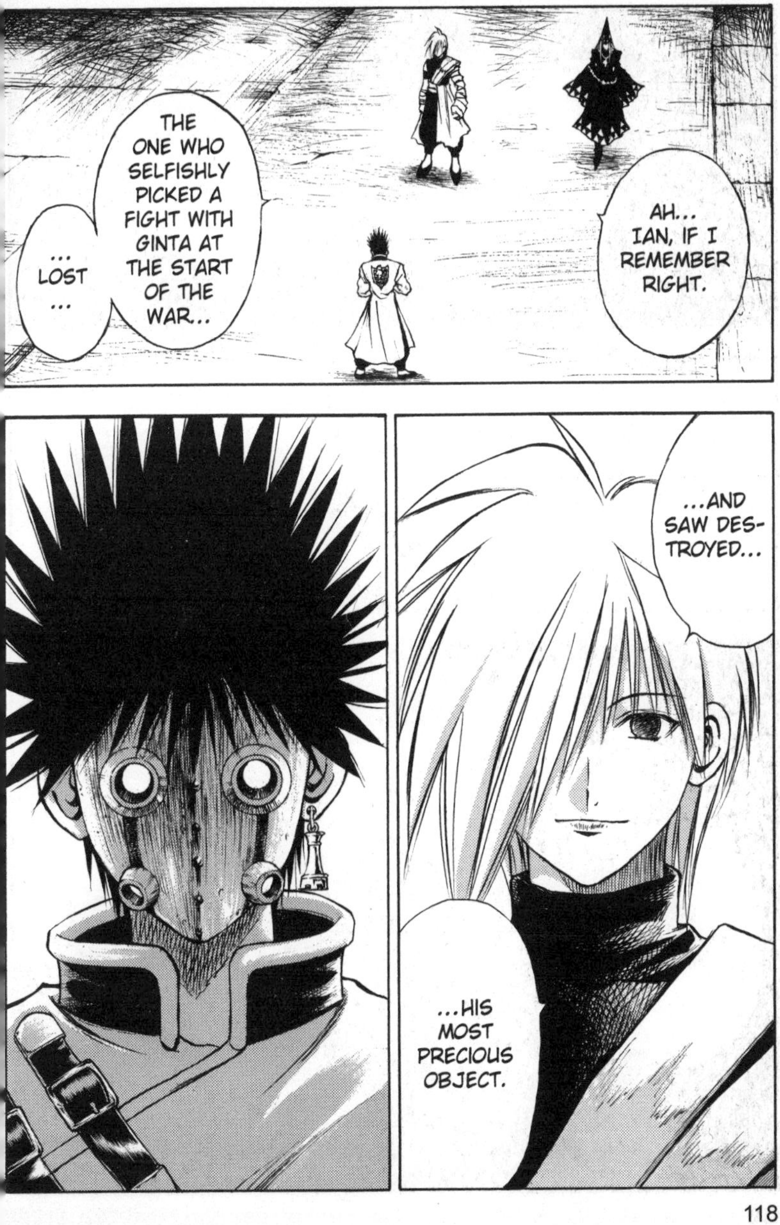
AH... IAN, IF I REMEMBER RIGHT.
THE ONE WHO SELFISHLY PICKED A FIGHT WITH GINTA AT THE START OF THE WAR...
...LOST...
...AND SAW DES-TROYED...
...HIS MOST PRECIOUS OBJECT.

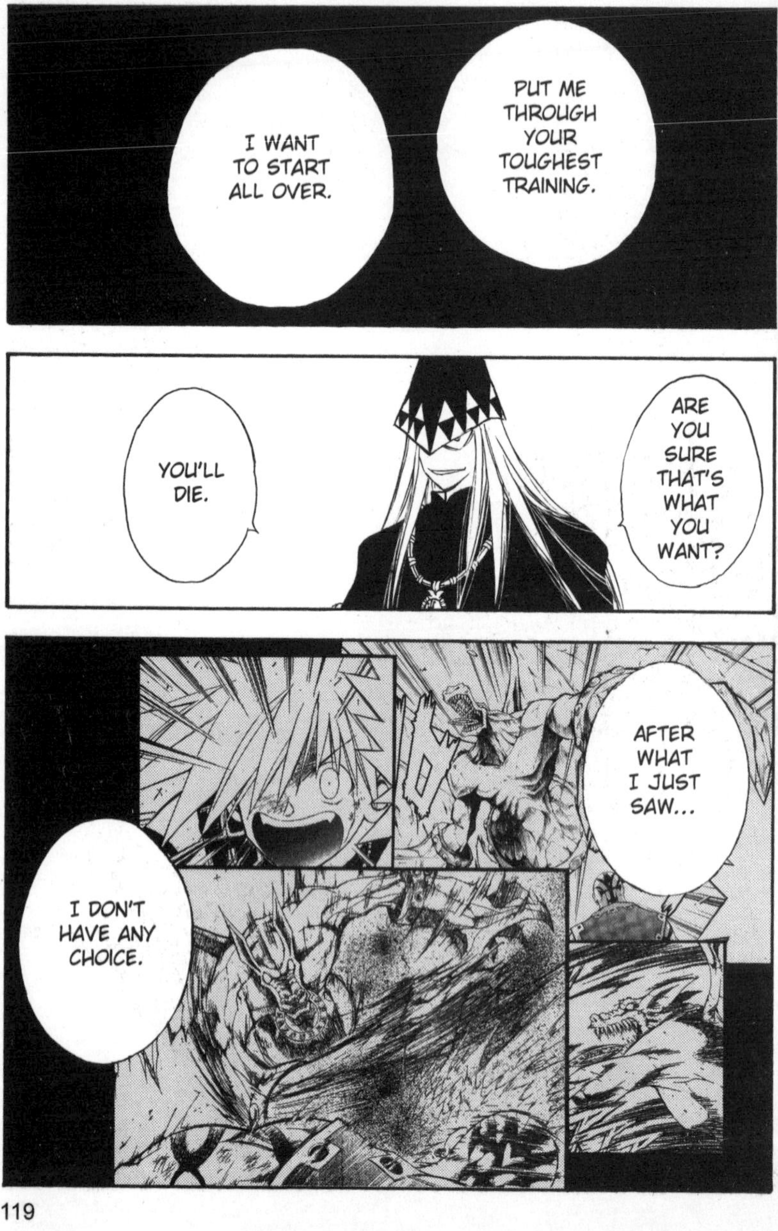
PUT ME THROUGH YOUR TOUGHEST TRAINING.
I WANT TO START ALL OVER.
ARE YOU SURE THAT'S WHAT YOU WANT?
YOU'LL DIE.
AFTER WHAT I JUST SAW...
I DON'T HAVE ANY CHOICE.

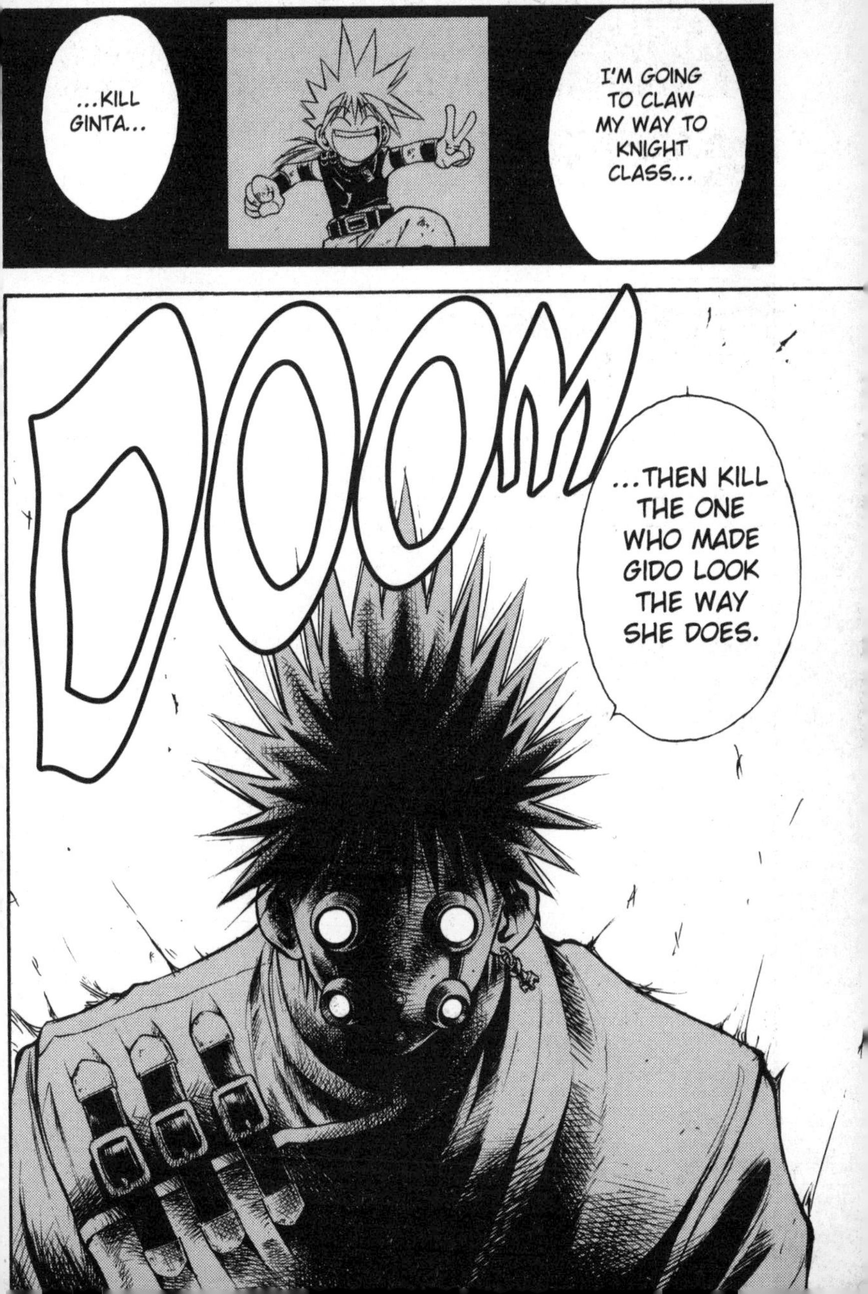
I'M GOING TO CLAW MY WAY TO KNIGHT CLASS...
...KILL GINTA...
...THEN KILL THE ONE WHO MADE GIDO LOOK THE WAY SHE DOES.
DOOM

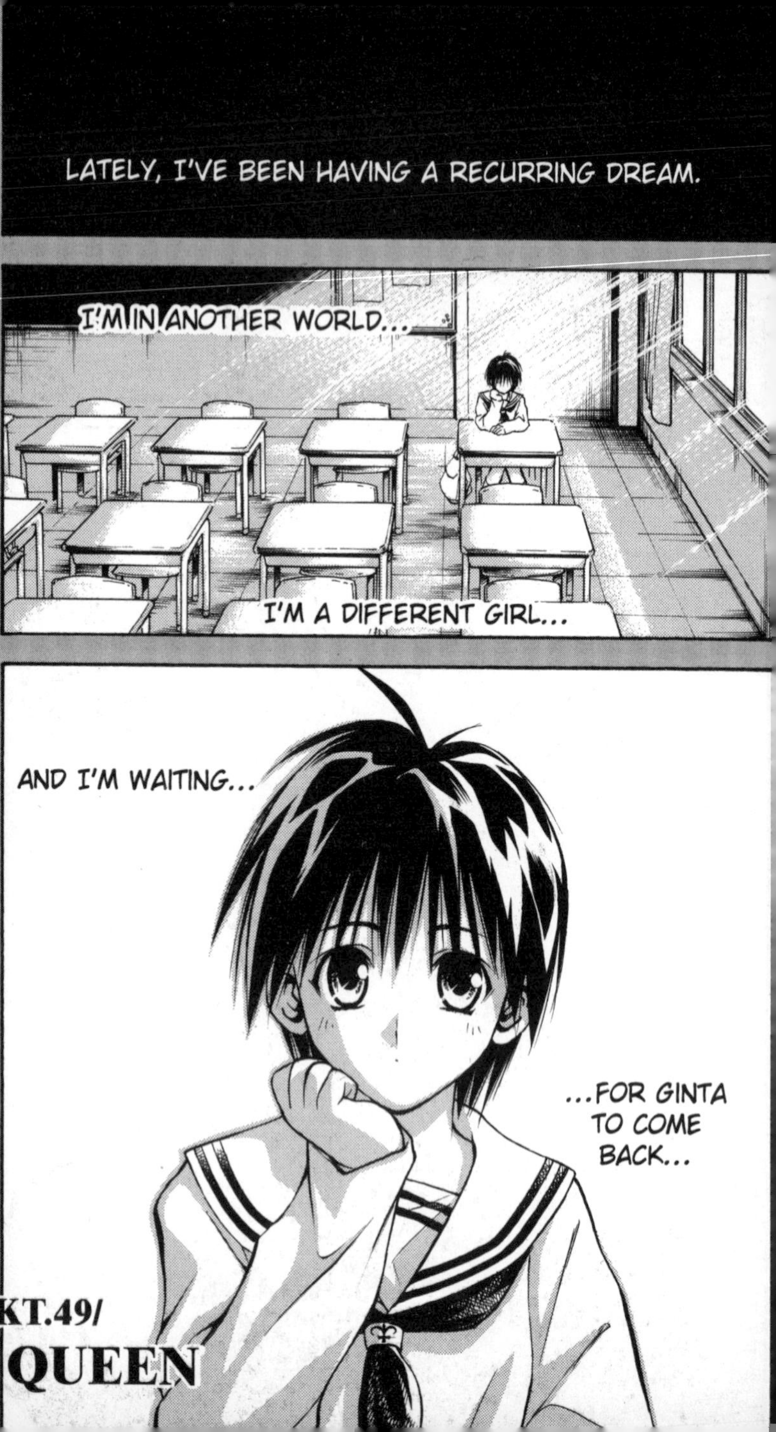

LATELY, I'VE BEEN HAVING A RECURRING DREAM.
I'M IN ANOTHER WORLD...
I'M A DIFFERENT GIRL...
AND I'M WAITING...
...FOR GINTA TO COME BACK...
AKT.49/
QUEEN

AKT.49/ QUEEN

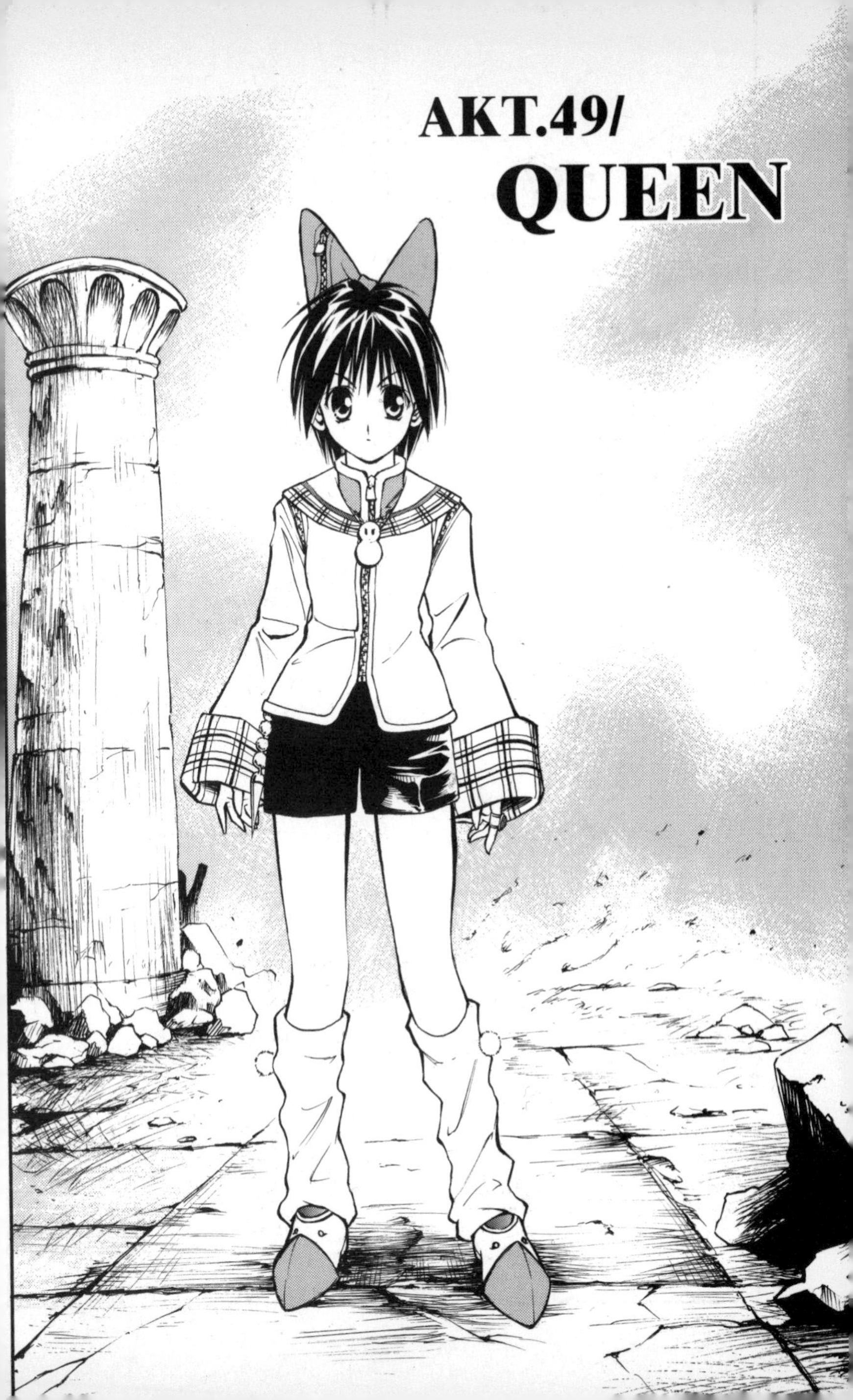

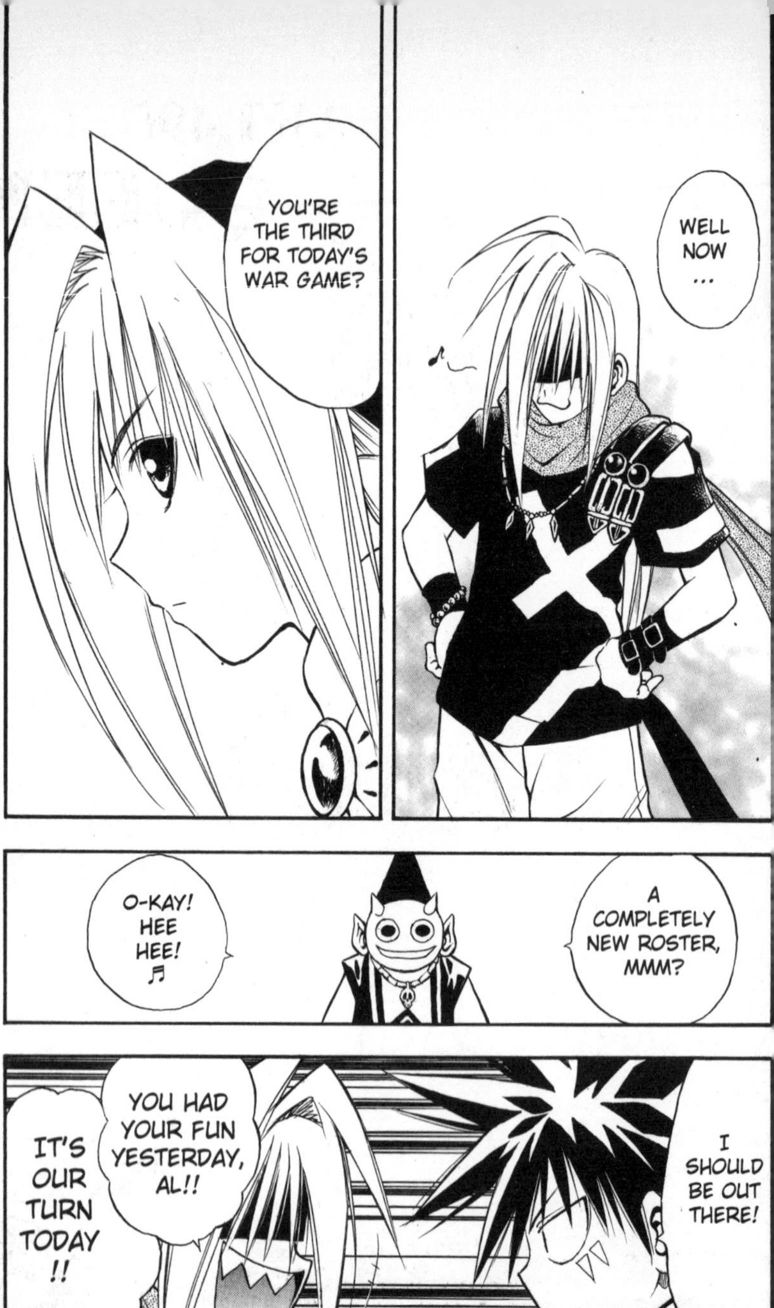
WELL NOW ...
YOU'RE THE THIRD FOR TODAY'S WAR GAME?
A COMPLETELY NEW ROSTER, MMM?
O-KAY! HEE HEE! ♬
I SHOULD BE OUT THERE!
YOU HAD YOUR FUN YESTERDAY, AL!!
IT'S OUR TURN TODAY !!

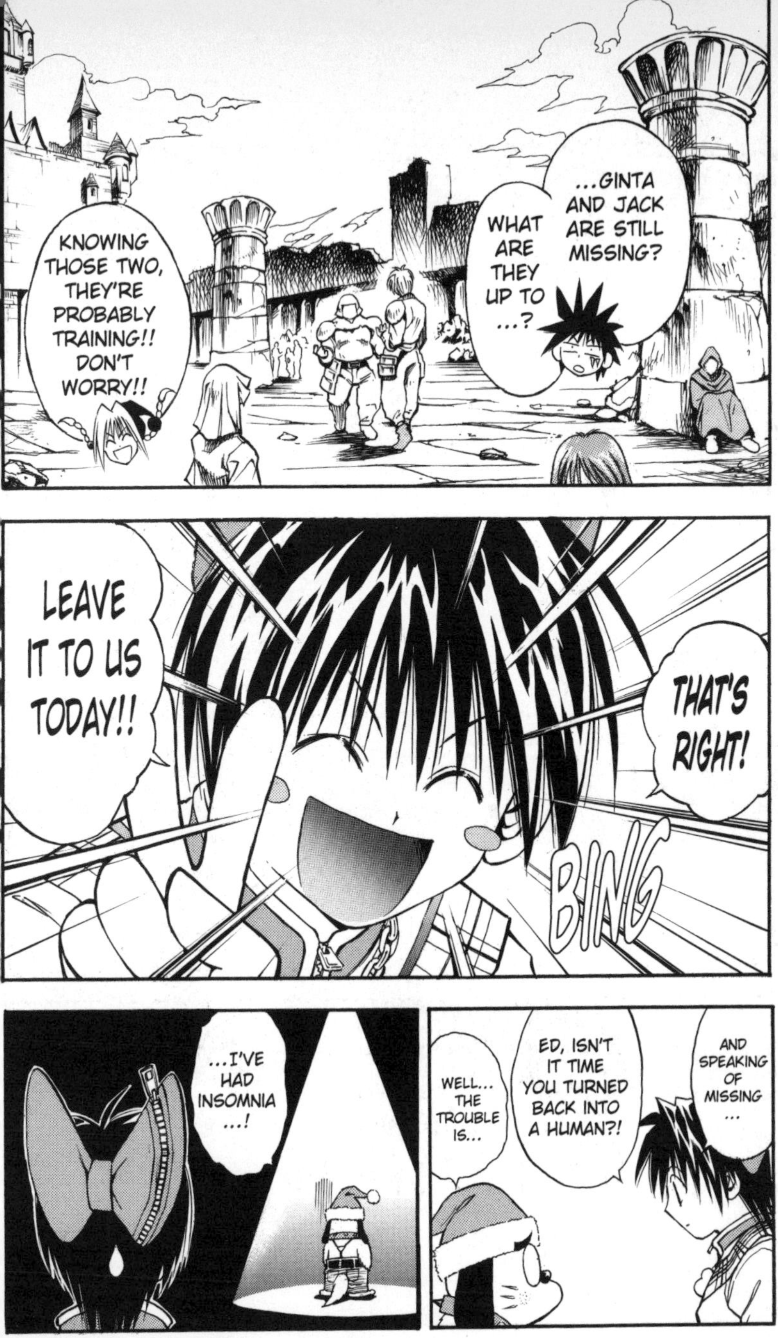
...GINTA AND JACK ARE STILL MISSING?
WHAT ARE THEY UP TO ...?
KNOWING THOSE TWO, THEY'RE PROBABLY TRAINING!! DON'T WORRY!!
THAT'S RIGHT!
LEAVE IT TO US TODAY!!
BING
AND SPEAKING OF MISSING...
ED, ISN'T IT TIME YOU TURNED BACK INTO A HUMAN?!
WELL... THE TROUBLE IS...
...I'VE HAD INSOMNIA...!

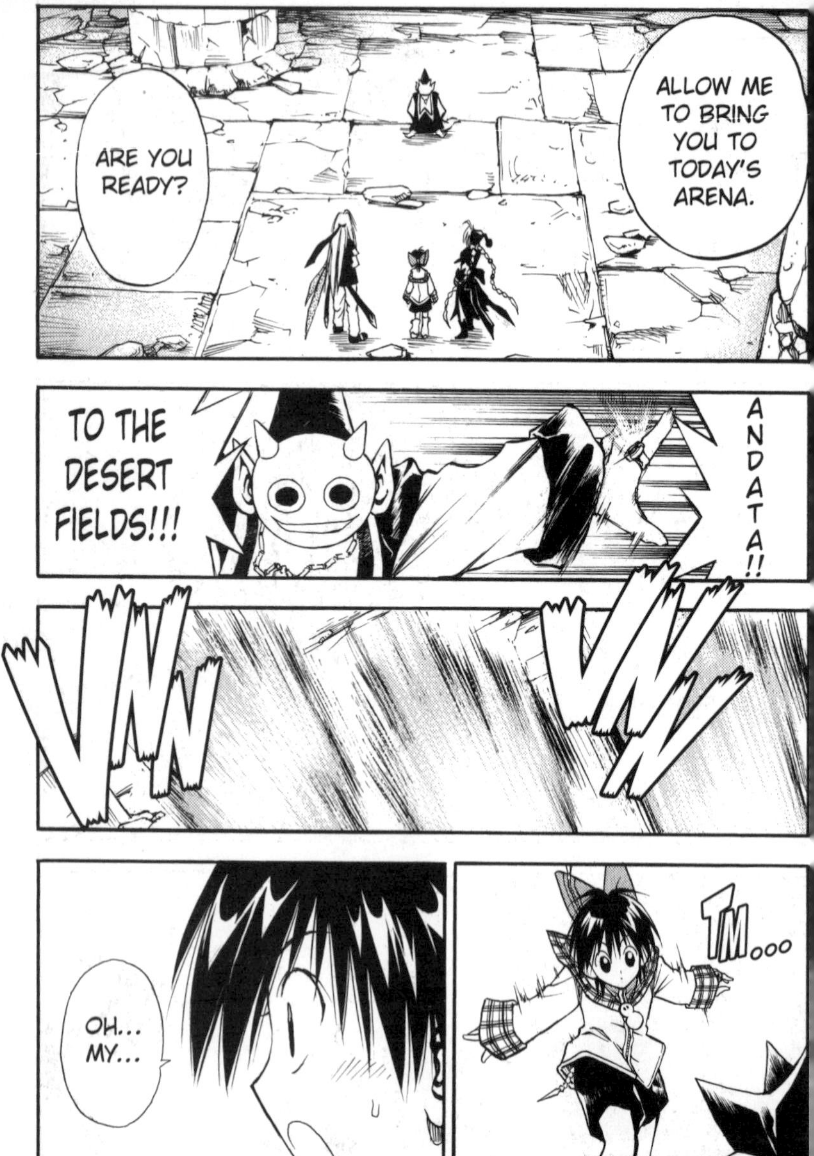

ALLOW ME TO BRING YOU TO TODAY'S ARENA.
ARE YOU READY?
ANDATA!!
TO THE DESERT FIELDS!!!
VNN
VNN
TM...
OH... MY...

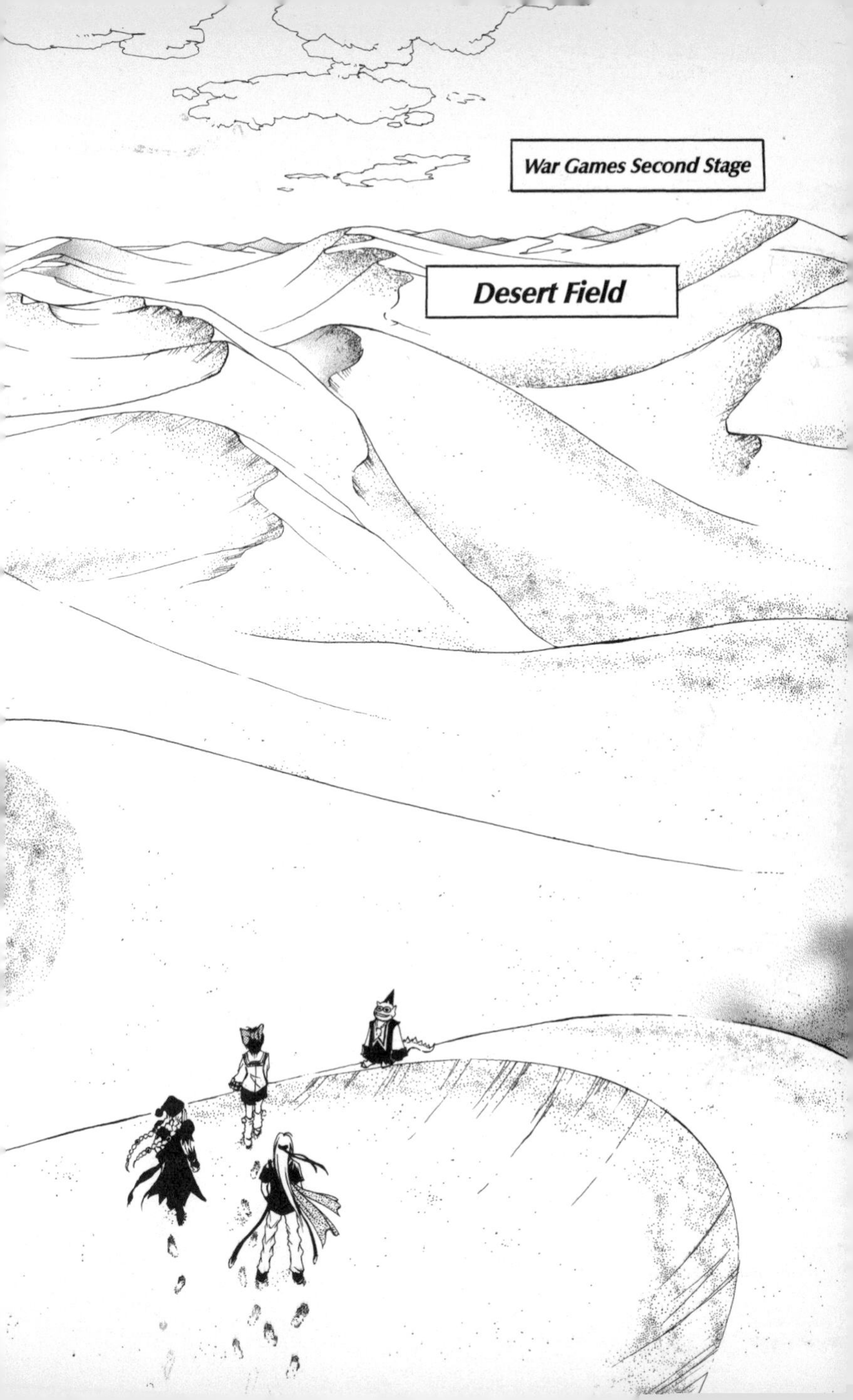
War Games Second Stage
Desert Field

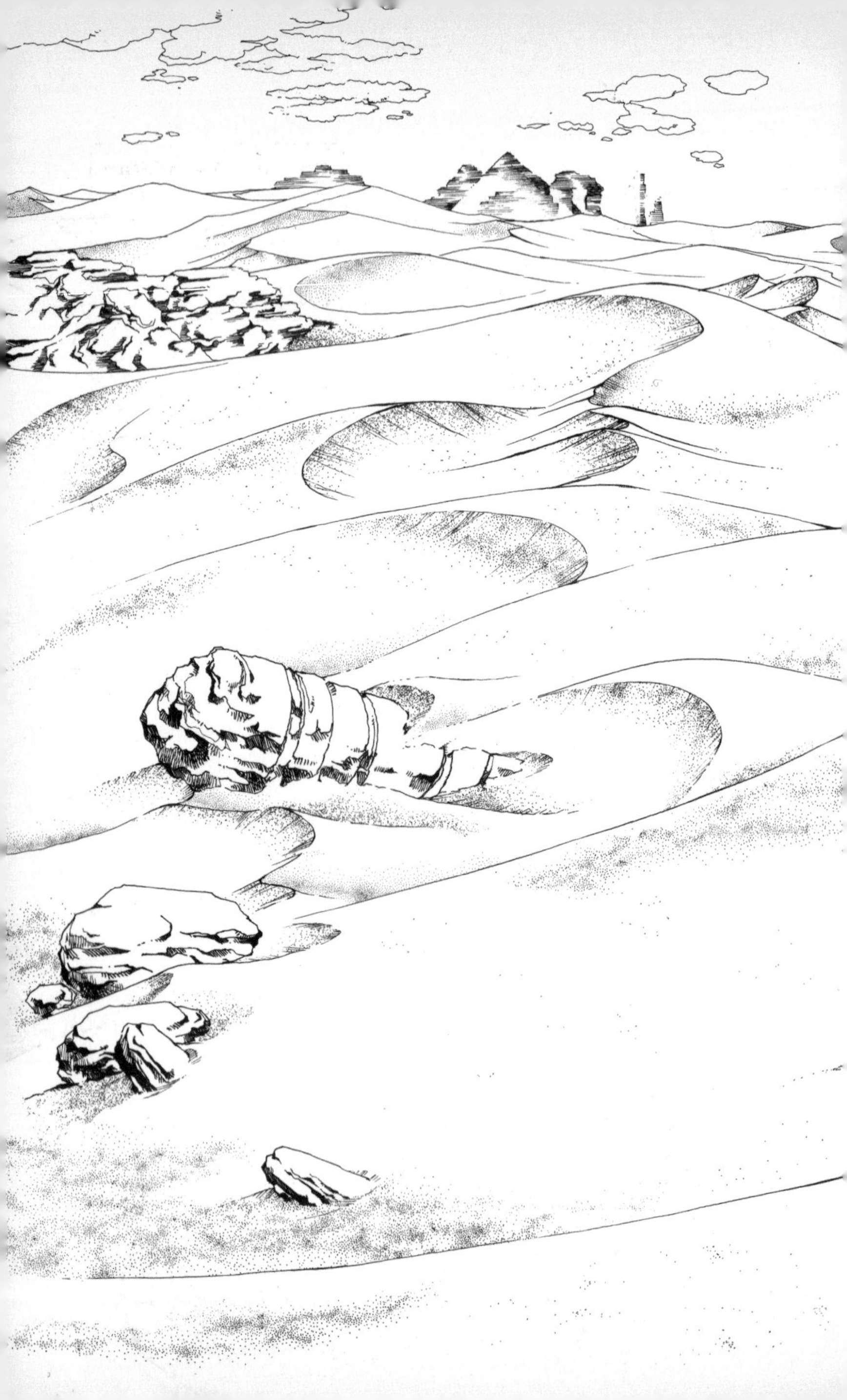

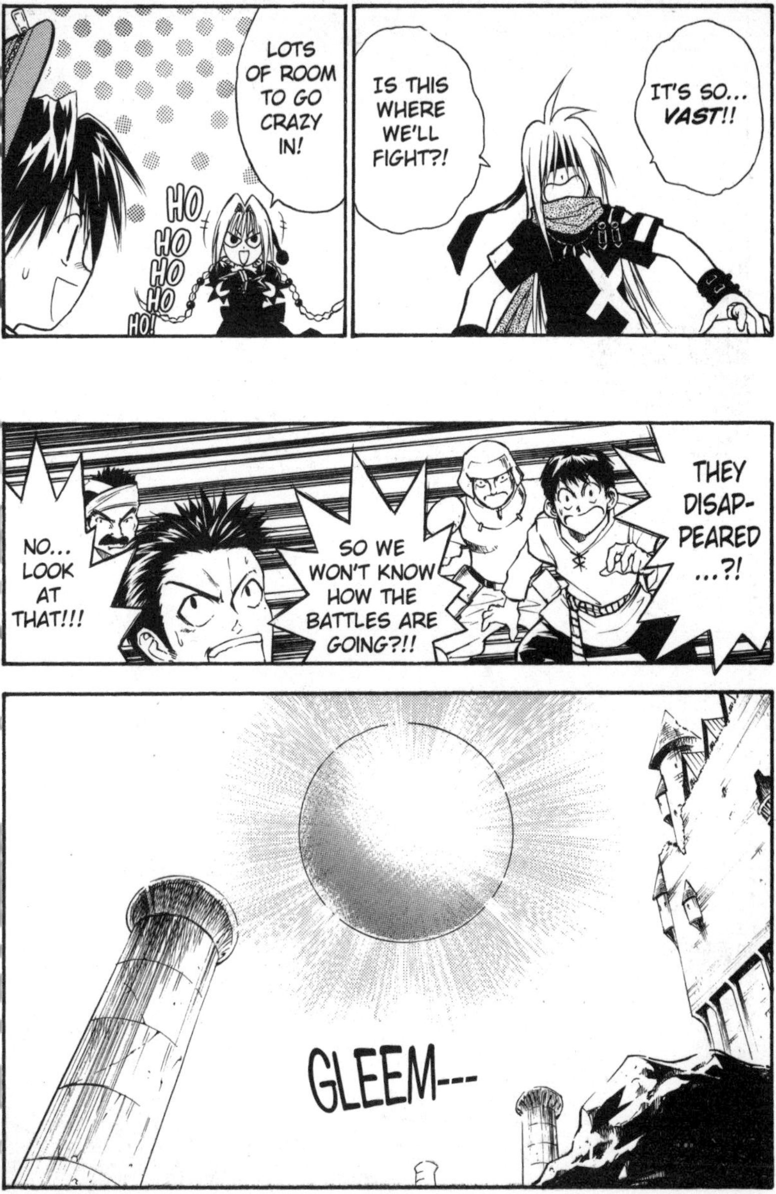
IT'S SO... *VAST*!!
IS THIS WHERE WE'LL FIGHT?!
LOTS OF ROOM TO GO CRAZY IN!
HO HO HO HO HO!
THEY DISAP-PEARED ...?!
SO WE WON'T KNOW HOW THE BATTLES ARE GOING?!!
NO... LOOK AT THAT!!!
GLEEM---

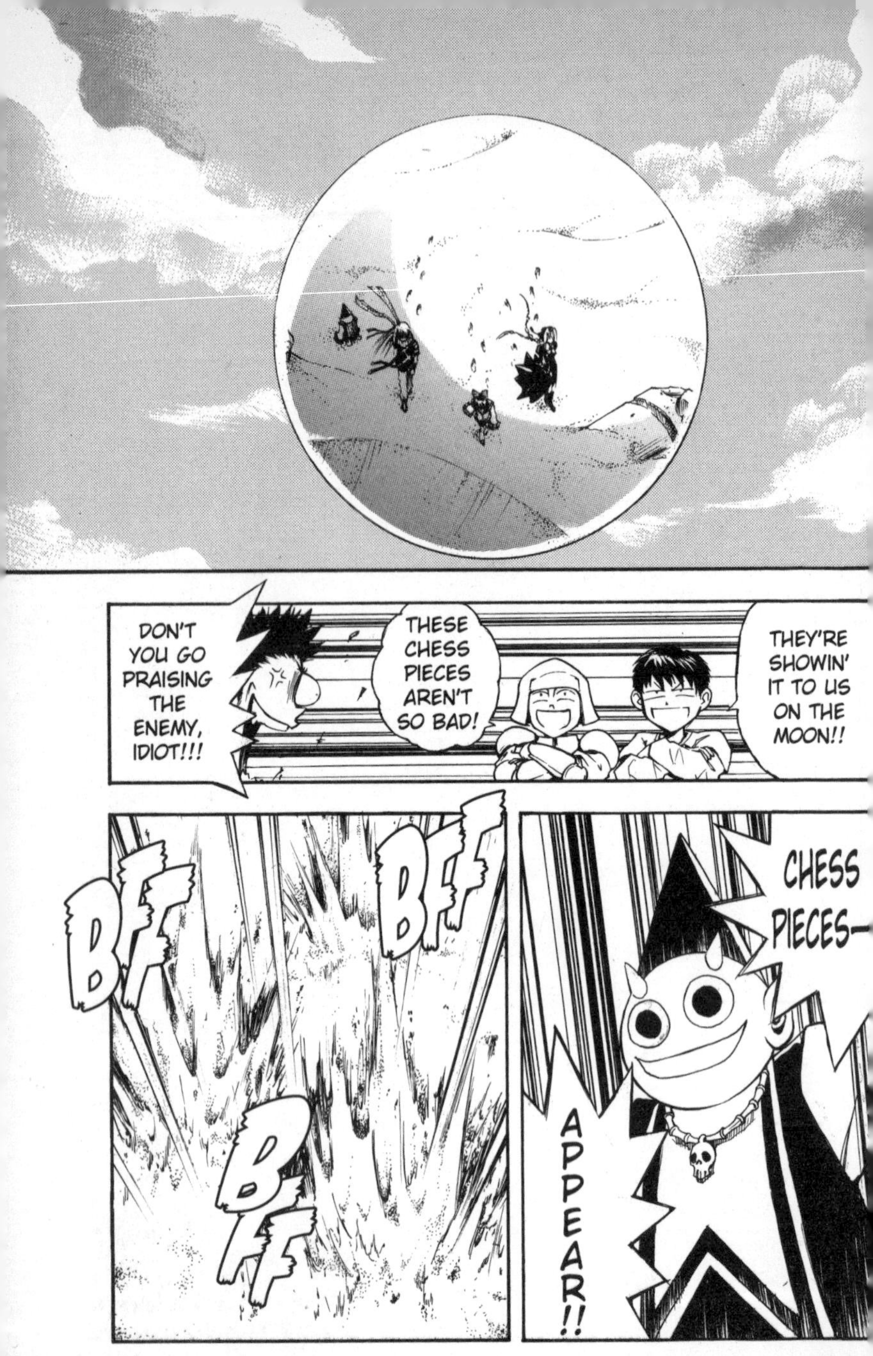
THEY'RE SHOWIN' IT TO US ON THE MOON!!
THESE CHESS PIECES AREN'T SO BAD!
DON'T YOU GO PRAISING THE ENEMY, IDIOT!!!
CHESS PIECES—
APPEAR!!
BFF
BFF
BFF

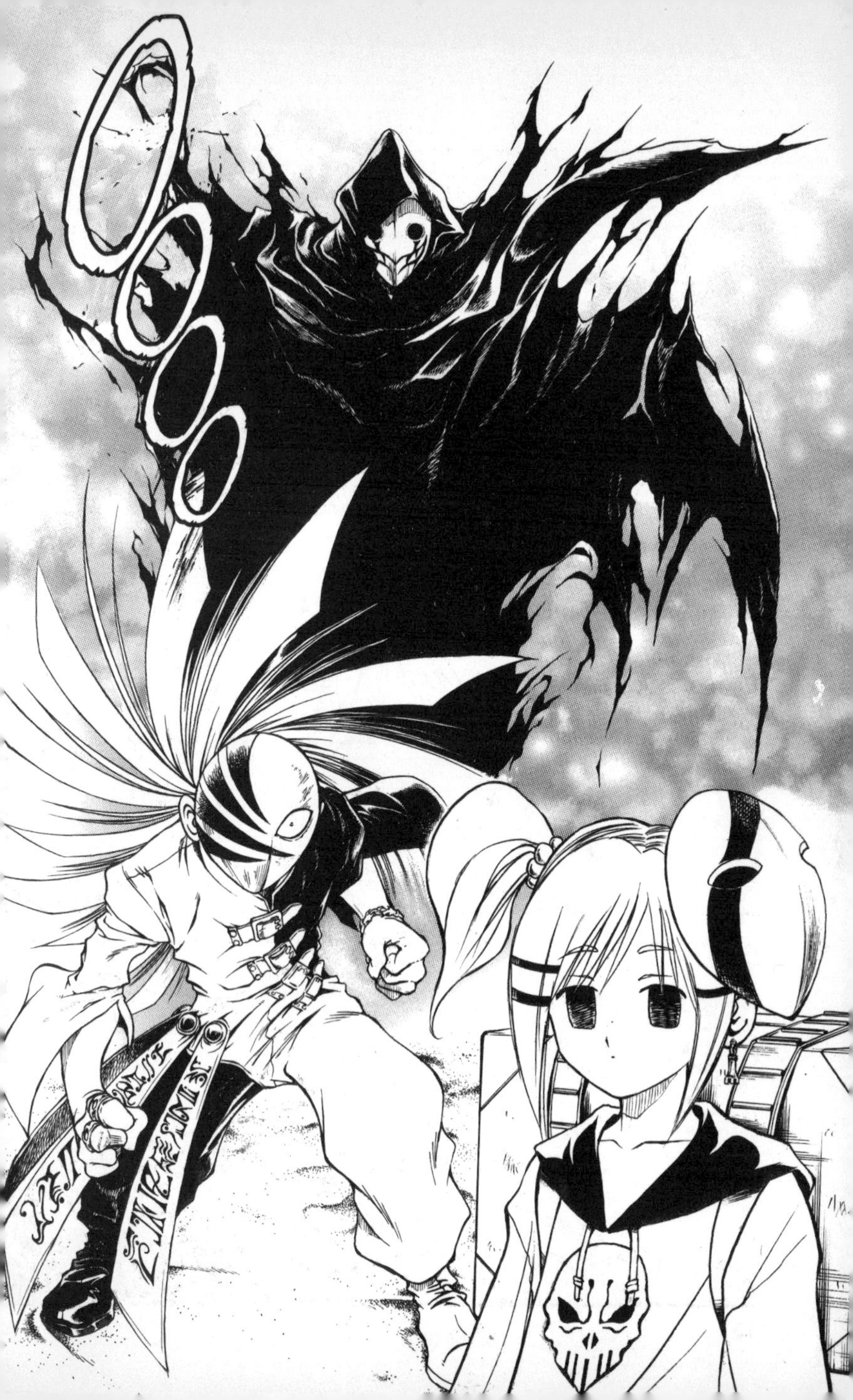

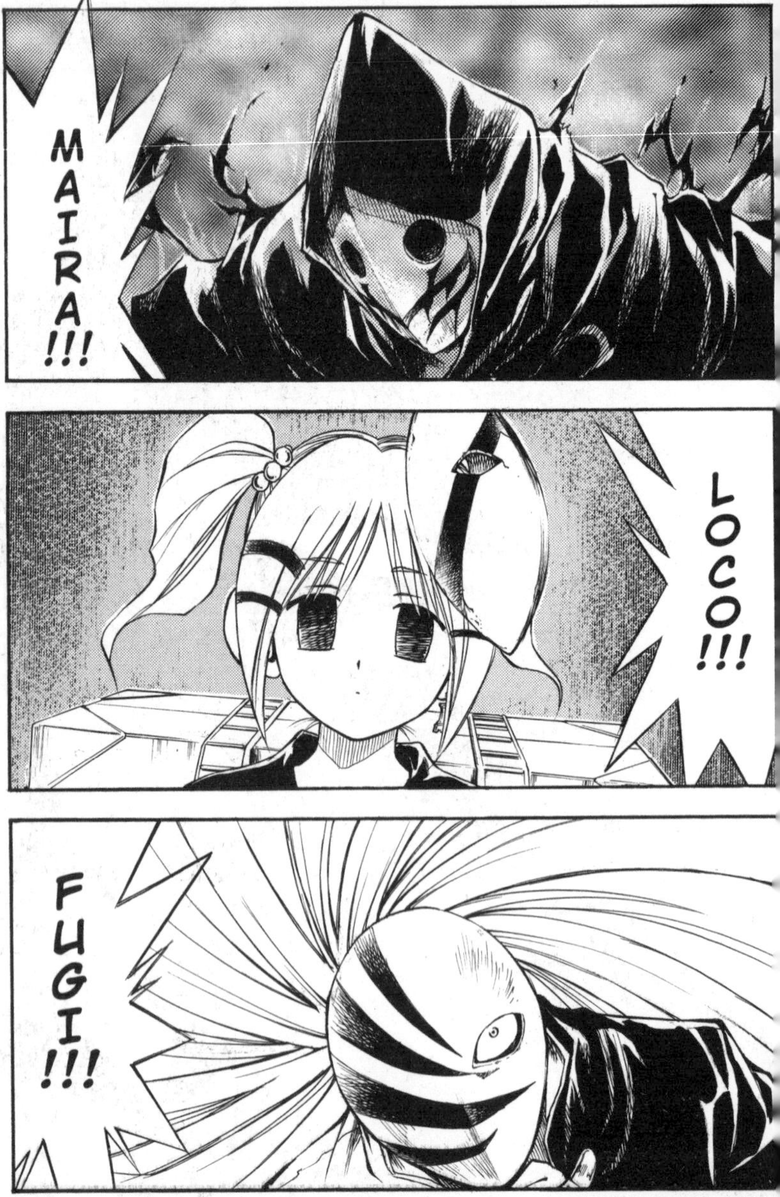
MAIRA!!!
LOCO!!!
FUGI!!!

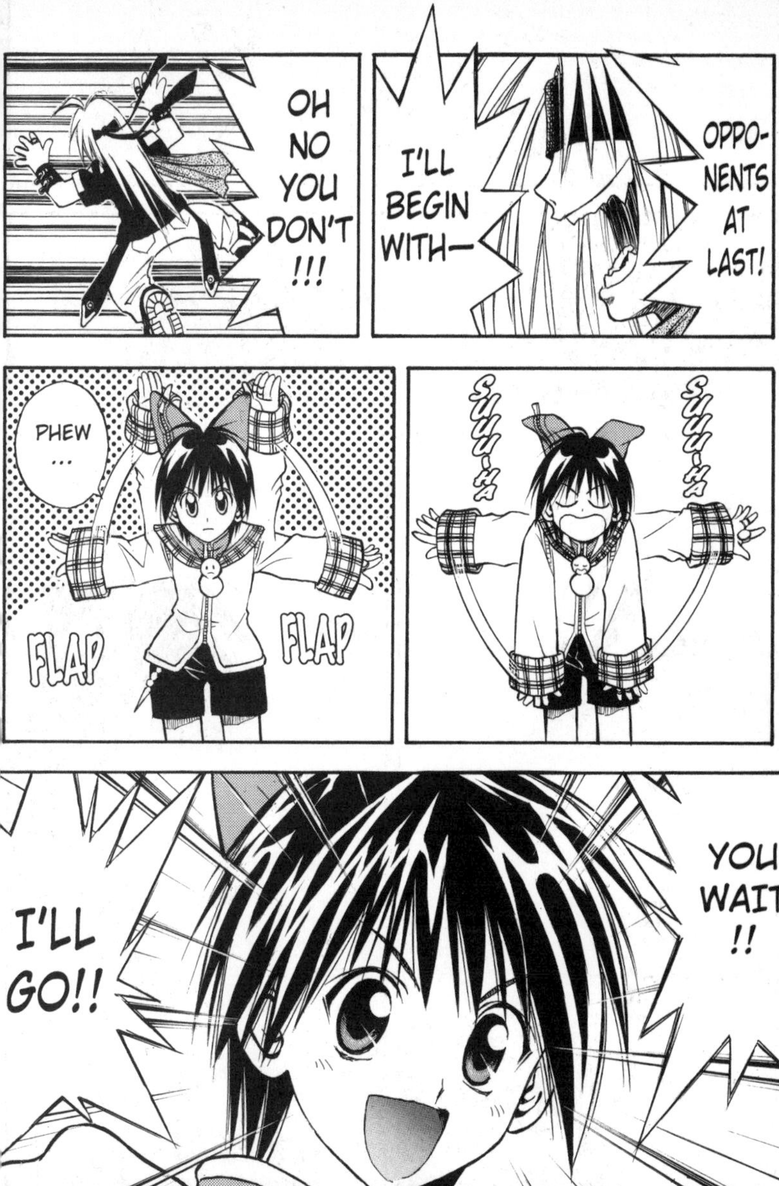
OPPO-NENTS AT LAST!
I'LL BEGIN WITH—
OH NO YOU DON'T !!!
SUUU-HA
SUUU-HA
PHEW ...
FLAP
FLAP
YOU WAIT !!
I'LL GO!!

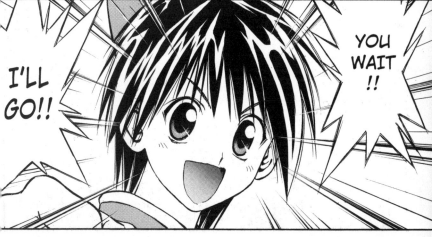

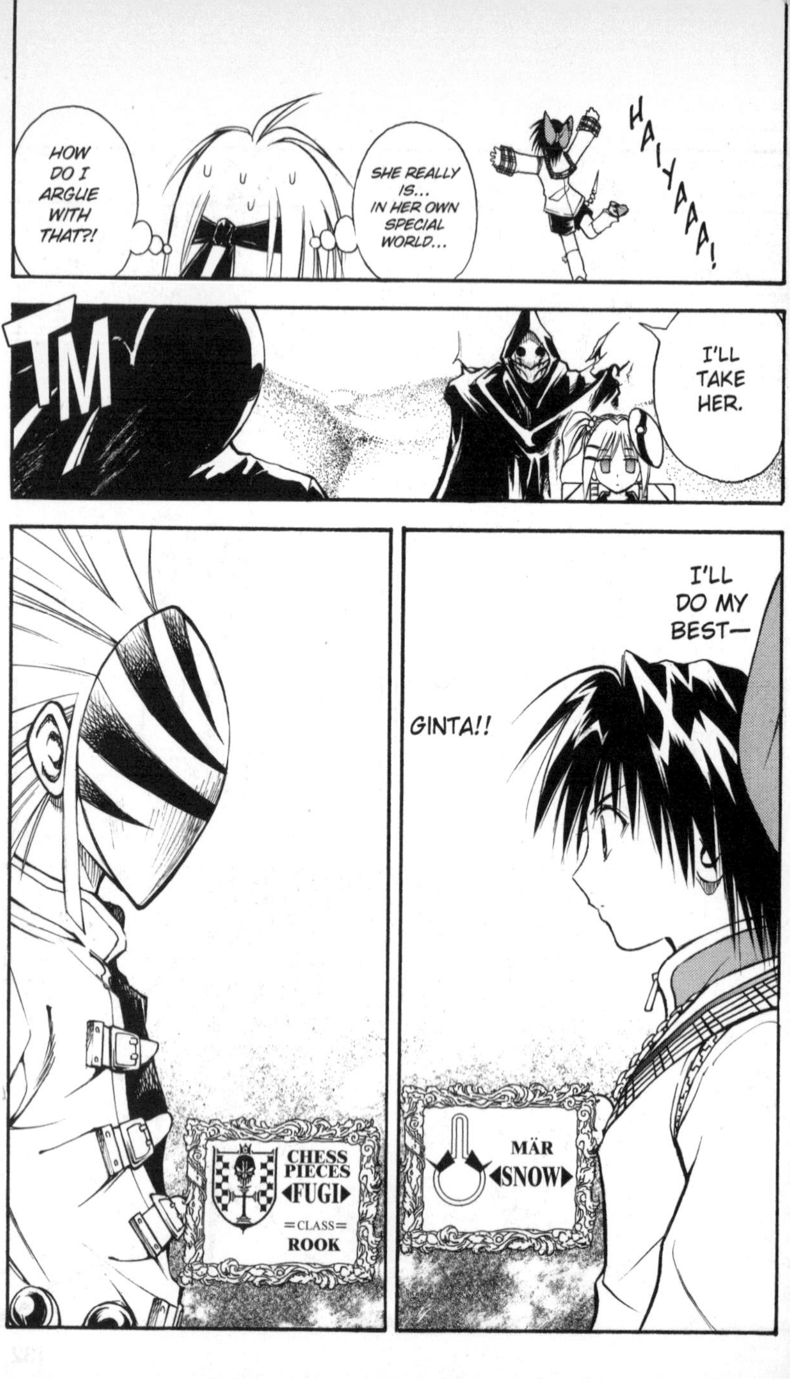
HAIYAAAA!
SHE REALLY IS... IN HER OWN SPECIAL WORLD...
HOW DO I ARGUE WITH THAT?!
I'LL TAKE HER.
TM
I'LL DO MY BEST—
GINTA!!
MÄR
SNOW
CHESS PIECES
FUGI
=CLASS=
ROOK

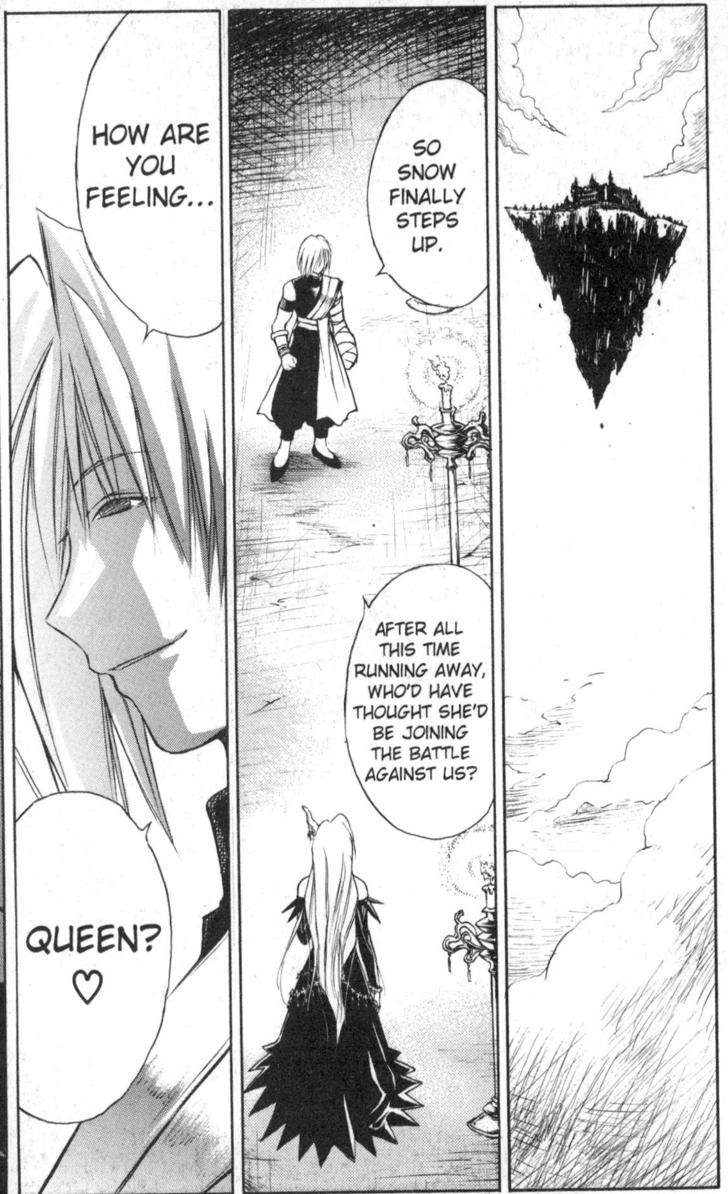
SO SNOW FINALLY STEPS UP.
AFTER ALL THIS TIME RUNNING AWAY, WHO'D HAVE THOUGHT SHE'D BE JOINING THE BATTLE AGAINST US?
HOW ARE YOU FEELING...
QUEEN? ♡

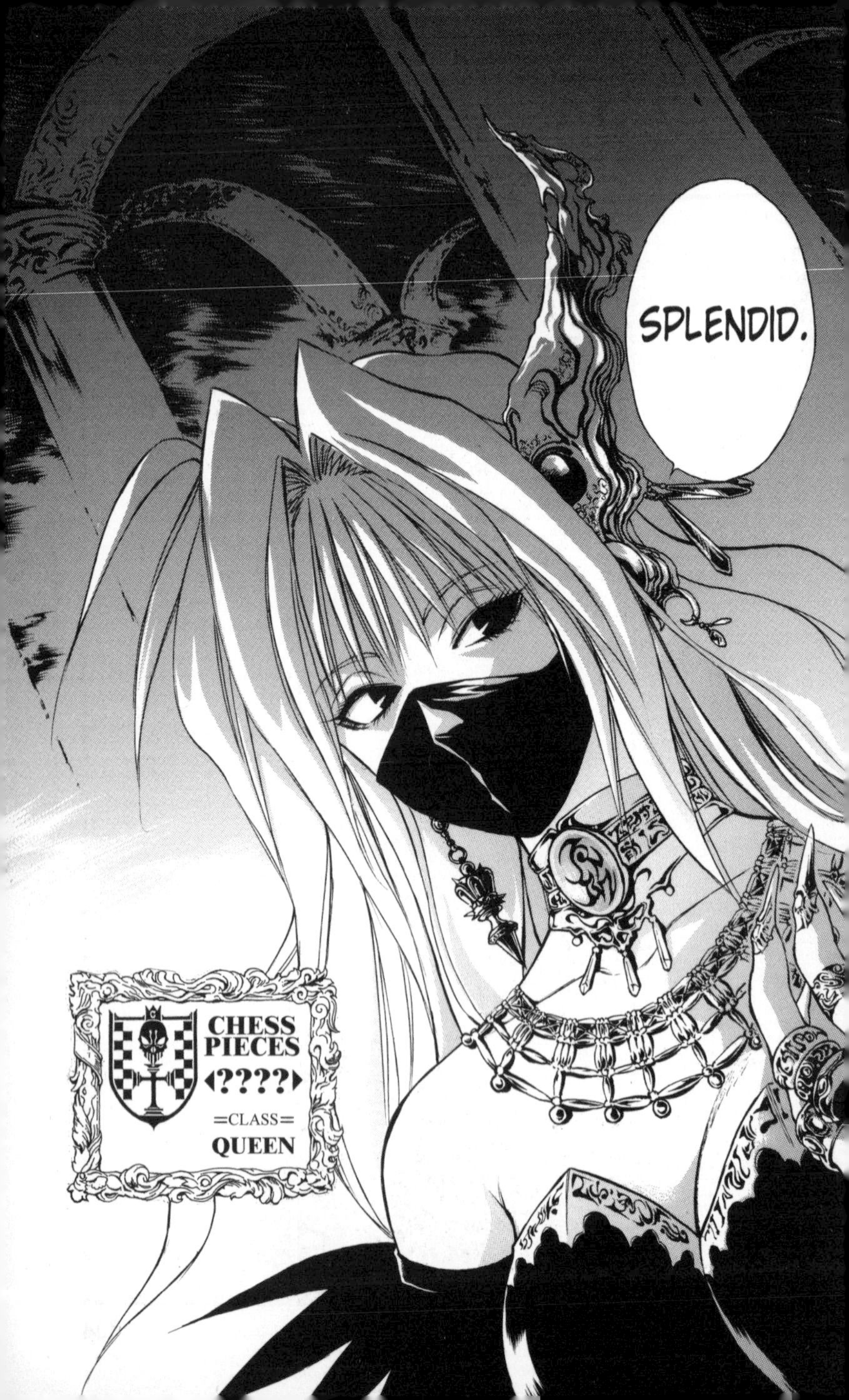
SPLENDID.
CHESS PIECES
◂????▸
=CLASS=
QUEEN

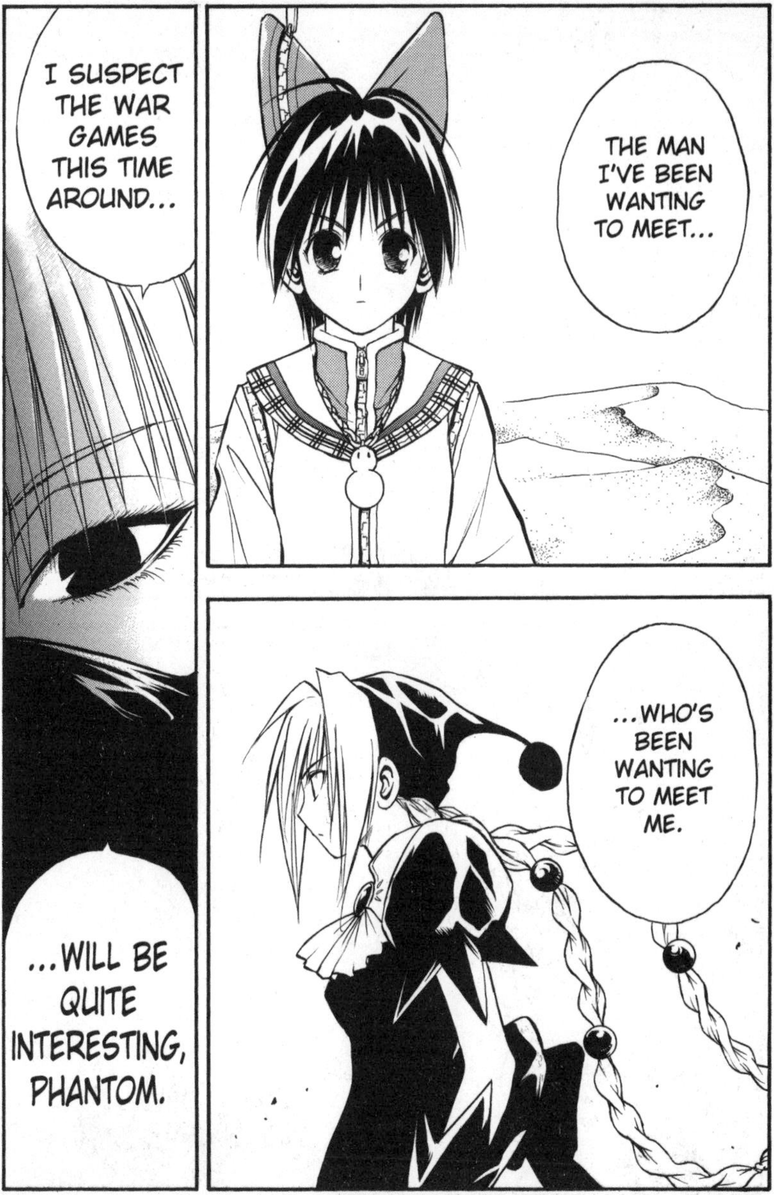
THE MAN I'VE BEEN WANTING TO MEET...
...WHO'S BEEN WANTING TO MEET ME.
I SUSPECT THE WAR GAMES THIS TIME AROUND...
...WILL BE QUITE INTERESTING, PHANTOM.

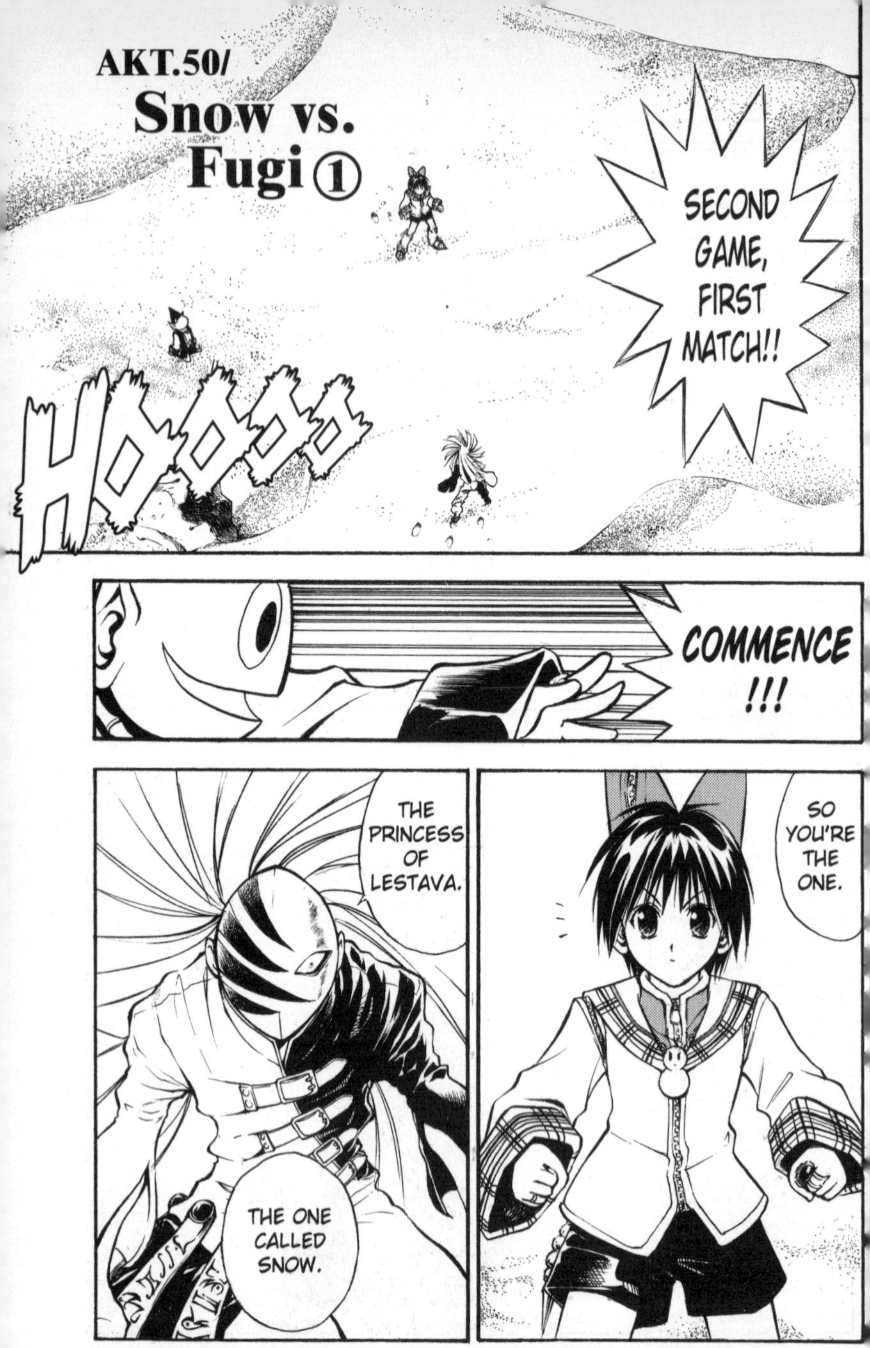
AKT.50/ Snow vs. Fugi ①
SECOND GAME, FIRST MATCH!!
HOOOO
COMMENCE!!!
SO YOU'RE THE ONE.
THE PRINCESS OF LESTAVA.
THE ONE CALLED SNOW.

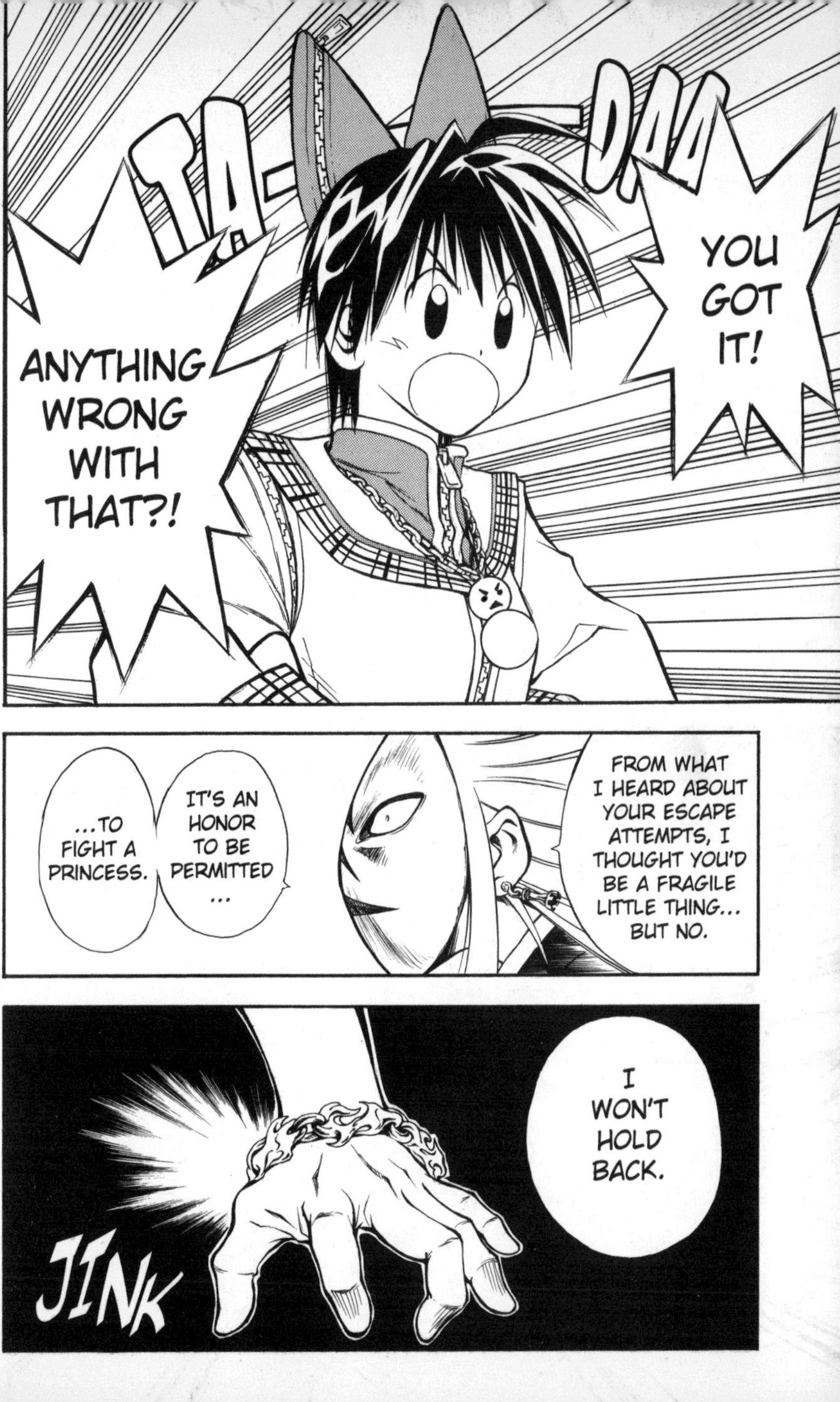
TA-DAA
YOU GOT IT!
ANYTHING WRONG WITH THAT?!
FROM WHAT I HEARD ABOUT YOUR ESCAPE ATTEMPTS, I THOUGHT YOU'D BE A FRAGILE LITTLE THING... BUT NO.
IT'S AN HONOR TO BE PERMITTED ...
...TO FIGHT A PRINCESS.
I WON'T HOLD BACK.
JINK

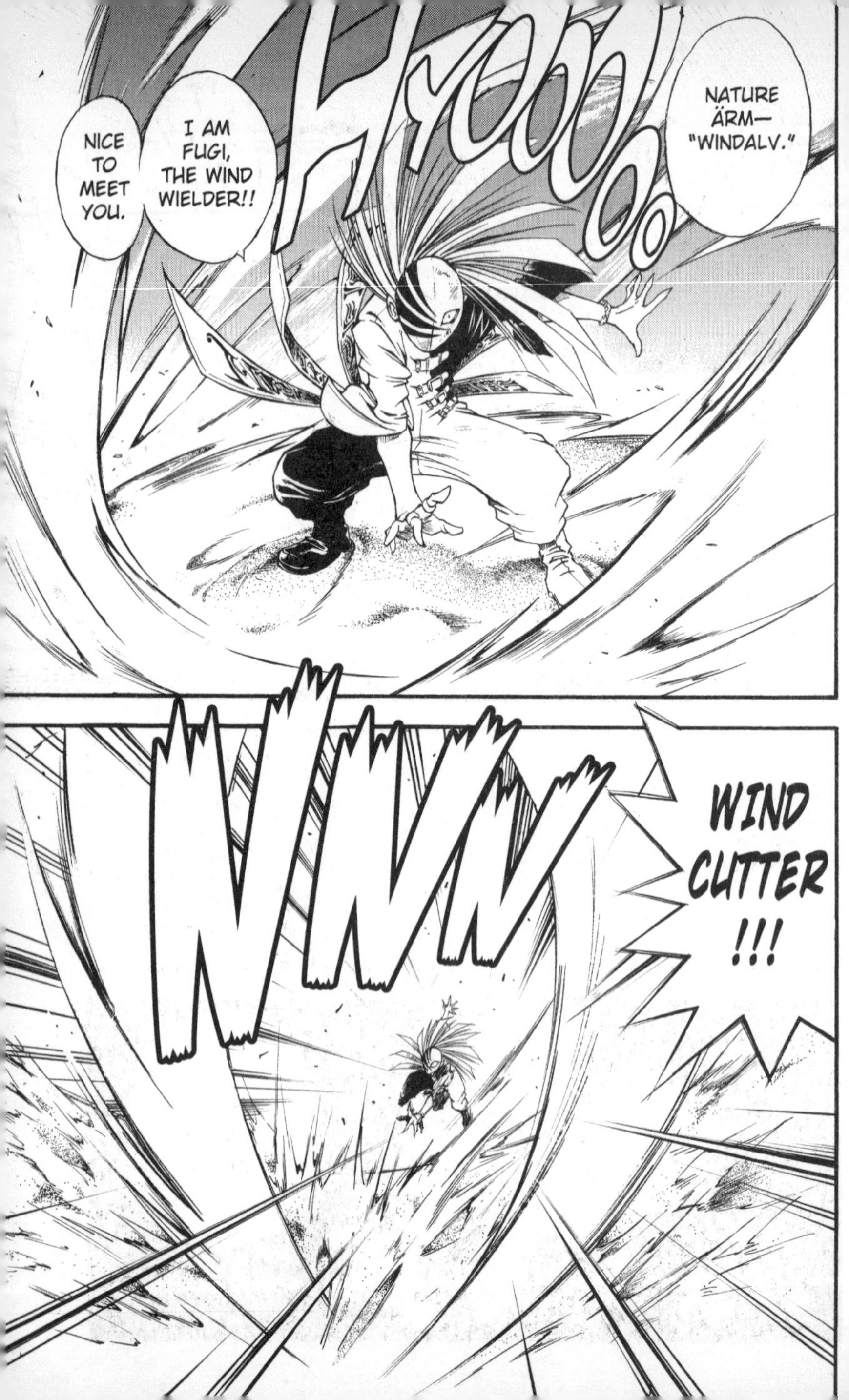
NATURE ÄRM— "WINDALV."
I AM FUGI, THE WIND WIELDER!!
NICE TO MEET YOU.
WIND CUTTER !!!
WNN

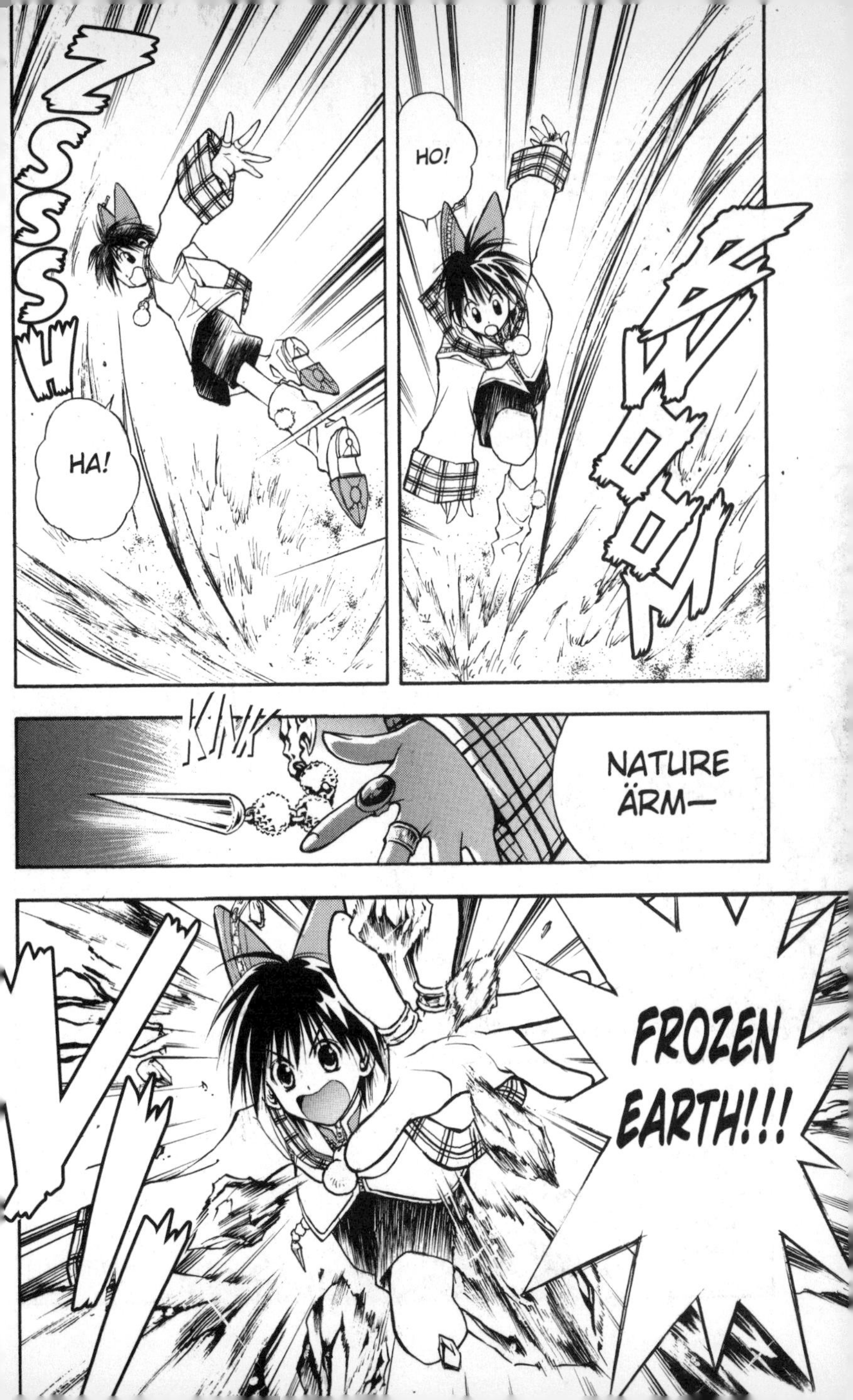
HO!
HA!
KINK
NATURE ÄRM—
FROZEN EARTH!!!

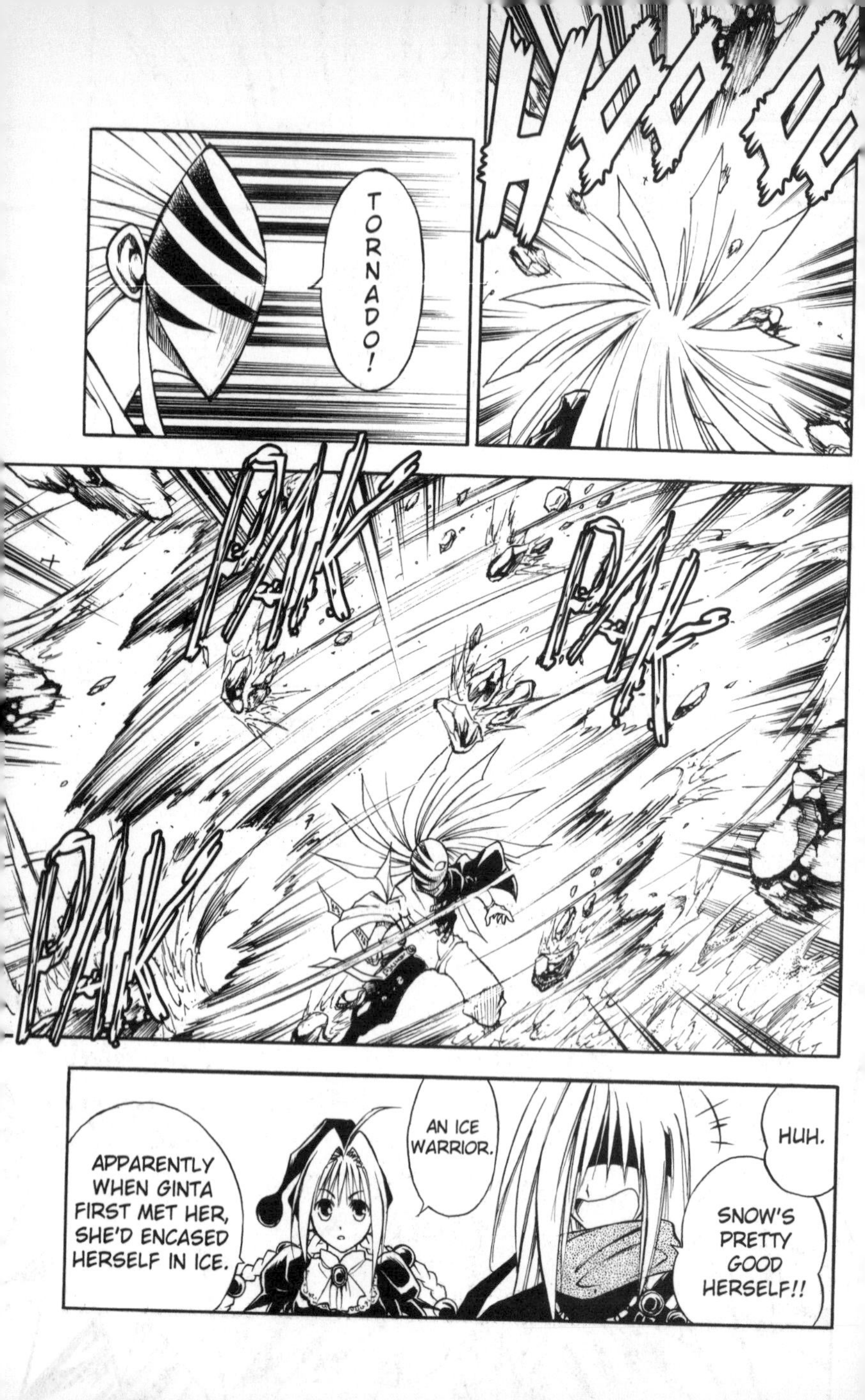
TORNADO!
PAK
PAK
PAK
HUH.
SNOW'S PRETTY GOOD HERSELF!!
AN ICE WARRIOR.
APPARENTLY WHEN GINTA FIRST MET HER, SHE'D ENCASED HERSELF IN ICE.

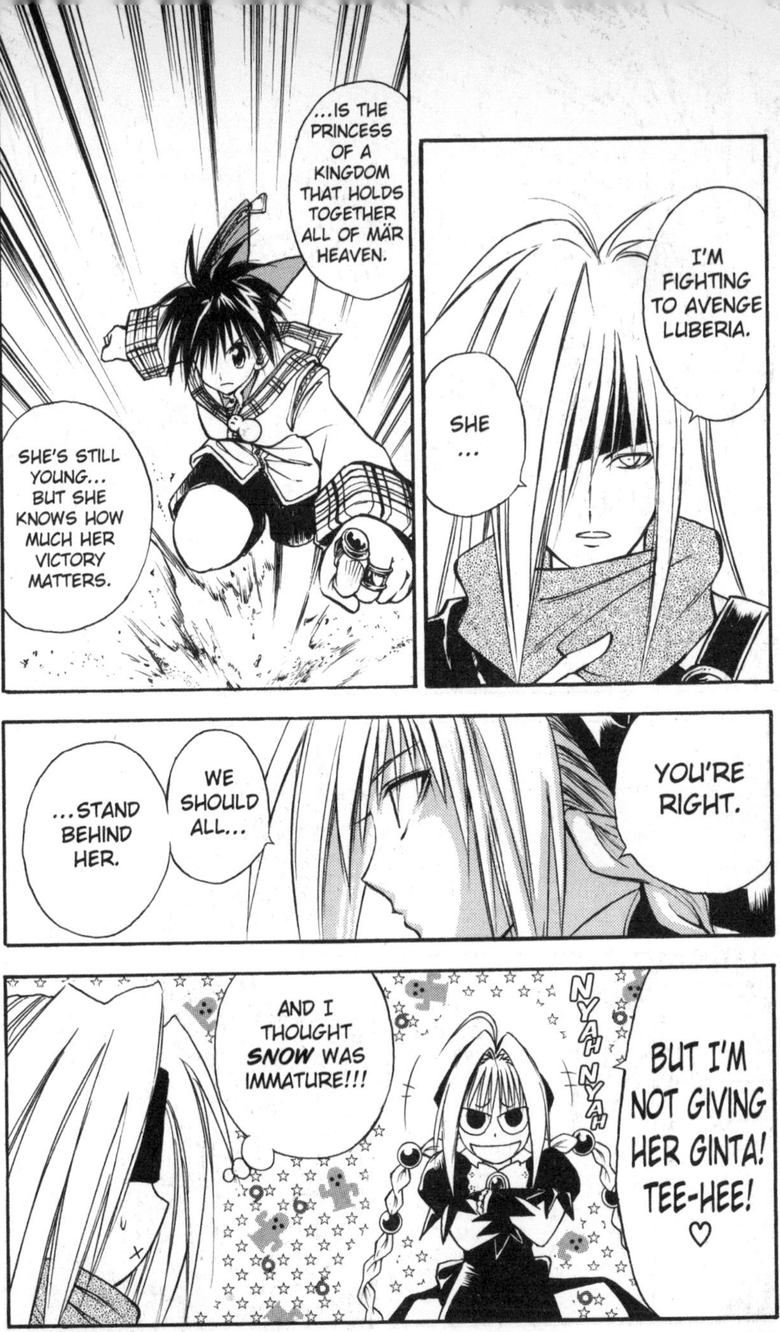

I'M FIGHTING TO AVENGE LUBERIA.
SHE ...
...IS THE PRINCESS OF A KINGDOM THAT HOLDS TOGETHER ALL OF MÄR HEAVEN.
SHE'S STILL YOUNG... BUT SHE KNOWS HOW MUCH HER VICTORY MATTERS.
YOU'RE RIGHT.
WE SHOULD ALL...
...STAND BEHIND HER.
BUT I'M NOT GIVING HER GINTA! TEE-HEE! ♡
NYAH NYAH
AND I THOUGHT *SNOW* WAS IMMATURE!!!

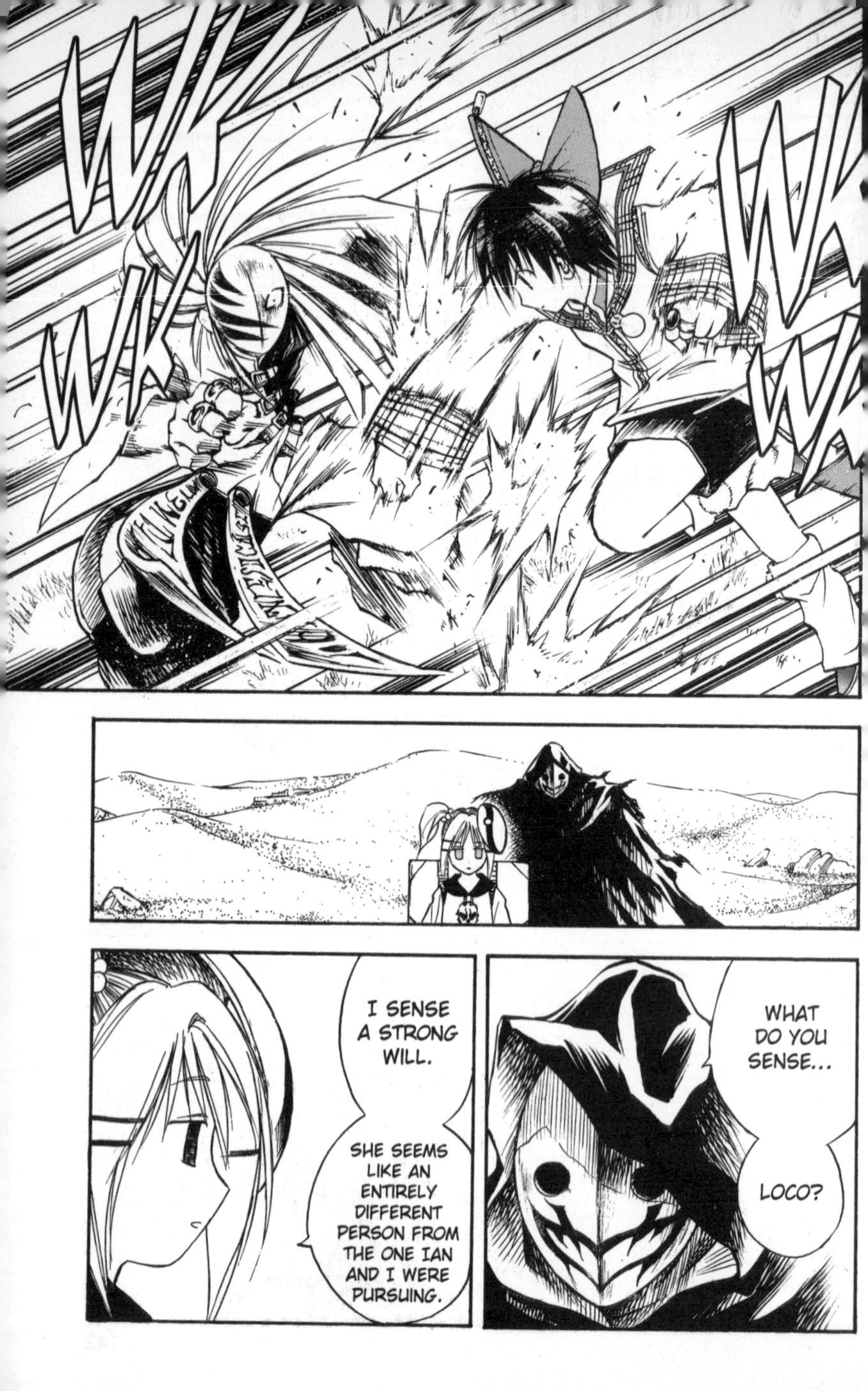
WK
WK
WK
WK
WHAT DO YOU SENSE...
LOCO?
I SENSE A STRONG WILL.
SHE SEEMS LIKE AN ENTIRELY DIFFERENT PERSON FROM THE ONE IAN AND I WERE PURSUING.

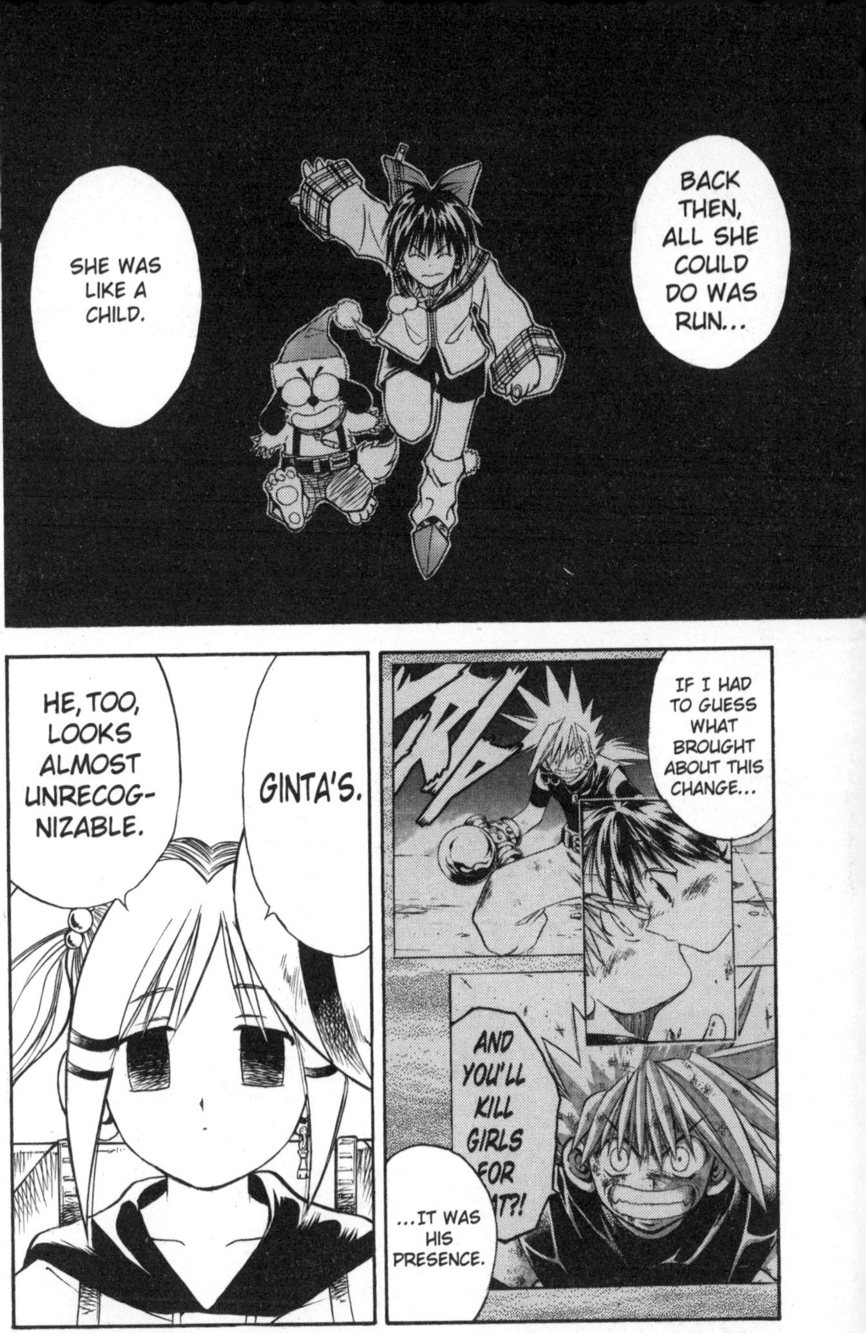
BACK THEN, ALL SHE COULD DO WAS RUN...
SHE WAS LIKE A CHILD.
IF I HAD TO GUESS WHAT BROUGHT ABOUT THIS CHANGE...
AND YOU'LL KILL GIRLS
...IT WAS HIS PRESENCE.
GINTA'S.
HE, TOO, LOOKS ALMOST UNRECOG-NIZABLE.

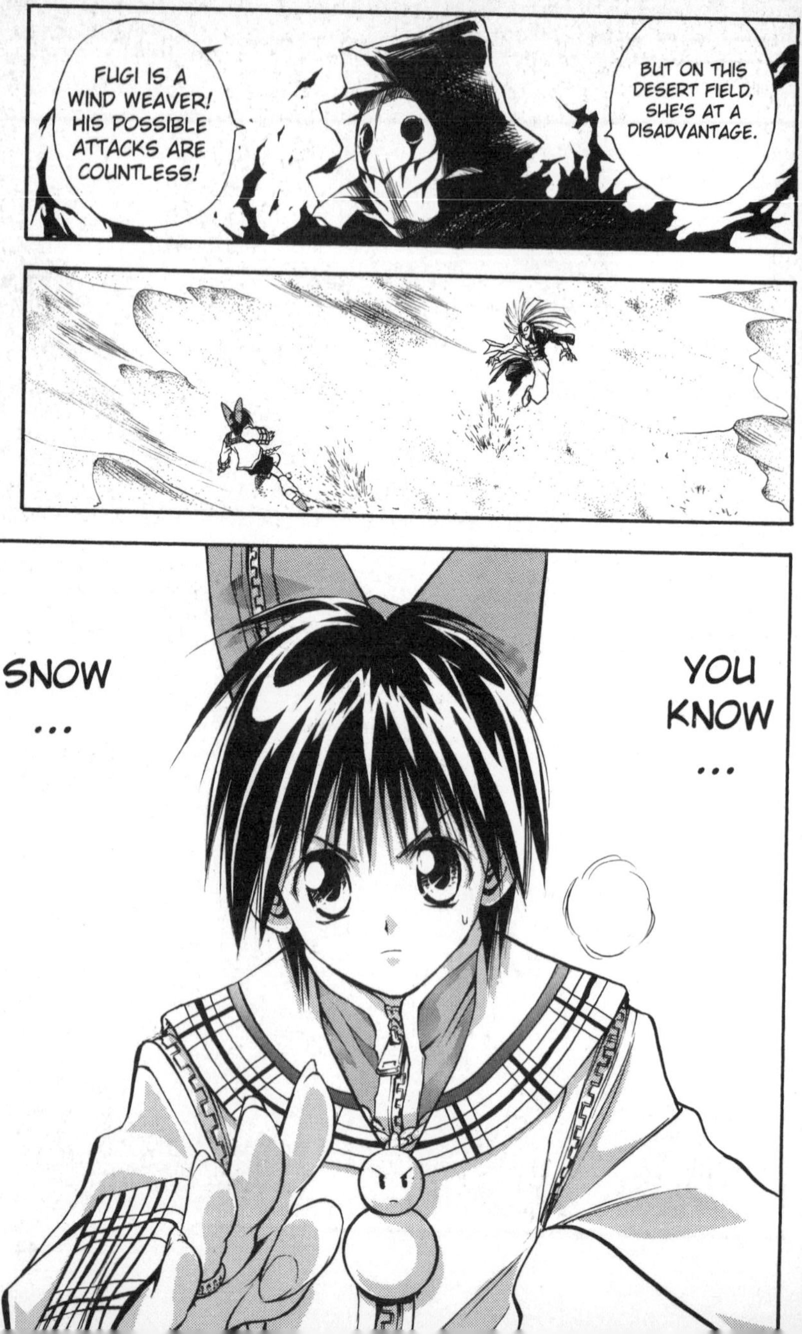
BUT ON THIS DESERT FIELD, SHE'S AT A DISADVANTAGE.
FUGI IS A WIND WEAVER! HIS POSSIBLE ATTACKS ARE COUNTLESS!
YOU KNOW ...
SNOW ...

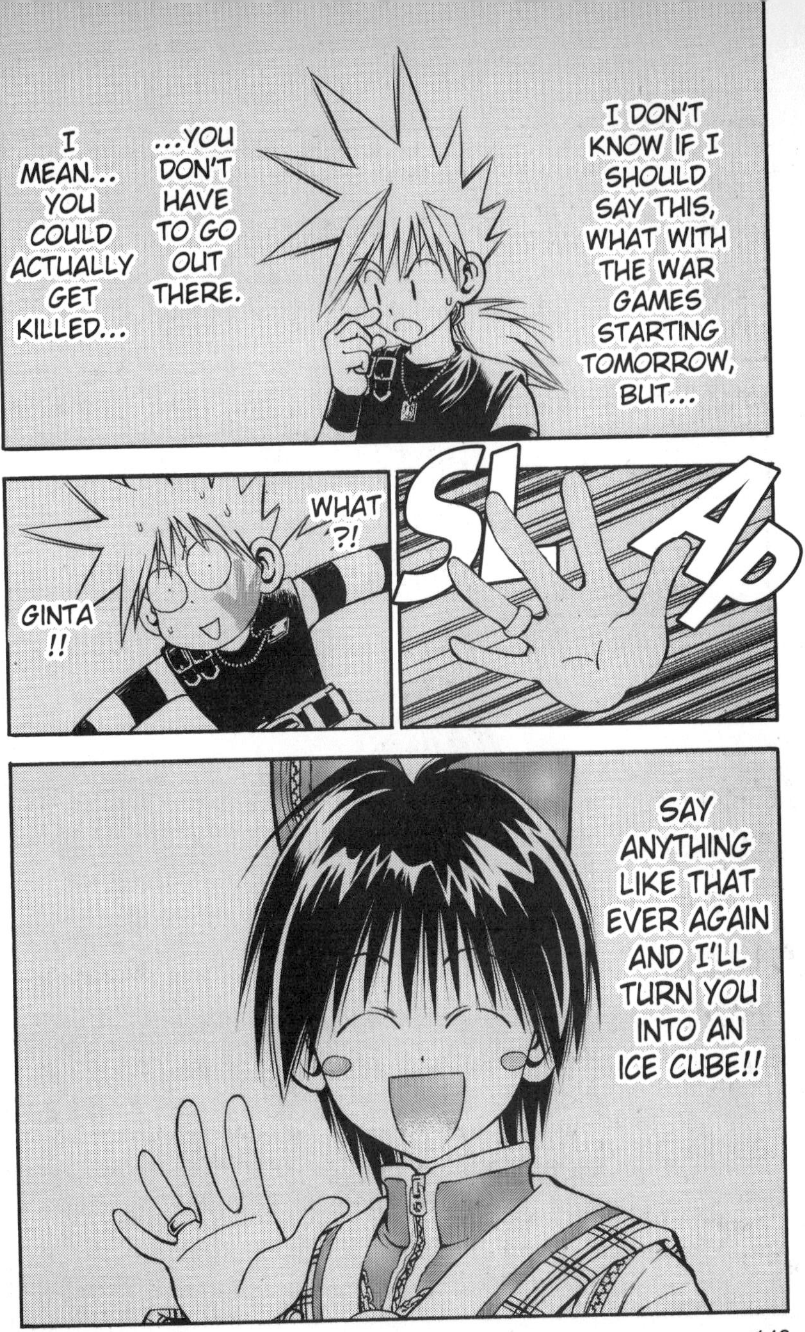
I DON'T KNOW IF I SHOULD SAY THIS, WHAT WITH THE WAR GAMES STARTING TOMORROW, BUT...
...YOU DON'T HAVE TO GO OUT THERE.
I MEAN... YOU COULD ACTUALLY GET KILLED...
SLAP
WHAT ?!
GINTA !!
SAY ANYTHING LIKE THAT EVER AGAIN AND I'LL TURN YOU INTO AN ICE CUBE!!

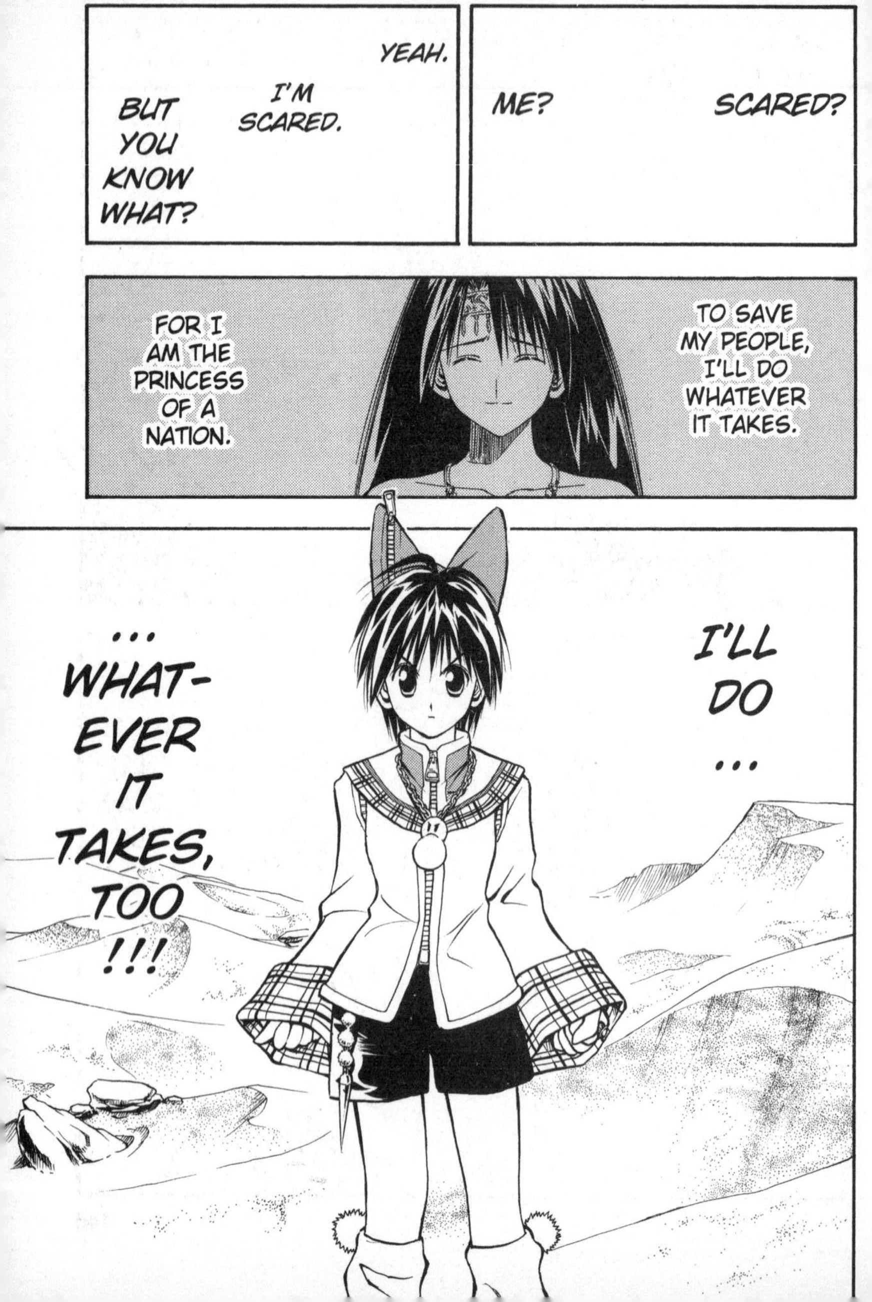
SCARED?
ME?
YEAH.
I'M SCARED.
BUT YOU KNOW WHAT?
TO SAVE MY PEOPLE, I'LL DO WHATEVER IT TAKES.
FOR I AM THE PRINCESS OF A NATION.
I'LL DO ...
... WHAT-EVER IT TAKES, TOO !!!

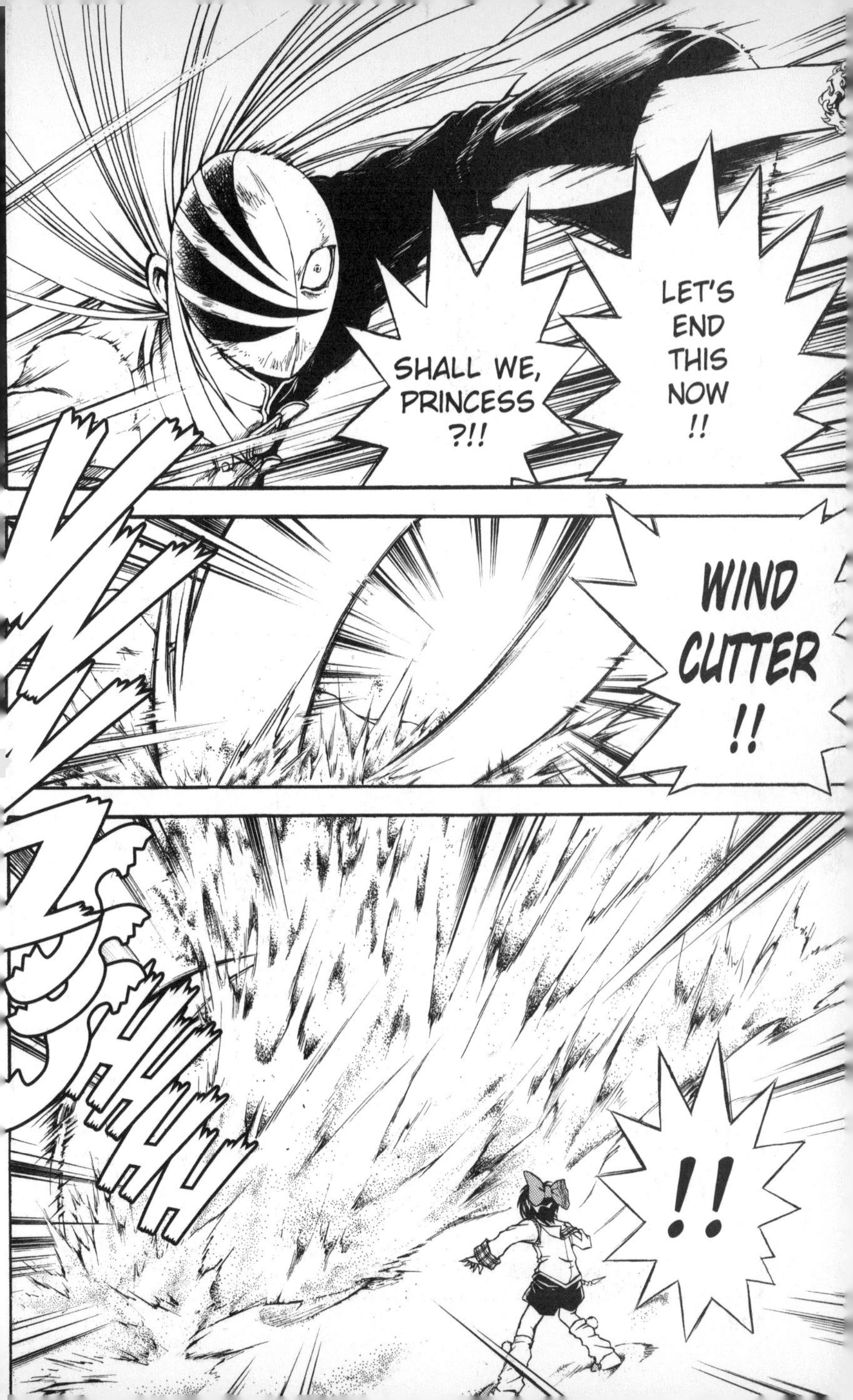
LET'S END THIS NOW!!
SHALL WE, PRINCESS?!!
WIND CUTTER!!
!!

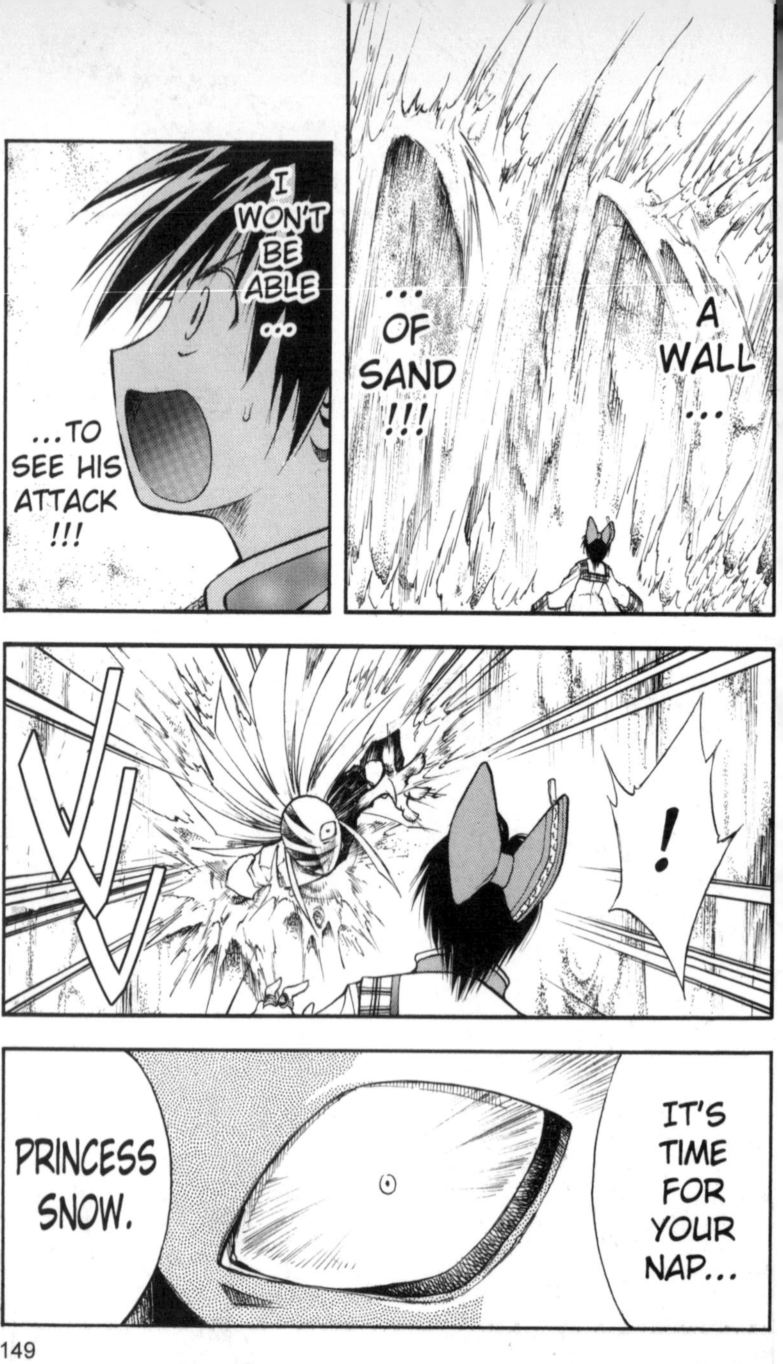
A WALL ...
... OF SAND !!!
I WON'T BE ABLE ...
...TO SEE HIS ATTACK !!!
!
IT'S TIME FOR YOUR NAP...
PRINCESS SNOW.

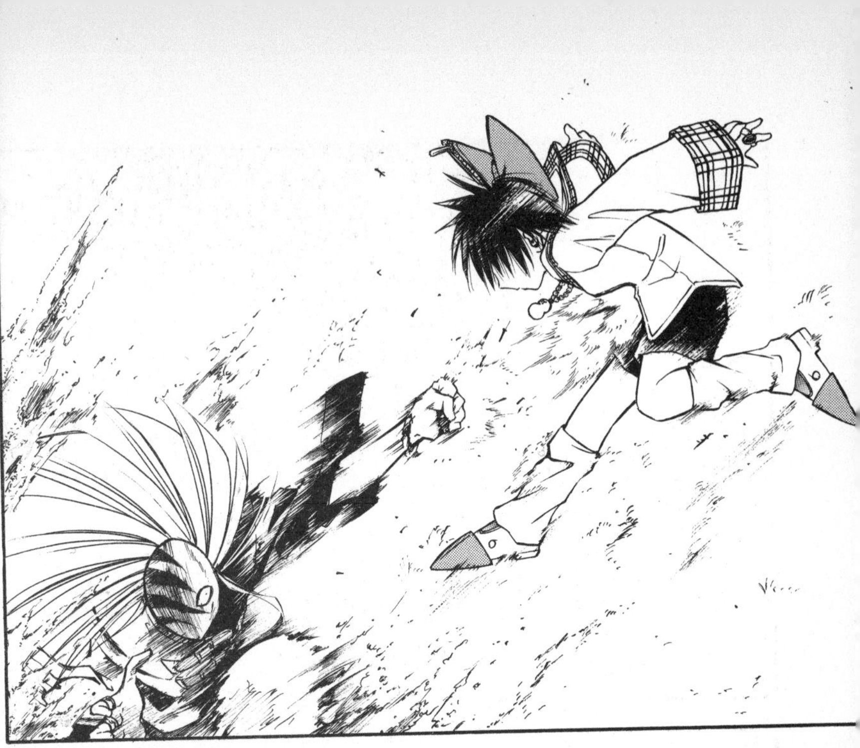

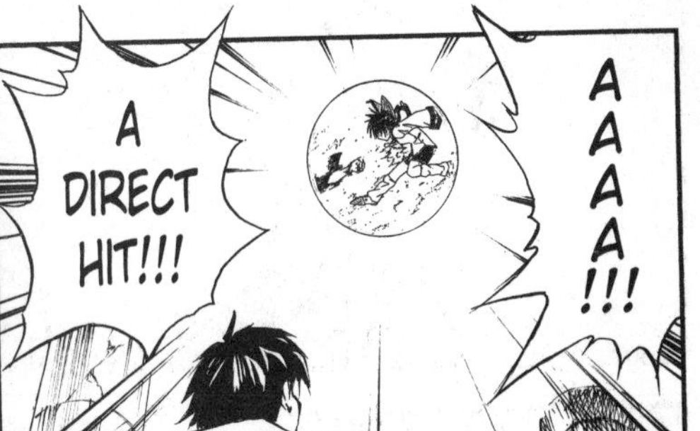
AAAA!!!
A DIRECT HIT!!!

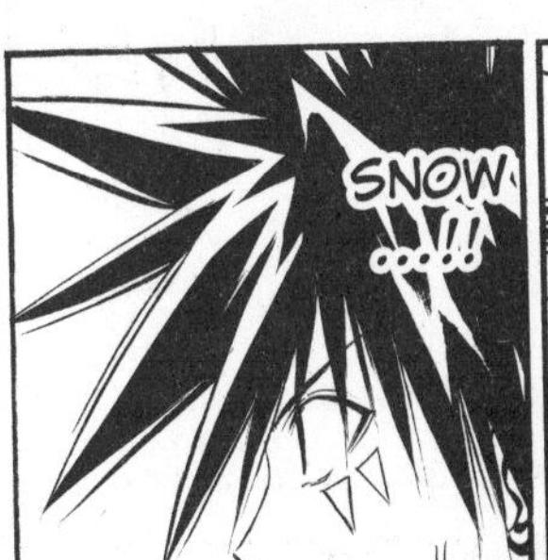
SNOW...!!

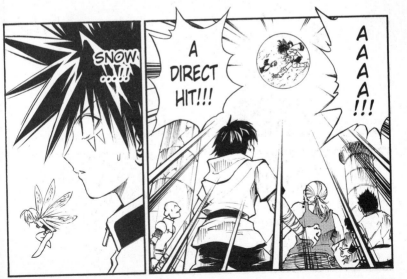

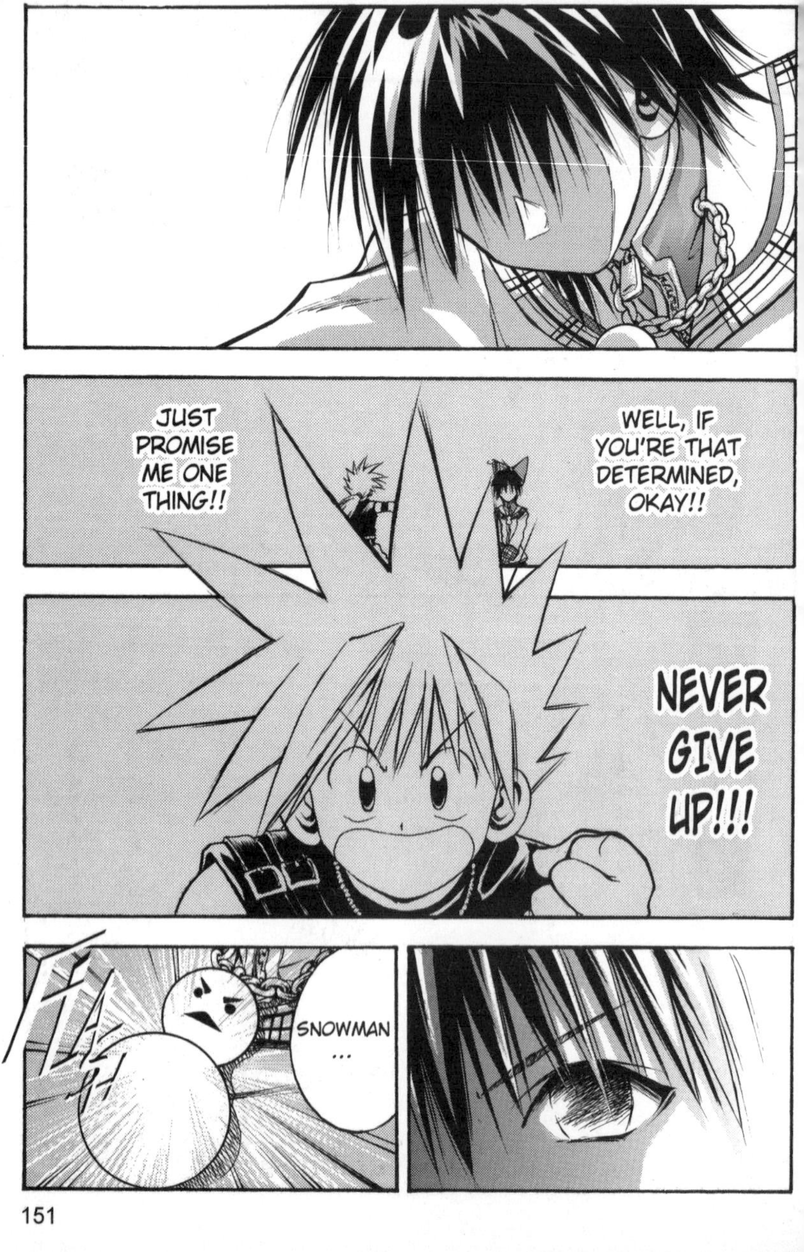
WELL, IF YOU'RE THAT DETERMINED, OKAY!!
JUST PROMISE ME ONE THING!!
NEVER GIVE UP!!!
SNOWMAN ...

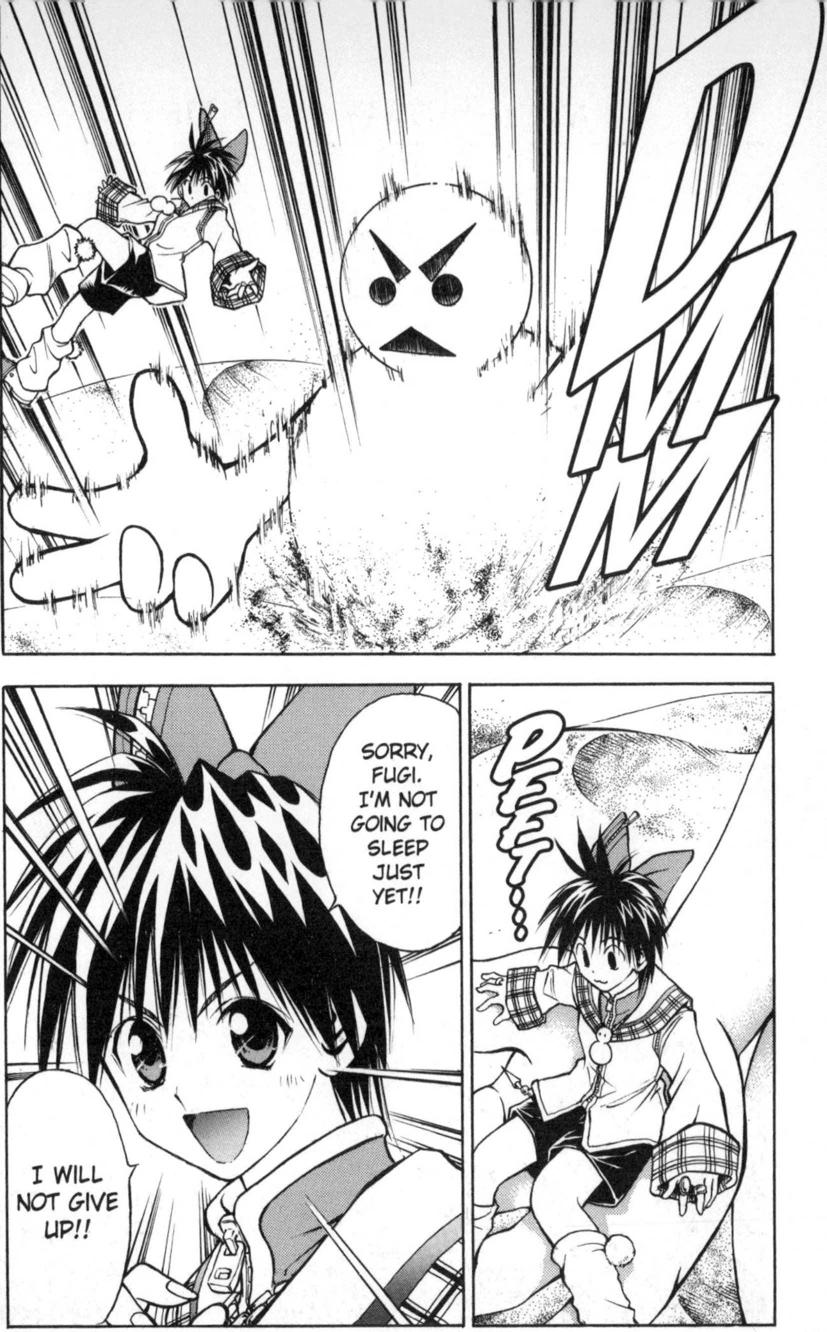
SORRY, FUGI. I'M NOT GOING TO SLEEP JUST YET!!
I WILL NOT GIVE UP!!

AKT.51/ Snow vs. Fugi②

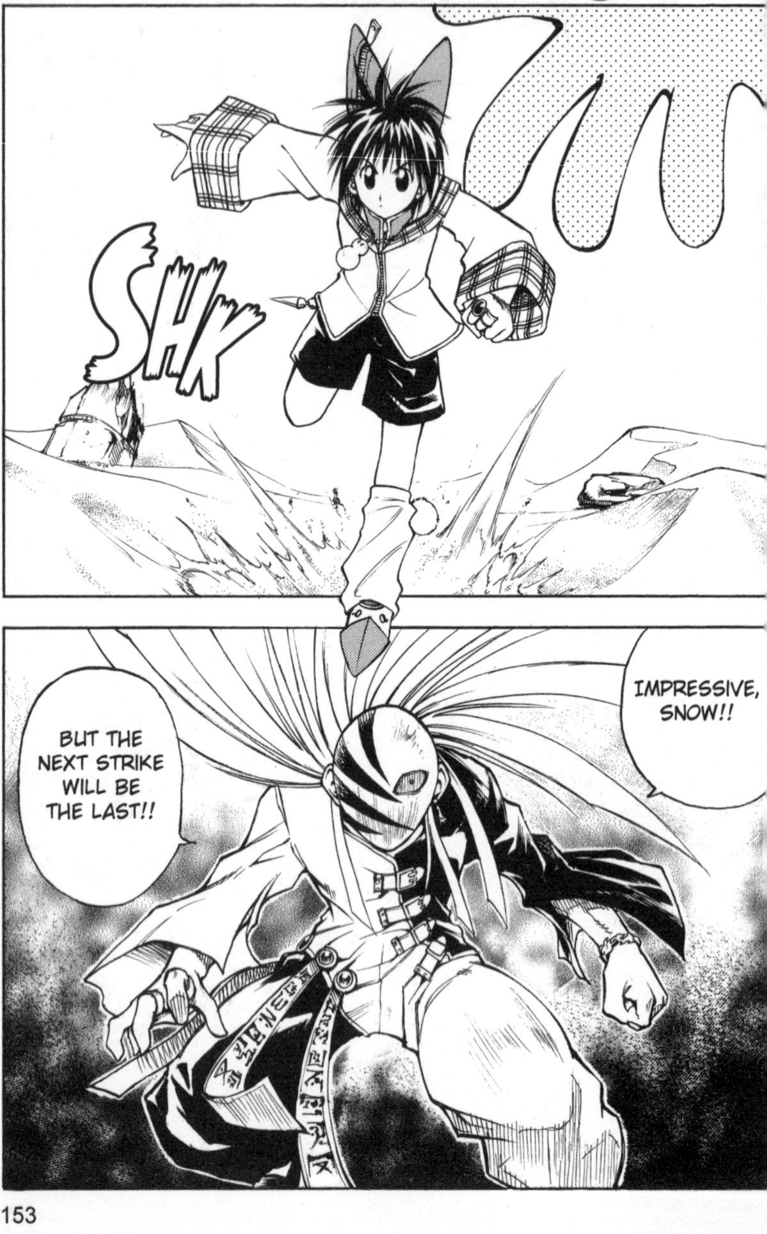
SHK
IMPRESSIVE, SNOW!!
BUT THE NEXT STRIKE WILL BE THE LAST!!

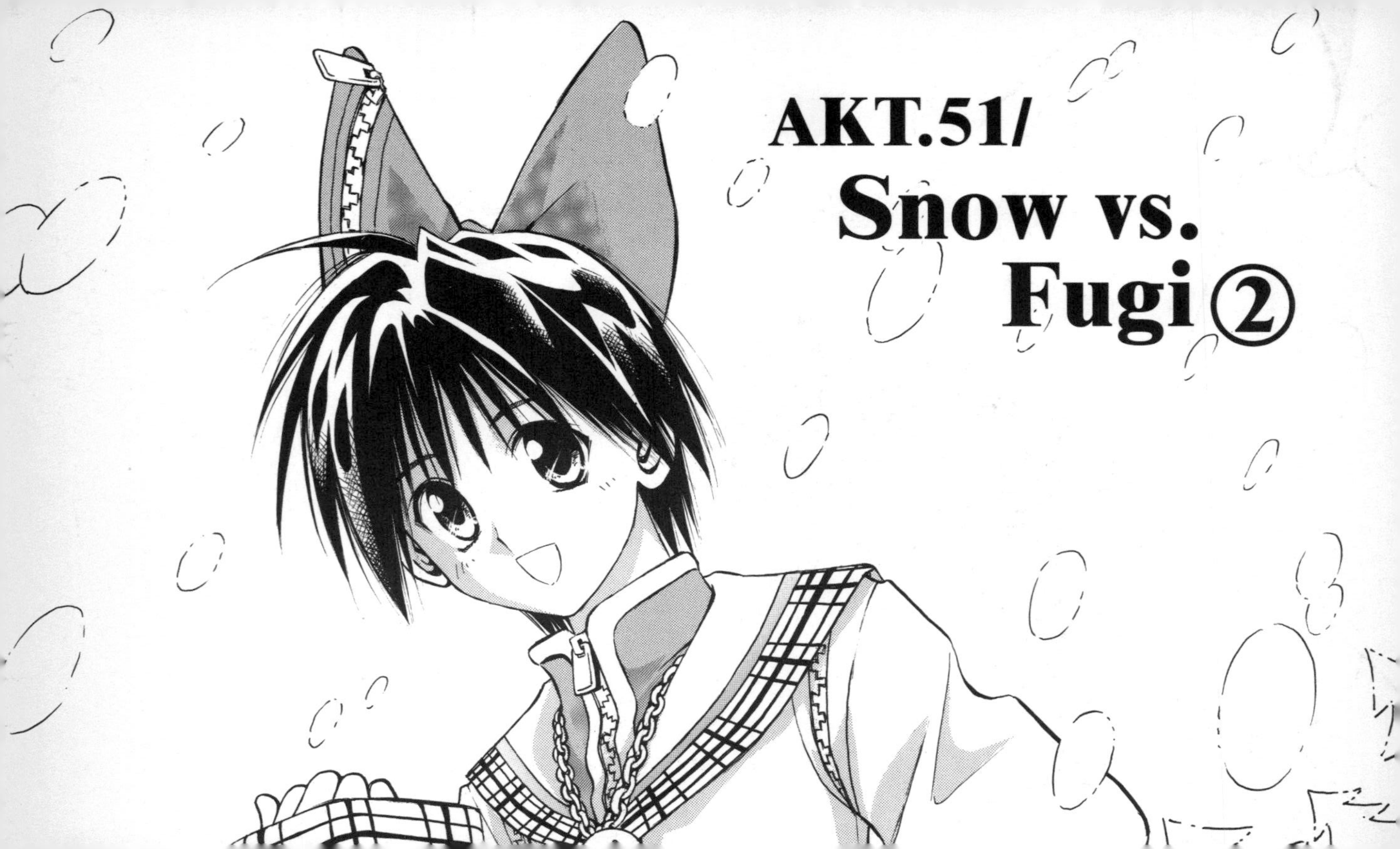

AKT.51/ Snow vs. Fugi ②

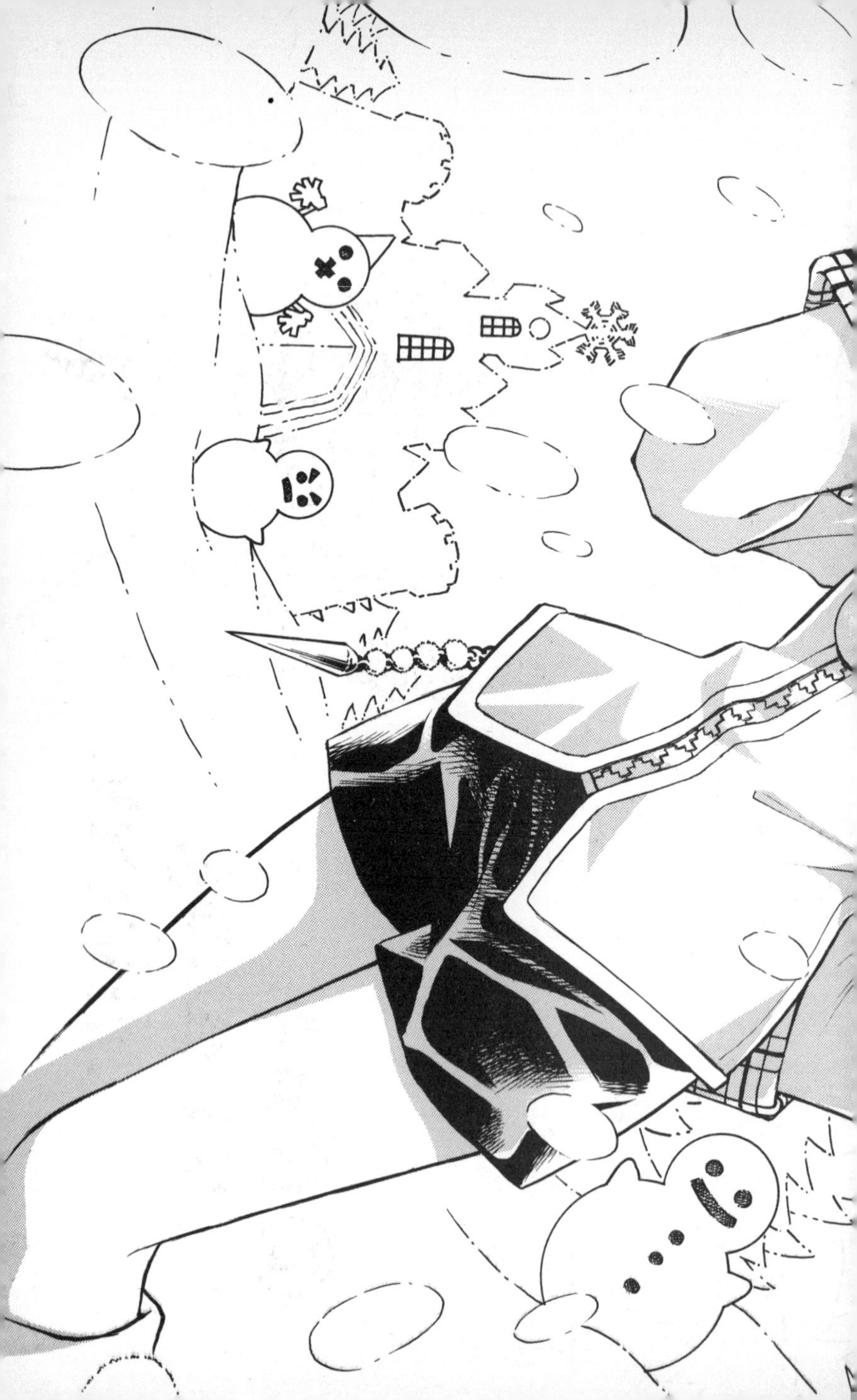

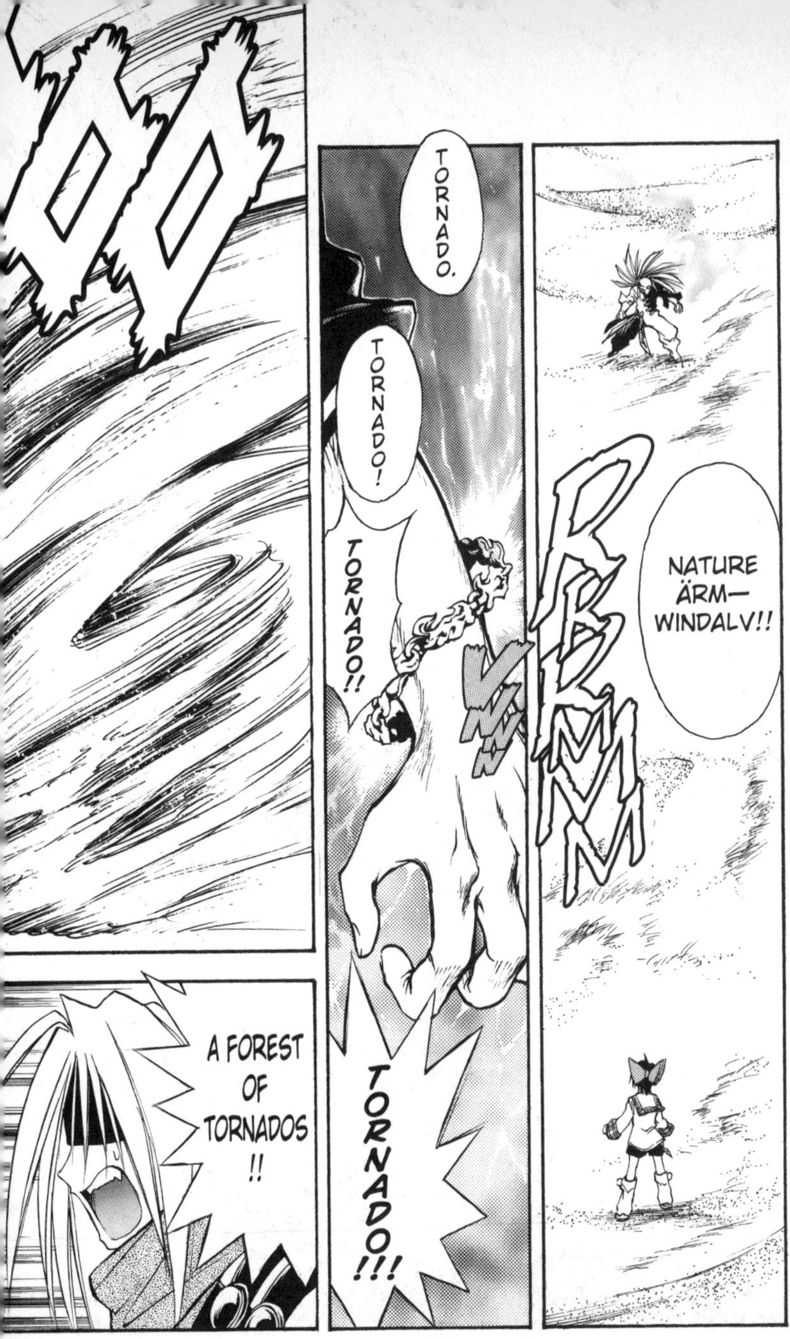
NATURE ÄRM—WINDALV!!
TORNADO.
TORNADO!
TORNADO!!
TORNADO!!!
A FOREST OF TORNADOS!!

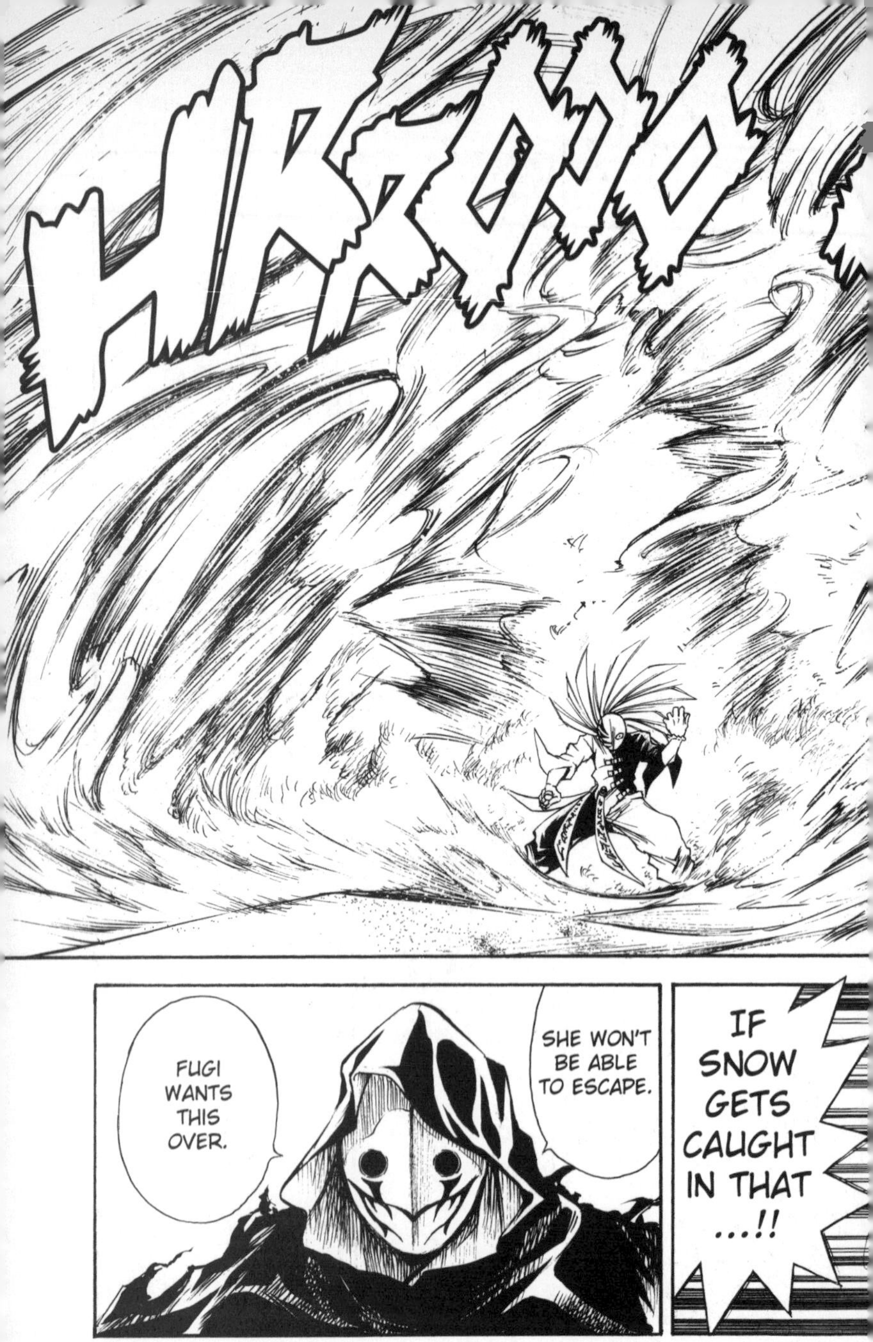
IF SNOW GETS CAUGHT IN THAT ...!!
SHE WON'T BE ABLE TO ESCAPE.
FUGI WANTS THIS OVER.

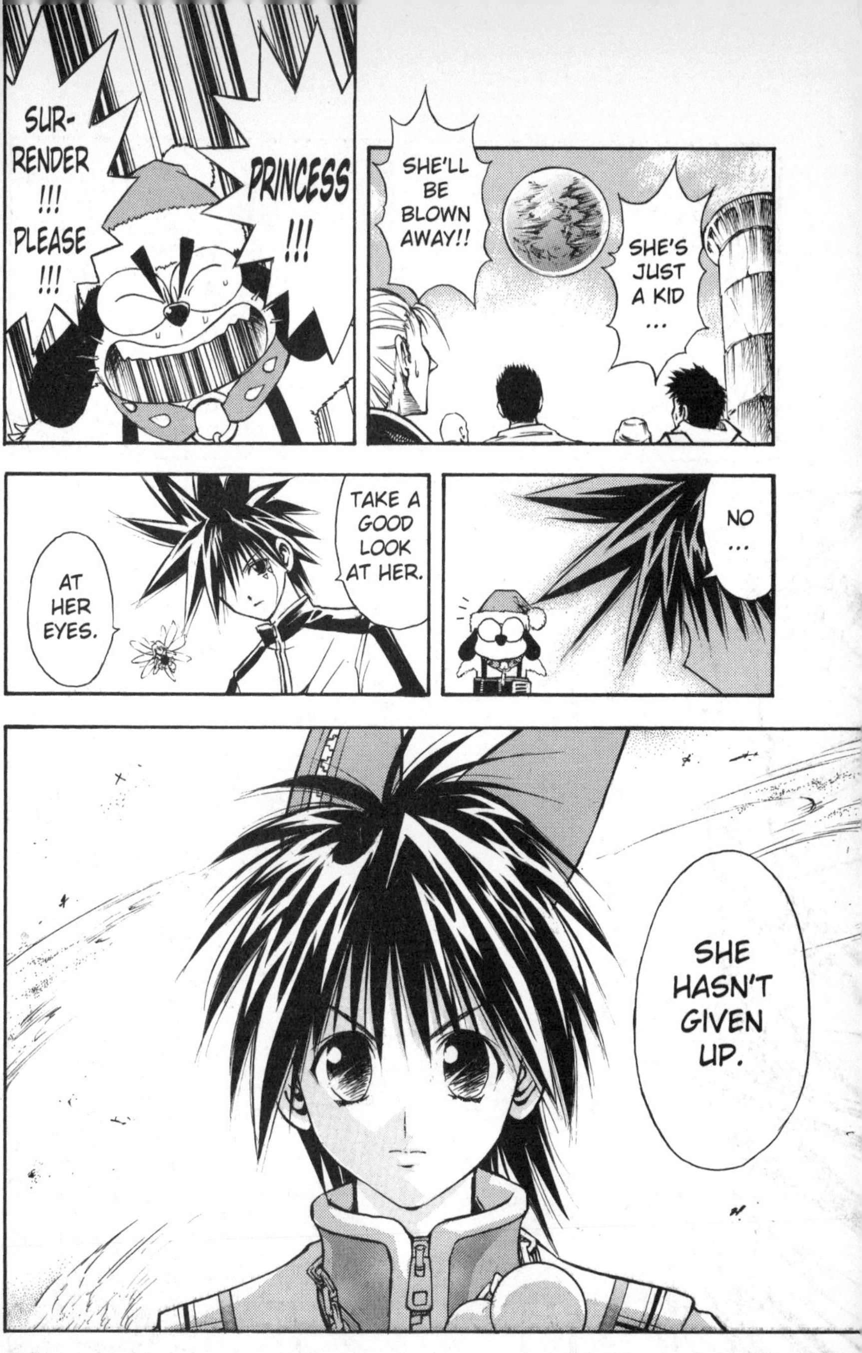
SHE'S JUST A KID ...
SHE'LL BE BLOWN AWAY!!
PRINCESS !!!
SUR-RENDER !!! PLEASE !!!
NO ...
TAKE A GOOD LOOK AT HER.
AT HER EYES.
SHE HASN'T GIVEN UP.

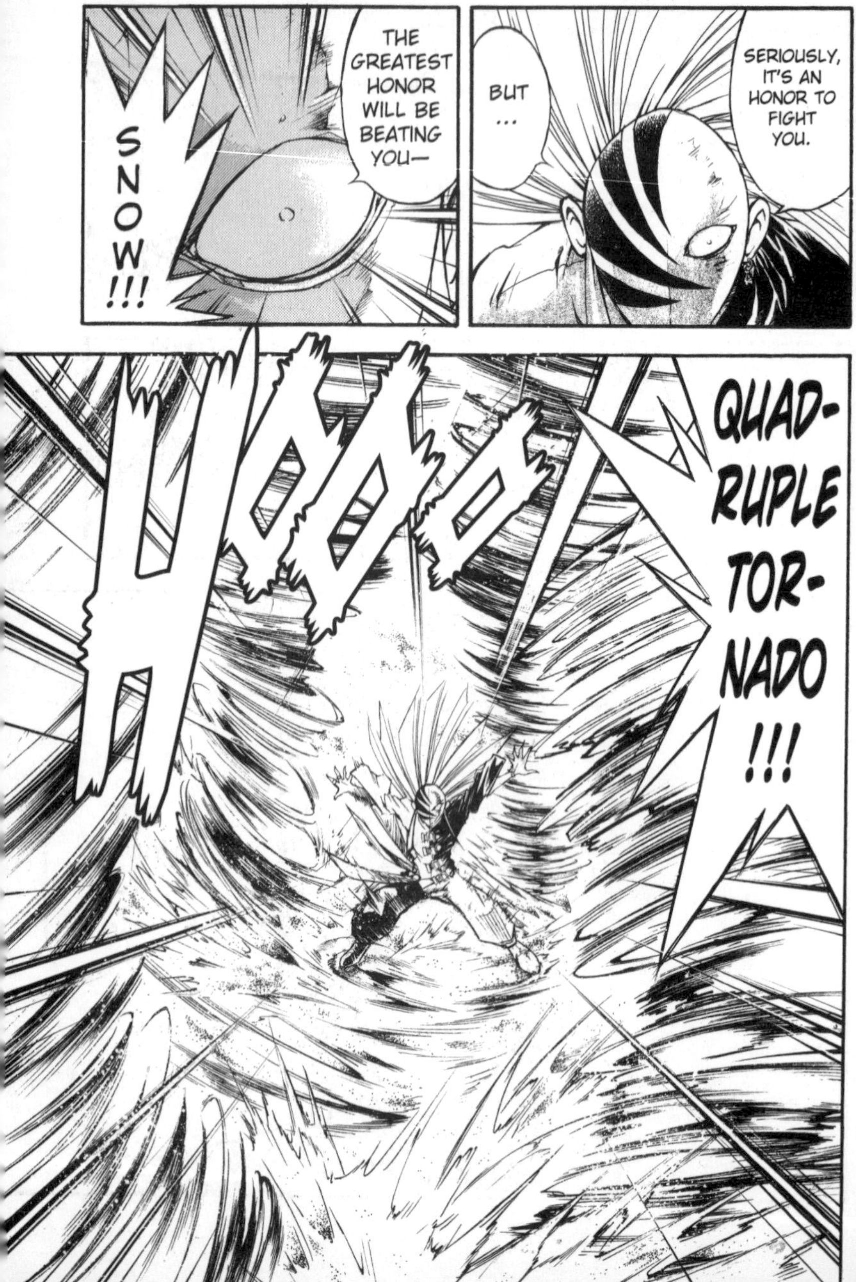
SERIOUSLY, IT'S AN HONOR TO FIGHT YOU.
BUT ...
THE GREATEST HONOR WILL BE BEATING YOU—
SNOW!!!
QUAD-RUPLE TOR-NADO!!!

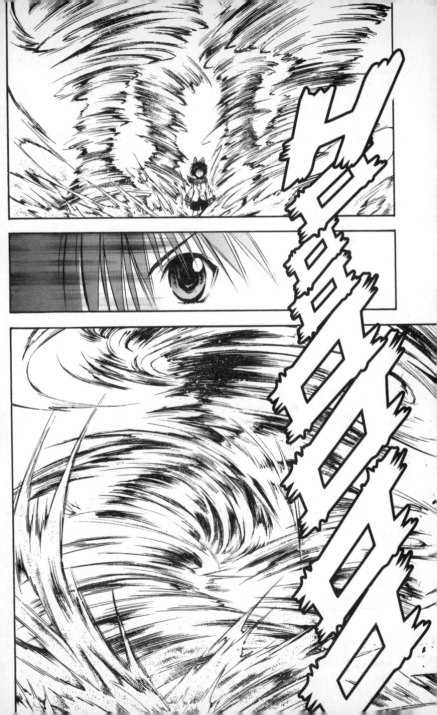

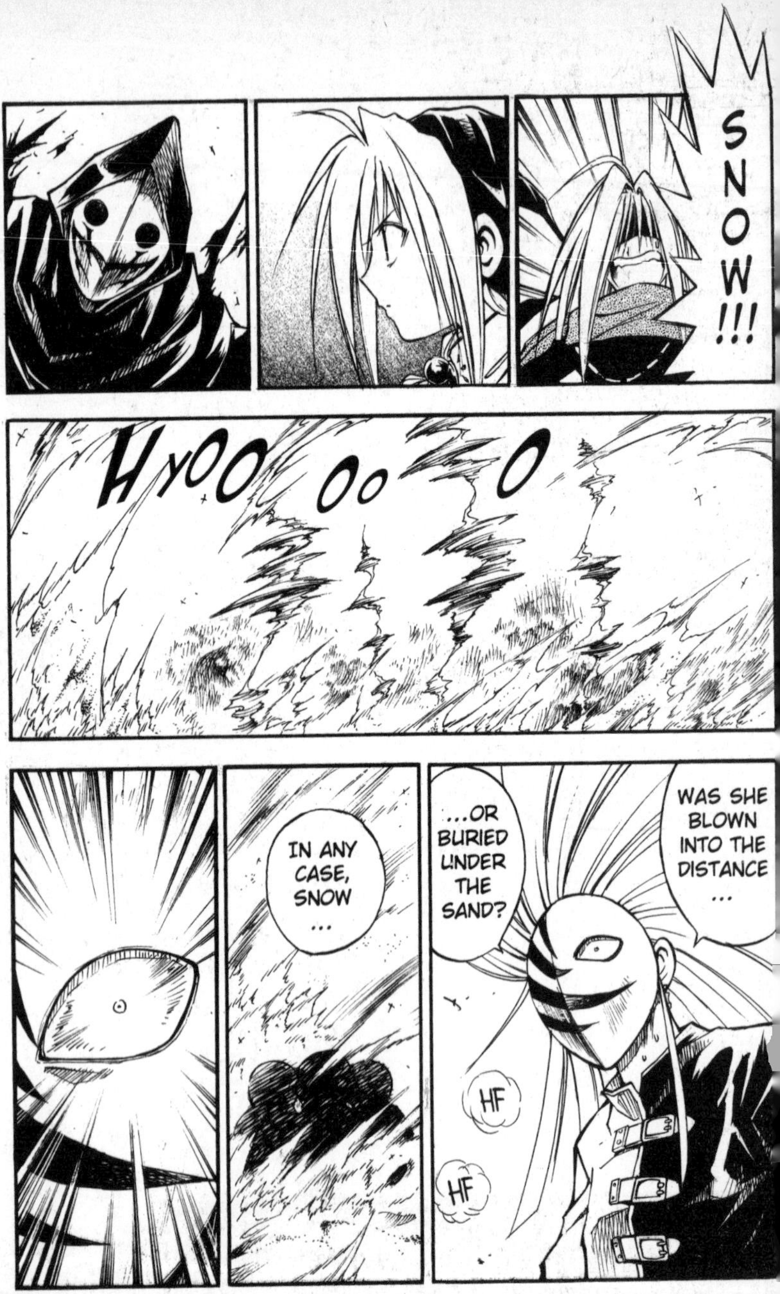
SNOW!!!
HYOOO OO O
WAS SHE BLOWN INTO THE DISTANCE...
...OR BURIED UNDER THE SAND?
HF
HF
IN ANY CASE, SNOW...

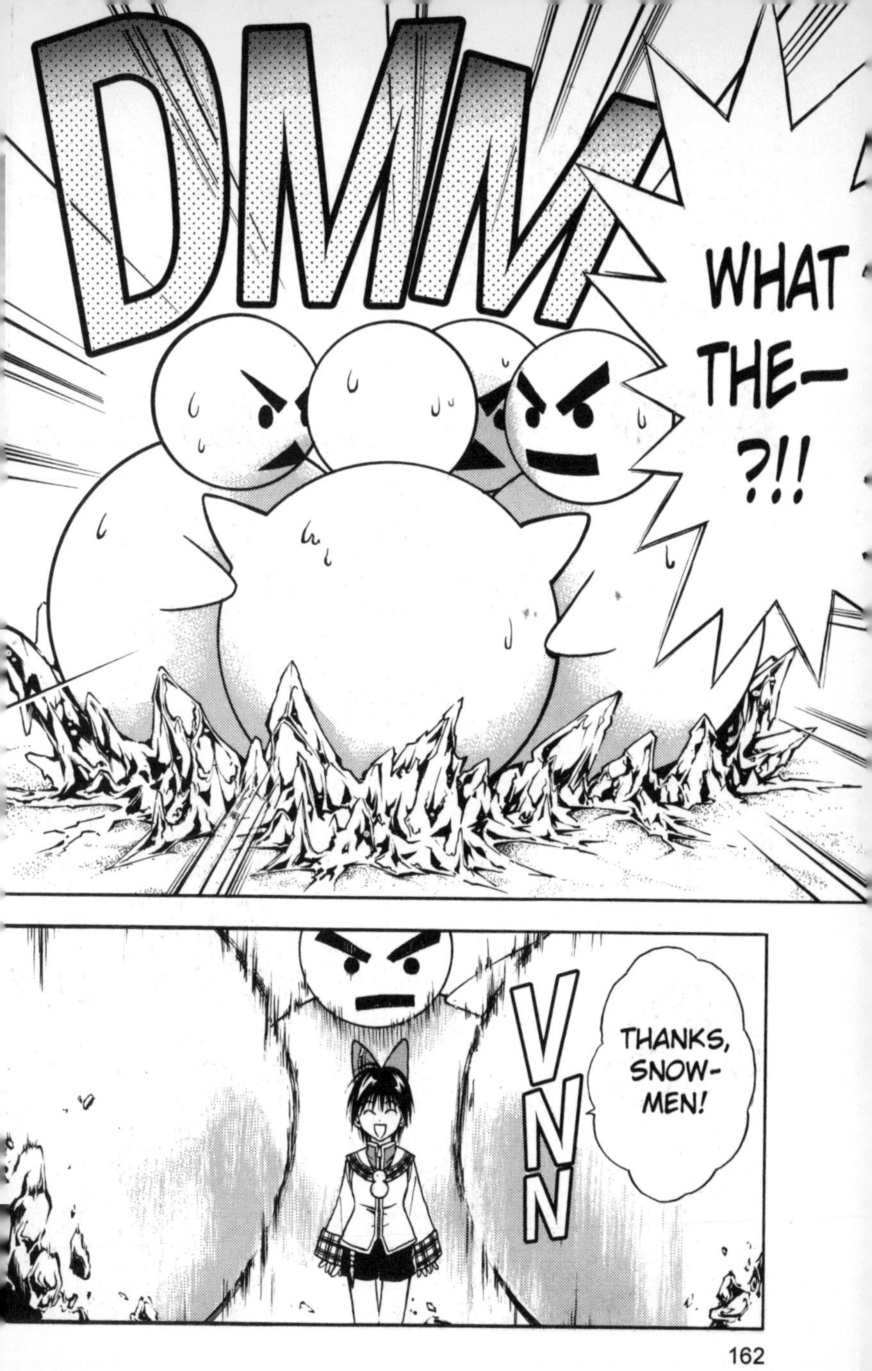
DMM
WHAT THE—?!!
VNN
THANKS, SNOW-MEN!

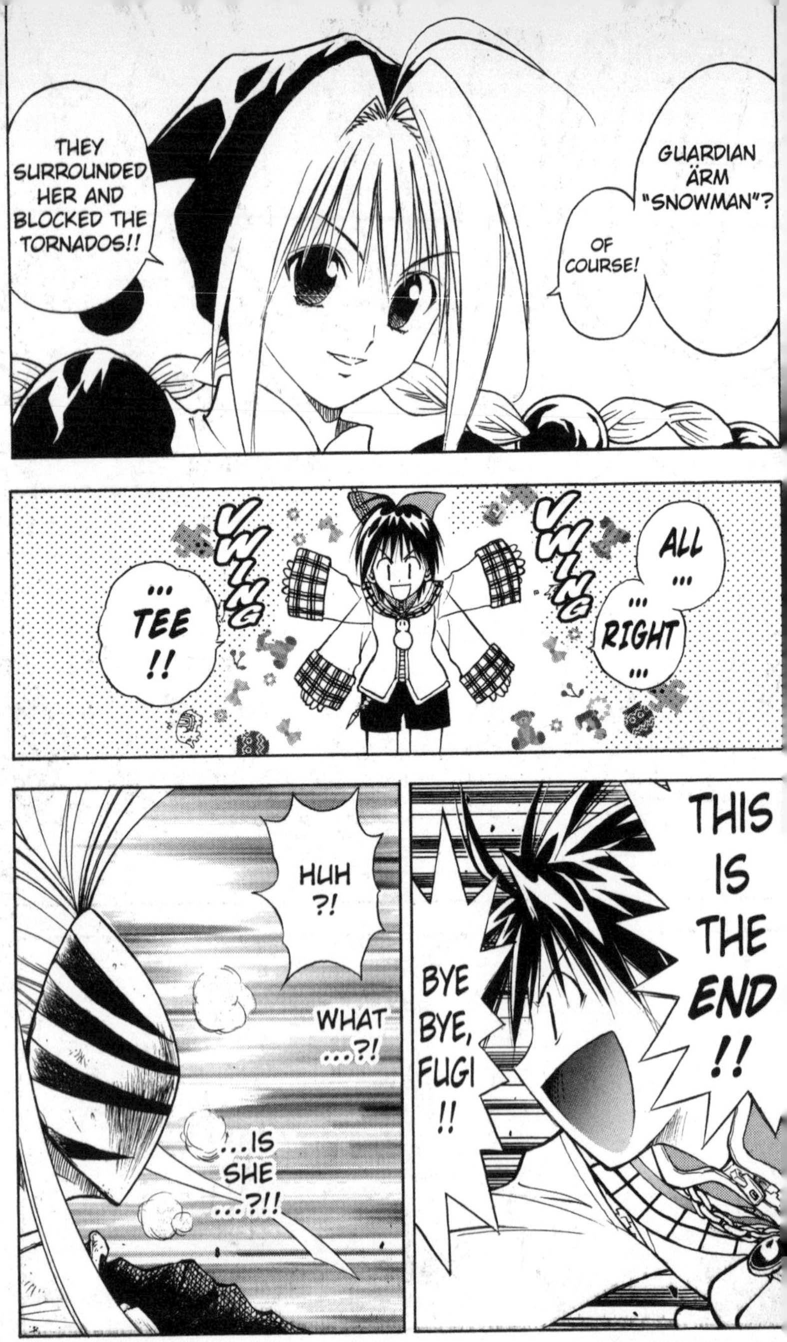
GUARDIAN ÄRM "SNOWMAN"?
OF COURSE!
THEY SURROUNDED HER AND BLOCKED THE TORNADOS!!
ALL ... ... RIGHT ...
VWING
VWING
... TEE !!
THIS IS THE END!!
BYE BYE, FUGI!!
HUH ?!
WHAT ...?!
...IS SHE ...?!!

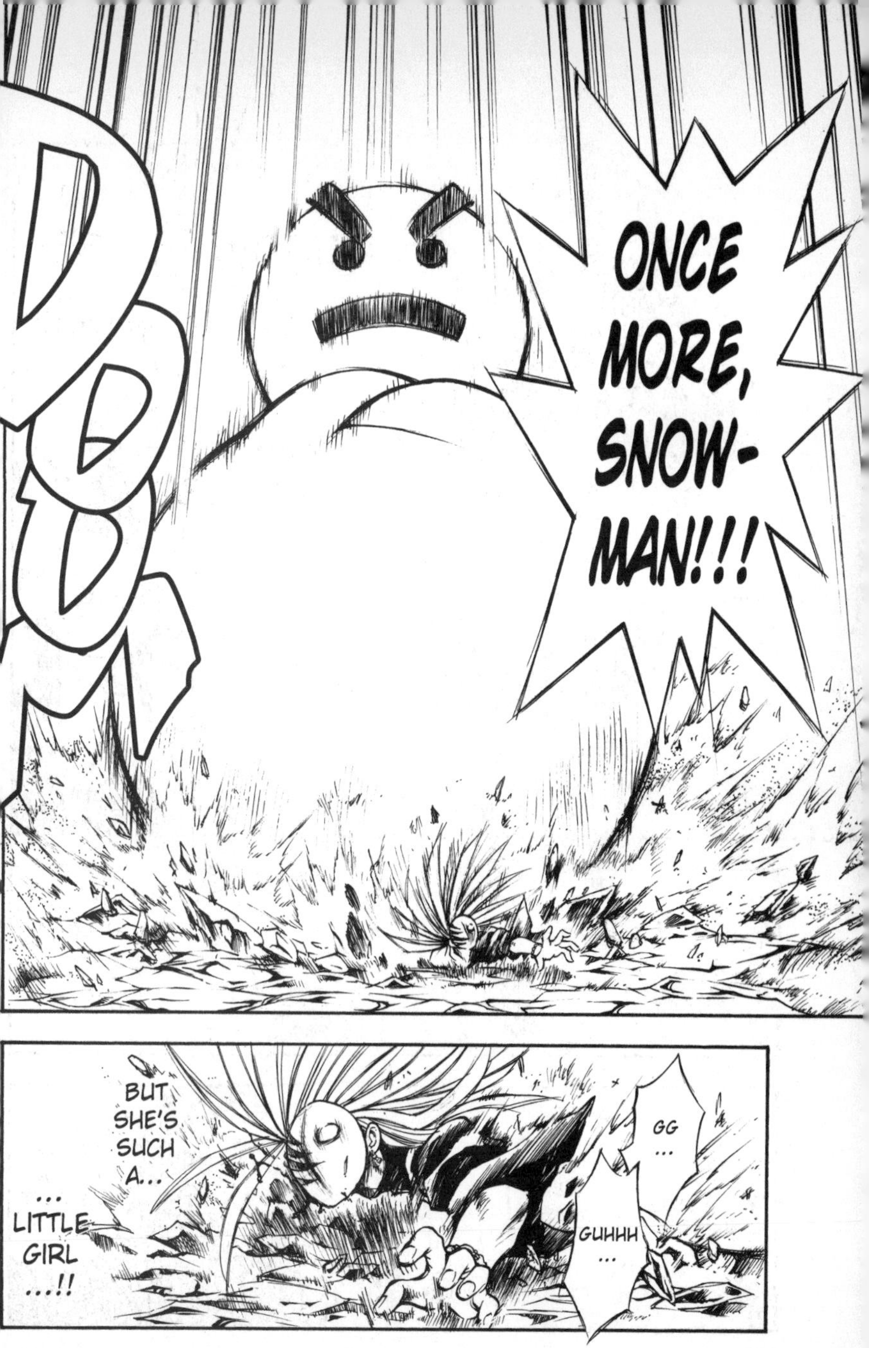
ONCE MORE, SNOWMAN!!!
GG ...
GUHHH ...
BUT SHE'S SUCH A...
... LITTLE GIRL ...!!

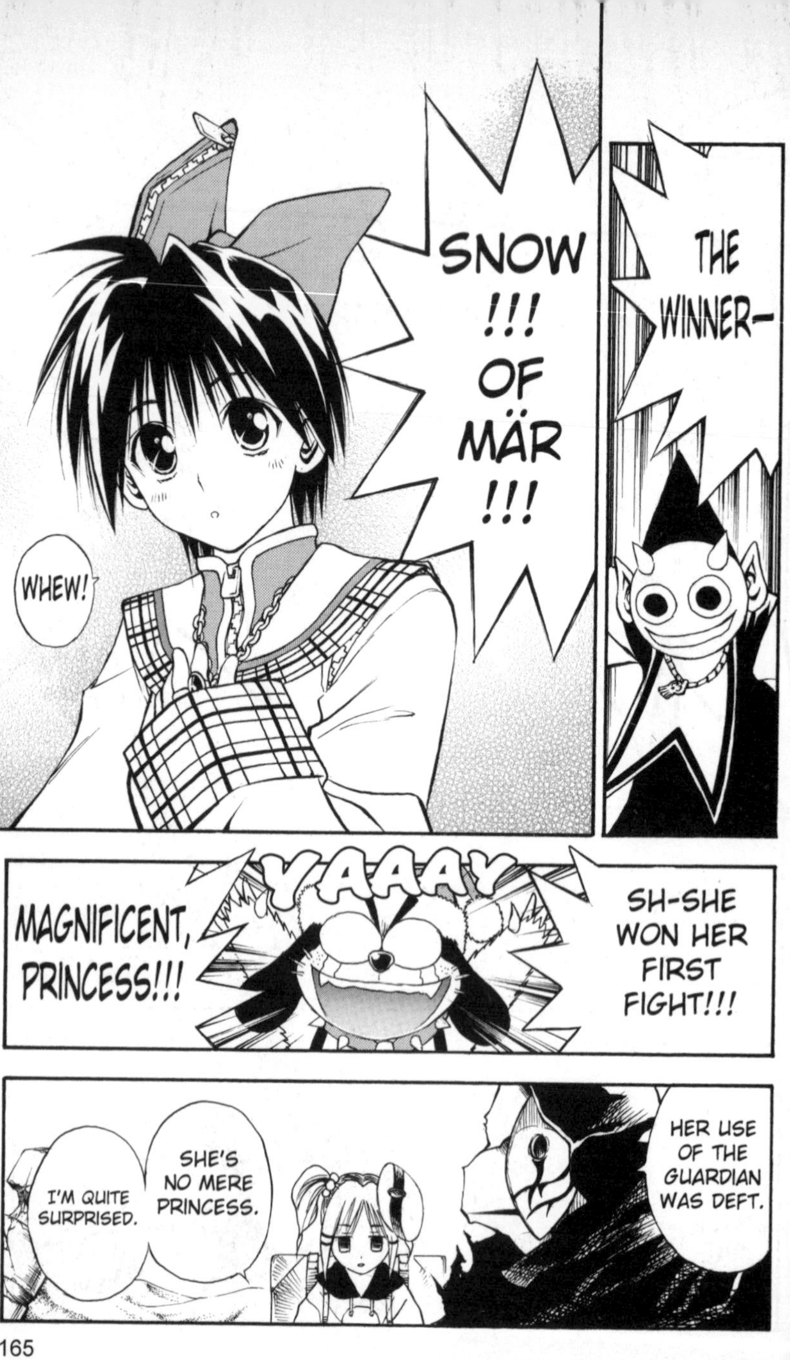
THE WINNER—
SNOW!!! OF MÄR!!!
WHEW!
SH-SHE WON HER FIRST FIGHT!!!
YAAAY
MAGNIFICENT, PRINCESS!!!
HER USE OF THE GUARDIAN WAS DEFT.
SHE'S NO MERE PRINCESS.
I'M QUITE SURPRISED.

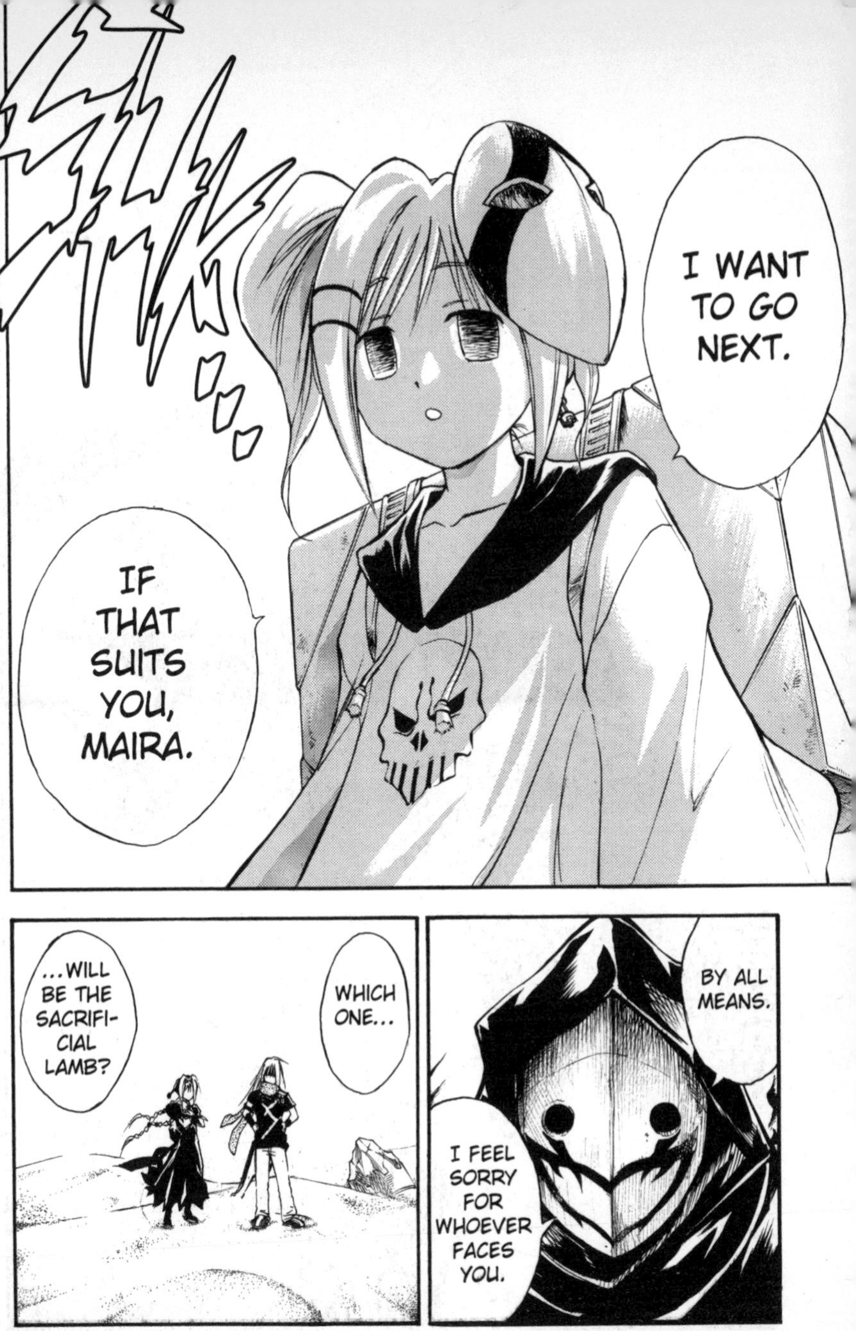
I WANT TO GO NEXT.
IF THAT SUITS YOU, MAIRA.
BY ALL MEANS.
I FEEL SORRY FOR WHOEVER FACES YOU.
WHICH ONE...
...WILL BE THE SACRIFICIAL LAMB?

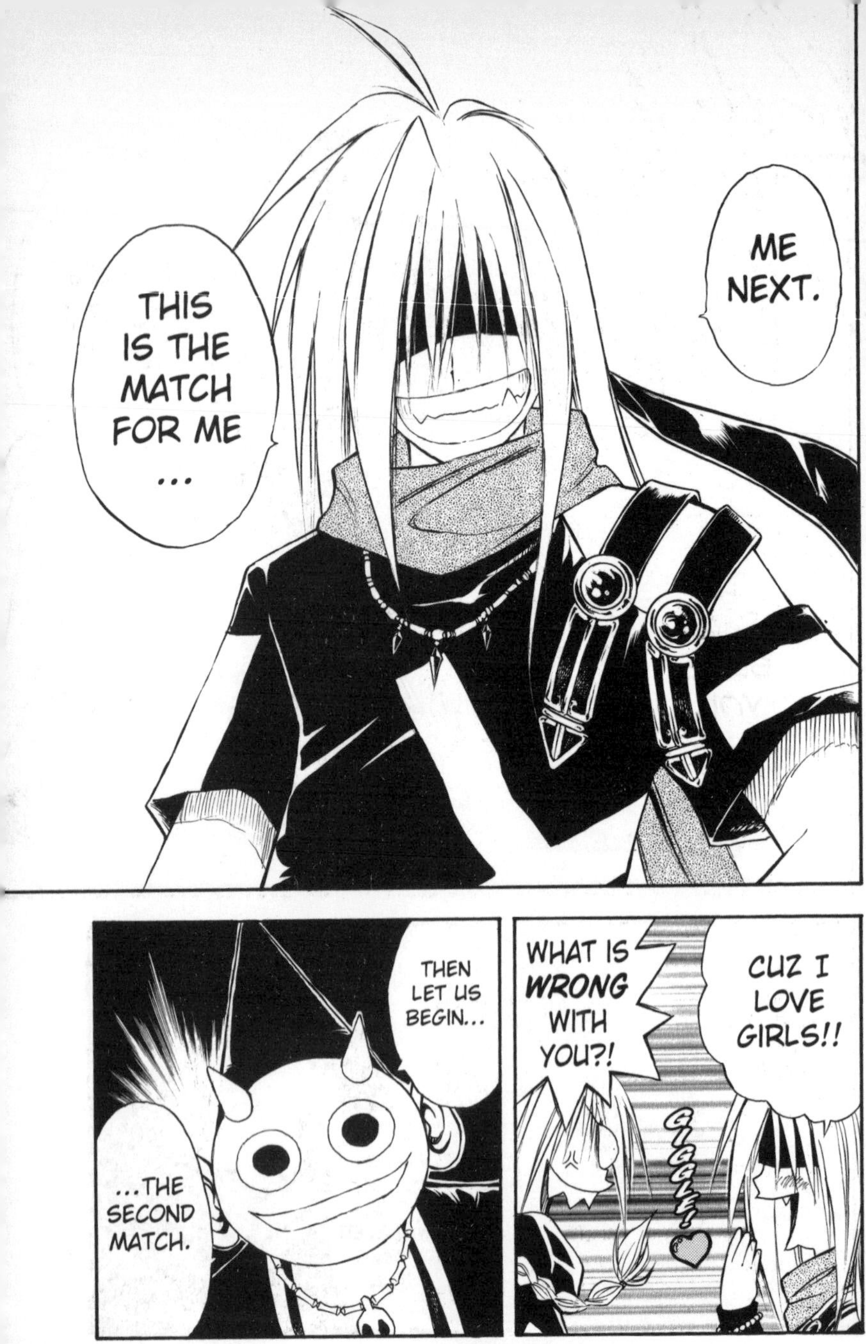
ME NEXT.
THIS IS THE MATCH FOR ME ...
CUZ I LOVE GIRLS!!
WHAT IS WRONG WITH YOU?!
GIGGLE!
THEN LET US BEGIN...
...THE SECOND MATCH.

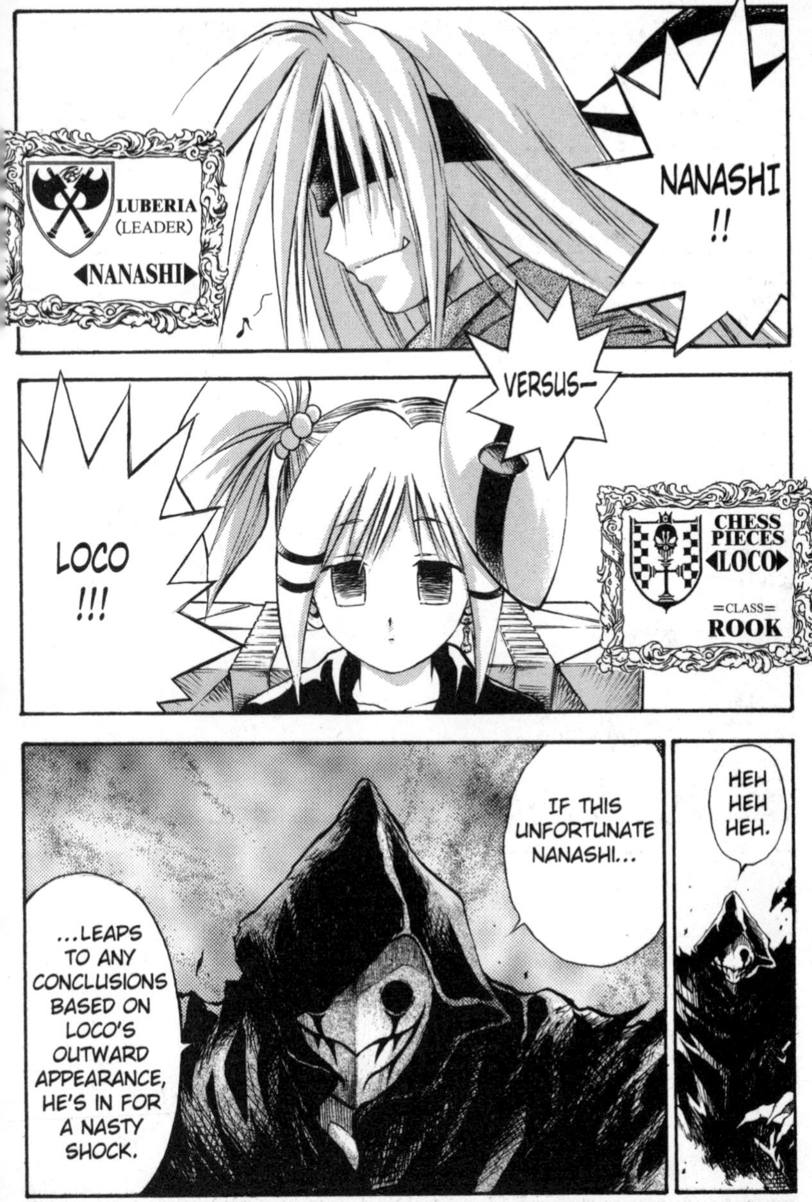
NANASHI !!
LUBERIA (LEADER)
NANASHI
VERSUS—
CHESS PIECES
LOCO
=CLASS=
ROOK
LOCO !!!
HEH HEH HEH.
IF THIS UNFORTUNATE NANASHI...
...LEAPS TO ANY CONCLUSIONS BASED ON LOCO'S OUTWARD APPEARANCE, HE'S IN FOR A NASTY SHOCK.

AKT.52/ Nanashi v.s. Loco

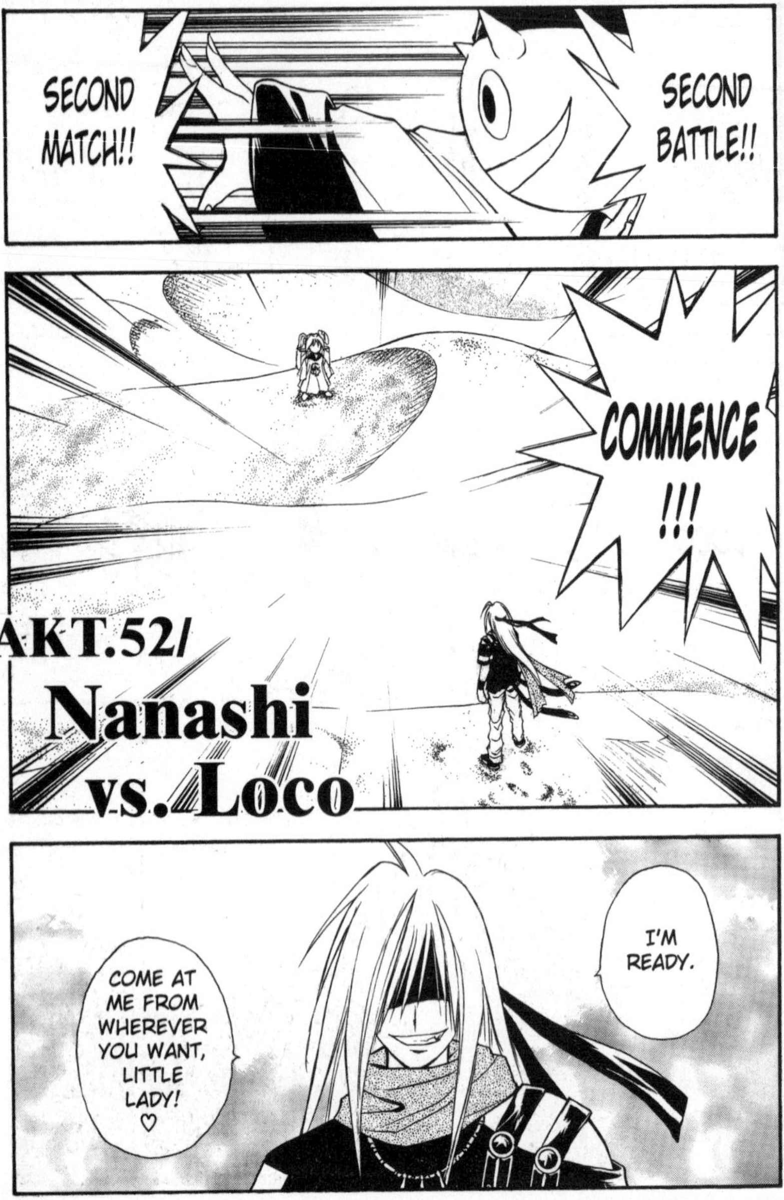
SECOND BATTLE!!
SECOND MATCH!!
COMMENCE!!!
I'M READY.
COME AT ME FROM WHEREVER YOU WANT, LITTLE LADY! ♡

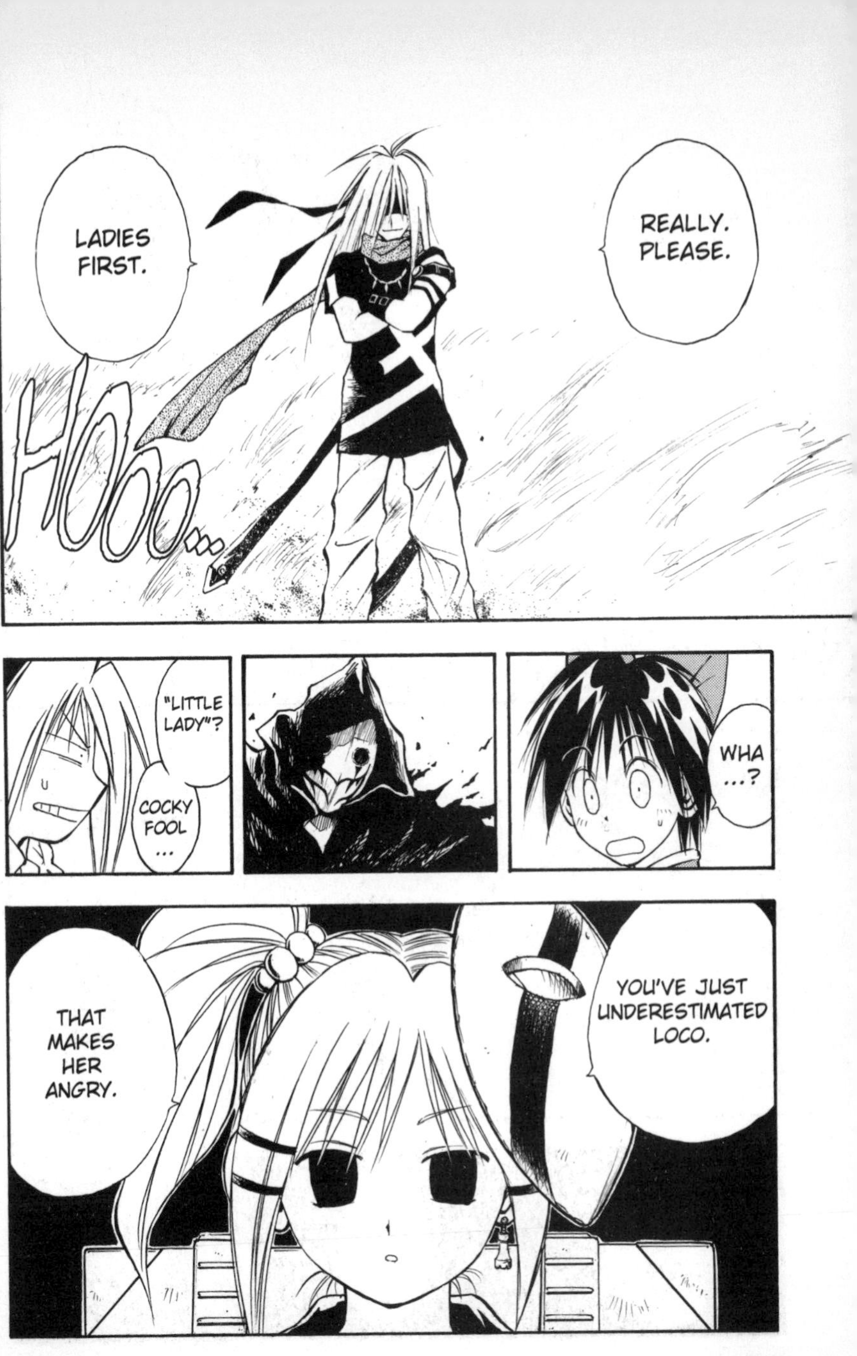
REALLY. PLEASE.
LADIES FIRST.
HOOO...
WHA ...?
"LITTLE LADY"?
COCKY FOOL ...
YOU'VE JUST UNDERESTIMATED LOCO.
THAT MAKES HER ANGRY.

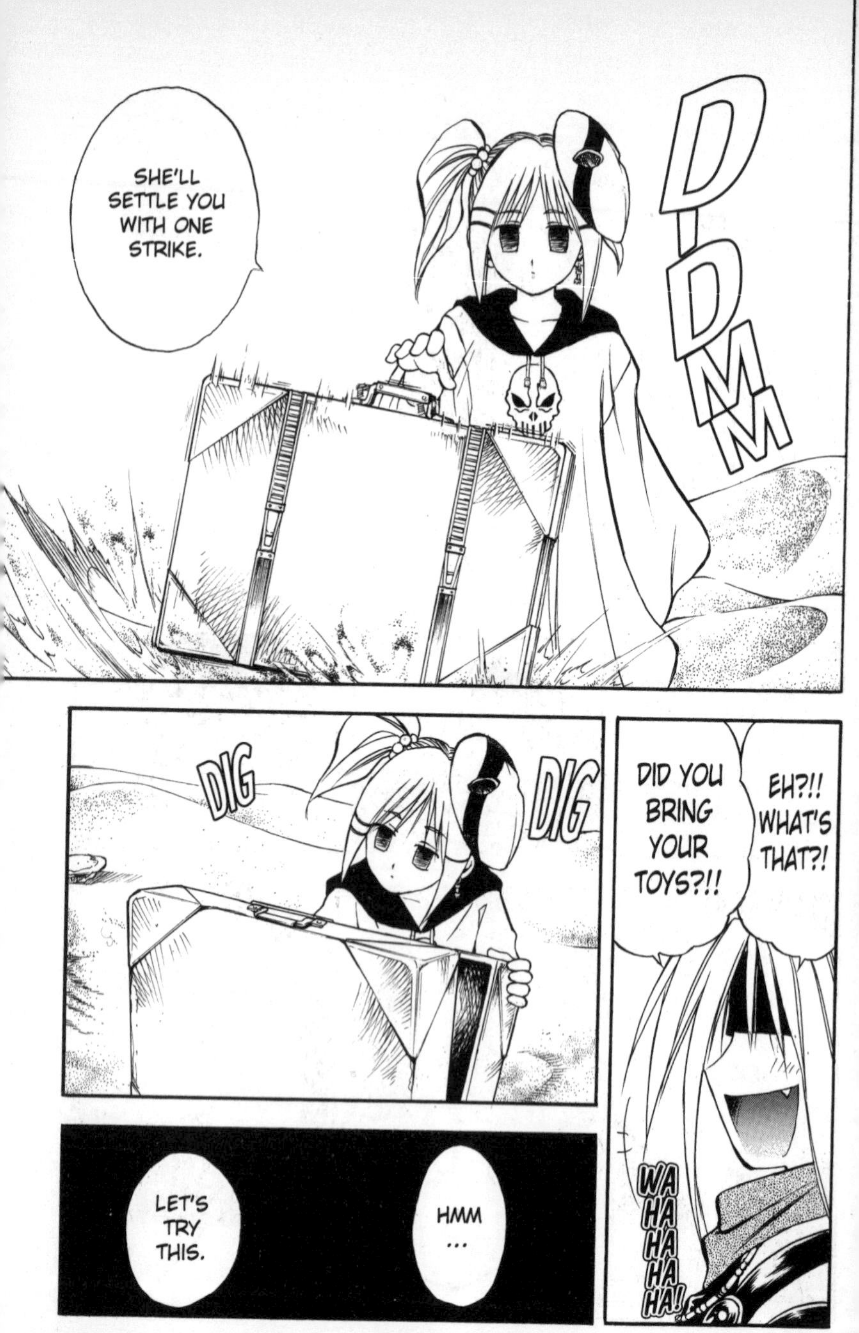
DDMM
SHE'LL SETTLE YOU WITH ONE STRIKE.
EH?!! WHAT'S THAT?!
DID YOU BRING YOUR TOYS?!!
WAHAHAHAHA!
DIG DIG
HMM...
LET'S TRY THIS.

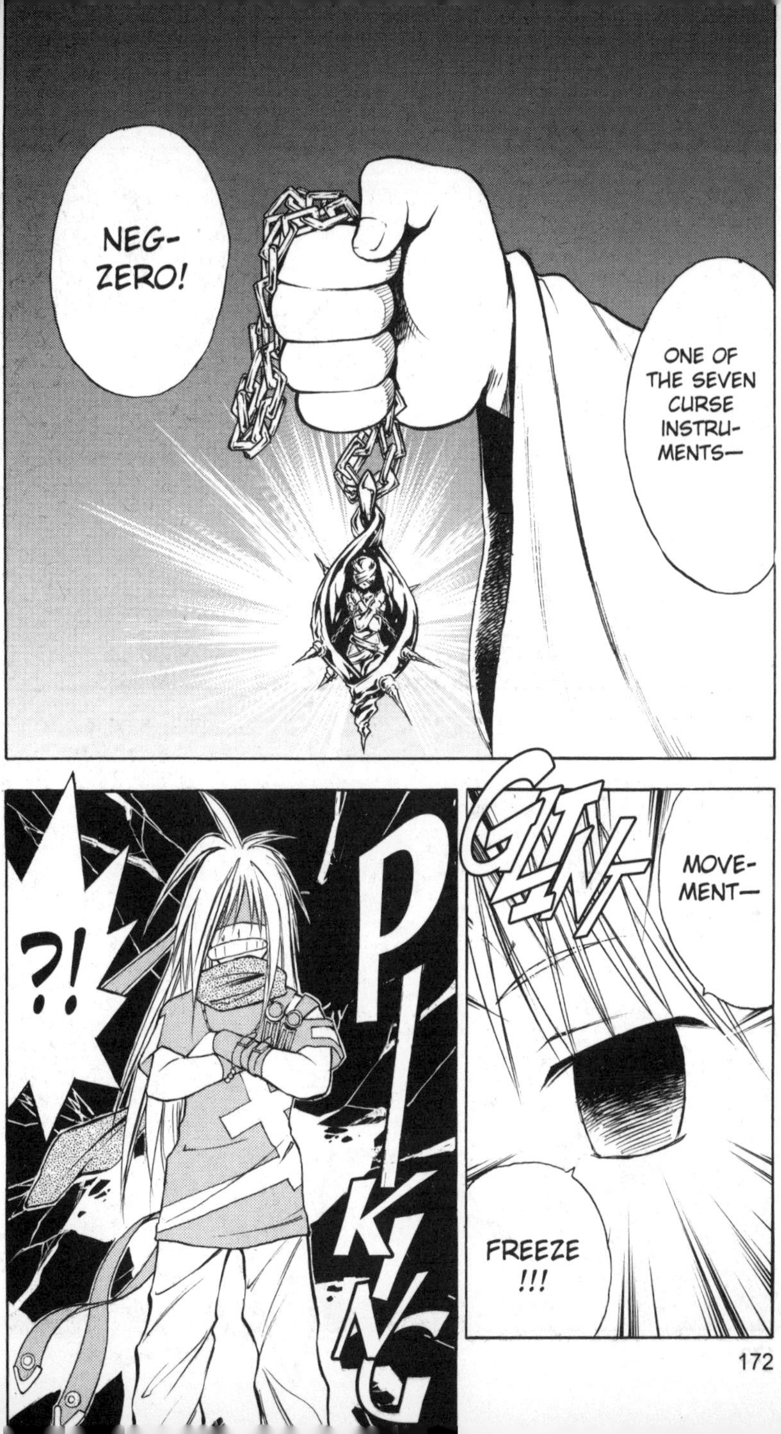
ONE OF THE SEVEN CURSE INSTRUMENTS—
NEG-ZERO!
GIN
MOVEMENT—
FREEZE !!!
PI KING
?!

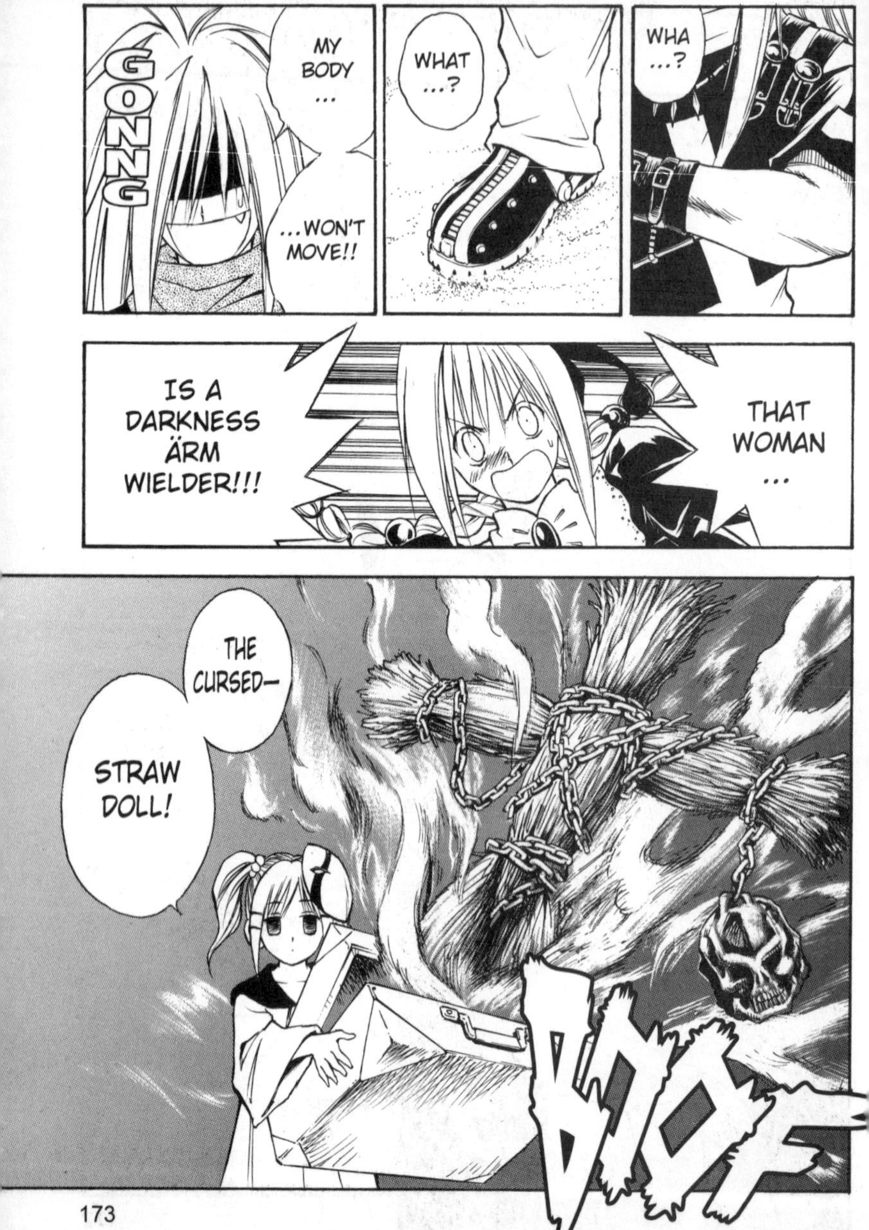
WHA ...?
WHAT ...?
MY BODY ...
...WON'T MOVE!!
GONNG
THAT WOMAN ...
IS A DARKNESS ÄRM WIELDER!!!
THE CURSED—
STRAW DOLL!

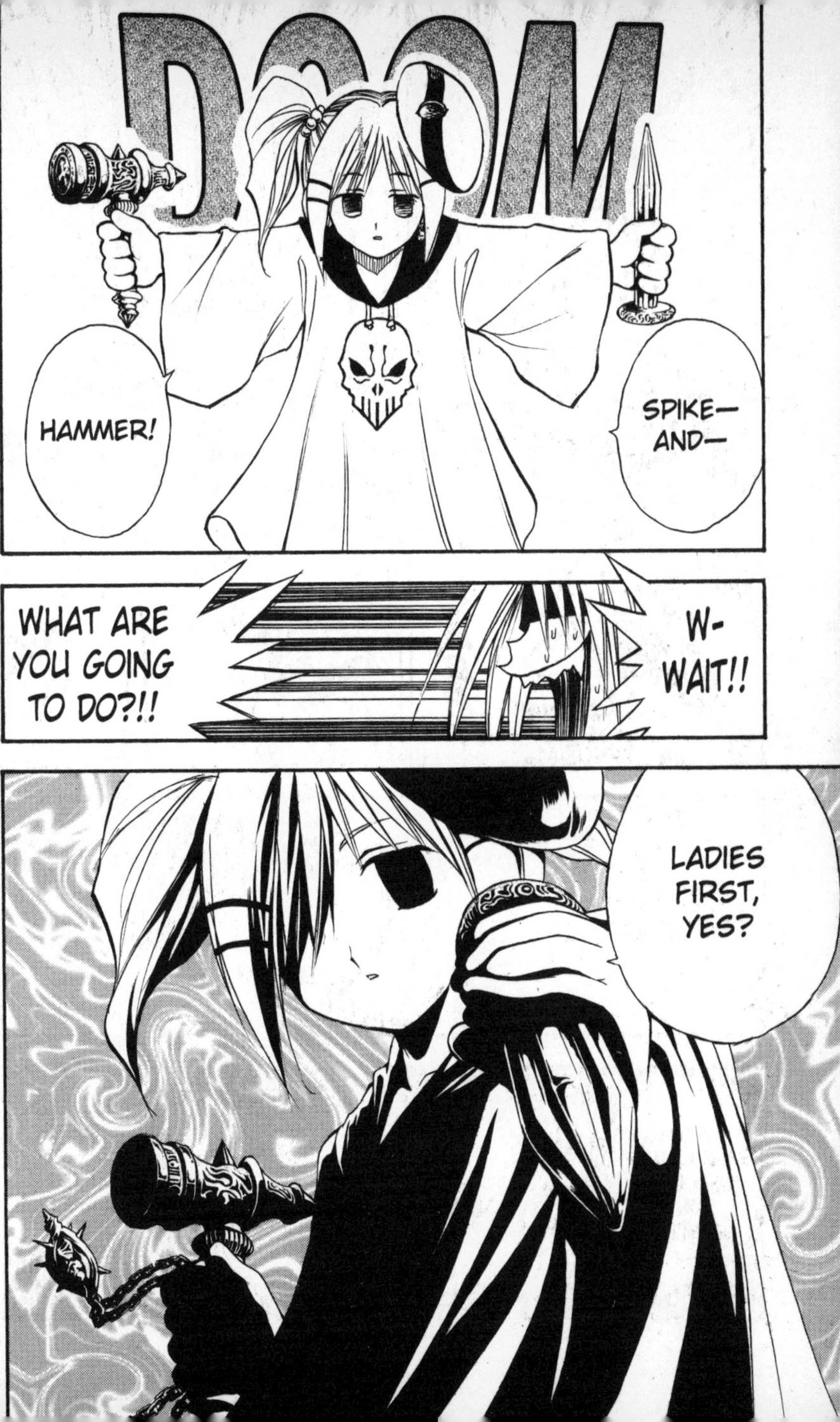
DOOM
SPIKE— AND—
HAMMER!
W- WAIT!!
WHAT ARE YOU GOING TO DO?!!
LADIES FIRST, YES?

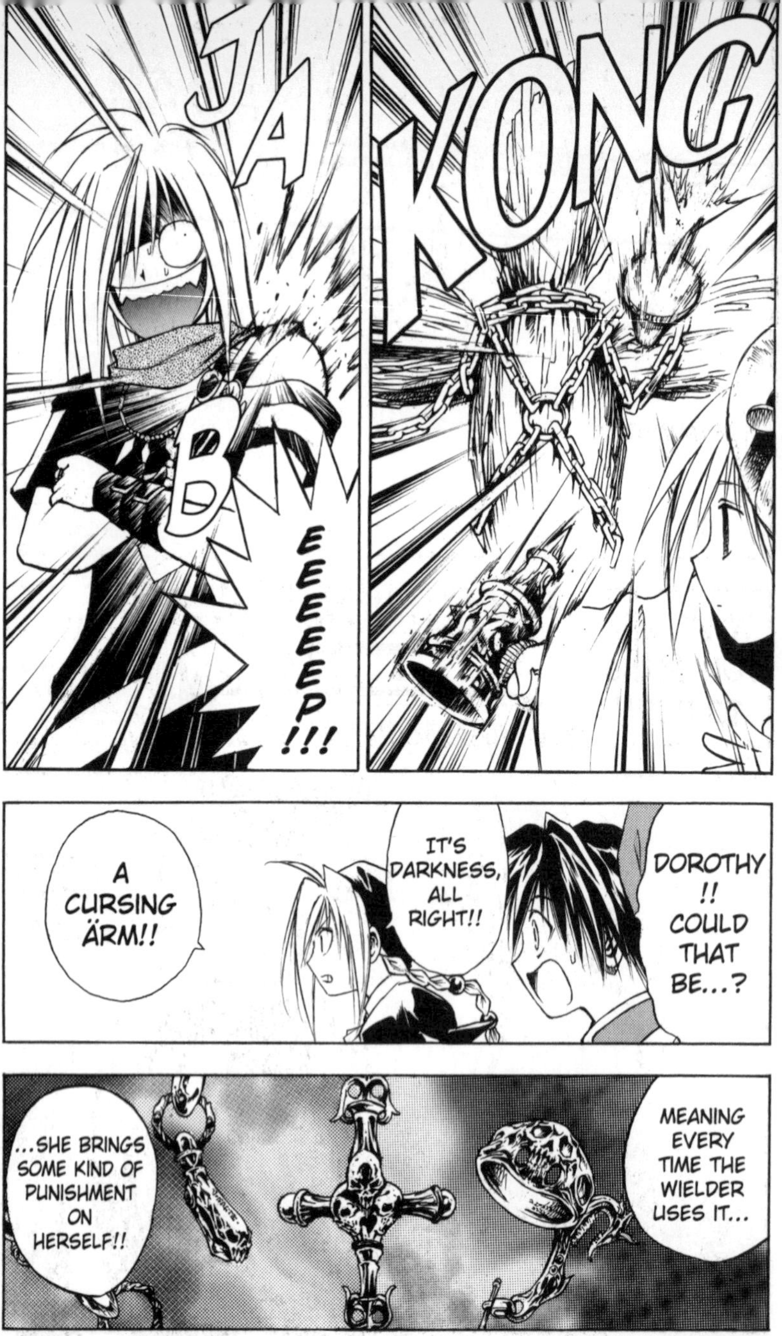
JAKONG
BEEEEEEEP!!!
DOROTHY!! COULD THAT BE...?
IT'S DARKNESS, ALL RIGHT!!
A CURSING ÄRM!!
MEANING EVERY TIME THE WIELDER USES IT...
...SHE BRINGS SOME KIND OF PUNISHMENT ON HERSELF!!

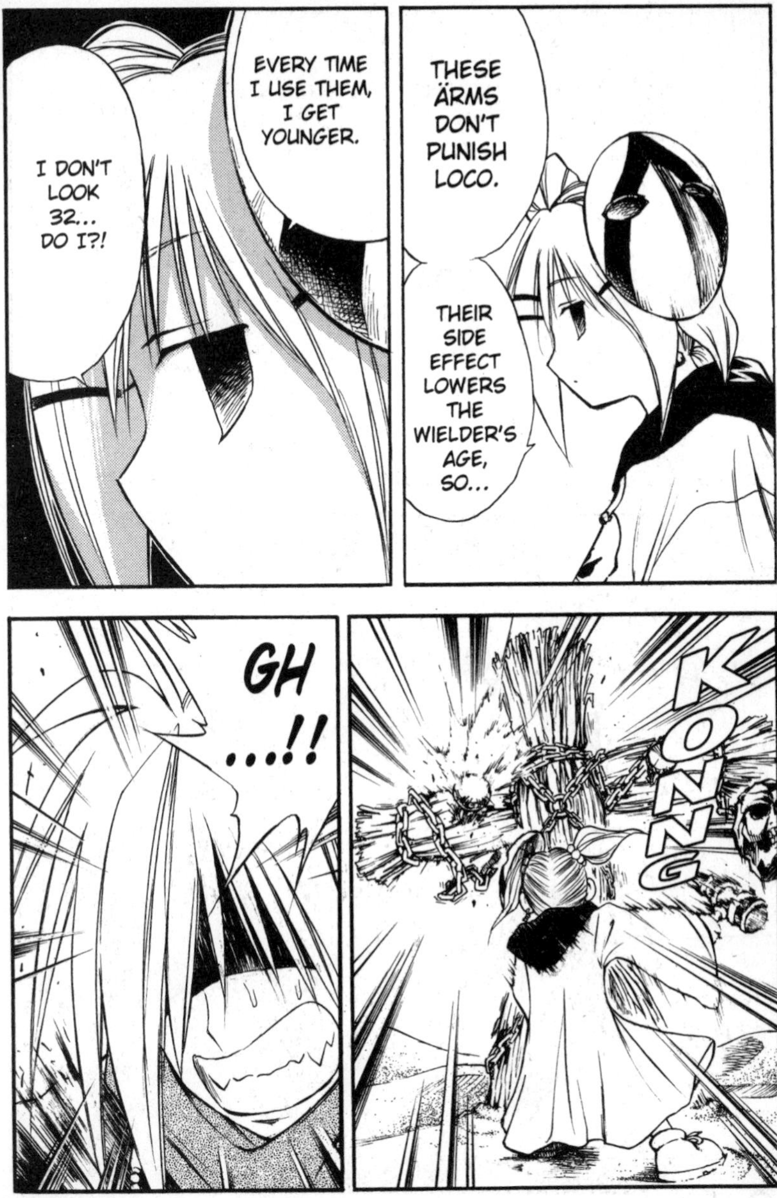
THESE ÄRMS DON'T PUNISH LOCO.
THEIR SIDE EFFECT LOWERS THE WIELDER'S AGE, SO...
EVERY TIME I USE THEM, I GET YOUNGER.
I DON'T LOOK 32... DO I?!
KONNG
GH ...!!

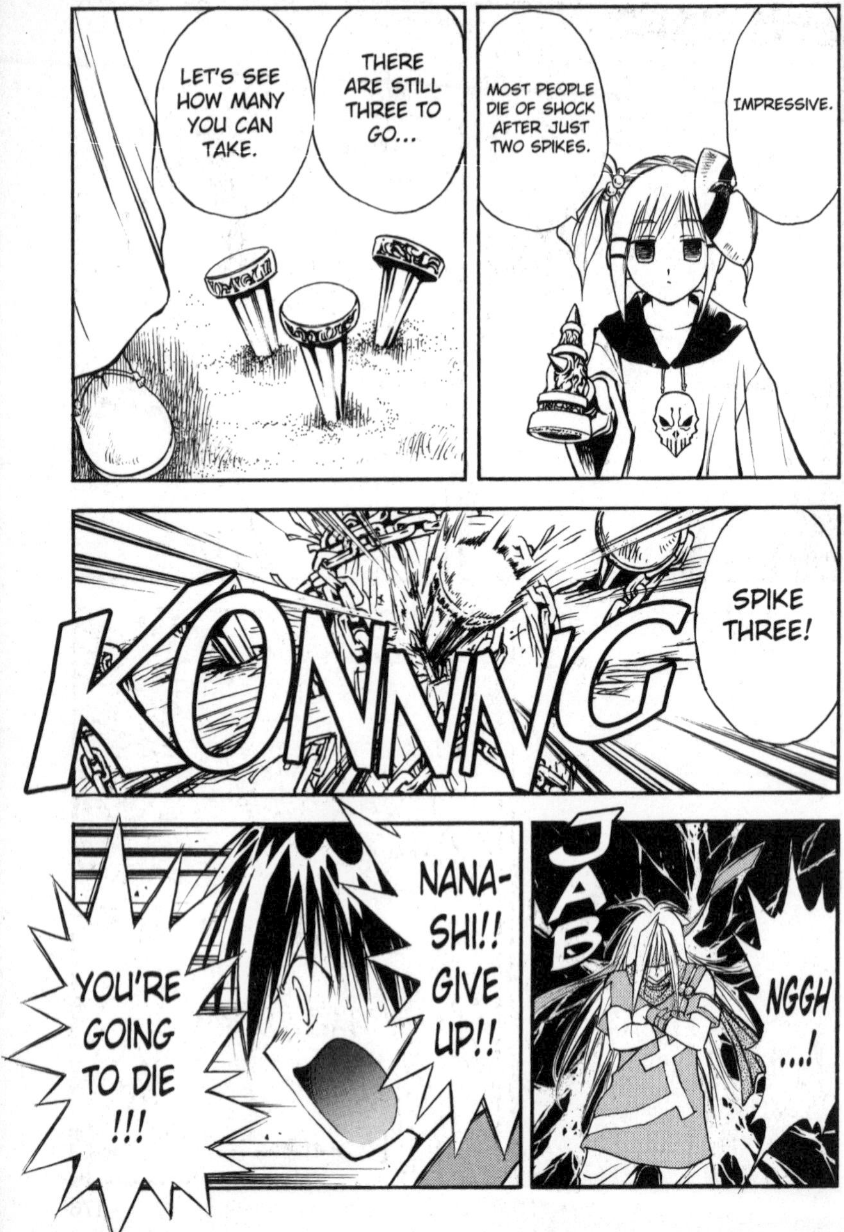
IMPRESSIVE.
MOST PEOPLE DIE OF SHOCK AFTER JUST TWO SPIKES.
THERE ARE STILL THREE TO GO...
LET'S SEE HOW MANY YOU CAN TAKE.
SPIKE THREE!
KONNNG
JAB
NGGH ...!
NANA-SHI!! GIVE UP!!
YOU'RE GOING TO DIE !!!

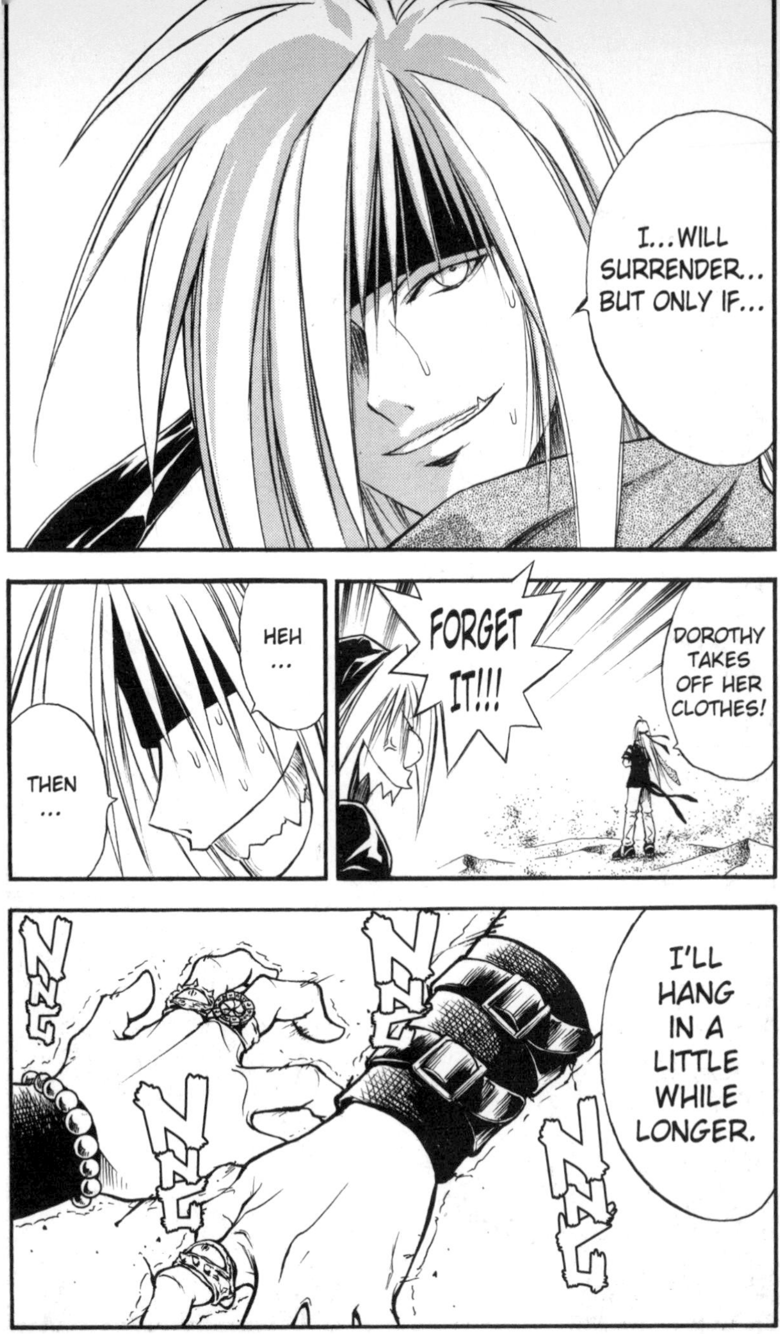
I...WILL SURRENDER... BUT ONLY IF...
DOROTHY TAKES OFF HER CLOTHES!
FORGET IT!!!
HEH ...
THEN ...
I'LL HANG IN A LITTLE WHILE LONGER.
NNG
NNG
NNG
NNG
NNG

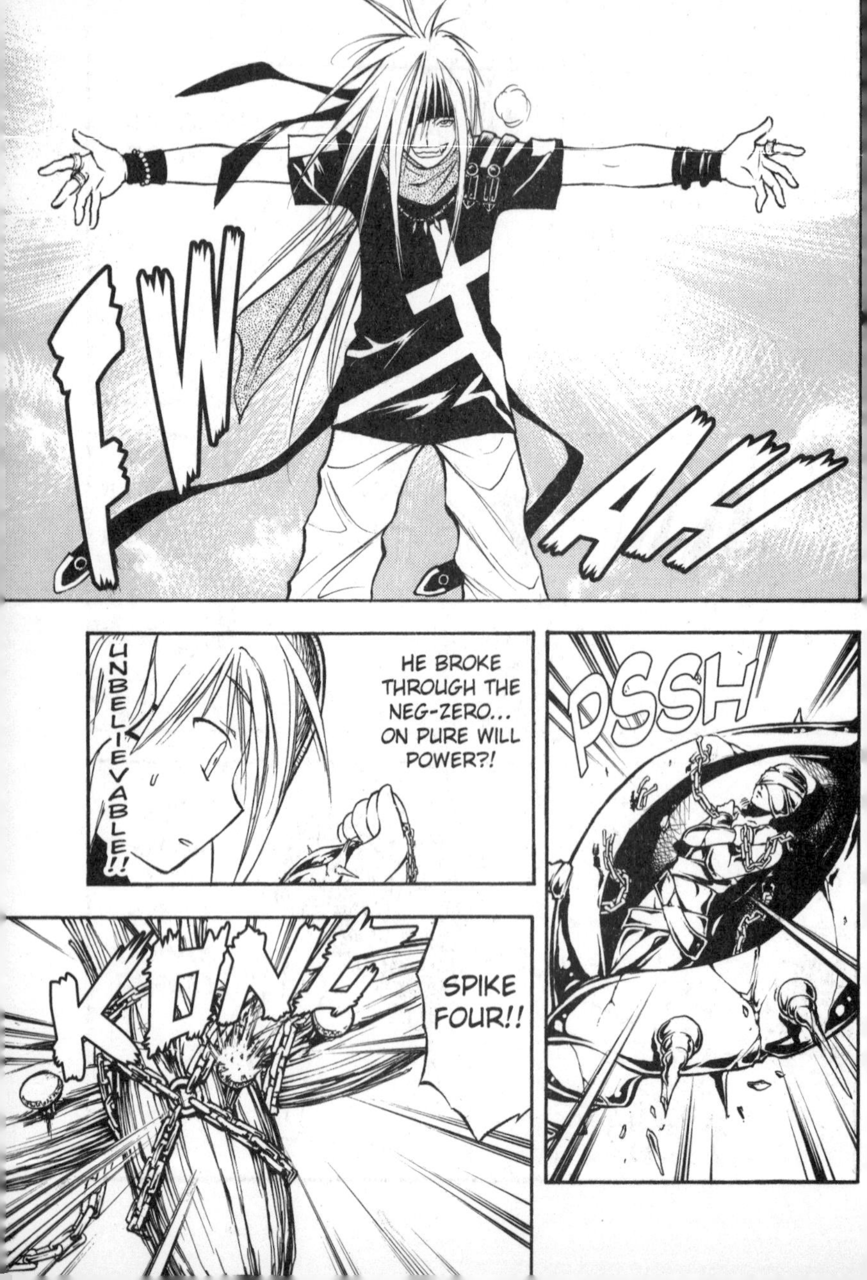
FWAH
PSSH
HE BROKE THROUGH THE NEG-ZERO... ON PURE WILL POWER?!
UNBELIEVABLE!!
SPIKE FOUR!!
KONG

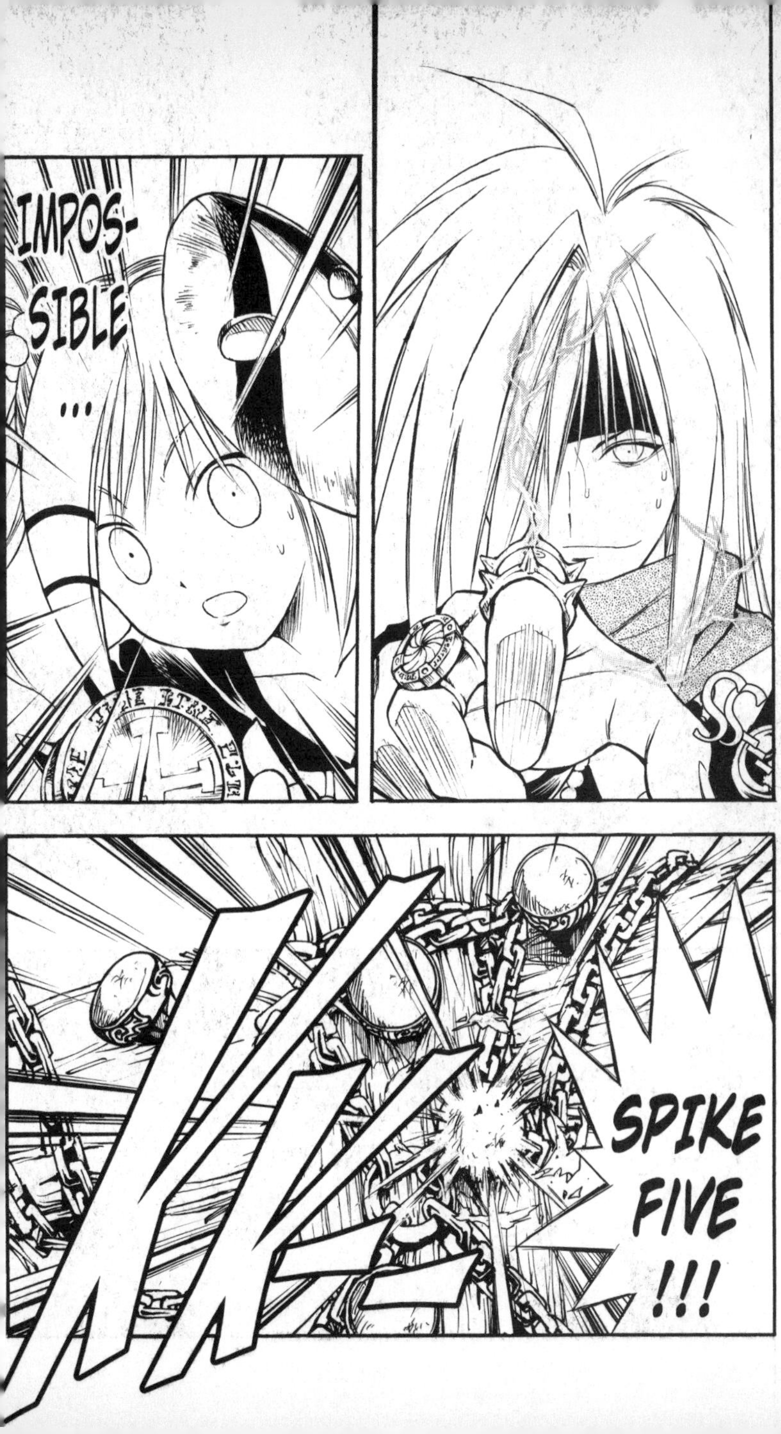
IMPOS-SIBLE ...
SPIKE FIVE !!!

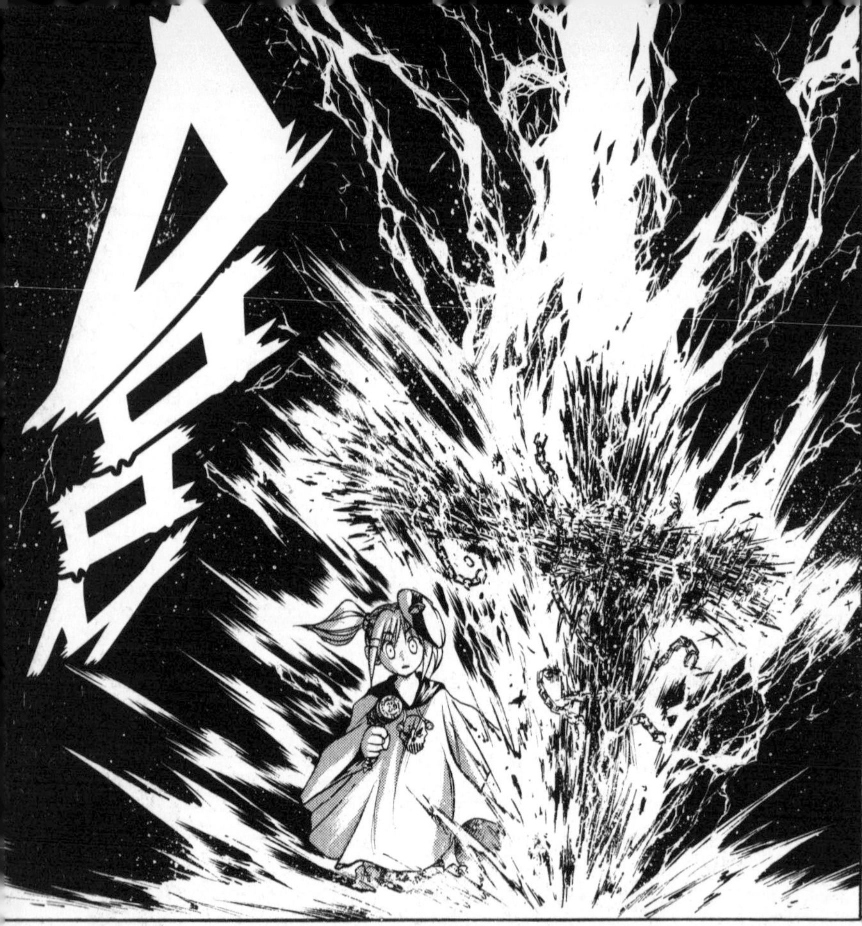

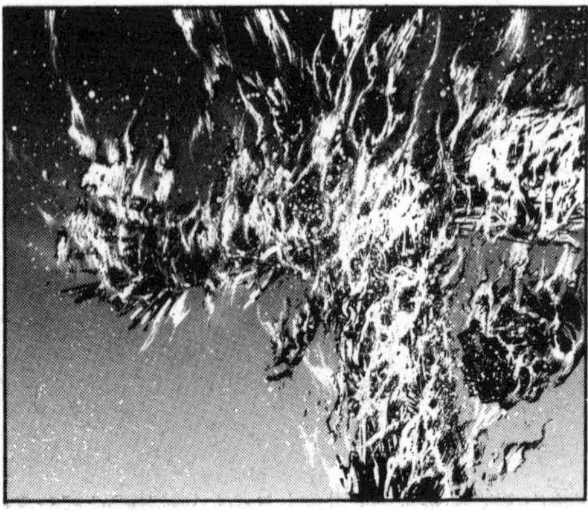

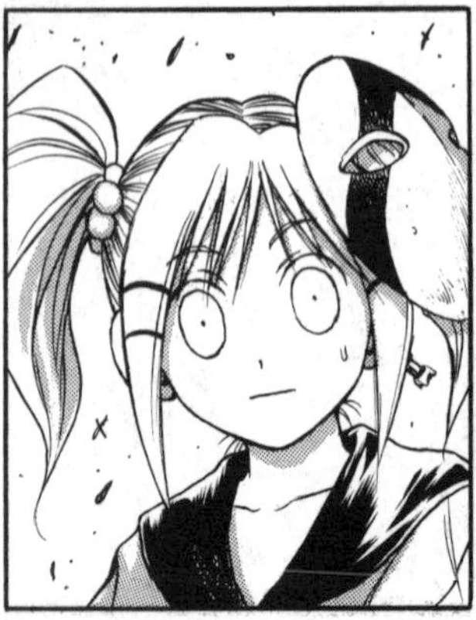

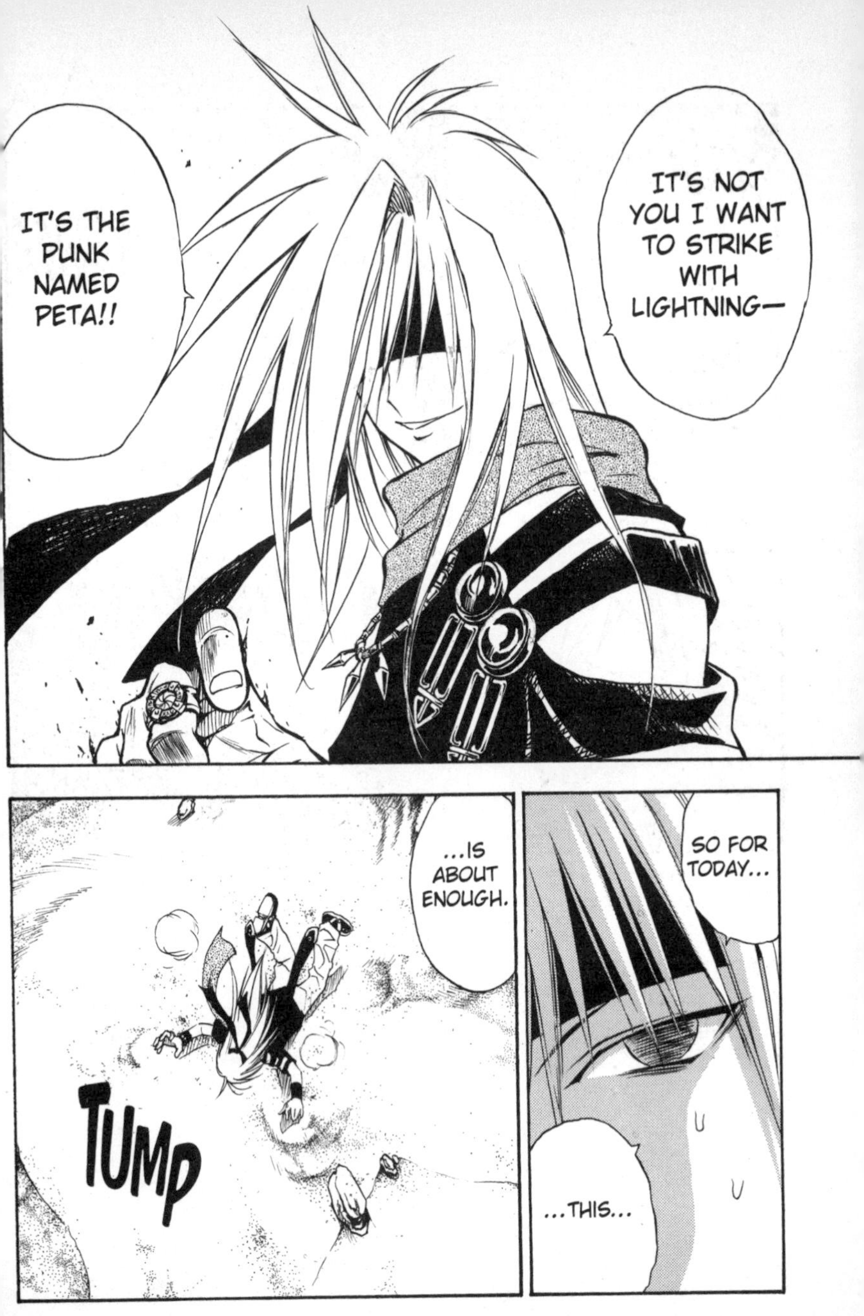
IT'S NOT YOU I WANT TO STRIKE WITH LIGHTNING—
IT'S THE PUNK NAMED PETA!!
SO FOR TODAY...
...THIS...
...IS ABOUT ENOUGH.
TUMP

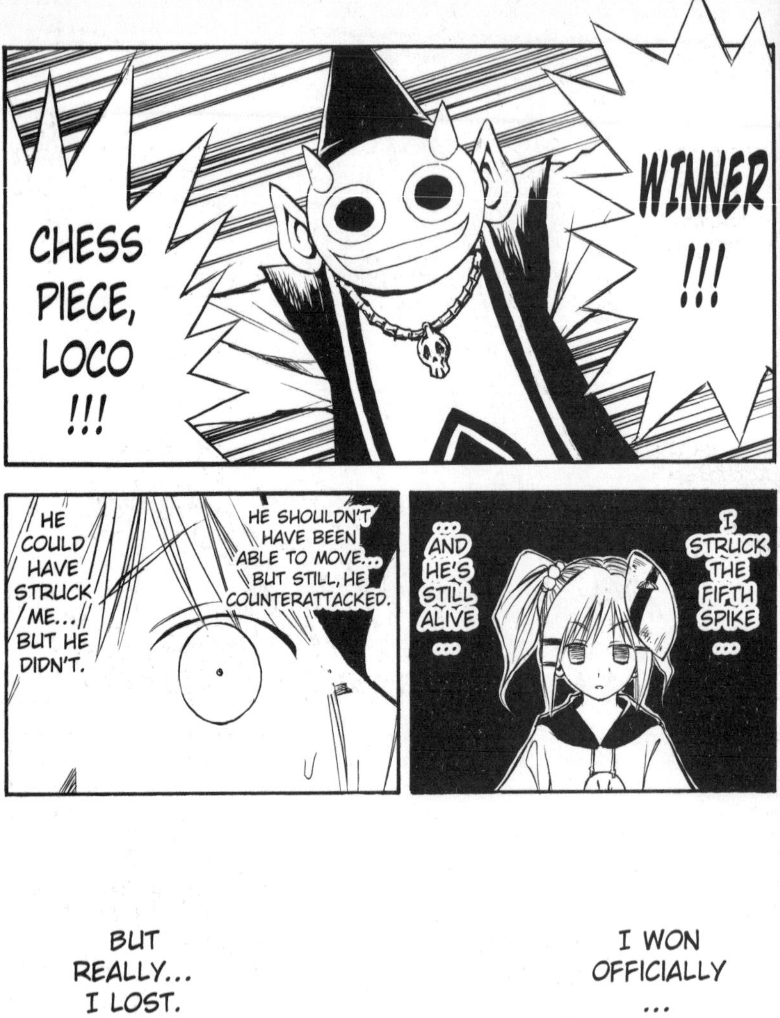
WINNER !!!
CHESS PIECE, LOCO !!!
I STRUCK THE FIFTH SPIKE ...
...AND HE'S STILL ALIVE ...
HE SHOULDN'T HAVE BEEN ABLE TO MOVE... BUT STILL, HE COUNTERATTACKED.
HE COULD HAVE STRUCK ME... BUT HE DIDN'T.
I WON OFFICIALLY ...
BUT REALLY... I LOST.

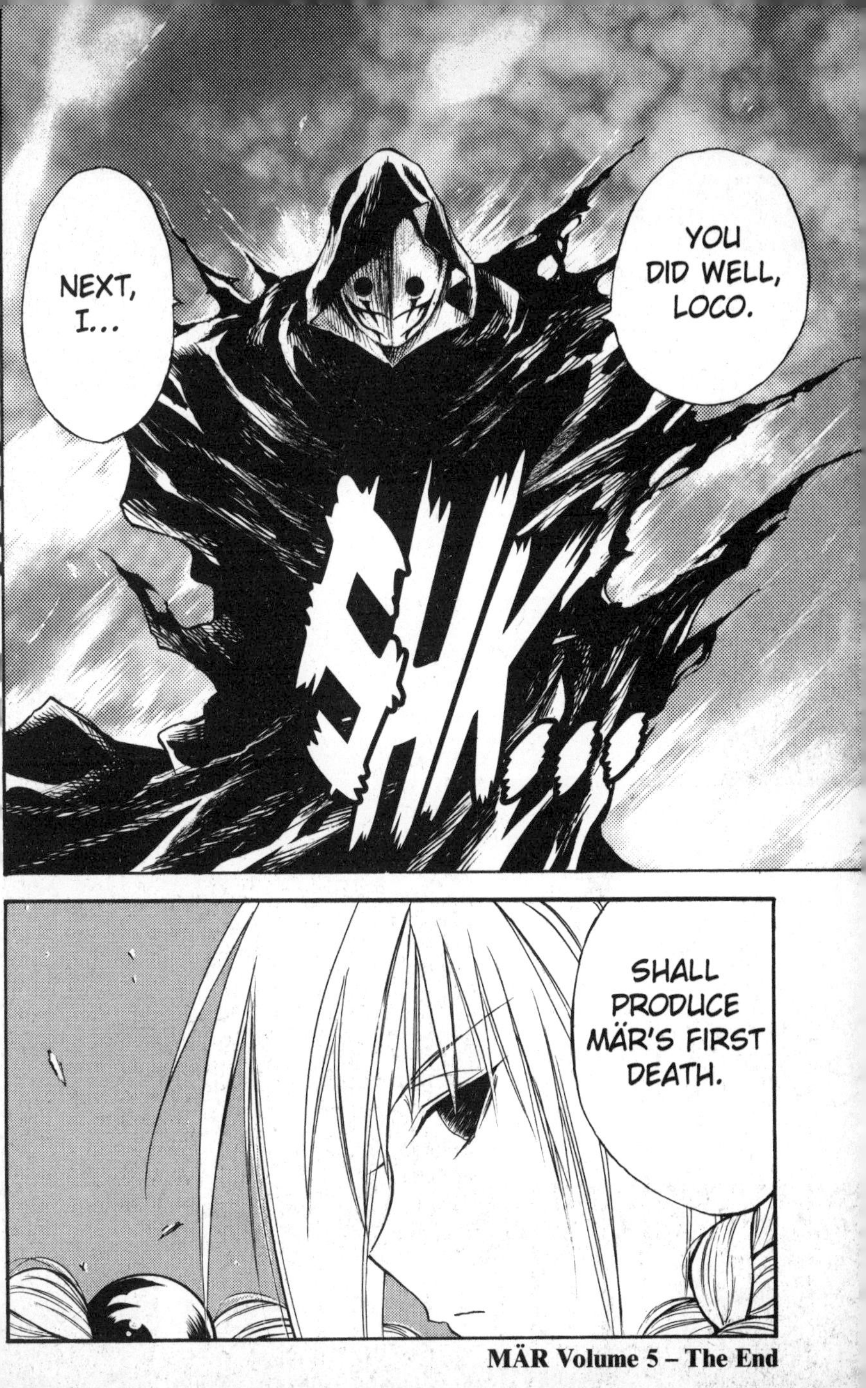
YOU DID WELL, LOCO.
NEXT, I...
SHK...
SHALL PRODUCE MÄR'S FIRST DEATH.

MÄR Volume 5 – The End

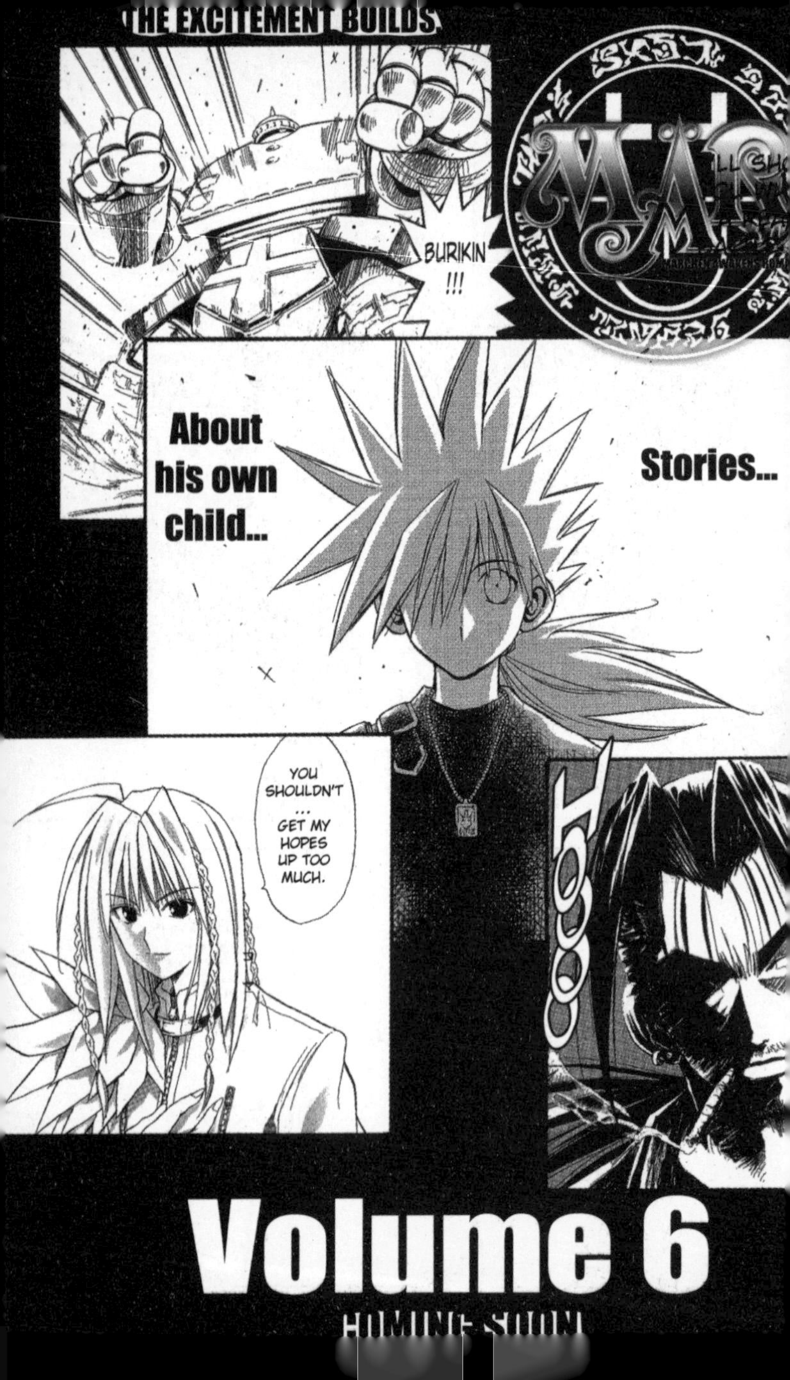
THE EXCITEMENT BUILDS
BURIKIN !!!
Stories...
About his own child...
YOU SHOULDN'T ... GET MY HOPES UP TOO MUCH.
Volume 6
COMING SOON

ALAN AND ED'S TRUE FEELINGS BOP

AniKi

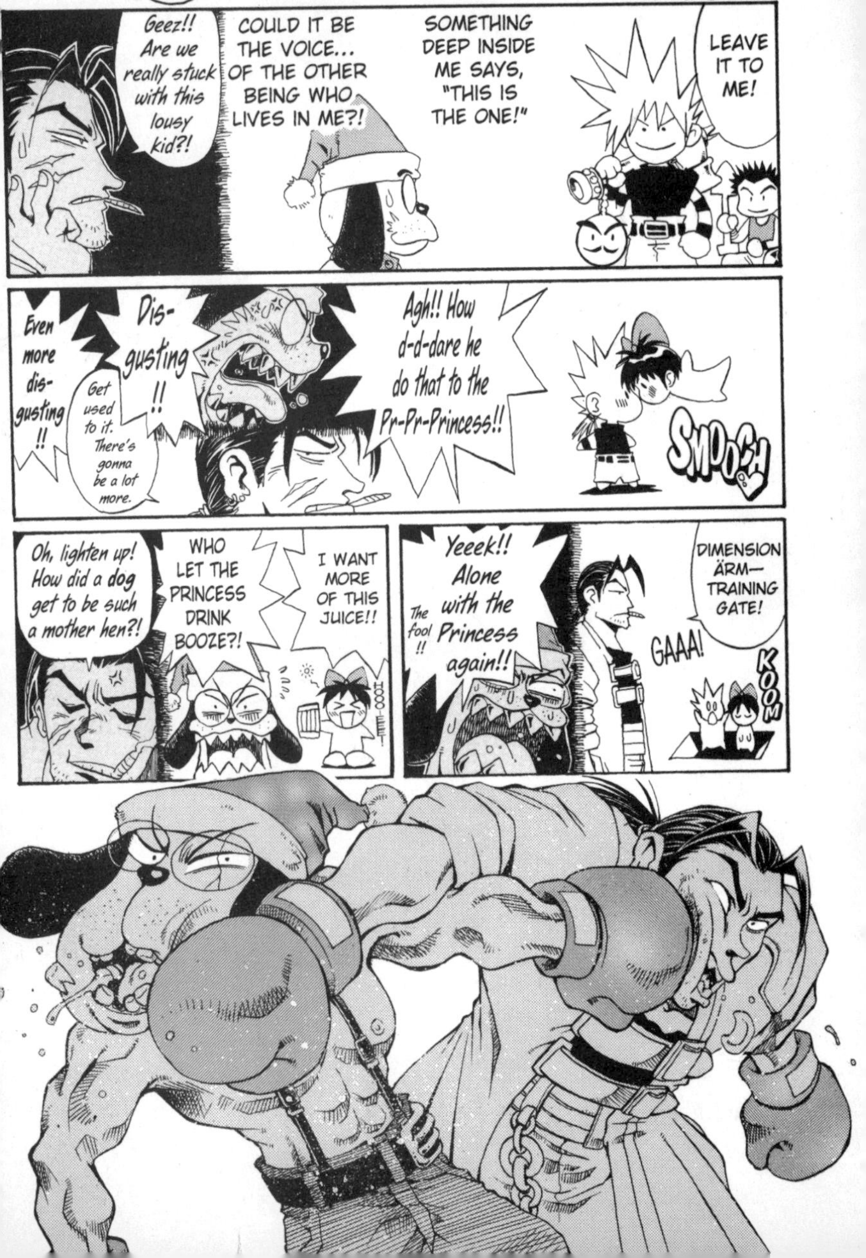
LEAVE IT TO ME!
SOMETHING DEEP INSIDE ME SAYS, "THIS IS THE ONE!"
COULD IT BE THE VOICE... OF THE OTHER BEING WHO LIVES IN ME?!
Geez!! Are we really stuck with this lousy kid?!
SMOOCH
Agh!! How d-d-dare he do that to the Pr-Pr-Princess!!
Dis-gusting!!
Get used to it. There's gonna be a lot more.
Even more dis-gusting!!
DIMENSION ÄRM—TRAINING GATE!
KOOM
GAAA!
Yeeek!! Alone with the Princess again!!
The fool!!
I WANT MORE OF THIS JUICE!!
WHO LET THE PRINCESS DRINK BOOZE?!
Oh, lighten up! How did a dog get to be such a mother hen?!

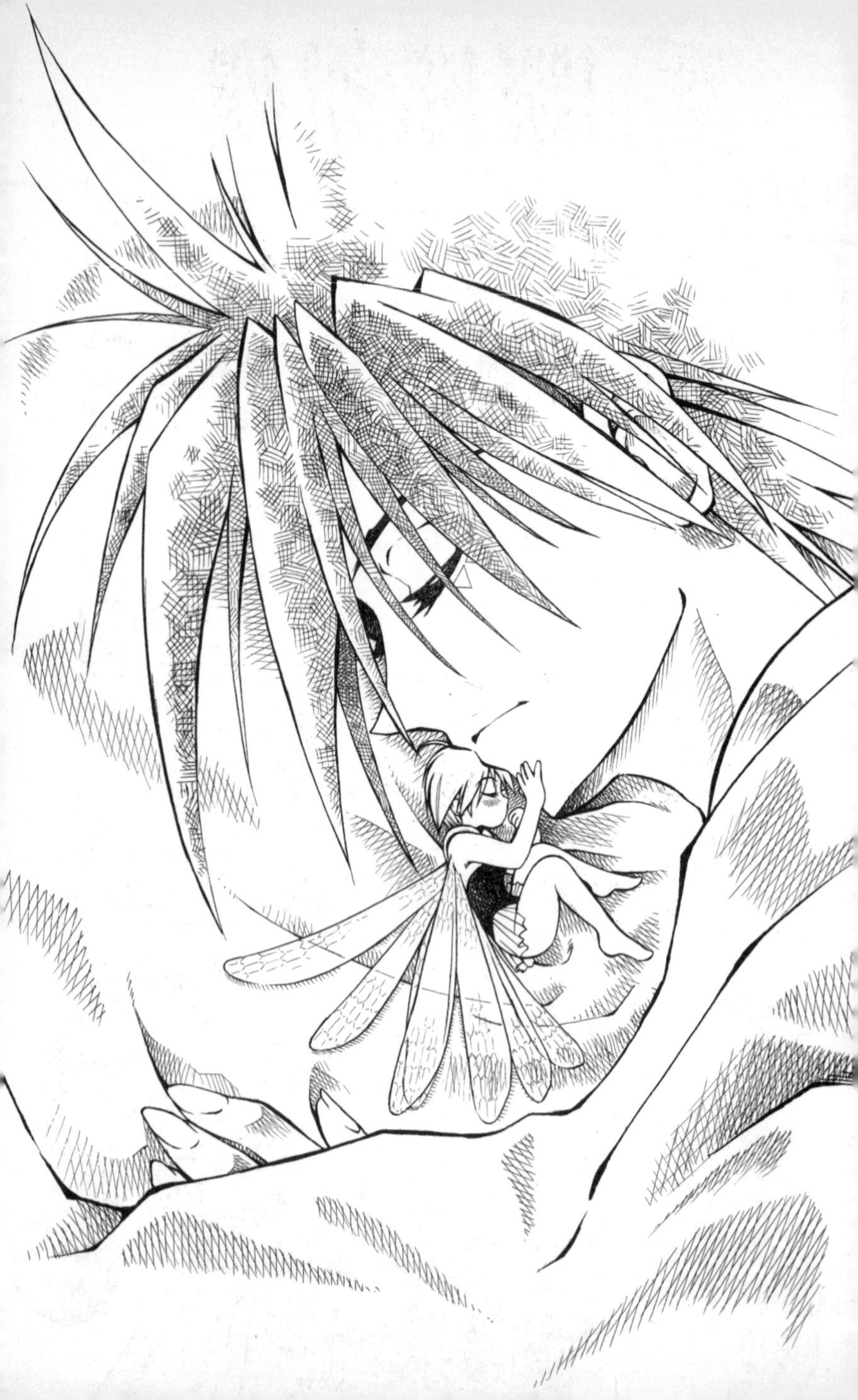

FIND THE MISTAKES

By: GB

- There are eight differences between the top and bottom picture.
(Differences in the border or line thickness don't count!)
Good luck!!

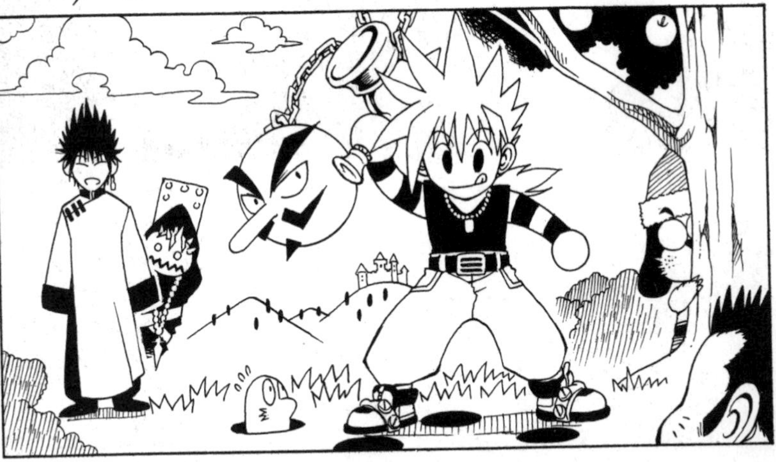

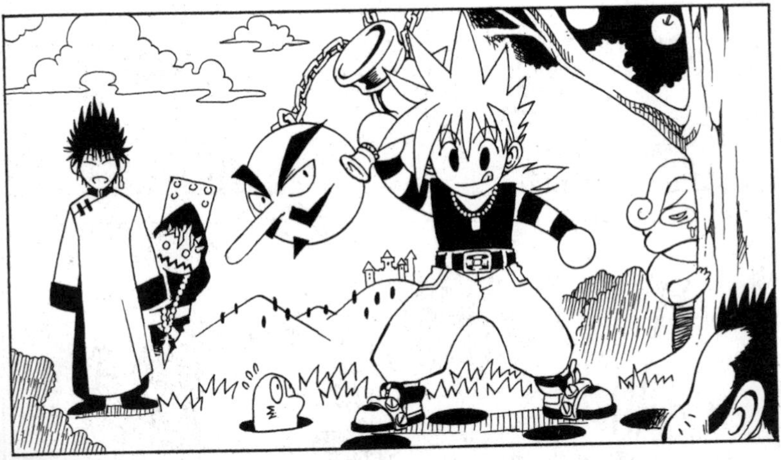

ACID VOMIT

By: G B
Title lettering: Anzo

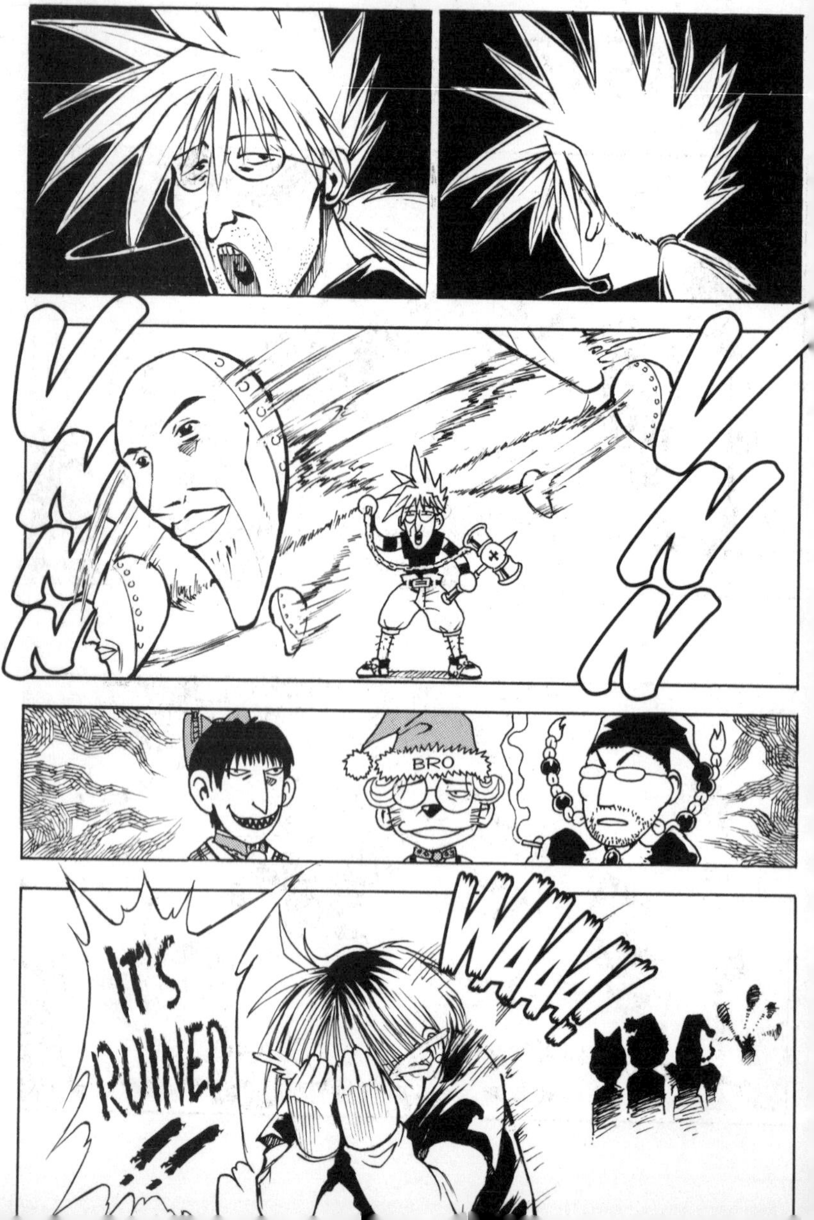
VNNN
VNNN
BRO
WAAA!!
IT'S RUINED!!

BONUS— POP!

Nobuyuki Anzai

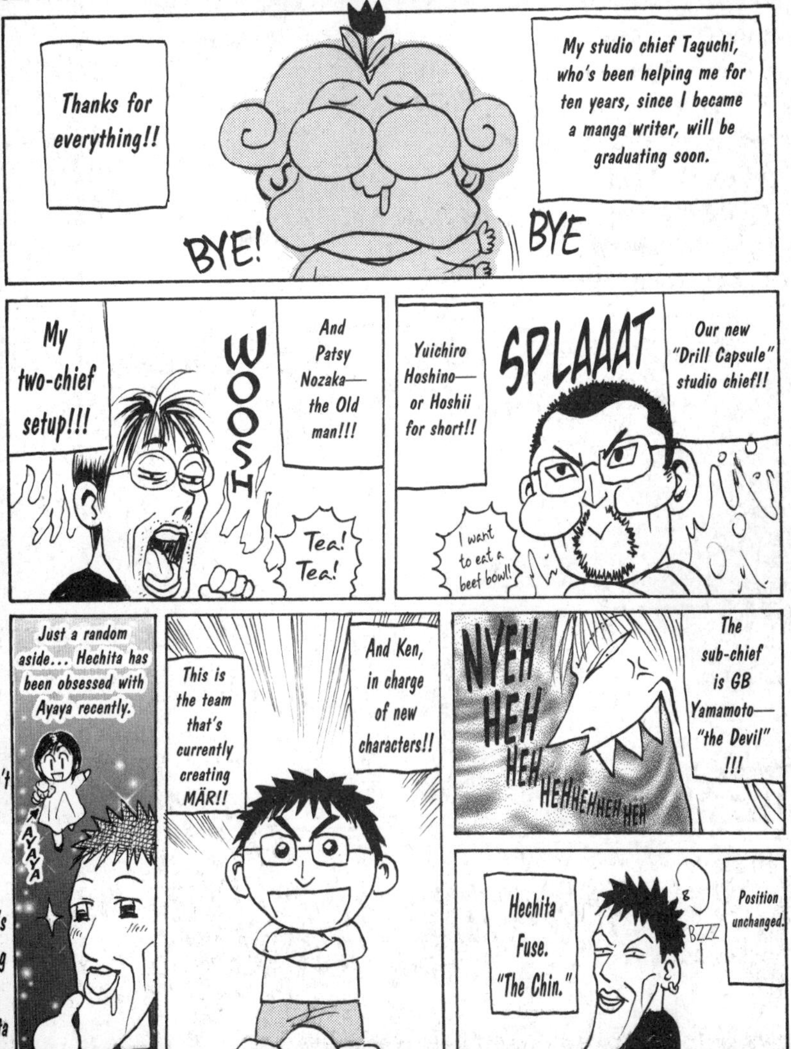

My studio chief Taguchi, who's been helping me for ten years, since I became a manga writer, will be graduating soon.
Thanks for everything!!
BYE
BYE!
Our new "Drill Capsule" studio chief!!
SPLAAT
Yuichiro Hoshino— or Hoshii for short!!
I want to eat a beef bowl!
And Patsy Nozaka— the Old man!!!
WOOSH
My two-chief setup!!!
Tea! Tea!
The sub-chief is GB Yamamoto— "the Devil" !!!
NYEH HEH HEH HEHHEHHEH HEH
Position unchanged.
BZZZ
Hechita Fuse. "The Chin."
And Ken, in charge of new characters!!
This is the team that's currently creating MÄR!!
Just a random aside... Hechita has been obsessed with Ayaya recently.
AYAYA

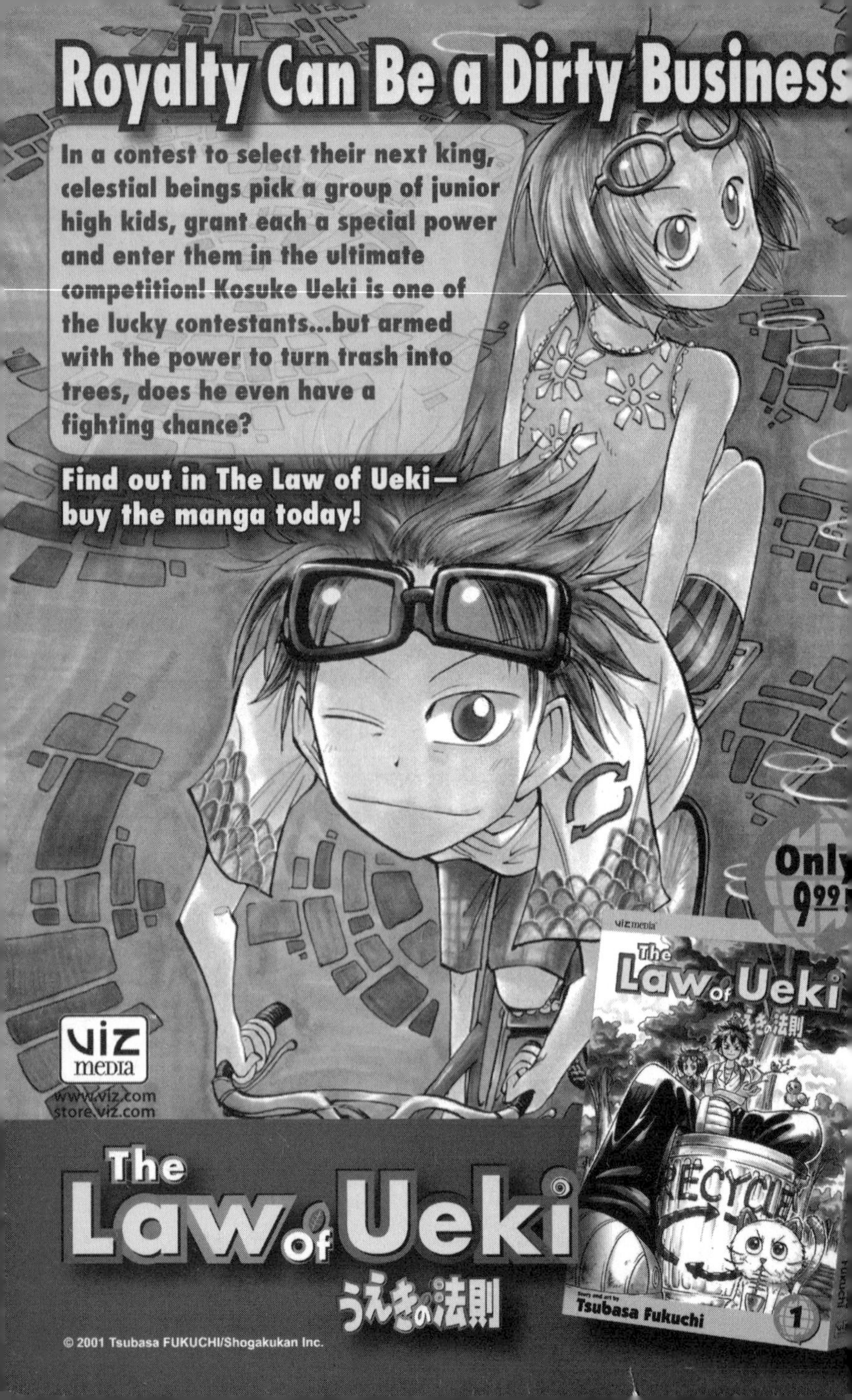
Royalty Can Be a Dirty Business
In a contest to select their next king, celestial beings pick a group of junior high kids, grant each a special power and enter them in the ultimate competition! Kosuke Ueki is one of the lucky contestants...but armed with the power to turn trash into trees, does he even have a fighting chance?
Find out in The Law of Ueki—buy the manga today!
Onl
9.99
viz media
www.viz.com
store.viz.com
The Law of Ueki
うえきの法則
© 2001 Tsubasa FUKUCHI/Shogakukan Inc.
viz media
The Law of Ueki
うえきの法則
RECYCLE
Story and art by
Tsubasa Fukuchi
1

LOVE MANGA?

LET US KNOW WHAT YOU THINK!

KU-195-841

OUR MANGA SURVEY IS NOW
AVAILABLE ONLINE. PLEASE VISIT:
VIZ.COM/MANGASURVEY

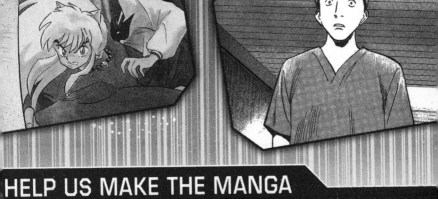

HELP US MAKE THE MANGA
YOU LOVE BETTER!